T0289747

ROUTLEDGE LIBRARY EDITIONS: ECONOMETRICS

Volume 2

ECESIS: AN INTERREGIONAL ECONOMIC-DEMOGRAPHIC MODEL OF THE UNITED STATES

ECESIS: AN INTERREGIONAL ECONOMIC-DEMOGRAPHIC MODEL OF THE UNITED STATES

PAUL M. BEAUMONT

LONDON AND NEW YORK

First published in 1989 by Garland

This edition first published in 2018
by Routledge
2 Park Square, Milton Park, Abingdon, Oxon OX14 4RN

and by Routledge
711 Third Avenue, New York, NY 10017

Routledge is an imprint of the Taylor & Francis Group, an informa business

British Library Cataloguing in Publication Data
A catalogue record for this book is available from the British Library

ISBN: 978-0-8153-9640-6 (Set)
ISBN: 978-1-351-14012-6 (Set) (ebk)
ISBN: 978-0-8153-5026-2 (Volume 2) (hbk)
ISBN: 978-1-351-14100-0 (Volume 2) (ebk)

Publisher's Note
The publisher has gone to great lengths to ensure the quality of this reprint but points out that some imperfections in the original copies may be apparent.

Disclaimer
The publisher has made every effort to trace copyright holders and would welcome correspondence from those they have been unable to trace.

ECESIS

An Interregional Economic-Demographic Model of the United States

Paul M. Beaumont

GARLAND PUBLISHING, INC.
New York London
1989

Library of Congress Cataloging-in-Publication Data

Beaumont, Paul M.
ECESIS : an interregional economic-demographic model of the United States / Paul M. Beaumont
p. cm. — (Garland studies in historical demography)
Originally presented in 1984 as the author's thesis (Ph. D.)—University of Pennsylvania
Includes bibliographical references.
ISBN 0-8240-3398-1 (alk. paper)
1. Population—Economic aspects—Mathematical models. 2. United States—Economic conditions—1945- —Econometric models.
3. United States—Population—Econometric models.
I. Title. II. Series.
HB849.41.B43 1989
304.6'01'1—dc20 89-37798

Printed on acid-free, 250-year-life paper

Manufactured in the United States of America

Acknowledgments

I am grateful for financial support from the Economics Research Unit at the University of Pennsylvania and from the National Science Foundation's American Statistical Association/ U.S. Bureau of the Census Special Project to improve Economic-Demographic Modeling

There are many people to whom I owe a great debt. I would like to thank my dissertation supervisor, Professor Lawrence R. Klein, for his many helpful suggestions and his patience. From the Census Bureau I would like to thank John Long, Signe Wetrogan, and, especially, David McMillen. Without David's help and encouragement I would never have finished this thesis. David Plane and Peter Rogerson, the other members of the ECESIS research team, deserve most of the credit for the demographic submodels of ECESIS. Professor Andrew Isserman guided the research team and provided eternal optimism. I am very grateful for his help over the years. Finally, I want to thank Vicki and Derek.

Preface

Not a great deal has changed in economic-demographic modeling in the years since ECESIS was built. I think that this reflects both the current state of large-scale model building and the innovative nature of the ECESIS model.

ECESIS was designed to investigate the linkages between interregional economic and demographic models. To carry this off, each component of the model had to be fairly complete. Supply and demand interaction, and the flow of labor, capital, and goods, all had to be accounted for. I believe that ECESIS was about as good a model for its purpose as could be built at that time. The model was able to address linkage issues that could not be addressed with any other empirical or analytical tool available. The price that one must pay to accomplish this is a very large and complex model.

The trend today is toward smaller models whose properties are more easily understood. The cost of this approach is that the models lack the richness of detail that the users of models require. I believe that it has been useful to step back from large-scale models to re-examine the basic tenets of empirical model building. I will be curious to see what kinds of models or methods of analysis this reflection produces in the next generation of economic-demographic models.

TABLE OF CONTENTS

LIST OF TABLES

LIST OF FIGURES

CHAPTER ONE: INTRODUCTION, OVERVIEW AND SUMMARY

1.1 INTRODUCTION AND OUTLINE

Since the dramatic but unsubstantiated claims of Malthus that population grows geometrically and food supply grows arithmetically, a vast literature has accumulated on the interactions between economic activity and demographic forces.[1] However, the principal question remains--what and how strong are the interactions between population dynamics and economic activity?

The interdependence of economic and demographic variables suggests the need for their simultaneous determination. This seems clear at the theoretical level (Beyers 1980; Gordon and Ledent 1981), but it remains to test the strength of the interactions at the empirical level.

The purpose of this research is to determine to what extent a simultaneous economic-demographic interregional model provides improved projection and simulation properties over regional economic and demographic models used independently of one another. If economic-demographic

---

[1] Leibenstein (1954), Kuznets (1960), Easterlin (1968) and Simon (1977) are a few notable examples.

feedbacks are strong in both directions then simulations by either purely economic or purely demographic models will be subject to large errors. Otherwise, partial models will be adequate simulation tools.

ECESIS[2], an interregional economic-demographic model of the United States, has been developed to address this research issue. ECESIS is eclectic. It includes econometric models, spatial interaction models, and cohort-component models. It incorporates theories and methods from economics, regional science, geography, demography, and sociology, which, in many cases, have been extended and modified in recognition of the important differences between the national and subnational levels of analysis.

ECESIS consists of four major model elements. First, there are fifty-one regional economic models. These regional models are linked by an interregional trade model so that wages, employment and production are simultaneously determined in all regions. An interregional cohort-component demographic accounts model simultaneously determines age-sex disaggregated population, births and deaths for each region. The economic and demographic models are linked by an interregional migration model that determines flows of people. The system is completely

---

[2] The name ECESIS is borrowed from biology and means the movement of an organism from one habitat to another.

simultaneous. A change in any submodel will require adjustments in all other submodels.

This chapter introduces the research issue and gives an overview of the ECESIS model. Section 1.2 reviews the issues that motivated this research. The structure of the model is summarized in Section 1.3. First, general modelling strategies are discussed. Next, the economic submodel, presented in detail in Chapters Two through Six, is summarized. The demographic submodel, summarizing Chapters Seven, Eight and Nine is discussed next. Section 1.3 concludes with a brief discussion of the economic-demographic linkages in ECESIS. The properties and applications of ECESIS are summarized in Section 1.4. The multiplier, structural and simulation experiments discussed in that section provide a summary of Chapters Ten through Twelve.

1.2 MOTIVATION FOR ECESIS

ECESIS is a large and expensive project. While the academic issues involved are fundamental and even interesting, these are not sufficient conditions for funding. Instead, it was a political issue that provided the impetus to build this model.

While economic-demographic interactions have been discussed by academicians for many years, government policy planners have only recently become cognizant of this inter-relationship. Accurate population projections are now recognized as critical for long-term government financing plans.

Consider, for example, the high cost of unemployment benefits due to chronically high unemployment rates over the past several years. This trend could have been anticipated twenty years ago. The post World War II baby boom reached its peak around 1960. The first contingents of the baby boom would enter the labor force in the late 1960's with the peak occurring in the late 1970's and early 1980's. The share of teenagers in the labor force has grown from under seven percent in the early fifties to over ten percent in the early eighties.[3] Traditionally, the unemployment rate among teenagers has been three to three and a half times that of persons over twenty. The result is that the aggregate unemployment rate will increase due to the changed composition of the labor force (Easterlin 1968; Easterlin, Wachter and Wachter 1978). This trend has been reinforced by the rapid increase in the participation rates of women--whose unemployment rate is generally one to two points above

[3] This trend would be even more dramatic except that over the same period the participation rate of teenagers has dropped.

that of men.[4]

Decreased productivity of the labor force has partially offset the increase in unemployment rates. Even this trend could have been predicted as the labor force has become younger and less experienced.

Obviously, circumstances have been more complex and issues more obtuse than hindsight would make it seem. Nevertheless, the basic trends could have been, and in fact were (Easterlin 1968), predicted many years ago. Policy makers were either unaware of or put low priorities on this information.

The U.S. Social Security system provides another example of the importance of demographic trends in government planning. The Social Security Act of 1935 established the Old Age and Survivors Insurance (OASI) program to provide benefits to workers and their dependents upon retirement or death of the worker. The program was designed as a "pay as you go" system with the current work force providing the funds to cover current benefit payments. A wage tax of two percent, split between the employee and the employer, was paid on a base of about $3000 to finance the system through the 1940's.

---

[4] This latter trend could not have been easily predicted but its influence is much smaller than the influx of teenagers into the labor supply.

In 1945 there were approximately fifty workers per beneficiary in the system. By 1955 the program had expanded so that the worker-to-beneficiary ratio fell to about ten. To cover the increased costs the wage tax was increased to five percent on a $5500 base. Due to the high worker-beneficiary ratio the Social Security system was able to expand dramatically over the decades of the 1950's and 1960's. In 1956 disability insurance was added and in 1965 Medicare was added to the system. As a result, a person retiring in 1979 with a dependent spouse will receive approximately eleven times in benefits what he has paid into the system (Ginzberg 1982). The entrance of the baby boom generation into the labor force helped make this expansion possible in a pay as you go system.

By the year 2000 the first members of the baby boom will begin to retire; the peak will occur in about the year 2025. There will be so many people eligible to receive Social Security benefits by 2025 that there will be only two workers for each beneficiary in the system. It is estimated (Ginzberg 1982) that the wage tax would have to increase to twenty-four percent in order to maintain the solvency of the pay as you go system.

Policy makers planning the future of the Social Security system have a great deal of information at hand. Much may be predicted with a fair degree of accuracy because of the long lags involved in demographic trends. Nearly everyone who will be in the labor force in the year 2000, and approximately ninety six percent of the Social Security benefits paid in the next seventy-five years will go to people who are alive today (Ginzberg 1982).

The funding arrangements of the Social Security system would surely have been different had policy makers understood the implications of demographic trends on the system. Demographic projections will play a key role in future debates on the Social Security system.

Two federal agencies are currently assigned the task of providing population projections for use in planning government finance and policy. One, the Bureau of Economic Analysis (BEA), uses an economic-base model, while the other, the Bureau of the Census, uses a cohort-component model. The philosophies behind these two models are very different. The BEA model projects population almost solely on the basis of economic data; excluding available demographic data. The Census model, on the other hand, largely ignores economic data and uses a purely demographic approach to projecting population. The result not surprisingly, is that the two agencies (both within the U.S. Department of Commerce) project populations for the same regions that are quite different from one another. This would be a mere curiosity except that many federal government programs distribute funds to states on the basis of these population projections.

A specific example involves the Environmental Protection Agency (EPA) which distributes funds to states to build sewage treatment facilities. The EPA funding formula used population projections that were generated by the states. The higher the projected population, the more money the state would receive. As one might expect, "These projections were generally too optimistic, as they summed to a population many tens of millions in excess of the projected United States population for 1990 even under the highest fertility model. Using the nonuniform set of projections, facilities would be built providing excess capacity in many areas and wasting billions of dollars (Griffith 1980, p. 57)." The EPA's response was to order the use of the BEA figures for funding purposes. States which received reduced funding appealed the ruling and noted that many states would receive more money if Census projections were used rather than BEA projections.

Finally, after several committees, one new agency and a special task force were created, several recommendations on the generation and use of population projections were made. One of the recommendations reads,

> The Department of Commerce should assume the responsibility for developing, in consultation with other Federal agencies, a single set of baseline State

> population projections which would incorporate economic and demographic variables for use, whenever projections are included as a factor in Federal funding allocations (Griffith 1980, p. 58).

The ECESIS model is an attempt at meeting this recommendation. Unfortunately, as the project was nearing completion, the Reagan administration dropped the program for a uniform population projection series in fear that the state appeals process would be too expensive. The new U.S. Department of Commerce procedure to provide uniform economic-demographic population projections will be to add the Census and BEA population projections and divide by two. So it goes.

Nonetheless, the key issue remains--how important are economic-demographic interactions when making simulations and projections? ECESIS was designed to meet both the political and academic needs raised by this issue.

1.3 OVERVIEW OF ECESIS

1.3.1 MODEL DESIGN

Several decisions concerning the design of a model must be made before any model building effort can begin. Since ECESIS is such an eclectic model many techniques are used. For example, the economic models are organized in a time-series format while the demographic model is organized in a cross-sectional format. Even this classification has exceptions since the economic subsystem contains a cross-sectional trade model and the migration component of the demographic subsystem contains some time-series elements. All of these systems are described in detail later. For now it is sufficient to note that data availability and model requirements were used to determine the data structure of each element of the model.

A behavioral model approach is used over a pure auto-regressive integrated moving average (ARIMA) model because the model is intended to be used for simulation experiments. ARIMA models are parsimonious with data, easy to build, and simple to use for projections, but their simulation capabilities are severely limited.

The question of the appropriate time interval to use is a difficult one. Demographic models are generally designed with five year time intervals and five year age groups so that the entire cohort moves into the next age group for each period of the model. Economic models, on the other hand, are generally designed with no more than one year time intervals. Since an entire economic cycle might be missed with five year intervals, ECESIS is designed as an annual model. This creates some compromises in the demographic model; these will be discussed later.

A micro-simulation model design is appealing because many of the key linkage variables in an economic-demographic model (labor force participation, fertility, migration) are micro level decisions. however, these types of models are relatively new and their properties are not well tested; thus, ECESIS will rely on a conventional macroeconomic modelling approach.

The appropriate level of geographic disaggregation for a regional model generally evokes endless debate. If place-to-place migration flows are of interest, an area large enough to wash out local household moves but small enough to capture moves to new labor markets is appropriate. This suggests the use of Standard Metropolitan Statistical Areas (SMSA's) or BEA labor market areas. Complete coverage is also required; people should not be allowed to move in and out of undefined areas. This speaks against SMSA's. Also, there are 273 (in 1980) BEA regions so a model based on that level of disaggregation would be quite large.

On theoretical grounds practically no one likes to define areas using state boundaries. The practical considerations, however, are overwhelming. Much of the regional economic and demographic data available at the subnational level are available only at the state level. State boundaries have been fixed for a long period of time, whereas county, SMSA and BEA region boundaries are frequently redefined. In addition, the reasonably small number of states allows a model of complete coverage to be constructed. ECESIS consists of fifty-one regions--each state and the District of Columbia. Region and division names referred to in this and the following chapters use the conventions established by the U.S. Bureau of the Census. These are illustrated in Figure 1.3.1.

ECESIS is primarily a bottom-up as opposed to a top-down model design. There are exceptions. Interest rates and most price variables are determined at the national level and some demographic variables are constrained to projected national totals. This issue is probably over emphasized in the regional modelling literature. A compromise design is inevitably chosen by proponents of either philosophy when the model is actually built. In general, bottom-up models are preferred in theory while top-down models are preferred in practice (Klein and Glickman 1977).

Another important issue to be addressed before model building begins is where to put the emphasis of the modelling effort. There are three basic elements in an economic- demographic model: the economic submodel, the demographic submodel and the linkages between the two. A model may be designed to emphasize all or any subset of these elements. ECESIS was designed to put equal emphasis on all three elements.

FIRGURE 1.3.1

Regions and Census Divisions of the United States

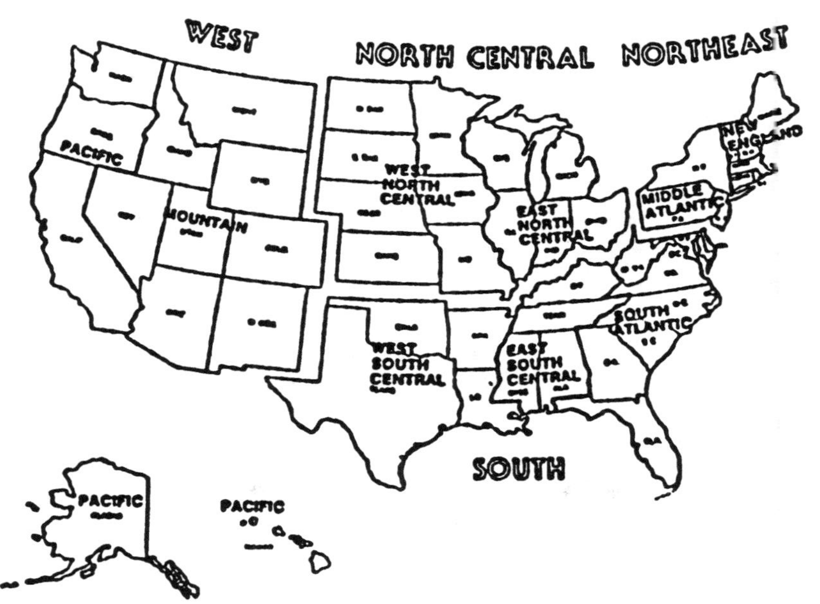

1.3.2 THE ECONOMIC SUBMODEL

The economic submodel of ECESIS is a time-series structural model estimated over the sample period 1958 to 1974. Because of time and resource constraints, the same model structure is used for each of the fifty-one regions in the model.

The economic model in each region is disaggregated into three sectors: manufacturing, nonmanufacturing (including agricultural services, forestry, fisheries and other; mining; construction; transportation, communications and public utilities; wholesale trade; retail trade; finance, insurance and real estate; services; and government), and agriculture. This disaggregation scheme allows a rough correspondence with the basic-nonbasic disaggregation commonly used in regional models.

The manufacturing (basic) sector is modelled with considerable detail. The manufacturing sector was chosen for this purpose because that sector comprises twenty-five to thirty percent of national income and is also the largest sector in over three-quarters of the states. Also, the available data for the manufacturing sector are more complete than for any other sector.

Supply and demand factors interact in determining the output of manufacturing sector of each state. Demand is a function of the states's manufacturing wage and of income in every state weighted by a trade matrix. A production function and the related factor demand equations are key elements in the supply side of each model. Increased demand from outside the state cannot induce increased production unless the factors are available for expansion.

The nonmanufacturing (nonbasic) sector is dominated by the trade, services and government industries, each accounting for approximately fifteen percent of national income (although considerable variation exists among states). This rather aggregated sector is treated very simply with reduced form equations. The farm sector, which accounts for less than two percent of nation income, is exogenous for all states.

A detailed description of the economic model along with complete estimation results is given in Chapters Two through Six. This section provides a general overview of the economic model design. A complete listing of the equation specifications in the economic models is given in Appendix 1.1 at the end of this chapter. The equation numbers in this section correspond to those in Appendix 1.1. Appendix 1.2 provides a complete list of the variables used in the model along with their definitions and sources. These appendices should prove useful references throughout this and the following chapters. Figure 1.3.2 shows a flow chart of a state economic model and its linkages to the interstate trade and demographic models. In order to make the chart more readable, the model is depicted in a somewhat simplified form. Generally each box represents several variables. Lagged relationships are denoted by dashed lines and exogenous variables do not appear on the chart.

Manufacturing output is determined from an interregional supply and demand model. Let Q_{ij} be the amount of region i's manufacturing output that is shipped to region j. Then $Q_{i\cdot}=\Sigma_j Q_{ij}$ is region i's total manufacturing output and $Q_{\cdot j}=\Sigma_i Q_{ij}$ is region j's total demand for manufactured goods. A matrix of the Q_{ij}'s is available from the 1977 Commodity Transportation Survey of the U.S. Bureau of the Census (1980).[5] A time-series of $Q_{i\cdot}$ is available from the Annual Survey of Manufactures but no further data for $Q_{\cdot j}$ are available. Thus, it is not possible to model the interregional trade flows and develop a Project LINK (Ball 1973) style trade model.

ECESIS uses a modified trade model approach. Let region j's real total personal income ($YT72_j$) serve as a proxy for that region's total demand for manufactured goods. Then define r_{ij} as the total shipments of manufactured goods from

---

[5] The CTS is also available for 1967 and 1972 but the data cannot be compared across time due to definitional and procedural changes in the surveys.

FIGURE 1.3.2

FLOW CHART OF STATE ECONOMIC MODELS

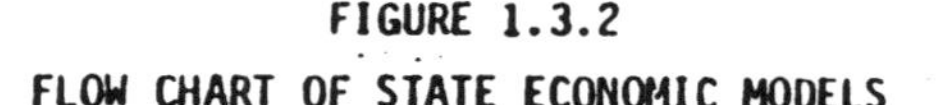

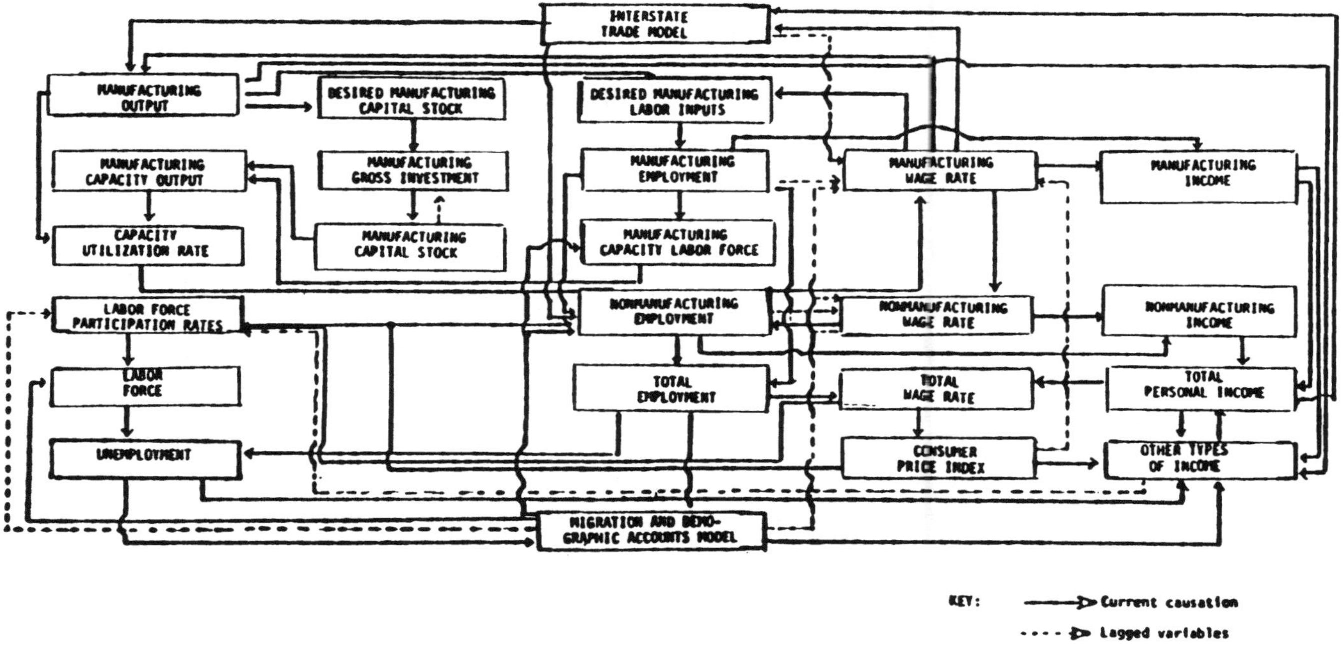

region i to region j as a fraction of the total real income of the receiving region in the year 1977,

$$r_{ij} = Q_{ij}/YT72_j.$$

The r_{ij} are assumed to remain fixed over time. A proxy for the interregional demand for region i's manufactured output in any year is then calculated as,[6]

$$RYT72_{i,t} = \Sigma_j r_{ij} \cdot YT72_{j,t}.$$

Other factors influencing region i's output would be relative prices, approximated by the ratio of the hourly manufacturing wage rate in the region and the U.S. average manufactured output price ($WMH_i/USMP$),[7]

and an anticipated output variable (Q_i^a) to capture the inertia of the manufacturing process.

$$Q_i^a = Q_{i,-1}(IP/IP_{-1}),$$

where IP is an industrial production index for the U.S.

The final specification for the manufacturing output equation is,

$$\text{(A1)} \qquad Q_i = a_0 + a_1 Q_i^a + a_2(WMH_i/USMP) + a_3 RYT72_i.$$

---

[6] Time subscripts are omitted unless there is possible confusion.

[7] Subnational manufacturing output prices are not available. Since the wage bill comprises about sixty percent of the cost of manufactured goods, the wage rate is a reasonable approximation for production costs.

Because of the bottom-up design of ECESIS, there is no constraint to force the sum of the regions' manufacturing outputs to equal a predetermined U.S. manufacturing output level. Instead, each region has capacity constraints to control production.

Assuming a Cobb-Douglas production technology and that the utilization rate of capital is equal to the output capacity rate (CU), capacity manufacturing output (QCAP) may be calculated from,

$$\text{(A2)} \qquad QCAP_i = a_0 MLFC_i^{\alpha} \cdot K_i^{\beta} \exp(\gamma \cdot PRTR_i),$$

where MLFC is manufacturing labor force capacity, K is real manufacturing capital stock and PRTR is a productivity growth trend.

Labor inputs and capital stock are estimated from partial adjustment models whose coefficients are forced to be consistent with the parameters estimated in the production function. Using a simplified version of a method developed by Klein and Su (1979), capacity manufacturing labor inputs (MLFC) are calculated as,

$$\text{(A8)} \qquad MLFC_i = MHC_i \cdot (EM/PTOT)_i^{c} \cdot PTOT_i \cdot 52wk/yr/1000,$$

where MHC is peak hours worked per week, $(EM/PTOT)^c$ is the peak ratio of manufacturing employment to total population and PTOT is current total population in the region.

The capacity utilization rate is obtained from,

(A7) $CU = Q/QCAP$.

Capacity output is not directly observed and must be calculated from QCAP=Q/CU, but CU cannot be calculated until QCAP is known. The iterative estimation procedure used for the production function is described in Chapter Three.

Assuming that firms follow profit maximizing behavior, the desired level of factor inputs will be a function of desired output, expected output price, factor prices and the parameters from the production function. The desired real capital stock (MKD) equation is,

(A3) $MKD = \beta(1-1/\xi)PQ/UCC$,

where PQ is nominal manufacturing output , UCC is the user cost of capital, and ξ is the elasticity of demand (imperfect markets are assumed). The equation for desired labor inputs (MLD) is,

(A4) $MLD = \alpha(1-1/\xi)PQ/WMH$,

where WMH is the nominal hourly manufacturing wage rate. The estimates of returns to scale ($\alpha+\beta$) from the production function generally fall between 1.0 and 1.5, indicating moderate increasing returns. The estimates of the elasticity of demand generally fall in the range of two to three suggesting a moderately competitive climate.

Actual factor inputs are assumed to adjust to desired levels using a partial adjustment model. Labor inputs are estimated as,

(A6) $\log(MLAB) = a_0 + a_1 \log(MLD) + a_2 \log(MLAB_{-1})$,

where MLAB is actual labor inputs. Estimates of the labor adjustment rate are quite variable but are usually in the range of forty to seventy-five percent.

The change in manufacturing capital stock is modelled as a geometrically declining lag structure on past differences of desired and actual capital stock,

(A5) $MGI72_i = a_0 + a_1 MGI72_{i,-1} + a_2(MKD_i - K_{i,-1})$,

where MGI72 is real manufacturing gross investment. This specification works well given the poor quality of regional investment data.

If income in region j should increase, trade linkages between region j and, say, region i will increase the demand for manufactured goods in region i. The increased production in region i will raise the capital utilization rate and lower the unemployment rate in that region. Both effects tend to drive up the manufacturing wage rate in region i. The closer the factors are to full utilization, the faster the wage rate will increase. If production in region i becomes relatively more expensive than in other competing regions then the output demand created by the income increase in region j will be shifted to regions other than region i. Through this mechanism increases in demand will be met by those regions who have close trading ties with the demanding region and who also have the resources available for expanded production at a competitive cost structure.

Manufacturing sector employment is determined by dividing labor inputs by hours worked,

(A14) $EM = MLAB/(MHR \cdot 52/1000)$.

The nonmanufacturing sector is modelled with a reduced form employment equation. Since the trade, services, and government industries dominate this sector, the local population size should be an important determinant of nonmanufacturing employment (ENM). Distance weighted populations of other states are used in the specification in a manner analogous to the trade share variables of the manufacturing output equation. Using the total population in state j as a proxy for the market size in that state, an interregional demand variable may be constructed as,

$$DPTOT_i = \sum_j d_{ij}^{-1} \cdot PTOT_j,$$

where d_{ij} is the distance between the 1970 population centroids of state i and state j. This specification assumes that closer markets have more impact on the local nonmanufacturing sector than more distant markets.

The economic base approach is also incorporated by including manufacturing employment in the specification. The nonmanufacturing real wage is included with the demand effect expected to dominate. In a few states, lagged nonmanufacturing employment is included in the specification while in other states the wage variable is omitted. The final specification for nonmanufacturing employment is,

$$(A15)\qquad ENM_i = a_0 + a_1 ENM_{i,-1} + a_2 DPTOT_i + a_3 EM_i + a_4 (WNM_i / CPI72_i).$$

Wage rates are determined using a leading region and leading sector approach. The manufacturing sector is taken to be the leader with the nonmanufacturing sector following. Rather than declaring some state or subset of states as the leading region, a wage transmission variable is constructed that allows all states to have some impact on the manufacturing wage rate determination process. This transmission variable ($DW_i{}^*$) is defined as,

$$DW_i{}^* = \sum_j \{d_{ij}{}^{-1} [(YM_i / YTLPR_i)/(YM_{us}/YTLPR_{us})] S_i\} WM_j,$$

where the term in square brackets is the ratio of manufacturing income (YM) to total labor and proprietors' income (YTLPR) in state i relative to the same ratio for the U.S., S_i is a scaling factor (equal to the mean distance from state i to all other states), and WM_j is the manufacturing wage rate in state j. Every state's manufacturing wage rate has some influence on DW_i^* but nearby states and states with large manufacturing sectors have relatively more influence.

Local labor market conditions and an industry's ability to substitute for scarce resources are also important in determining the local wage. The local manufacturing employment to working age population ratio (EM/P1864) and capacity utilization rate (CU) are included in the equation to capture these effects. Inflationary effects are captured by the local consumer price index (CPI72). The final specification for the manufacturing wage equation is,

$$\text{(A18)} \quad \log(WM_i) = a_0 + a_1\log(DW_i^*) + a_2\log(EM_i/P1864_i)_{-1} + a_3\log(CU_i) + a_4\log(CPI72_i)_{-1}.$$

The nonmanufacturing wage rate (WNM) is assumed to be a simple function of the manufacturing wage rate and the local nonmanufacturing employment to working age population ratio.

(A19) $\log(WNM_i) = a_0+a_1\log(WM_i)+a_2\log(ENM_i/P1864_i)_{-1}$.

Wage income is solved by identity. Additional income equations which complete the personal income accounts are listed in Appendix 1.1. Demographic linkages are provided in the proprietors income and transfer payments equations. The latter includes both direct and indirect population effects and also age distribution effects.

Perhaps the most direct linkage between the demographic and economic models is in the determination of the labor force. Labor force participation rates disaggregated by age and sex are estimated in ECESIS. They are applied to the age-sex specific populations derived by the demographic model. The unemployment rate is then calculated by identity. This approach, while theoretically appealing, has the problem that the unemployment rate, when calculated by the identity, is very sensitive to minor errors in the forecast values of the labor force participation rates. Since the unemployment rate plays such an important role in an econometric model, this sensitivity can create serious problems when using the model for forecasting exercises.

An alternative is to use a stochastic equation to estimate the unemployment rate and then calculate the labor force or the labor force participation rate by identity.

The major problem with this approach is that there is no good way to derive the age-sex disaggregated labor force variables from the aggregate labor force variable determined by the identity. Another disadvantage is that simulation experiments become more difficult to interpret when the unemployment rate is calculated from a stochastic equation rather than the identity. Estimation of age-sex specific labor force participation rates is further complicated because there is no age-sex detail among the economic data.

The procedure used in ECESIS to deal with these problems is to model the labor force participation rates with a two-step procedure and then calculate the unemployment rate by identity. The total labor force participation rate is modelled as a function of the real wage, per capita property income and the inflation rate. Of the eight age-sex groups in ECESIS that participate in the labor force the participation rates of the 5-17 and 65+ age groups for both sexes are taken as exogenous. The remaining participation rates are modelled as ratios of the already determined total participation rate. For example, the participation rate for 18-44 year old females is modelled as,

(A37) $\quad {}^{3}R^{2}/RTOT = a_0 + a_1({}^{3}R^{2}/RTOT)_{-1} + a_2BRATE,$

where RTOT is the total labor force participation rate and BRATE is the birth rate.

The participation rates of 18-44 and 45-64 year old males is modelled similarly except that per capita property income is used in place of the birth rate. One rate must be calculated by identity and in this case it is the participation rate of 45-64 year old females.

1.3.3 THE DEMOGRAPHIC SUBMODEL

The ECESIS demographic model is an interregional cohort-component model in the tradition of those proposed by Rogers (1968), Stone (1971), and Rees and Wilson (1977). The basic demographic processes that must be addressed in such a model are: fertility, mortality, aging and migration. A demographic accounts model is used to age the surviving population into the next cohort and to compute the populations that are at-risk of giving birth, dying and migrating to other regions. The accounts model must rely upon fertility, mortality and migration rates that are determined by independent processes.

Population in ECESIS is disaggregated by sex, age and region. The age groups are: 0-4, 5-17, 18-44, 45-64 and 65 plus years. The regions are the fifty states and the District of Columbia. The historical age-sex specific population data are from the U.S. Bureau of the Census' State Population Projections. Some adjustments were made to make the data consistent over the entire 1958 to 1979 period. Birth and death data are obtained from Vital Statistics records and are computed as midyear averages. The fertility rate is calculated as total sex specific births over the female population aged 18 to 44. Mortality rates are also age-sex specific.

Demographic Accounts

The components of change for regional population are births, deaths and migration. The basic demographic equation summarizing this relationship is,

$$POP_{i,t} = POP_{i,t-1} + B_{i,t} - D_{i,t} + I_{i,t} - O_{i,t},$$

where $POP_{i,t-1}$ is the population in region i in the previous period, $B_{i,t}$ is total births and $D_{i,t}$ is total deaths in the region during the period t-1 to t, $I_{i,t}$ is inmigration to i and $O_{i,t}$ is outmigration from i during the period.

Because of the way demographic data are collected, the basic demographic equation is not completely accurate when used with published data. The addition of births to the population in region i incorrectly assumes that no infants migrate during the year of their birth. The subtraction of deaths fails to recognize that an inmigrant who dies was not part of the population of i in the beginning of the period and, therefore, should not be subtracted from it. Similarly, the outmigration figures do not include outmigrants between (t-1) and t who died before t. Because they died in another state, they are subtracted from its population as a death but not from state i's population as an outmigrant.

ECESIS contains a set of demographic accounts which corrects the basic demographic equation. It should be stressed that the equation is only incorrect because of the characteristics of the data for births, deaths, and migration. With correctly defined data, the equation would hold. The problem then is designing a set of accounts which provide correctly defined estimates of the components of population change. The age and sex disaggregated accounts built into ECESIS are based on the work of Rees and Wilson (1977). Their system is modified to work on gross inmigration and outmigration totals, rather than place-to-place flows. This change considerably reduces the amount of data which must be processed without significantly reducing the amount of information obtainable from the full accounts matrix.

The modified accounting equation is,

$$POP_{i,t}=POP_{i,t-1}+B_{i,t}-(D_{i,t}-ID_{i,t}-IBD_{i,t})$$
$$+(I_{i,t}+IB_{i,t})-(O_{i,t}+OB_{i,t}+OBD_{i,t}+OD_{i,t}),$$

where $IB_{i,t}$ is the number of inmigrants to i born during the period (t-1,t), $OB_{i,t}$ is the outmigrants from i born during the period, $ID_{i,t}$ is the inmigrants to i who die before t, $OD_{i,t}$ is outmigrants from i who die before t, $IBD_{i,t}$ is inmigrants to i born during the period who die before t, $OBD_{i,t}$ is outmigrants from i born during the period who die before t, and the remaining variables are defined as before. No data are available on the terms, IB, OB, ID, OD, IBD, and OBD. Therefore, these "minor flows", which are indeed small in magnitude, must be estimated for each age-sex group. This is a tedious procedure and is detailed in Chapter Eight.

The demographic model also goes to considerable lengths to define the appropriate population that is "at-risk" of migrating, dying or giving birth. For example, a thirty year old women who migrates from Iowa to Texas must be included in the populations at-risk of giving birth in both states. Also, the woman, during this period, may age into another cohort or die. All of these factors, and more, must be considered. The number of possible permutations is quite large and an elaborate accounting structure is required to keep track of things.

Since ECESIS is an annual model and the population age groups used are broader than one year, the number of persons leaving and entering each age group must be estimated for each year. No population data are available by single year of age at the state level, so U.S. population totals by sex for single year age groups are used to determine the proportion of individuals changing age groups during the year. These proportions are applied evenly to all states.

State fertility and mortality rates are treated as exogenous in ECESIS. The trends in these rates are closely linked to national trends as predicted by the U.S. Bureau of the Census for the national population projections. This procedure is more flexible than might appear since considerable effort goes into computing the at-risk populations to which these rates are applied. The computation of at-risk populations is completely endogenous to the model.

Using data from the Immigration and Naturalization Services, the demographic model distributes 400,000 immigrants annually throughout the United States.[8]

The Migration Submodel

Migration models come in many varieties but most have their foundations in the human capital theory of migration (Sjaastad 1962). Simply put, individuals will migrate if the net present discounted value of their move is positive. Single equation behavioral models generally determine net

[8] This figure includes the 270,000 immigration quota and an allowance, based on previous years, for refugees entering the U.S. Most refugees apply for immigrant status once they arrive in the U. S.

migration as a function of something like wage rate differentials (Borts and Stein 1964). Gravity and entropy models use attractiveness variables like wages and employment rates and mass variables like population and labor force (Lowry 1966; Feeney 1973). Other models stress the decision process by comparing all of the migrants alternative opportunities (Feder 1979).

In addition to these models which stress the economic incentives for migration, recent work focuses on several special population groups like the elderly, college age and military personnel that respond more to institutional settings than economic incentives (Long 1983).

No matter how they are specified, all migration models suffer from inadequate data. There are many sources of migration data but all of them have serious flaws that limit their usefulness (Bilsborrow and Akin 1982; Isserman, Plane and McMillen 1982). The migration model in ECESIS makes use of several data sources. A time-series modelling approach was abandoned in favor of a cross-sectional model because the time-series data sources proved to be unreliable (see Chapter Nine).

The migration model used in ECESIS is a merger of the gravity and Markov modelling approaches. A gravity model determines the migration flow from region i to region j during period t ($M_{ij}(t)$) as a function of distance weighted (d_{ij}) attractiveness (A_i,A_j) of the two regions,

(1.3.1) $$M_{ij}(t) = C \cdot A_i(t)^{\alpha} \cdot A_j(t)^{\beta} \cdot d_{ij}^{-\gamma}.$$

Only one migration flow matrix is required to solve for the parameters C, α, β and γ. A Markov model approach requires two flow matrices and some assumption about the stability of migration rates. In the simplest case, the rates are assumed constant,

(1.3.2) $$M_{ij}(t) = P_i(t-1)[M_{ij}(b)/P_i(b-1)],$$

where $P_i(t-1)$ is the population in region i in period t-1 (beginning of period t), and b refers to some base period.

The ECESIS migration model combines the attractiveness measures from the gravity model with the dynamics of the transition rates from the Markov model. Defining,

$$p_{ij}(t) = M_{ij}(t)/P_i(t-1),$$

the model may be written as,

(1.3.3) $$p_{ij}(t) = p_{ij}(t-1)[A_j(t)/A_j(t-1)]^{\gamma} \cdot D_i^{-1},$$

where,

$$D_i = \Sigma_k p_{ik}(t-1)[A_k(t)/A_k(t-1)]^{\gamma}.$$

The term D_i is a balancing factor to ensure that the rows of the Markov matrix sum to one. The attractiveness term measures the growth in attractiveness of region j relative to all other regions.

All transition rates are interdependent. Even if there are no changes in the attractiveness of regions i and j, the migration probability from i to j will change in response to the relative attractiveness changes of other regions in the system. If there are no attractiveness changes in any region, (1.3.3) reduces to the constant probability Markov model (1.3.1).

With two sets of migration flow matrices, γ can be estimated, for instance, to minimize the root mean square error between estimated and observed transition rates in the second year. γ is a close approximation to an elasticity. When $\gamma=0$, (1.3.3) is identical to the standard demographic Markov approach--there is no migration response to changing attractiveness.

The attractiveness measure in ECESIS varies by age group. For the four population groups in primary labor force ages (18-44 and 45-64), the attractiveness measure is related to regional labor market conditions. It is a proxy for the probability of gaining employment.

$$A_j(t) = \{[E_j(t)-E_j(t-1)]+sE_j(t-1)\}/[U_j(t-1)+sE_j(t-1)],$$

where $E_j(t)$ is the employment in region j in t, $sE_j(t-1)$ is the number of separations excluding layoffs, and $U_j(t-1)$ is the number of unemployed. The number of separations is estimated using the national rate of separations (s), because this statistic is not available for all fifty states. The numerator can be considered a measure of opportunity (the number of jobs available) and denominator a measure of competition (the number of people seeking employment).

Migration in the four population groups less than eighteen years of age is modelled with migration of fecund females (18-44 years of age) as the attractiveness index. If migration of women from region i to region j increases, the migration of children would be expected to increase also. Migration of the elderly is modelled with no attractiveness measure, i.e. in the standard demographic manner with fixed transition rates and no linkages to economic conditions.

The γ parameters for the four population groups of labor force age are estimated using migration data based on federal income tax records. Interstate migration is estimated by the U.S. Bureau of the Census for use in making population estimates to allocate General Revenue Sharing funds. An individual's tax return for one year is matched to the return for a subsequent year by social security number. If the addresses on the two returns are in different states the individual and any dependents claimed are counted as interstate migrants. Annual migration flows for 1975-76, 1976-77, and 1978-79 are currently available but with no age detail. Therefore, the age distribution of migrants was estimated using the age distribution of 1965-70 migration flows from the 1970 population census adjusted for subsequent changes in the national population composition.

The 1975-76 matrices of transition rates for each of the four labor force groups were modified to approximate the 1976-77 matrices using (1.3.3) and the opportunity-competition attractiveness index. The values of γ were chosen to minimize the root mean square error between the estimated and observed transition rates for 1976-77. These γ values are held constant in ECESIS. With no other annual migration flow matrices available for consecutive years, it is not possible to model γ endogenously.

In a simulation exercise, the 1976-77 matrix was used with the estimated γ's and the actual values for the attractiveness measures to estimate 1978-79 migration (see Chapter Nine). For the four labor force age groups this method was more accurate than the demographic approach by twenty percent in estimating net migration by state.

For the ECESIS model, a set of 1957-58 migration flow matrices were created to be compatible with the economic data that begin in 1958. These matrices were constructed from 1955-60 migration flows identified in the 1960 census, the 1965-70 age distribution of migration adjusted for changes in population composition from 1965-70 to 1958, and the ratio of one-year to five-year migration according to the Current Population Survey. The constructed matrices are used as base year values in ECESIS.

1.3.4 ECONOMIC-DEMOGRAPHIC LINKAGES

The components described above are interconnected through a set of linkage equations. These interregional linkages play an important role in ECESIS. A change in the economic conditions in any state will affect the economies of all other states through the output, wage and employment linkages. In addition, changes in the relative economic conditions in the states will induce changes in migration patterns. This, in turn, will feed back into the state economies.

A flow chart of these relationships is shown in Figure 1.3.3. First the individual state economic models are solved one at a time. These solutions are stored on a data file and selected data (about 120 variables per state) are passed to the trade and demographic models. These models update certain of the data on each state's data file. At this point every variable in the system in checked for

FIGURE 1.3.3

FLOW CHART OF ECESIS SYSTEM

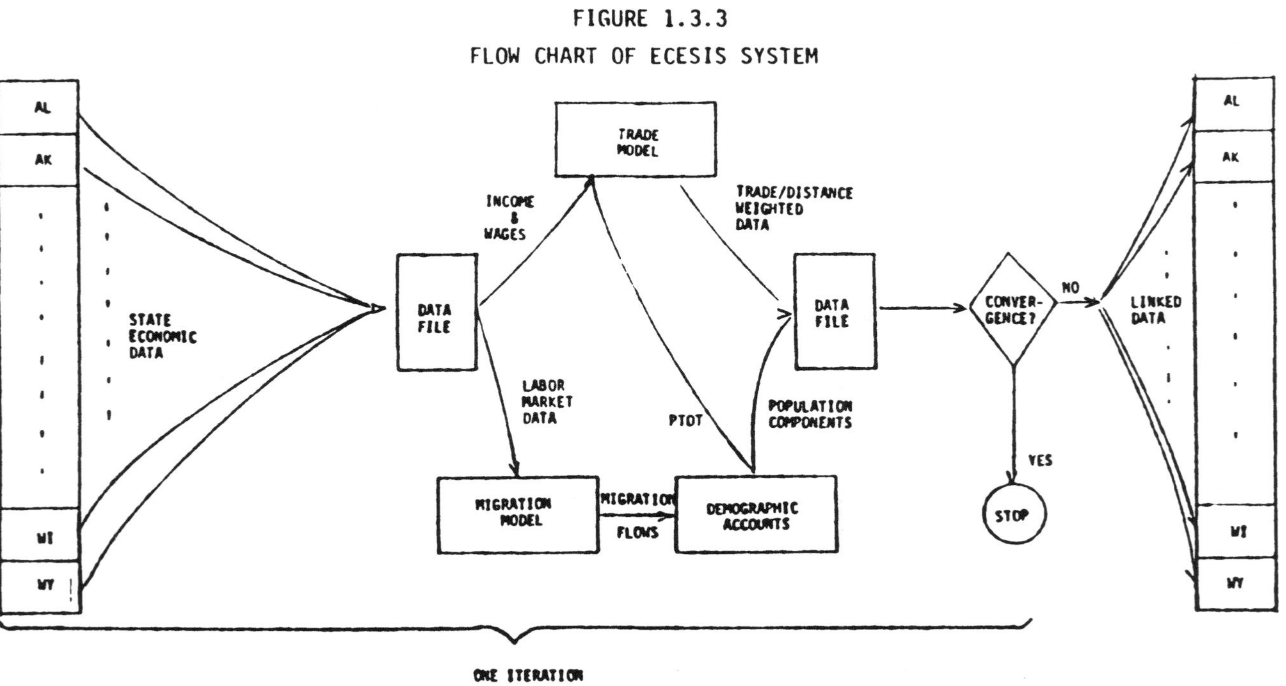

convergence. If the value of any variable, even manufacturing investment in North Dakota, changes by more than five hundredths of a percent the process is repeated. Once convergence is achieved, the final solution is stored and used as the initial point for the next period and the whole procedure is repeated.

For a typical simulation, ECESIS would require ten to twenty iterations per year for the twenty year horizon. Within each of these system iterations each of the fifty-one state models would iterate twenty to fifty times and the demographic and migration models would iterate ten to twenty times.

An example will help to illustrate the economic-demographic linkages in the model. Say there is an exogenous increase in government spending in Virginia. This will show up as an increase in total personal income which will stimulate output demand. The increased output will lead to increased employment and wages and thus higher income. This is the within state multiplier effect. Through the interregional trade model some of the increased demand would spill over to Virginia's trading partners--particularly if Virginia is close to full capacity. This stimulates the economies in other regions which also indirectly stimulates Virginia through the trade model. This is the interregional aspect of the multiplier effect.

Since Virginia is its own greatest trading partner, the biggest employment impact will likely be in Virginia. This will make Virginia relatively more attractive to migrants than other states. The increased inmigration to Virginia will further increase demand in that state--the demographic aspect of the multiplier effect. Also, the increased population will increase capacity output and increase the labor force. Both of these changes tend to counter act the affects of the increase in employment and hold down wages. Wages in Virginia may still rise faster than in surrounding states because of the relative size of the impact in Virginia. If so, Virginia will become less competitive and more of the increased demand from the stimulus will be met by Virginia's trading partners.

Adjustments in capital, goods and people flows will continue until a new interregional equilibrium is achieved. The net results are difficult to predict, depending on the relative elasticities in Virginia, how close to full capacity Virginia's manufacturing sector is to begin with and how many new migrants are attracted to Virginia. Experience with the model indicates that even a modest one-time stimulus would require at least a decade to arrive at a new equilibrium.

1.4 TESTING THE PROPERTIES OF ECESIS

Several experiments have been conducted with the ECESIS model in order to test its simulation properties. Multiplier experiments are used to determine how sensitive the regional economic models are to various levels of linkages to the other submodels. A second set of experiments test how the system responds when different types of demographic submodels are used. Finally, a set of simulation experiments show the potential uses of ECESIS and highlight some of its strengths and weaknesses.

1.4.1 MULTIPLIER EXPERIMENTS

A multiplier experiment is conducted by shocking some exogenous variable to the system and solving the model. The new solution path is compared to a control path to determine the effects of the shock.

In this case the CONTROL solution is the historical data from 1959 to 1980. First the ECESIS model is tracked to the historical data so that an unshocked simulation from 1959 to 1980 will reproduce the actual data over that period. This is accomplished in a two-step procedure. First, the residuals from the economic model equation estimations are added back to those equations as constant adjustments. Next, residuals from the demographic model are calculated by using actual economic data to drive the demographic model and then computing the forecast errors for each historical period. These errors are then added back to the demographic equations as in the economic model. This procedure is complicated by the cross-sectional nature of the migration model and the lack of a time-series of migration transition rates. The full procedure is outlined in Chapter Ten. Some of the actual data from 1975 to 1980 are incomplete and must be projected. The model is tracked to the projected values for those variables.

The experiment consists of subtracting one-half percent of each state's 1959 level of total personal income from an exogenous income item (YFARM) in that state. The shock is maintained throughout the 1959 to 1980 period. The experiment is carried out under three different linkage conditions. First, the model is shocked with no linkages active. All interstate trade and wage linkages and the entire demographic submodel is turned off. This is equivalent to shocking each state economic model on a stand-alone basis with no interregional or demographic feedbacks. Next, the interregional economic linkages are turned on but the demographic submodel remains exogenous. This is equivalent to shocking an interregional economic model with no demographic feedbacks. Finally, the model is shocked with all interregional economic and demographic linkages active.

With all linkages turned off the impact multipliers in the state models are quite low. The simple average of the fifty-one impact multipliers on total personal income is 1.18. The impact income multiplier for the total U.S. is 1.15. The multipliers are similar across states. The range is a low of 1.08 in North Dakota to a high of 1.35 in West Virginia with a variance of only .0025. This similarity is not surprising since each state model is based on the same structure and each is shocked by the same percent of income.

When the interregional economic wage, production and employment linkages are turned on the impact multipliers increase by about twenty-five percent. The range of the income impact multipliers is from 1.06 in Arkansas to 2.16 in North Carolina with a simple average of 1.44. The U.S. multiplier is 1.43. The variation in the multipliers increases to .053, still quite small. With the economic linkages on, the states still behave quite similarly to one another. The feedback effects increase the impact multipliers in all states except Arkansas, Mississippi, Rhode Island and Vermont.

There is virtually no change in the impact multipliers when the demographic linkages are activated. The U.S. income multiplier remains at 1.43 and the simple average remains at 1.44. The variation in the income multipliers across regions increases only slightly to .055. The greatest change in the income impact multipliers from the second (economic linkages only) to the third (economic and demographic linkages) experiments is .09 in Florida. As Florida's economy slows down due to the negative income shock, net inmigration into Florida slows. This relative decline in population feeds back into the state economy causing the fully linked impact multiplier to increase.

The long-run multiplier is the sum of the single period multipliers from 1959 to 1980. With no linkages active the long-run multipliers are small and similar across states. The static multipliers drop to approximately zero in the second year of the shock and remain there through 1980. After the initial shock, total income slowly (and nearly asymptotically) approaches the baseline level.

When the economic linkages are activated the long-run total income multiplier for the U.S. increases to 2.31 with the simple fifty-one region average up to 2.96, a 150% increase over the no linkages case. The variation of the multipliers across states also increases from .022 with no linkages on to 1.77 with the economic linkages on. The long-run income multiplier range is from -.96 in New York to 6.52 in Florida. There is also a dramatic change in the income adjustment path over the solution period. Rather than the monotonic adjustment in the no linkage case, the solution path now follows a damped cyclical pattern in most states. Four states (Delaware, District of Columbia, Hawaii and Wyoming) tended to follow explosive cyclical patterns. As a consequence, the economic models for these four states were left exogenous for these experiments. Also, a few states had periods when income was actually above the baseline level. The income growth in these states (Connecticut, New Jersey and New York) was so slow by the end of the baseline period that they actually gained relative to other states when the entire U.S. was shocked downward. In general, the states that are least sensitive to the economic linkages (those states where the long-run income multipliers change the least when the economic linkages are activated) are the Northeast, Middle Atlantic and East North Central states.

When the demographic linkages are activated in addition to the economic linkages, the long-run total income multiplier decreases to 2.07 for the U.S. and 2.71 for the fifty-one region average. Even though the multipliers have fallen in magnitude, the across state variation increases to 2.22. The range is from -1.43 in New York to 7.06 in Florida. There is no apparent spatial pattern to the states whose multipliers went up and those which went down. However, the fully linked long-run income multipliers tend to be highest in the Southern and Mountain states and lowest in the New England and East North Central states.

The income adjustment paths of the fully linked and economic only linked experiments are very similar. Even in Virginia, where the economic linked long-run multiplier drops to .42, the income adjustment paths are quite similar.

The interregional economic linkages clearly affect the basic properties of the state economic models. On a stand-alone basis, the state models are very stable and adjust monotonically to shocks. With interregional economic linkages, the state models are more volatile and follow a cyclical adjustment pattern. An individual state's adjustment is influenced by the type of states that surround it. The New England and East North Central states, for example, are in a pocket of slow growth. As a consequence, their sluggish economies interact with one another resulting in relatively low multiplier responses for the whole region.

The introduction of the demographic linkages (population movements) does not seem to change the basic properties of the state models. The demographic linkages do, however, significantly influence the state economies. In New York, for example, the economic trough comes in 1965 in response to the income shock. When the demographic linkages are exogenous, income is $850 million below the baseline value in that year. When population is made endogenous, nearly fourteen thousand people choose to leave New York in 1965 in search of job opportunities in other states less hard hit by the down-turn. As a result, employment falls by five thousand and income falls to $900 million below baseline in 1965. Thus, the economic adjustment cycle in New York is amplified when population dynamics are taken into account. In other states, California, for example, the adjustment cycles are muted when population is made endogenous.

1.4.2 ALTERNATIVE DEMOGRAPHIC SUBMODELS

This group of experiments is designed to test how sensitive the ECESIS model is to the type of demographic submodel used. The ECESIS demographic model is an interregional cohort-component model similar to the demographic model used by the U.S. Bureau of the Census for state population projections. Such a model takes full advantage of accounting information available to demographers but, as a consequence, is quite complex. In the Census model, the migration decision is made solely on the basis of past migration patterns. In ECESIS, the migration decision is at least partially motivated by economic factors.

In contrast, the demographic model used by the Bureau of Economic Analysis (BEA) makes little use of demographic accounting techniques and is thus quite simple. Regional population is determined by regional employment growth. The implication of this is that the implicitly determined net inmigration of a region is completely motivated by economic factors.

The experiments in this section compare the economic and demographic trends projected by ECESIS when the differing types of demographic models discussed above are linked to the economic models. The details of these experiments as well as a complete analysis of the results are presented in Chapter Eleven. Only a brief overview is given here.

The CONTROL solution for these experiments is the 1981 to 2000 period. Because ECESIS has two levels of linkages (interregional economic and economic-demographic), a first approximation of all data must be available for the first iteration in all forecast years. This first guess obviously influences the final forecast. The ideal forecast procedure would be to produce a forecast for each state economy and the demographic model on a stand-alone basis and use this as a starting point for the fully linked forecasts. Time and resource constraints dictate a simpler procedure. First, the economic and demographic data are projected to the year 2000 using a simple trend procedure. Next, residual terms are calculated for these data on an individual model basis. This procedure is in lieu of individual model forecasts. No attempt is made at this point to make the projected data consistent with identities and across state restrictions. Using these projected data and calculated residuals as a starting point, the ECESIS model is run in fully linked mode to produce a projection for the period 1981 to 2000.

The advantage of this procedure, other than cost and time savings, is that the CONTROL solution is relatively smooth. By comparison, the actual historical data for some states are quite volatile--more so than can be comfortably believed. The smooth CONTROL solution makes the task of comparing the results of the various experiments easier. The disadvantage of this procedure is that the CONTROL projection is a function of the starting point and this starting point was derived mechanically rather than by considering the particulars of each region.

Two of the experiments in this section alter the elasticity of the migrants' response to the economic attractiveness variable in the ECESIS migration model. Recall,

$$p_{ij}(t) = p_{ij}(t-1)[A_j(t)/A_j(t-1)]^{\gamma} \cdot D_i^{-1},$$

where

$$p_{ij}(t) = M_{ij}(t)/P_i(t-1), \text{ and}$$

$$D_i = \sum_k p_{ik}(t-1)[A_k(t)/A_k(t-1)]^{\gamma}.$$

A separate γ coefficient is estimated for each of the four age-sex groups in the labor force ages. The estimated γ's range from .43 to .53. In the first experiment (GAMMA0) all of the γ's are set to zero. This implies that migration flows are not sensitive to economic attractiveness and reduces the migration model to the simple fixed transition rate Markov model. The next experiment (GAMMA1) sets all of the γ's to one. This essentially doubles the sensitivity of the migration rates to the attractiveness variable.

The next experiment, BEAPOP, completely replaces the ECESIS demographic model with a BEA type demographic model. In this case, the migration decision is completely motivated by economic factors. Using the BEA hypothesis, population in state i is determined from,

(1.4.1) $$PTOT_{i,t} = PTOT_{i,t-1}(ET_{i,t-1}/ET_{i,t-2}).$$

Age-sex detail is added to the total state population by a simple RAS procedure. Birth, death, and place-to-place migration flows are not calculated by this model and the formal aging procedure used in the ECESIS demographic model is ignored. Note that the BEA demographic model is completely postrecursive to the economic model, just as in the case of the BEA projections model. Also, in keeping with the BEA projection technique, the unemployment rate in each state is taken as exogenous. Thus, the labor force and labor force participation rates must be determined by identity. This approach tends to reduce the demographic feedbacks on the system, precisely what the BEA intends.

The final experiment considered in the section is the case where net migration for each state is forced to be zero for each forecast year. This NONET scenario is commonly used at the Bureau of the Census because net migration estimates are so volatile and difficult to project. The question is whether or not this simple net migration assumption, which replaces the entire migration submodel, performs significantly differently than other versions of the ECESIS model. Technical problems prevented the completion of this final experiment. The problems encountered, however, are enlightening. The demographic submodel of ECESIS, based on the Rees and Wilson procedure, calculates minor population flows. As the name suggests, these flows are small in magnitude. These minor flows, however, are a mechanically crucial part of the Rees-Wilson algorithm. If net migration is assumed to be zero, the minor flow calculations break down and the Rees-Wilson demographic model cannot be solved. This suggests that the Rees-Wilson model may be far too sensitive to the minor flow variables.

In terms of economic incentives for interstate migration, the experiments in this section may be ranked in the order: GAMMA0, CONTROL, GAMMA1, and BEAPOP. Economic factors play no role in migrants' decisions in GAMMA0 and rule the migrants' decision completely in BEAPOP.

In general, as the economic incentives for migration increase, the "efficiency" of the moves also increases. In other words, as migrants pay less attention to established migration patterns and more attention to economic opportunities, the economies of most regions benefit. For example, total employment in the U.S. in 1999 is projected in the CONTROL solution to be 129.462 million. For this same date, GAMMA0 projects 173 thousand fewer and GAMMA1 projects 157 thousand more persons employed. These experiments simply change the elasticity of migration with respect to the economic attractiveness of a region. When economic motives completely determine migration patterns (BEAPOP), total U.S. employment in 1999 increases by 1500 thousand persons. This order of magnitude differential indicates that long-term economic projections are quite dependent upon the type of demographic model used.

Not all regions benefit equally as available labor is used more efficiently. Most of the additional employment growth takes place in the eastern half of the U.S. Indeed, the only state east of the Mississippi River that suffers reduced employment as economic incentives for migration increase is Florida. Historically, Florida has had a high rate of positive net inmigration. GAMMA0 simply projects this trend to the year 2000 independently of the relative economic growth of Florida. The CONTROL and GAMMA1 experiments reduce this pattern somewhat but still the historical trend plays an important role. The BEAPOP scenario, however, completely ignores Florida's history of inmigration and moves people in and out of Florida solely on the basis of relative economic opportunities in Florida. As a consequence, Florida's population is 400 thousand persons less under BEAPOP than under GAMMA0. Similar arguments can be made, to a lesser extent, for California and some of the Mountain states.

The East North Central and Middle Atlantic states benefit most by the more efficient allocation of workers. Employment, real income and population are all up in those states. The big losers, other than Florida, are the Plains states (particularly Kansas, Missouri, Arkansas and Oklahoma) and the Pacific states.

The BEA's economic and demographic forecasts have been criticized for overstating growth in the North Central and Northeast states and understating growth in the Southern and Western states. This group of experiments indicates that the implicit migration assumption made by the BEA is a primary cause. If migrants are allowed to entertain noneconomic motives for their migration decisions, the long-term regional growth patterns of the US. are quite different.

1.4.3 SIMULATION EXPERIMENTS

Two simulation experiments have been chosen to demonstrate the usefulness of an interregional economic-demographic model of the U.S. First, the impact of increased Asian immigration to the U.S. is examined. The issue is not only how this increased immigration will affect long term economic growth in the U.S. but also how regional growth patterns will be affected. The second simulation explores the usefulness of regional policies for stimulating the U.S. economy and aiding depressed regions. Providing tax incentives for firms in depressed areas may be a cost effective way of stimulating growth in the entire U.S. economy. Details of both of these simulations are given in Chapter Twelve.

Increased Asian Immigration

A nation of immigrants is a term often applied to the U.S. But ambivalence toward immigration has long existed in America. Many factors, including cultural, racial and ethnic attitudes, are involved. A common argument is that immigrants will drive down wages and displace citizen workers in the labor force. Recent media coverage of illegal Mexican and Haitian immigration and Cuban and Southeast Asian refugees have amplified social and political awareness of the issue. Little, however, has been done to measure the quantitative effects of immigration (Greenwood 1979). ECESIS provides a framework for analyzing this issue at both the national and regional levels.

The most dramatic change in recent U.S. immigration trends is the rapid increase in Asian immigration over the last two decades. In 1965, Asia accounted for only seven percent of total U.S. immigration; by 1979 that share rose to over forty percent. Changes in U.S. immigration laws and socio-political conditions in parts of Asia have accounted for this rapid increase. From 1977 to 1979 nearly 600 thousand Asians immigrated to the U.S. Asian immigration has quickly become a significant source of demographic change within the U.S.--even more so when regional factors are taken into consideration. Thirty-eight percent of all Asian immigrants list California as their state of intended residence. New York is second with eleven percent. Over two-thirds of all Asian immigrants settle in just six U.S. states: California, Hawaii, Illinois, New Jersey, New York, and Texas.

Measuring the quantitative effects at the regional and national level of this immigration trend is the purpose of this simulation. There are obviously supply effects as the immigrants enter the labor force and reduce wages. In addition, there are demand effects as immigrants rent or purchase homes, and buy food, cars, and other consumer goods. Which effect dominates is an empirical question.

The simulation exercise to estimate these impacts was carried out by increasing Asian immigration by 100,000 persons annually in each year between 1981 and 2000. This simulation is compared to the CONTROL solution which assumes a total of 400,000 immigrants annually--forty percent of which are Asian. The extra immigration is allocated among the states using the 1979 distribution of Asian immigration. The immigrants in each state were given the age and sex distribution of total 1979 immigration. Once allocated, the 500,000 total immigrants assume the same birth, death, migration and labor force participation rates as the rest of the states' population.

Since the spatial distribution of Asian immigrants is not uniform, some states are more affected than others. For example, under the CONTROL solution, California receives 21.6 percent of all migrants or 86,400 persons. In the Asian simulation, since 38 percent of all Asians settle there, California receives 24.8 percent or 124,200 migrants.

Wyoming, on the other hand, receives less than fifty additional migrants per year.

The first three years of the simulation show the supply side effects dominating at the national level. The unemployment rate increases and real wages fall. By the mid 1980's, however, the demand effects begin to dominate. By the year 2000, two million additional immigrants have been added to the U.S. population. Wages, income, productivity, and output are all above the baseline levels. Employment is up by 1,099,810 and unemployment is up by 425,520. The unemployment rate increases by one quarter of a point. This does not imply, however, that "citizen workers" have been displaced by immigrants. Assuming that immigrants have the same unemployment rate as nonimmigrants, approximately 55,000 immigrants would be unemployed. This leaves about 370,000 additional nonimmigrants in the unemployment ranks. The expansion in economic activity, however, increases the labor force participation rate over the baseline, inducing over 475,000 additional nonimmigrants into the labor force. Thus, employment of "citizen workers" is likely to be higher than under the baseline scenario. Further, the adjustment path is quite cyclical and the year 2000 occurs at a down period of the cycle.

The scenario differs substantially across different regions of the U.S. California, for example, the largest recipient of the additional immigrants, grows at a faster rate than the U.S. average. By 2000 the unemployment rate is lower than the baseline and employment, income and real wages are up.

Michigan suffers the most adverse effects in the simulation. Early in the period Michigan benefits from increased output demand from other states. But few immigrants move to Michigan. Eventually a tight labor market drives the wage rate in Michigan to an uncompetitive level and employment in Michigan actually declines. Increased unemployment rates do not significantly reduce Michigan's wage (see Chapter Five) to make the state more competitive.

In general, the North Central and Northeast states benefit less from the expansion than do the Southern and Western states. Relatively high wages in the former appear to be a major reason for the slower growth. An interesting exception is New York, the second leading destination of Asian immigrants. New York's labor force increases enough to offset the demand effects and to keep wages lower than in surrounding states. Still New York's unemployment rate is up seven-tenths of a percent and workers are moving to faster growing areas.

This simulation experiment suggests that, for the nation as a whole, increased Asian immigration will not result in the dire consequences predicted by many displacement hypotheses. Regional aspects of the scenario, however, are less encouraging. Not all regions benefit and some states suffer substantial economic losses. The empirical results support adding another dimension to immigration policy. They strongly hint at something that regional economists and other regional scientists have long argued. The impact of a policy depends on its locational characteristics. Immigration policy probably should be concerned with the origins of immigrants as well as with their destinations.

Regional Stimulus Policies

Differential regional growth rates again became a political issue in the 1970's. A period of moderate growth for the U.S. as a whole, the seventies were a period of rapid growth for the Mountain and Southern states and slow or negative growth for the Northeast and North Central states. Several factors have led to these growth rate differentials. The North Central and Northeast states are heavily weighted with manufacturing industries which, historically, have been more sensitive to economic cycles than nonmanufacturing industries. The sharp economic downturn of the mid 1970's affected the Northeast and North Central states quite severely. In addition, in recent years, there has been a relative decline in the importance of the manufacturing industries in the U.S. This structural shift away from manufacturing and into the services, trade and government sectors has benefited the Western and Southern states. Another factor has been a shift in the migration patterns in the U.S. The seventies saw a dramatic increase in "frost belt" to "sun belt" migration. This phenomenon is only partially explained by changes in the relative economic conditions in the regions. This population shift has augmented the decline of the Northeast and North Central and advance of the Western and Southern states.

In this simulation experiment the feasibility of a federal policy to stimulate manufacturing investment in depressed areas is examined. The experiment is conducted over the period 1981 to 2000 and is compared to the CONTROL solution for that period. The experiment introduces a five year program that increases the investment tax credit for manufactured goods in selected states. The target area is the East North Central and Middle Atlantic states (Illinois, Indiana, Michigan, New Jersey, New York, Ohio, Pennsylvania, and Wisconsin).[9] The program is initiated in 1981 with an effective 5.66 percent reduction in the user cost of

---

[9] As in previous experiments, Delaware, District of Columbia, Hawaii, and Wyoming are exogenous in this simulation exercise.

manufacturing capital stock in the target areas. The tax credit is gradually phased out so that by 1985 the tax credit is back to the CONTROL level. At issue is whether or not this policy will lead to any long-term growth gains for the target states and by how much other regions are affected by this policy.

The program creates a spurt of real gross manufacturing investment in the target area. The peak impact is in 1982 with a three percent increase in real gross manufacturing investment. As the program is phased out, investment quickly falls back to the CONTROL solution level. For the U.S. as a whole, real gross manufacturing investment is up by just over one percent in 1982 (421 million 1972 dollars) and is nearly back to the CONTROL solution level by 1987. Nontarget states also show an increase in investment but the effect is much smaller and the peak does not occur until about 1988.

The tax credit program creates a cyclical adjustment path. The stimulus peaks in about 1988 then turns down and eventually turns up again in 1996. By the year 2000 most variables are approximately back at their baseline values--completing one full cycle. The amplitude of the cycle is greater in the target states than in the nontarget states. This is primarily due to the large manufacturing sectors in the target states and the sensitivity of manufacturing to economic cycles. Since the investment cycle has ended, the next economic cycle should be shorter and more damped.

The increased manufacturing investment in the target states leads to increased in manufacturing capital stock and manufacturing output which, in turn, lead to employment and income increases. Forty percent of the new jobs created are in the manufacturing sector. That is about twice as large as one would normally expect but this shock was designed to stimulate manufacturing output.

Increased job opportunities in the target regions reduce the net outmigration from the area. All of the target states, except New Jersey, increase their populations during the simulation. Population movements follow the economic cycle in the target area. During the boom, the target states attract more than twenty thousand people over the CONTROL solution. During the decline, however, people leave the target area in large numbers so that by the year 2000 the target area has attracted only about two thousand additional residents.

If the population flows are not allowed--by exogenizing the demographic model and holding population constant--the simulation adjustment paths tend to be less cyclical. The demographic model reinforces the economic cycles. People move to fast growing regions which induces further growth.

Conversely, slow growing regions lose population. This pattern is quite evident in this experiment. Only one state, Pennsylvania, attracts enough migrants during the stimulus period to create sufficient demand to significantly soften the cyclical downturn. Pennsylvania is the only target state that enjoys long-term gains from the stimulus policy.

That such a policy as carried out here would only lead to short-term gains for the target areas would not surprise most economists. Essentially the policy tested is a subsidy program. Such policies disrupt markets and lead to gains only at the expense of distorting market incentives. When the subsidy is removed, the subsequent adjustment back to market equilibrium is bound to be costly. This simulation indicates that any such regional policy, to be effective, would have to be in place for a long period of time--perhaps over a decade. This is an expensive proposition, particularly if the policy is thought of as a tax on nontarget regions. That is not to say that such policies are unreasonable. Many factors other than economic efficiency determine optimal policies.

APPENDIX 1.1

SPECIFICATION OF ECONOMIC MODEL EQUATIONS

OUTPUT AND FACTOR DEMANDS

(A1) OUTPUT DEMAND

$$Q = a_0 + a_1Q^* + a_2(WMH/P) + a_3RYT72_j$$

Q - real manufacturing value added; 10^6 72 \$.
Q^* - $Q_{-1} \cdot IP/IP_{-1}$.
IP - U.S. index of industrial production; 1967=100.
WMH - manufacturing hourly wage rate; \$/hr.
P - manufacturing output deflator; 1972 = 1.
RYT72 = $\sum_j r_{ij} YT72_j$; trade weighted real income.
r_{ij} - interstate trade share matrix for manufactured goods.
YT72 - real total personal income; 10^6 72 \$.

(A2) CAPACITY OUTPUT

$$QCAP = a_0 MLFC^{\alpha} MKS72^{\beta} \exp(\gamma PRTR)$$

QCAP - capacity real manufacturing output; 10^6 72 \$.
MLFC - capacity manufacturing labor inputs; 10^6 hr/yr.
MKS72 - real manufacturing capital stock; 10^6 72 \$.
PRTR - productivity trend (function of past productivity growth).

(A3) DESIRED CAPITAL INPUTS

$$MKD = \beta(1 - 1/\xi)PQ/UCC$$

MKD - desired manufacturing capital stock; 10^6 72 \$.
UCC - user cost of capital.
β - elasticity of capital inputs from production
PQ - nominal manufacturing value added; 10^6 \$. function.
ξ - elasticity of demand for manufactured goods.

(A4) DESIRED LABOR INPUTS

$$MLD = \alpha(1 - 1/\xi)PQ/WMH$$

MLD - desired manufacturing labor inputs; 10^6 hr/yr.
α - elasticity of labor inputs from production function.
WMH - manufacturing hourly wage rate; \$/hr.

(A5) CAPITAL ADJUSTMENT - INVESTMENT

$$MGI72 = a_0 + a_1 MGI72_{-1} + a_2(MKD - MKS72_{-1})$$

MGI72 - real manufacturing gross investment; 10^6 72 \$.
MKD - desired manufacturing capital stock; 10^6 72 \$.
MKS72 - real manufacturing capital stock; 10^6 72 \$.

(A6) LABOR DEMAND ADJUSTMENT

$$\log(MLAB) = a_0 + a_1 \log(MLD) + a_2 \log(MLAB_{-1})$$

MLAB - manufacturing labor inputs; 10^6 hr/yr.
MLD - desired manufacturing labor inputs; 10^6 hr/yr.

(A7) CAPACITY UTILIZATION RATE

$$CU = Q/QCAP$$

CU - manufacturing capacity utilization rate.
Q - real manufacturing value added; 10^6 72 \$.
QCAP - capacity real manufacturing output; 10^6 72 \$.

(A8) CAPACITY MANUFACTURING LABOR INPUTS

$$MLFC = MHC(EM/PTOT)^c PTOT \cdot 52/1000$$

MLFC - capacity manufacturing labor inputs; 10^6 hr/yr.
MHC - capacity hours per week (past peak); hr/wk.
$(EM/PTOT)^c$ - capacity manufacturing employment to population ratio (past peak).
PTOT - total state population; 10^3 persons.

(A9) MANUFACTURING CAPITAL STOCK DEPRECIATION

$$MD72 = \delta \cdot MKS72_{-1}$$

MD72 - depreciation of real manufacturing capital stock; 10^6 72 \$.
MKS72 - real manufacturing capital stock; 10^6 72 \$.
δ - capital depreciation rate.

(A10) NET MANUFACTURING INVESTMENT

$$MNI72 = MGI72 - MD72$$

MNI72 - real net manufacturing investment; 10^6 72 \$.
MGI72 - real gross manufacturing investment; 10^6 72 \$.
MD72 - depreciation of real manufacturing capital stock; 10^6 72 \$.

(A11) MANUFACTURING CAPITAL STOCK

$$MKS72 = MKS72_{-1} + MNI72$$

MKS72 - real manufacturing capital stock; 10^6 72 \$.
MNI72 - real net manufacturing investment; 10^6 72 \$.

(A12) NOMINAL MANUFACTURING OUTPUT

$$PQ = P \cdot Q$$

PQ - nominal manufacturing value added; 10^6 \$.
Q - real manufacturing value added; 10^6 72 \$.
P - manufacturing output deflator; 1972 = 1.

(A13) MANUFACTURING GROSS PROFITS

$$MGP\$ = PQ - YM$$

MGP\$ - nominal manufacturing gross profits; 10^6 \$.
PQ - nominal manufacturing value added; 10^6 \$.
YM - manufacturing income; 10^6 \$.

EMPLOYMENT

(A14) MANUFACTURING EMPLOYMENT

$$EM = MLAB/(MHR \cdot 52/1000)$$

EM - manufacturing employment; 10^3 jobs.
MLAB - manufacturing labor inputs; 10^6 hr/yr.
MHR - manufacturing hours per week per employee; hr/wk.

(A15) NONMANUFACTURING EMPLOYMENT

$$ENM = a_0 + a_1 ENM_{-1} + a_2(\sum_j d_{ij}^{-1} \cdot PTOT_j) + a_3 EM + a_4(WNM/CPI72)$$

ENM - nonmanufacturing employment; 10^3 jobs.
d_{ij} - distance between 1970 population centroids of state i and state j.
PTOT - total state population; 10^3 persons.
EM - manufacturing employment; 10^3 jobs.
WNM - nonmanufacturing average earnings; 10^3 \$/yr.
CPI72 - consumer price index; 1972 = 1.

(A16) TOTAL EMPLOYMENT

$$ET = EM + ENM + EOTHER$$

ET - total state employment; 10^3 persons.
EM - manufacturing employment; 10^3 jobs.
ENM - nonmanufacturing employment; 10^3 jobs.
EOTHER - other employment (farming) plus jobs to people employed conversion.

(A17) AVERAGE LABOR PRODUCT

$$APL = Q/EM$$

APL - average labor product; 10^3 72 \$/employee.
Q - real manufacturing value added; 10^6 72 \$.
EM - manufacturing employment; 10^3 jobs.

WAGES and PRICES

(A18) MANUFACTURING WAGES

$$\log(WM) = a_0 + a_1 \log(DW^*_i)_{-1} + a_2 \log(EM/P1864)_{-1}$$

$$+ a_3 \log(CU) + a_4 \log(CPI72)_{-1}$$

WM - manufacturing average earnings; 10^3 \$/yr.
$DW^*_i = \sum_j d_{ij}^{-1} WM_j [(YM_j/YTLPR_j)/(USYM/USYTLPR)]$; distance weighted and share adjusted manufacturing wage rates.
d_{ij} - distance between 1970 population centroids of state i and state j.
YM - manufacturing income; 10^6 \$.
YTLPR - total labor and proprietors income; 10^6 \$.
US... - US aggregate variables.
EM - manufacturing employment; 10^3 jobs.
P1864 - state population aged 18 to 64; 10^3 persons.
CU - manufacturing capacity utilization rate.
CPI72 - consumer price index; 1972 = 1.

(A19) NONMANUFACTURING WAGES

$$\log(WNM) = a_0 + a_1 \log(WM) + a_2 \log(ENM/P1864)_{-1}$$

WNM - nonmanufacturing average earnings; 10^3 \$/yr.
WM - manufacturing average earnings; 10^3 \$/yr.
ENM - nonmanufacturing employment; 10^3 jobs.
P1864 - state population aged 18 to 64; 10^3 persons.

(A20) NOMINAL MANUFACTURING HOURLY WAGE RATE

$$WMH = WM/(MHR \cdot 52/1000)$$

WMH - nominal manufacturing hourly wage rate; \$/hr.
WM - manufacturing average earnings; 10^3 \$/yr.
MHR - manufacturing hours per week per employee; hr/wk.

(A21) REAL MANUFACTURING HOURLY WAGE RATE

$$WMH72 = WMH/CPI72$$

WMH72 - real manufacturing hourly wage rate; 72 \$/hr.
WMH - nominal manufacturing hourly wage rate; \$/hr.
CPI72 - consumer price index; 1972 = 1.

(A22) TOTAL AVERAGE EARNINGS

$$WT = (YM + YNM)/(EM + ENM)$$

WT - total average earnings; 10^3 \$/yr.
YM - manufacturing income; 10^6 \$.
YNM - nonmanufacturing income; 10^6 \$.
EM - manufacturing employment; 10^3 jobs.
ENM - nonmanufacturing employment; 10^3 jobs.

(A23) REAL TOTAL AVERAGE EARNINGS

$$WT72 = WT/CPI72$$

WT72 - real total average earnings; 10^3 72 \$.
WT - nominal total average earnings; 10^3 \$.
CPI72 - consumer price index; 1972 = 1.

(A24) CONSUMER PRICE INDEX

$$\log(CPI72) = a_0 + a_1 \log(WT)$$

CPI72 - consumer price index; 1972 = 1.
WT - nominal total average earnings; 10^3 \$.

INCOME

(A25) MANUFACTURING INCOME

$$YM = WM \cdot EM$$

YM - manufacturing income; 10^6 \$.
WM - manufacturing average earnings; 10^3 \$.
EM - manufacturing employment; 10^3 jobs.

(A26) NONMANUFACTURING INCOME

$$YNM = WNM \cdot ENM$$

YNM - nonmanufacturing income; 10^6 \$.
WNM - nonmanufacturing average earnings; 10^3 \$.
ENM - nonmanufacturing employment; 10^3 jobs.

(A27) NONFARM PROPRIETORS INCOME

$$YPROP = a_0 + a_1 YT + a_2 PTOT$$

YPROP - nonfarm proprietors income; 10^6 \$.
YT - total state personal income; 10^6 \$.
PTOT - total state population; 10^3 persons.

(A28) TOTAL LABOR AND PROPRIETORS INCOME

$$YTLPR = YM + YNM + YPROP + YFARM$$

YTLPR - total labor and proprietors income; 10^6 \$.
YM - manufacturing income; 10^6 \$.
YNM - nonmanufacturing income; 10^6 \$.
YPROP - nonfarm proprietors income; 10^6 \$.
YFARM - total farm income; 10^6 \$.

(A29) PROPERTY INCOME

$$YDIR = a_0 + a_1 YDIR_{-1} + a_2 (GP\$+GP\$_{-1})/2 + a_3 PR$$

$$+ a_4 CPI72$$

YDIR - total dividend, interest and rent income; 10^6 \$.
GP\$ - nominal gross manufacturing profits; 10^6 \$.
PR - US average prime lending rate.
CPI72 - consumer price index; 1972 = 1.

(A30) TRANSFER PAYMENT INCOME

$$YTP = PTOT[a_0 + a_1 (YT/PTOT) + a_2 (P65+/PTOT)$$

$$+ a_3 (U/PTOT)]$$

YTP - total transfer payment income; 10^6 \$.
PTOT - total state population; 10^3 persons.
YT - total state personal income; 10^6 \$.
P65+ - state population age 65 years and over; 10^3 persons.
U - unemployment; 10^3 persons.

(A31) SOCIAL INSURANCE CONTRIBUTIONS

$$YSIC = YTLPR(a_0 + a_1 USSICR)$$

YSIC - social insurance contributions; 10^6 \$.
YTLPR - total labor and proprietors income; 10^6 \$.
USSICR - US social insurance contribution rate.

(A32) TOTAL STATE PERSONAL INCOME

$$YT = YTLPR + YDIR + YTP + YRA - YSIC$$

YT - total state personal income; 10^6 \$.
YTLPR - total labor and proprietors income; 10^6 \$.
YDIR - total dividend, interest and rent income; 10^6 \$.
YTP - total transfer payments; 10^6 \$.
YRA - residence adjustment; 10^6 \$.
YSIC - social insurance contributions; 10^6 \$.

(A33) REAL INCOME VARIABLES

$$Yxxx72 = Yxxx/CPI72$$

Yxxx72 - real income variables; 10^6 72 \$.
xxx - T, TLPR, DIR, etc.

LABOR FORCE AND UNEMPLOYMENT

Notation: ${}^aX^s$ - variable X for age group a and sex group s.

Age groups: a = 1 : 0-4 yrs.
= 2 : 5-17 yrs.
= 3 : 18-44 yrs.
= 4 : 45-64 yrs.
= 5 : 65 + yrs.

Sex groups: s = 1 : male
= 2 : female

R - labor force participation rate.

${}^aR^s$; a = 2,5; s = 1,2 are exogenous.

(A34) TOTAL LABOR FORCE PARTICIPATION RATE

$$RTOT = a_0 + a_1(YDIR/P1864)_{-1} + a_2WT72 + a_3\%CPI72$$

RTOT - total LFPR.
YDIR - total dividend, interest and rent income; 10^6 \$.
P1864 - state population aged 18 to 64; 10^3 persons.
WT72 - total real average earnings; 10^3 72 \$.
%CPI72 - percentage change in the consumer price index.

(A35) TOTAL LABOR FORCE

$$LF = RTOT \cdot PTOT$$

(A36) LFPR FOR 18-44 YEAR OLD MALES

$${}^3R^1/RTOT = a_0 + a_1({}^3R^1/RTOT)_{-1} + a_2(YDIR/P1864)_{-1}$$

(A37) LFPR FOR 18-44 YEAR OLD FEMALES

$${}^3R^2/RTOT = a_0 + a_1({}^3R^2/RTOT)_{-1} + a_2BRATE$$

BRATE - births per female aged 18-44.

(A38) LFPR FOR 45-64 YEAR OLD MALES

$${}^4R^1/RTOT = a_0 + a_1({}^4R^1/RTOT)_{-1} + a_2(YDIR/P1864)_{-1}$$

(A39) AGE-SEX SPECIFIC LABOR FORCE

$${}^aLF^s = {}^aR^s \cdot {}^aPOP^s;\ a \neq 4,\ s \neq 2$$

(A40) LF FOR 45-64 YEAR OLD FEMALES

$${}^4LF^2 = LF - \sum_{a,s} {}^aLF^s;\ a \neq 4,\ s \neq 2$$

(A41) LFPR FOR 45-64 YEAR OLD FEMALES

$${}^4R^2 = {}^4LF^2/{}^4POP^2$$

(A42) UNEMPLOYMENT RATE

$$UR = (LF - ET)/LF$$

APPENDIX 1.2

VARIABLE NAMES, DESCRIPTIONS AND SOURCES

Primary sources are listed at the end of this appendix and are referred to in the following by number--i.e. [2]. Variables constructed by transformation are indicated by "TRAN" and the transformation is given in the description section. The output variable "Q" referred to in the text is listed here as "MVA72". In many cases in the text the leading "M" is dropped from the manufacturing variables.

LABEL	DESCRIPTION, UNITS AND SOURCES
CPI72	Consumer price index; 1972=1.0; [1].
W*	Wage transmission variable; 10^3\$/person; WM[(YM/YTLPR)/(USYM/USYTLPR)]; tran.
DW*	Distance weighted wage transmission variable; $\Sigma_j d_{ij}^{-1} W*_j$; TRAN.
YTL72	Real total labor and proprietors income; 10^6 1972 \$; YTLPR/CPI72; TRAN.
YDR72	Real dividend, interest and rent income; 10^6 1972 \$; YDIR/CPI72; TRAN.
YT72	Real total personal income; 10^6 1972 \$; YT/CPI72; TRAN.
DYT72	Distance weighted real total personal income; $\Sigma_j d_{ij}^{-1} YT72_j$; TRAN.
RYT72	Trade weighted real total personal income; $\Sigma_j r_{ij} YT72_j$; TRAN.
DPTOT	Distance weighted total population; $\Sigma_j d_{ij}^{-1} PTOT_j$; TRAN.
MGP72	Real manufacturing gross profits; 10^6 1972 \$; MGP\$/CPI72; TRAN.
MLD	Desired manufacturing labor inputs; 10^6 hours; see Chapter Four; TRAN.

MKD	Desired manufacturing capital stock; 10^6 1972 $; see Chapter Four; TRAN.
MLAB	Actual manufacturing labor inputs; 10^6 hours; EM·MHR·52/1000; TRAN.
MAPL	Manufacturing average labor product; 10^3 1972 $/person; MVA72/EM; TRAN.
MGPR	Manufacturing gross profit rate; fraction; GP$/MVA; TRAN.
MEPC	Capacity manufacturing employment to population ratio; fraction; see Chapter Three; TRAN.
MHC	Capacity manufacturing hours worked; hours/week; see Chapter Three; TRAN.
MLFC	Capacity manufacturing labor inputs; 10^6 hours; MHC·MEPC·PTOT·52/1000; TRAN.
QCAP	Capacity manufacturing output; 10^6 1972 $; see Chapter Three; TRAN.
MCU	Manufacturing capacity utilization rate; fraction; MVA72/QCAP; TRAN.
MHR	Manufacturing hours worked per week per employee; hours; [19].
MPRTR	Manufacturing productivity trend; index; see Chapter Three; TRAN.
MGI72 or I	Real manufacturing gross investment; 10^6 1972 $; [2], [3].
MD72	Real manufacturing capital stock depreciation; 10^6 1972 $; see Chapter Three; TRAN.
MGP$	Manufacturing gross profits; 10^6 $; MVA–YM; TRAN.
MKS72 or K	Real manufacturing capital stock; 10^6 1972 $; see Chapter Three and Four; TRAN from [2], [13].
MNI72	Real manufacturing net investment; 10^6 1972 $; MGI72–MD72; TRAN.
MVA or PQ	Manufacturing value added; 10^6 $; [3].

MVA72 or Q	Real manufacturing value added; 10^6 1972 \$; MVA/USMP72; TRAN.
ET	Total employment; 10^3 persons; [18], [19].
EM	Manufacturing employment; 10^3 jobs; [18].
ENM	Nonmanufacturing employment; 10^3 jobs; [18].
EOTHER	Other employment; jobs to people; TRAN from [16], [17], [18], [19].
YTLPR	Total labor and proprietors income; 10^6 \$; [13].
YPROP	Nonfarm proprietors' income; 10^6 \$; [13].
YFARM	Farm income; 10^6 \$; [13].
YM	Manufacturing income; 10^6 \$; [13].
YNM	Nonmanufacturing income; 10^6 \$; [13].
YSIC	Social insurance contributions; 10^6 \$; [13].
YRA	Residence adjustment; 10^6 \$; [13].
YDIR	Dividend, interest and rent income; 10^6 \$; [13].
YTP	Transfer payments; 10^6 \$; [13].
YT	Total personal income; 10^6 \$; [13].
WM	Manufacturing average earnings; 10^3 \$/job; YM/EM; TRAN.
WNM	Nonmanufacturing average earnings; 10^3 \$/job; YNM/ENM; TRAN.
WT	Total average earnings; 10^3 \$/job; (YM+YNM)/(EM+ENM); TRAN.
WT72	Real total average earnings; 10^3 1972 \$/job; WT/CPI72, TRAN.
U	Total unemployment; 10^3 persons; [16], [17], [19].
UR	Unemployment rate; percent; U/LF·100, TRAN.
WMH	Manufacturing hourly wages; \$/hour; WM/(MHR·52/1000); TRAN.

WMH72 Real manufacturing hourly wages; 1972 $/hour; WMH/CPI72; TRAN.

PTOT Total resident population; 10^3 persons; [4], [6], [7], [8], [9].

PMALE Total male population; 10^3 persons; [4], [6], [7], [8], [9].

PFEM Total female population; 10^3 persons; [4], [6], [7], [8], [9].

P04 Total population 0 to 4 years old; 10^3 persons; [4], [6], [7], [8], [9].

P04M Male population 0 to 4 years old; 10^3 persons; [4], [6], [7], [8], [9].

P04F Female population 0 to 4 years old; 10^3 persons; [4], [6], [7], [8], [9].

P517 Total population 5 to 17 years old; 10^3 persons; [4], [6], [7], [8], [9].

P517M Male population 5 to 17 years old; 10^3 persons; [4], [6], [7], [8], [9].

P517F Female population 5 to 17 years old; 10^3 persons; [4], [6], [7], [8], [9].

P1844 Total population 18 to 44 years old; 10^3 persons; [4], [6], [7], [8], [9].

P1844M Male population 18 to 44 years old; 10^3 persons; [4], [6], [7], [8], [9].

P1844F Female population 18 to 44 years old; 10^3 persons; [4], [6], [7], [8], [9].

P4564 Total population 45 to 64 years old; 10^3 persons; [4], [6], [7], [8], [9].

P4564M Male population 45 to 64 years old; 10^3 persons; [4], [6], [7], [8], [9].

P4564F Female population 45 to 64 years old; 10^3 persons; [4], [6], [7], [8], [9].

P65 Total population 65 years and older; 10^3 persons; [4], [6], [7], [8], [9].

P65M	Male population 65 years and older; 10^3 persons; [4], [6], [7], [8], [9].
P65F	Female population 65 years and older; 10^3 persons; [4], [6], [7], [8], [9].
BIRTHS	Total live births; 10^3 persons; [15].
BRATE	Fertility rate; births per thousand women; BIRTHS/P1844F, corrected for calender year; TRAN.
DEATHS	Total deaths; 10^3 persons; [15].
ITOT	Total inmigration; 10^3 persons; [5], [8], [9].
IMALE	Total male inmigration; 10^3 persons; [5], [8], [9].
IFEM	Total female inmigration; 10^3 persons; [5], [8], [9].
I04	Total inmigration in 0 to 4 age group; 10^3 persons; [5], [8], [9].
I04M	Male inmigration in 0 to 4 age group; 10^3 persons; [5], [8], [9].
I04F	Female inmigration in 0 to 4 age group; 10^3 persons; [5], [8], [9].
I517	Total inmigration in 5 to 17 age group; 10^3 persons; [5], [8], [9].
I517M	Male inmigration in 5 to 17 age group; 10^3 persons; [5], [8], [9].
I517F	Female inmigration in 5 to 17 age group; 10^3 persons; [5], [8], [9].
I1844	Total inmigration in 18 to 44 age group; 10^3 persons; [5], [8], [9].
I1844M	Male inmigration in 18 to 44 age group; 10^3 persons; [5], [8], [9].
I1844F	Female inmigration in 18 to 44 age group; 10^3 persons; [5], [8], [9].
I4564	Total inmigration in 45 to 64 age group; 10^3 persons; [5], [8], [9].

I4564M — Male inmigration in 45 to 64 age group; 10^3 persons; [5], [8], [9].

I4564F — Female inmigration in 45 to 64 age group; 10^3 persons; [5], [8], [9].

I65 — Total inmigration in 65 and over age group; 10^3 persons; [5], [8], [9].

I65M — Male inmigration in 65 and over age group; 10^3 persons; [5], [8], [9].

I65F — Female inmigration in 65 and over age group; 10^3 persons; [5], [8], [9].

OTOT — Total outmigration; 10^3 persons; [5], [8], [9].

OMALE — Total male outmigration; 10^3 persons; [5], [8], [9].

OFEM — Total female outmigration; 10^3 persons; [5], [8], [9].

O04 — Total outmigration in 0 to 4 age group; 10^3 persons; [5], [8], [9].

O04M — Male outmigration in 0 to 4 age group; 10^3 persons; [5], [8], [9].

O04F — Female outmigration in 0 to 4 age group; 10^3 persons; [5], [8], [9].

O517 — Total outmigration in 5 to 17 age group; 10^3 persons; [5], [8], [9].

O517M — Male outmigration in 5 to 17 age group; 10^3 persons; [5], [8], [9].

O517F — Female outmigration in 5 to 17 age group; 10^3 persons; [5], [8], [9].

O1844 — Total outmigration in 18 to 44 age group; 10^3 persons; [5], [8], [9].

O1844M — Male outmigration in 18 to 44 age group; 10^3 persons; [5], [8], [9].

O1844F — Female outmigration in 18 to 44 age group; 10^3 persons; [5], [8], [9].

O4564 Total outmigration in 45 to 64 age group; 10^3 persons; [5], [8], [9].

O4564M Male outmigration in 45 to 64 age group; 10^3 persons; [5], [8], [9].

O4564F Female outmigration in 45 to 64 age group; 10^3 persons; [5], [8], [9].

O65 Total outmigration in 65 and over age group; 10^3 persons; [5], [8], [9].

O65M Male outmigration in 65 and over age group; 10^3 persons; [5], [8], [9].

O65F Female outmigration in 65 and over age group; 10^3 persons; [5], [8], [9].

NTOT Total netmigration; 10^3 persons; [5], [8], [9].

NMALE Total male netmigration; 10^3 persons; [5], [8], [9].

NFEM Total female netmigration; 10^3 persons; [5], [8], [9].

N017 Total netmigration in 0 to 17 age group; 10^3 persons; [5], [8], [9].

N017M Male netmigration in 0 to 17 age group; 10^3 persons; [5], [8], [9].

N017F Female netmigration in 0 to 17 age group; 10^3 persons; [5], [8], [9].

N1864 Total netmigration in 18 to 64 age group; 10^3 persons; [5], [8], [9].

N1864M Male netmigration in 18 to 64 age group; 10^3 persons; [5], [8], [9].

N1864F Female netmigration in 18 to 64 age group; 10^3 persons; [5], [8], [9].

N65 Total netmigration in 65 and over age group; 10^3 persons; [5], [8], [9].

N65M Male netmigration in 65 and over age group; 10^3 persons; [5], [8], [9].

N65F — Female netmigration in 65 and over age group; 10^3 persons; [5], [8], [9].

RTOT or ρ — Total labor force participation rate; percent; LF/PTOT; TRAN.

RMALE — Male labor force participation rate; percent; LMALE/PMALE; TRAN.

RFEM — Female labor force participation rate; percent; LFEM/PFEM; TRAN.

R517 — Total labor force participation rate of 5 to 17 year olds; percent; L517/P517; TRAN.

R517M — Labor force participation rate of 5 to 17 year old males; percent; L517M/P517M; TRAN.

R517F — Labor force participation rate of 5 to 17 year old females; percent; L517F/P517F; TRAN.

R1844 — Total labor force participation rate of 18 to 44 year olds; percent; L1844/P1844; TRAN.

R1844M — Labor force participation rate of 18 to 44 year old males; percent; L1844M/P1844M; TRAN.

R1844F — Labor force participation rate of 18 to 44 year old females; percent; L1844F/P1844F; TRAN.

R4564 — Total labor force participation rate of 45 to 64 year olds; percent; L4564/P4564; TRAN.

R4564M — Labor force participation rate of 45 to 64 year old males; percent; L4564M/P4564M; TRAN.

R4564F — Labor force participation rate of 45 to 64 year old females; percent; L4564F/P4564F; TRAN.

R65 — Total labor force participation rate of age group 65 and over; percent; L65/P65; TRAN.

R65M — Labor force participation rate of males aged 65 and over; percent; L65M/P65M; TRAN.

R65F — Labor force participation rate of females aged 65 and over; percent; L65F/P65F; TRAN.

LTOT or LF — Total labor force; 10^3 persons; [16], [17], [18], [19].

LMALE	Male labor force; 10^3 persons; [16], [17], [18], [19].
LFEM	Female labor force; 10^3 persons; [16], [17], [18], [19].
L517	Total labor force of 5 to 17 year olds; 10^3 persons; [16], [17], [18], [19].
L517M	Labor force of 5 to 17 year old males; 10^3 persons; [16], [17], [18], [19].
L517F	Labor force of 5 to 17 year old females; 10^3 persons; [16], [17], [18], [19].
L1844	Total labor force of 18 to 44 year olds; 10^3 persons; [16], [17], [18], [19].
L1844M	Labor force of 18 to 44 year old males; 10^3 persons; [16], [17], [18], [19].
L1844F	Labor force of 18 to 44 year old females; 10^3 persons; [16], [17], [18], [19].
L4564	Total labor force of 45 to 64 year olds; 10^3 persons; [16], [17], [18], [19].
L4564M	Labor force of 45 to 64 year old males; 10^3 persons; [16], [17], [18], [19].
L4564F	Labor force of 45 to 64 year old females; 10^3 persons; [16], [17], [18], [19].
L65	Total labor force of age group 65 and over; 10^3 persons; [16], [17], [18], [19].
L65M	Labor force of males aged 65 and over; 10^3 persons; [16], [17], [18], [19].
L65F	Labor force of females aged 65 and over; 10^3 persons; [16], [17], [18], [19].
USIP or IP	U.S. index of industrial production; 1967=100.; [13].
USSICR	U.S. social insurance contribution rate; fraction; [13].
USPR or PR	U.S. prime lending rate; percent; [20].

USMP72 or P U.S. manufacturing price index; 1972=100; [20[.

USMIP72 U.S. gross private domestic investment deflator; 1972=100; [20].

USSEPR or S U.S. separation rate; percent; [19].

PRIMARY SOURCES

[1] The First National Bank of Boston. General Revenue Sharing Technical Papers, mimeographed. 1980.

[2] U.S. Department of Commerce. Bureau of the Census. Annual Survey of Manufactures, Special Geographic Supplement: Data on Book Value of Fixed Assets and Rental Payments for Buildings and Equipment, Washington, D.C.

[3] U.S. Department of Commerce. Bureau of the Census. Annual Survey of Manufactures (various years), Washington, D.C.

[4] U.S. Department of Commerce. Bureau of the Census. Current Population Reports, Series P-25, "Annual Estimates of the Population of States", (various years), Washington, D.C.

[5] U.S. Department of Commerce. Bureau of the Census. "Internal Revenue Service Based Migration Files", Unpublished data.

[6] U.S. Department of Commerce. Bureau of the Census. Current Population Reports, Series P-25, "Estimates of the Population of States, by Age", (various years), Washington, D.C.

[7] U.S. Department of Commerce. Bureau of the Census. Current Population Reports, Series P-25, "Estimates of the Population of the United States and Components of Change", (various issues), Washington, D.C.

[8] U.S. Department of Commerce. Bureau of the Census. 1960 Census of Population, Vol. 1, Table 16, "Age by Color and Sex", Washington, D.C.

[9] U.S. Department of Commerce. Bureau of the Census. 1970 Census of Population, Vol. 1, Table 20, "Age by Race and Sex 1970", Washington, D.C.

[10] U.S. Department of Commerce. Bureau of the Census. Current Population Reports, Series P-25, No. 704, "Projections of the Population of the United States: 1977 to 2050", Washington, D.C., 1977.

[11] U.S. Department of Commerce. Bureau of the Census. Current Population Reports, Series P-25, No. 796, "Illustrative Projections of State Populations by Age, Race and Sex: 1975 to 2000", Washington, D.C., 1979.

[12] U.S. Department of Commerce. Bureau of the Census. Transportation Division. 1977 Census of Transportation, Commodity Transportation Survey, Washington, D.C.

[13] U.S. Department of Commerce. Bureau of Economic Analysys. Survey of Current Business, (various issues and working tapes), Washington, D.C.

[14] U.S. Department of Commerce. Bureau of Economic Analysis. Regional Work Force Characteristics and Migration Data: A Handbook on the Social Security Continuous Work History Sample and Its Application. Washington, D.C., 1976.

[15] U.S. Department of Health, Education, and Welfare. Monthly Vital Statistics Report (various issues), Washington, D.C.

[16] U.S. Department of Labor. Employment and Training Administration. Area Trends in Employment and Unemployment (various issues), Washington, D.C.

[17] U.S. Department of Labor. Employment and Training Administration. Employment and Training Report of the President (various issues), Washington, D.C.

[18] U.S. Department of Labor. Bureau of Labor Statistics. Employment and Earnings, States and Areas, 1939-78, Bulletin 1370-13. Washington, D.C.

[19] U.S. Department of Labor. Bureau of Labor Statistics. Handbook of Labor Statistics 1978, Bulletin 2000. Washington, D.C.

[20] U.S. Department of Commerce. Bureau of Economic Analysis. Business Conditions Digest (various issues), Washington, D.C.

CHAPTER TWO: OUTPUT AND PRICE DETERMINATION

2.1 INTRODUCTION

This chapter describes the determination of output and prices in the ECESIS model. Section 2.2 gives a brief review of spatial competition theory and its implied assumptions. The plausibility of the various sets of assumptions is discussed in Section 2.3 and a case is made for a particular version of the spatial model. Section 2.4 incorporates the spatial model into an aggregate supply and demand framework and describes the specifications and estimations in ECESIS. The complete estimation results are given in Appendix 2.1 at the end of this chapter. The final section presents the specification and estimation results of the state level consumer price index equations.

Since this report is intended for both economists and demographers, it is necessary to provide some background material for each of these disciplines. Much of this chapter is a review of results from economic theory. Readers already familiar with this material may want to skim over the reviews. Most of the material that is specific to ECESIS begins in the middle of Section 2.4. Other readers may want to spend more time on the theory discussion in the beginning of the chapter. In later chapters, when the demographic model is discussed, most readers will find that their roles are reversed.

2.2 SPATIAL COMPETITION THEORY

2.2.1 ASSUMPTIONS

Consumers are assumed to be identical and uniformly distributed on an unbounded and homogeneous two dimensional plane. Demand of the spatially separable consumers is sensitive to the delivered product price and consumer income. The delivered price is the mill price of the production unit from which the product is purchased plus the transportation cost of delivering the product to the consumer. Transportation costs are constant per unit distance, invariant to location and fully paid by consumers.

Production is of a single aggregate commodity that is produced at discrete points on the plane. The assumption of an aggregate output variable implies some further restrictions. Let the actual multiproduct production process be represented by the general function

$$G(Q_1, Q_2, \ldots, Q_m, X_1, X_2, \ldots, X_n) = 0,$$

where Q_i $(i=1,\ldots,m)$ are outputs and X_i $(i=1,\ldots,n)$ are inputs. If there exists a separable transformation process h, such that

$$g(h(Q_1,Q_2,\ldots,Q_m),X_1,X_2,\ldots,X_n) = 0,$$

then the function G may be written in the form

$$Q = h(Q_1,Q_2,\ldots,Q_m) = f(X_1,X_2,\ldots,X_n),$$

where Q is aggregate output. Further, the production function is homogeneous of degree d if and only if the dual joint cost function is homogeneous of degree 1/d in outputs (Brown, Caves and Christensen 1979).[1]

The function g also implies that the corresponding cost function is separable in outputs.

$$C = c(h(Q_1,Q_2,\ldots,Q_m),P_1,P_2,\ldots,P_n),$$

where P_j (j=1,...,n) are input prices.

Firms are assumed to have identical production functions, however, cost structures are allowed to vary regionally. New firms may enter the production process in a region if the most efficient existing firms in that region earn profits above some minimum amount. A further barrier to entry is represented by nonzero entry costs. Firms establish a uniform mill price and do not practice price

---

[1] The restrictive homogeneity and separability assumptions associated with the aggregate production function could be tested using flexible function forms (Christensen, Jorgenson, Lau 1975). That will not be done here.

discrimination. Product differentiation, due either to the aggregation process or to uncertainties in the market is allowed.

Since explicit solutions to the spatial competition problem will not be worked out here, these complicating assumptions will not cause serious problems. The product differentiation assumption offers an explanation of the commonly observed cross-hauling phenomenon.

2.2.2 THE THEORETICAL MODEL

The demand per consumer is

(2.2.1) $q = q(p_j+tu,\ y)$,

where q is demand per consumer, p_j is producer j's mill price, t is unit transportation cost, u is distance from consumer to the point of production, and y is consumer income.

If the shape of the market area of firm j is an s-sided regular polygon, the total demand within that market area is (Greenhut and Ohta 1975)

(2.2.2) $Q^*_j = 2Ds\int_0^\alpha\int_0^\beta q(p_j+tu,y)ududθ$,

where Q^*_j is total demand from within market area j, D is density of consumers, s is the number of sides of the polygon, $\alpha=\Pi/s$, $\beta=R_j/\cos\theta$, R_j is the distance from the center to the edge of the polygon, and p_j is the mill price of firm j.

Product differentiation implies that not all of the demand of market area j will be satisfied by firm j. Some of the consumers in this area will choose to purchase from firms outside of the area even though j is closer. Let r_{jj} be the proportion of consumers in area j that actually purchase from firm j. Denote by r_{ij} the proportion of demand in region j that is met by firm i. Then the total demand faced by firm i in region i may be written as

(2.2.3) $Q_i = \sum_j r_{ij} Q^*_j$.

Profits for the firm in market area i are

(2.2.4) $\Pi_i = p_i Q_i - c_i(Q_i, F_i)$,

where Π_i is profits of firm i, Q_i is total sales of firm i, c_i is total costs of firm i, F_i is fixed costs of firm i, and p_i is the mill price of firm i.

Firms will establish their mill price at the level at which profits are maximized. Substituting (2.2.2) and (2.2.3) into (2.2.4) and maximizing (2.2.4) with respect to price yields a curve in the (R,p) plane. Equating profits to some minimum level, say Π^*, above which new firms would be encouraged to enter, yields another curve in (R,p) space for each level of fixed costs. Thus, the two equations

(2.2.5a) $\partial\Pi_i/\partial p_i = 0$, and

(2.2.5b) $\Pi_i = \Pi^*$,

may be solved together to obtain the size of the market area (R_i) and the mill price (p_i) for firm i. These values are then substituted back into (2.2.3) to obtain Q_i.

To solve the system of equations (2.2.5), which must be solved for all firms simultaneously because of the product differentiation assumption, some assumption must be made about the response of one firms price level to changes of its competitors' prices.

Consider two producers, A and B, located a distance of U units apart on a line segment. As shown in Figure 2.2.1, the market boundary on the segment AB is located at the point R^{ab}--where the delivered price of each firm is equal. If firm A were to raise its price (p^a), by say dp, and firm B maintained its price (p^b) ($dp^b/dp^a = 0$), then the market boundary would shift to $R^{ab\prime}$--closer to A. Thus, barring product allegiance, those consumers on the segment $R^{ab\prime}R^{ab}$ would shift their purchases from firm A to firm B. If, however, firm B matched the price increase of firm A ($dp^b/dp^a = 1$), then the market boundary remains unchanged at R^{ab}.

FIGURE 2.2.1
COMPETITOR PRICE RESPONSES AND
MARKET BOUNDARIES

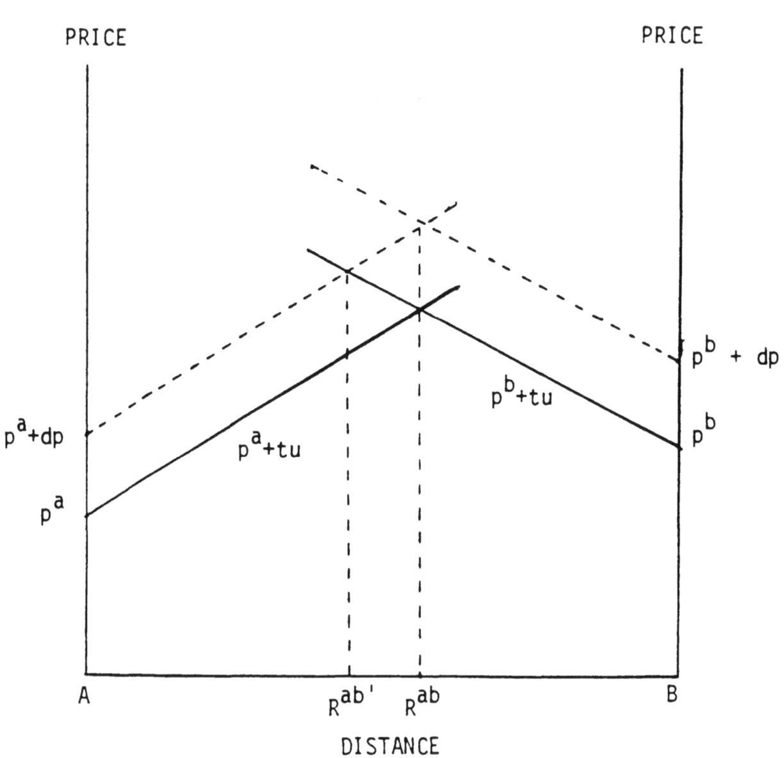

Normalizing such that firm A is at zero and firm B is at U on the line segment, the intersection of the delivered price lines occurs at the point where

$$p^a + tR = p^b + t(U-R).$$

Solving for R and differentiating with respect to p^a yields

(2.2.6) $$dR/dp^a = (1/(2t))(dp^b/dp^a - 1).$$

The value of the term dp^b/dp^a, referred to as the price conjectural variation (PCV), is a matter of assumption and plays an important role in the solution of the system of equations (2.2.5).

Capozza and Van Order (1977a, 1977b, 1978, 1980) have examined the properties of several spatial models with various price conjectural variation assumptions. For the pure spatial monopolist there are no competitors within the boundaries of the maximum market area (i.e., the point where transportation costs make the delivered price so high that consumers demand no product) so that the PCV does not apply. A PCV of minus one describes a situation in which the boundary price is fixed. If firm A raises its price firm B must lower its price to maintain the fixed boundary price. The boundary location, of course, is shifted toward B. While this price reaction is unlikely in a spatial competition context, it was originally discussed in the context of regulated and zonal pricing markets (Greenhut,

Hwang and Ohta 1975). A PCV of zero characterizes the type of spatial competition discussed by Hotelling (1929) and Smithies (1941). In the limit, as transport costs and fixed costs approach zero, the price in the Hotelling-Smithies model approaches the perfect competition price (Capozza and Van Order 1978). If competitors match each others price changes dollar for dollar (a PCV of one) a Loschian (1967) type competition is implied. For this model the limiting price is the nonspatial monopoly price. Intermediate values for the PCV are also possible and some of these are discussed by Capozza and Van Order (1979, 1980).

2.3 INTERPRETING THE ASSUMPTIONS

Most of the assumptions in the previous section are made to make the problem tractable and thus cannot be easily avoided. Consumers, for instance, are not likely to be identical and uniformly distributed on a homogeneous plane. Similarly, firms do not have identical production functions and many do practice various forms of price discrimination. The combination of these assumptions, however, yields nicely shaped market areas that greatly simplify the problem. The assumptions of uniform mill prices, constant per distance transport costs, varying cost structures and product differentiation, on the other hand, are quite reasonable.

Data collection conventions require that regional models, and the ECESIS model in particular, treat market areas in terms of state boundaries and the local "firm" as the aggregate industry within that state.

In ECESIS the uniform product is all manufactured goods. This assumption is quite severe[2] but could be alleviated by disaggregating the manufacturing sector.

Perhaps the most severe restriction is the lack of regional output price data. This, along with fixed market areas, implies a Loschian type price competition; a price conjectural variation of one. How closely this assumption reflects reality is debatable. The Loschian price competition model, however, is not unheard of in nature and even garners a substantial amount of support under the rubric of administered prices.

2.3.1 ADMINISTERED PRICES

The fact that price conjectural variation assumptions are discussed at all implies that firms are assumed to have some influence over pricing decisions. In his classic article that serves as a foundation for the field of Industrial Organization, Mason (1939, pg. 61) writes,

---

[2] The aggregate manufactured outputs of Michigan and North Dakota are quite different in composition.

> Policy implies some degree of control over the course of events and, at the same time, the use of judgment as to the probable consequences of alternative lines of action. In perfect markets, whether monopolistic or competitive, price is hardly a matter of judgment and where there is no judgment there is no policy. The area of price policy, then, embraces the deliberative action of buyers and sellers able to influence price; that is to say, it covers practically the whole field of industrial prices.

Stability is a primary goal of price policy. Concluding a study of industry pricing decisions, Oxenfeldt (1967) notes, "[m]anagement strives to achieve and preserve stability in the industry; outbreaks of competitive activity are regarded as an infectious disease--something that could be fatal if allowed to spread (pg. 226)."

Large variations in output and employment create organizational and administrative problems for firms; thus prices are 'administered' to create some stability in an otherwise whimsical market place. In fact, industry prices appear to be quite insensitive to demand changes (Weiss 1966). Lack of response to market conditions is more the rule than the exception. Yorden (1961, pg. 287) finds that "insensitivity of prices to demand change is not confined to highly oligopolistic industries, but is characteristic of most manufacturing industries."

Responding to short run market fluctuations is costly and risky. A firm's output capacity is not easily altered without costly retooling. Also, hiring and firing of skilled labor is an expensive process. Profit stability is more appealing to risk averse stock shareholders than profits with a higher mean and larger variance. Under such circumstances, managers may act to stabilize profits and thus maximize the value of the firm (Schramm and Sherman 1977).

Seldom is a firm so fortunate as to have detailed information on the demand function it is facing. Indeed, few firms even try to measure the price elasticity of their demand functions (Oxenfeldt 1967). Under conditions of uncertainty regarding current demand a stable price policy can be the profit maximizing price policy (Wu 1979, Schramm and Sherman 1977).

If price stability is a goal of a firm and industry then competitors' price behavior becomes a key issue. A competitor trying to capture a greater share of the market by price cutting can be a very destabilizing factor. This strategy is fairly uncommon in established industries since "the unprofitability of price wars is generally recognized (Zelomek 1967, pg. 205)." A more common pattern is for industries to establish informal pricing agreements. In some industries a particular firm is tacitly recognized as the price leader with other firms in the industry quickly matching its price changes. In other instances no single firm acts consistently as the price leader. Any firm may post a price change and if its competitors do not respond the new price will be withdrawn. In either case, the general rule is "when competitors do something notable, other firms follow (Oxenfeldt 1967, pg. 225)."

A spatial model with an organized price-leader market is well represented by the Loschian spatial competition model with its assumption that price conjectural variation is equal to one.

Equation (2.2.6) shows that the Loschian PCV assumption implies that the market radius of a firm is not sensitive to its established mill price. This is not surprising since the model by assumption eliminates price competition. Not all competition is eliminated however, "the competitive struggle moves into the area of nonprice competition, with the accent on service, quality, product-development, engineering, and similar considerations (Zelomek 1967, pg. 205)." By differentiating its product from its competitors, a firm may increase demand for its product. Also, a firm may be more effective than its competitors in competing for expanding markets by cutting its costs and having greater expansion capabilities. Thus, several factors other than price may determine the size of market areas.

It has already been assumed that each region produces the same aggregate manufacturing output. The Loschian market assumption implies that a uniform price is established for this aggregate output across all regions. While this is a strong assumption, it is not unreasonable and is consistent with some versions of spatial competition theory. In any case, it is an assumption that the applied regional modeller must learn to live with.

2.4 THE ECESIS MODEL OF OUTPUT, PRICE AND EMPLOYMENT

2.4.1 POST KEYNESIAN AGGREGATE DEMAND AND SUPPLY THEORY

A simple post Keynesian aggregate demand and supply framework allows both supply and demand factors to be incorporated into the manufacturing sector of ECESIS.

One of the basic tenets of post Keynesian theory is that the location of the consumer demand curve is not independent of the general price level because of the close relationship between the general price level and the money-wage rate and thus consumer income.

Figure 2.4.1 represents a set of demand curves in region I for consumers who are at a distance of u from the producer. At the expected sales price p^1, anticipated production and employment are such that the relevant demand curve is D^1; quantity $Q_I{}^1$ is demanded. If the expected sales price rises to p^2, the anticipated increase in output

FIGURE 2.4.1
DEMAND-OUTLAY CURVE

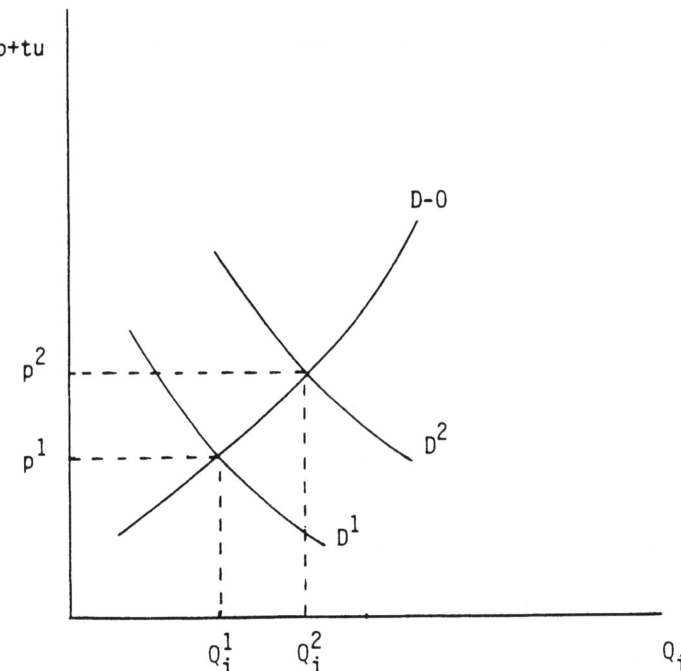

and employment and thus, consumer income, shifts the demand curve to D^2; where anticipated demand is Q_i^2. The values $p^1Q_i^1$ and $p^2Q_i^2$ are the intended demand-outlays for the expected sales prices p^1 and p^2 respectively. By varying the expected sales price and connecting the appropriate points on the relevant demand curves, the intended demand-outlay curve (D-O) can be traced out as in Figure 2.4.1. A D-O curve may be constructed for each firm or industry and each point on the D-O curves has associated with it some level of anticipated employment (L_i). By summing the demand-outlay curves over all firms in region i, anticipated expenditures (pQ_i) can be related to anticipated employment levels (L_i). The result is the aggregate demand curve shown in Figure 2.4.2.

The aggregate supply curve is derived from the production and cost functions. Assume that each firm produces its aggregate output (Q) with two inputs; capital (K) and labor (L). The general production function for the firm in region i may be written as

(2.4.1) $$Q_i = f_i(K_i, L_i).$$

The cost structure of the firm is

(2.4.2) $$C_i = c_i(Q_i, w_i, r_i, F_i),$$

where w_i is the price of labor, r_i is the price of capital,

FIGURE 2.4.2
AGGREGATE DEMAND FUNCTION

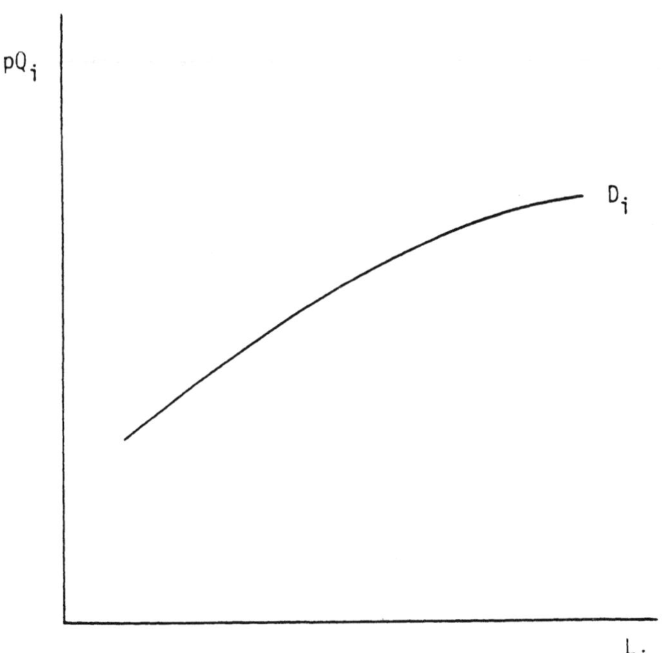

and F_i is fixed costs. For a given set of factor costs and fixed costs, (2.4.2) leads to a Marshallian type supply curve that is assumed to have a positive slope. Thus, as the expected sales price increases, anticipated production increases. At an expected sales price of p^1, firm i will expect to produce Q_i^1; and, assuming that firm i operates its plant efficiently, (2.4.1) associates labor inputs of L_i^1 with this output level. If the expected sales price rises to p^2, anticipated output and employment increase to Q_i^2 and L_i^2.

Aggregate proceeds expected at supply price p^1 are

$$Z^1 = \sum_i p^1 Q_i^1.$$

Similarly, aggregate anticipated employment at this price is

$$L^1 = \sum_i L_i^1.$$

By varying the expected sales price, a relationship between anticipated aggregate proceeds and employment may be constructed as in Figure 2.4.3.

If firms follow profit maximizing behavior, they will hire labor to the point where marginal revenue product equals the money-wage rate. Or,

(2.4.3) $\quad MPL_i MR_i = w_i,$

where MPL_i is the marginal product of labor for firm i, MR_i is the marginal revenue of firm i, and w_i is the money-wage

FIGURE 2.4.3
AGGREGATE SUPPLY FUNCTION

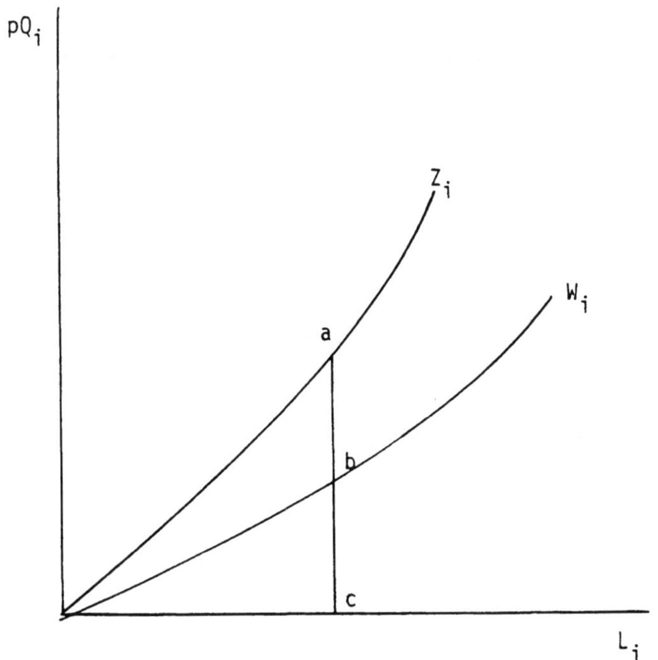

rate paid by firm i. If, as previously assumed, the firm faces a negatively sloped demand curve, marginal revenue equals

(2.4.4) $MR_i = p(1 - 1/\xi_i)$,

where ξ_i is the elasticity of demand. Thus, (2.4.3) becomes

(2.4.5) $MPL_i p(1 - 1/\xi_i) = w_i$.

Dividing both sides of (2.4.5) by the average product of labor ($APL_i = Q_i/L_i$) and again by expected sales price yields an expression for labors' share of income,

$$(w_i L_i)/(pQ_i) = (1-1/\xi_i)(MPL_i/APL_i).$$

Renormalizing yields the aggregate supply curve for firm i,

(2.4.6) $pQ_i = (1-1/\xi_i)^{-1}(APL_i/MPL_i)w_i L_i$.

The aggregate demand and supply functions, Figures 2.4.2 and 2.4.3 respectively, are combined in Figure 2.4.4 to yield equilibrium values for labor inputs (L_i) and total proceeds (pQ_i). If the anticipated sales price were such that entrepreneurs in region i expected proceeds of less than Z_i^*, say Z_i^a, then they would have hired labor to the point of L_i^a. The intended expenditures (D_i^a) at this expected sales price and level of employment, however, exceeds aggregate supply so entrepreneurs will be induced to

FIGURE 2.4.4

EQUILIBRIUM OF AGGREGATE DEMAND AND SUPPLY

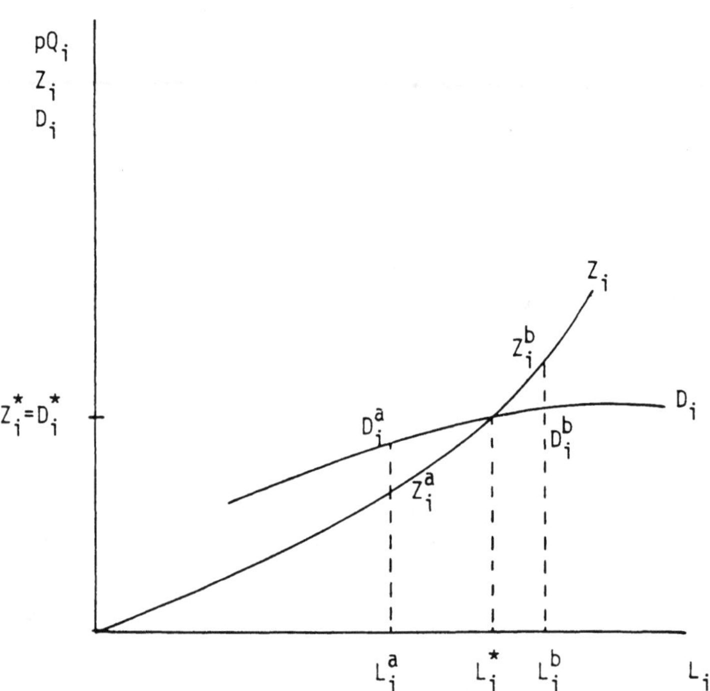

expand output. Similarly, if entrepreneurs expected proceeds of $Z_i^b > Z_i^*$ their sales expectations would be disappointed since the intended outlay at that implicit level of employment is less than Z_i^b. Equilibrium occurs at the intersection of Z_i and D_i where expected sales equals desired purchases.

Note that it is pQ_i and L_i that are determined by this equilibrium. An independent mechanism must be used to determine p and Q_i separately. In post Keynesian models this is accomplished with a wage-cost markup price equation to determine p (Weintraub 1958). But, since the Loschian market assumption implies an exogenous output price to the region, the demand equation may be normalized to solve for Q_i and the supply equation normalized to solve for L_i. Thus, output, price and employment are all determined.

Figure 2.4.4 shows the aggregate demand curve intersecting the aggregate supply curve from above. This is the requirement for a stable solution and, in general, is satisfied if the system has positive savings. This rather weak condition is consistent with Weintraub's (1958, pg. 41) observation that, "[a]part from some curious dissaving phenomena, [D] ought not, over an extended range, climb faster than Z."

The Loschian market assumption also implies that the market radius is fixed. In fact, the market radius concept is a theoretical fiction rather than an empirical reality. It is more useful to think of the size of the market area as a measure of the share of the total market. Thus, r_{ij} measures the share of market j that is captured by firm i.

The above analysis was carried out under the assumption of fixed money-wage rates. As the money-wage rate increases, the firm supply curves are shifted up; thus the aggregate supply curve shifts up. Similarly, an increase in the money-wage rate will increase money incomes and shift the firm demand curves out, increasing intended purchases at each employment (output) level and thus shifting the aggregate demand curve up. Depending on the elasticities of the aggregate demand and supply functions, total employment may decrease, remain the same or increase with an increase in the money-wage rate.

Note that if region i experienced relatively lower wage increases than neighboring regions with which it traded, then region i's aggregate demand curve should shift up faster than its aggregate supply curve. Thus, region i should be able to expand its output and employment at the expense of its neighbors. This is not necessarily a case of price competition. The cost structure in region i simply enables firm i to produce more output than its competitors before increasing marginal cost makes further production unprofitable.

A similar type of nonprice market competition results when the short run marginal cost curve is shifted via investments in new capital equipment.

2.4.2 SPECIFICATION AND ESTIMATION

Economic theories are seldom constrained by the realities of data collection. Spatial competition theory is no exception. Theoretical models of output and price determination in spatial economies are elegant, precise and very demanding of detailed data. The modeller, on the other hand, must face the fact that final demand accounts and output prices are seldom available at the regional level. Data, rather than theory, dictate the model design used to determine regional output and output prices. The ECESIS model must also live within these constraints. These theoretical discussions must now be translated to yield specifications that may be empirically estimated.

The demand equation should be negatively sloped with respect to price and a positive function of income. The total consumer demand facing firm i was shown to be

$$Q_i = \Sigma_j r_{ij} 2Ds \int_0^{\alpha} \int_0^{\beta} q(p_j + tu, y)\, u\, du\, d\theta,$$

where $\alpha=\Pi/s$ and $\beta=R_j/COS\theta$.

The Loschian model assumes that the market radius is independent of price

$$dR_j/dp_i = 0, \ \forall \ i,j.$$

Further, it was assumed that the individuals demand curves were negatively sloped

$$\partial q/\partial p_i \leq 0, \ \forall \ i.$$

Thus, it follows that

$$\partial Q_i/\partial p_j \leq 0, \ \forall \ i,j.$$

Also, if $\partial q/\partial y>0$, it follows that $\partial Q_i/\partial y>0$.

Let Q_{ij} be the amount of state i's manufacturing output that is shipped to state j. Define

$$(2.4.7) \qquad r_{ij} = Q_{ij}/Q_{\cdot j},$$

where $Q_{\cdot j} = \sum_i Q_{ij}$ is state j's total demand for manufacturing output. Multiplying (2.4.7) by $Q_{\cdot j}$ and summing over j gives state i's total manufacturing output,

$$(2.4.8) \qquad Q_{i\cdot} = \sum_j Q_{ij} = \sum_j r_{ij} Q_{\cdot j}.$$

The Q_{ij}'s are obtained from the 1977 Commodity Transportation Survey of the U.S. Bureau of the Census (1980). Since the total demand for manufactured goods in state j is not available, it is approximated by that state's real total personal income ($YT72_j$). To remain consistent, (2.4.7) must be redefined as,

$$(2.4.9) \qquad r_{ij} = Q_{ij}/YT72_j,$$

or the shipments from i to j as a fraction of total income of the receiving region. The r_{ij} are assumed to remain constant since there is no consistent time series for the Q_{ij} with which to estimate equations for the r_{ij}.

Although output prices are assumed constant across regions, production costs are allowed to vary. The wage bill, since it comprises about sixty percent of the cost of manufactured goods, is a good approximation of production costs. The hourly manufacturing money-wage rate over the U.S. average manufacturing output price index (WMH/USMP) serves as a proxy for the own price effect in the demand equation.

Since manufacturing output decisions are subject to long-run commitments, the inertia of the manufacturing process is captured with the anticipated demand variable,

$$Q_i^a = Q_{i,-1}(IP/IP_{-1}),$$

where IP is an industrial production index for the U.S. Trend effects should be captured by Q_i^a while relative price and interstate demand structure changes are captured by the other variables.

The final specification for the manufacturing output equation is

$$(2.4.10) \qquad Q_{i}. = a_0 + a_1 Q_i^{*} + a_2(WMH_i/USMP) + a_3(\textstyle\sum_j r_{ij} YT72_j).$$

During estimation, coefficient a_3 is constrained so that the elasticity of output with respect to income is equal to one. The equation is estimated over the period 1958 to 1974.

The complete estimation results are given in Appendix 2.1. In general, the estimations are good. The relative price coefficient was constrained to zero in some cases.

The aggregate supply curve is obtained by estimating the production function directly and then computing the average and marginal products of labor needed in expression (2.4.6). As noted above, the aggregate supply curve is renormalized to solve for labor inputs. The estimation procedure and results for the production function and factor demand equations are presented in Chapters Three and Four.

2.5 CONSUMER PRICE INDEX EQUATION

Since output prices are exogenous to the states in ECESIS and it is not intended to link ECESIS to a national model to drive these output prices, there is no endogenous price movement at all in the model. To alleviate this problem the Consumer Price Index (CPI) for each state was endogenized.

CPI data are not collected on a state basis but rather on a Standard Metropolitan Statistical Area (SMSA) basis. The twenty-eight SMSA's for which a time-series of CPI data is available do not provide good coverage for some regions of the country.

Slightly better regional coverage is offered by the Bureau of Labor Statistics Cost of Living Index. Figure 2.5.1 shows the spatial distribution of the forty SMSA's used in the BLS family budget surveys. Still many states are not represented by the data.

In a special study on the regional affects of General Revenue Sharing funds, the First National Bank of Boston (1980) used the BLS budget indices to construct a state level cost of living index. Assuming that the U.S. value is one, the 1978 values for this cost index are given in Table 2.5.1.

FIGURE 2.5.1

SPATIAL DISTRIBUTION OF BLS SMSA BUDGET DATA

TABLE 2.5.1

STATE LEVEL COST OF LIVING INDEX

UNITED STATES	1.000	MISSOURI	.9491
ALABAMA	.8775	MONTANA	.8968
ALASKA	1.260	NEBRASKA	.9455
ARIZONA	.975	NEVADA	.9866
ARKANSAS	.8524	NEW HAMPSHIRE	.9654
CALIFORNIA	1.004	NEW JERSEY	1.123
COLORADO	.9301	NEW MEXICO	.9058
CONNECTICUT	1.023	NEW YORK	1.146
DELAWARE	.9004	NORTH CAROLINA	.8594
DIST. OF COLUMBIA	1.040	NORTH DAKOTA	.9117
FLORIDA	.8933	OHIO	.9541
GEORGIA	.8408	OKLAHOMA	.8694
HAWAII	1.136	OREGON	.9512
IDAHO	.8827	PENNSYLVANIA	.9934
ILLINOIS	1.011	RHODE ISLAND	1.102
INDIANA	.9539	SOUTH CAROLINA	.8589
IOWA	.9349	SOUTH DAKOTA	.9150
KANSAS	.9367	TENNESSEE	.8580
KENTUCKY	.8634	TEXAS	.8731
LOUISIANA	.8564	UTAH	.9831
MAINE	.9379	VERMONT	.9300
MARYLAND	.9851	VIRGINIA	.9397
MASSACHUSETTS	1.169	WASHINGTON	.9370
MICHIGAN	.9920	WEST VIRGINIA	.8500
MINNESOTA	.9738	WISCONSIN	.9458
MISSISSIPPI	.8239	WYOMING	.8600

Using this state specific cost index for 1978 as a starting point, a time series of state specific CPI data is generated by multiplying the U.S. CPI time-series by each state's cost index. There is, of course, no additional information added to the data by this procedure. This pseudo time-series of state CPI data is then renormalized to base year 1972 and regressed against the total average money-wage rate of the state (WT),

(2.5.1) $\log(CPI_i) = a_0 + a_1 \log(WT_i)$.

The price elasticities with respect to wages from these estimations are given in Table 2.5.2.

TABLE 2.5.2

ESTIMATED PRICE ELASTICITIES

State	Elasticity	State	Elasticity
UNITED STATES	n.a.	MISSOURI	.632
ALABAMA	.639	MONTANA	.779
ALASKA	.892	NEBRASKA	.674
ARIZONA	.694	NEVADA	.781
ARKANSAS	.631	NEW HAMPSHIRE	.640
CALIFORNIA	.750	NEW JERSEY	.674
COLORADO	.668	NEW MEXICO	.875
CONNECTICUT	.669	NEW YORK	.633
DELAWARE	.733	NORTH CAROLINA	.599
DIST. OF COLUMBIA	.510	NORTH DAKOTA	.671
FLORIDA	.632	OHIO	.689
GEORGIA	.596	OKLAHOMA	.693
HAWAII	.628	OREGON	.726
IDAHO	.785	PENNSYLVANIA	.655
ILLINOIS	.658	RHODE ISLAND	.643
INDIANA	.706	SOUTH CAROLINA	.595
IOWA	.684	SOUTH DAKOTA	.728
KANSAS	.710	TENNESSEE	.631
KENTUCKY	.666	TEXAS	.670
LOUISIANA	.660	UTAH	.801
MAINE	.724	VERMONT	.592
MARYLAND	.662	VIRGINIA	.663
MASSACHUSETTS	.632	WASHINGTON	.686
MICHIGAN	.629	WEST VIRGINIA	.665
MINNESOTA	.662	WISCONSIN	.689
MISSISSIPPI	.645	WYOMING	.739

Equation (2.5.1) is only useful in the context of simulation experiments where the wage rate varies from the baseline values.

The wage rate is highly state specific (see Chapter Five) so (2.5.1) does allow some state specific price effects into the ECESIS model.

APPENDIX 2.1

OUTPUT EQUATION ESTIMATION RESULTS

The specification estimated is,

$$Q/1000 = a_0 + a_1[(Q_{-1}/1000)IP/IP_{-1}] + a_2(WMH/P)\cdot 100 + a_3(\textstyle\sum_j r_{ij} YT72_j/1000).$$

The estimation sample period is 1958 to 1974. The coefficient a_3 is calculated as

$$a_3 = \frac{\sum_t(\sum_j r_{ij} YT72_{j,t}/1000)/17}{\sum_t(Q_t/1000)/17}$$

so that the output elasticity with respect to trade weighted income is equal to one. Then the dependent variable is transformed appropriately and coefficients a_0, a_1 and a_2 are estimated with least squares.

The first three columns after the state names in the table below give the estimated coefficient values with their respective t-statistics reported directly below. The critical value for the five percent two-tailed test on a_0 is 2.145. The critical value for the five percent one-tailed test for a_1 and a_2 is 1.761. The next column gives the calculated value for a_3. The final column gives the coefficient of multiple correlation corrected for degrees of freedom with the Durbin-Watson statistic reported directly below that. The uncertainty range for the D-W test is .90 to 1.40.

STATE	a_0	a_1	a_2	a_3	$\bar{R}^2$/D-W
ALABAMA	-.168 0.26	.560 3.46	-.623 1.48	2.795	.89 1.47
ALASKA	-.067 3.24	.506 3.58	0 -	2.891	.42 1.33
ARIZONA	-.242 0.58	.750 4.67	-.140 0.90	2.713	.92 2.31
ARKANSAS	-.866 35.6	.545 41.1	0 -	3.532	.99 1.36
CALIFORNIA	3.506 1.41	.595 5.37	-4.135 3.50	2.223	.82 1.96
COLORADO	-.546 7.36	.352 8.40	0 -	2.769	.81 1.80
CONNECTICUT	.943 2.01	.661 5.62	-1.324 5.75	1.475	.67 1.68
DELAWARE	.087 0.47	.575 3.61	-.134 2.06	2.691	.53 2.13
DIST. OF COLUMBIA	-.031 1.18	.115 0.83	-.001 0.06	1.618	.00 1.84
FLORIDA	-1.107 11.8	.334 14.1	0 -	2.531	.93 2.28
GEORGIA	-.873 1.57	.535 3.88	-.608 1.38	3.242	.90 1.54
HAWAII	-.087 1.16	.275 1.31	0 -	2.251	.04 1.24
IDAHO	-.271 9.43	.521 10.6	0 -	2.989	.87 1.37
ILLINOIS	.046 0.05	.459 4.82	-2.443 3.76	2.191	.61 1.07
INDIANA	-.632 0.75	.474 4.35	-1.131 2.35	2.379	.73 0.80

IOWA	-.674 1.67	.676 4.23	-.455 1.73	3.416	.85 1.12
KANSAS	-.143 0.58	.493 5.22	-.274 2.12	3.448	.84 1.81
KENTUCKY	-1.556 13.6	.419 15.2	0 -	2.910	.94 1.66
LOUISIANA	-1.165 0.85	.597 1.10	-.159 0.18	4.716	.63 1.23
MAINE	-.079 1.13	.372 2.43	-.119 1.49	2.223	.46 1.75
MARYLAND	.933 4.53	.365 2.83	-.647 4.61	1.967	.68 0.80
MASSACHUSETTS	1.676 5.71	.493 5.53	-1.717 7.24	1.583	.80 2.51
MICHIGAN	.271 0.15	.457 3.35	-1.864 2.41	2.538	.40 1.90
MINNESOTA	-.573 1.47	.542 4.56	.455 1.92	2.539	.90 2.13
MISSISSIPPI	-.751 2.20	.604 3.89	-.090 0.37	3.574	.95 1.84
MISSOURI	-.158 0.51	.387 4.02	-.612 2.53	2.528	.75 2.35
MONTANA	-.093 3.45	.281 3.72	0 -	3.779	.45 2.35
NEBRASKA	-.489 14.4	.430 16.1	0 -	3.595	.94 2.35
NEVADA	-.030 0.55	.482 1.83	-.009 0.45	2.926	.35 1.83
NEW HAMPSHIRE	-.155 3.40	.514 4.24	-.114 2.28	2.011	.78 1.69
NEW JERSEY	2.888 4.70	.478 4.29	-2.381 5.06	1.894	.62 2.10
NEW MEXICO	.126 1.20	.668 6.91	-.082 2.20	4.346	.79 2.26

NEW YORK	5.986 7.84	.479 6.51	-4.635 9.91	1.541	.90 1.98
NORTH CAROLINA	-2.545 21.8	.377 25.1	0 -	2.761	.98 1.09
NORTH DAKOTA	-.081 6.04	.634 7.13	0 -	4.876	.76 2.79
OHIO	.576 0.35	.470 3.38	-2.651 2.49	2.166	.49 1.27
OKLAHOMA	-.105 0.34	.730 5.05	-.206 1.88	4.091	.91 2.64
OREGON	-.652 1.60	.458 2.38	-.107 0.47	2.657	.71 1.13
PENNSYLVANIA	.566 0.42	.471 3.23	-2.724 2.84	1.929	.35 1.08
RHODE ISLAND	.170 1.78	.577 4.29	-.318 4.26	1.837	.52 1.37
SOUTH CAROLINA	-.352 0.98	.610 4.65	-.623 2.03	2.769	.93 1.27
SOUTH DAKOTA	-.060 1.19	.406 2.09	-.007 0.24	4.019	.44 1.88
TENNESSEE	-1.366 2.96	.283 3.50	0 -	2.628	.41 2.51
TEXAS	1.842 0.55	.835 3.14	-3.158 1.75	3.814	.79 1.41
UTAH	.159 0.42	.351 0.94	-.129 0.66	2.621	.00 1.64
VERMONT	-.096 2.80	.693 4.76	-.080 2.80	2.085	.70 1.68
VIRGINIA	-.400 0.89	.481 3.08	-.554 1.48	2.650	.82 1.23
WASHINGTON	-.006 0.01	.556 2.44	-.520 1.74	2.174	.25 1.51
WEST VIRGINIA	.740 3.14	.521 3.76	-.501 4.36	1.878	.52 1.11

WISCONSIN	-.155 0.37	.531 4.13	-1.019 3.00	2.557	.63 1.01
WYOMING	.010 0.20	.527 2.20	-.018 0.94	5.479	.27 1.55

CHAPTER THREE: PRODUCTION FUNCTION AND CAPACITY CONSTRAINTS

3.1 INTRODUCTION

A completely specified macroeconometric model will include a production function and the demand equations for those factors which enter the production function. The model builder is free to choose among various normalization rules for these sets of equations. The interrelationships among the parameters of these equations, however, are determined by the particular specification of the production function chosen and upon economic theory. If these interrelationships are ignored during the estimation of the factor demand and production relations then the parameter estimates will be inconsistent with the production technology intended by the model builder. These inconsistencies become particularly serious if the model is to be used for simulation or forecasting experiments because the results of these experiments may be misleading.

Joint estimation of all of the relevant functions using a simultaneous equation estimation procedure with appropriate parameter restrictions is one way of accounting for the interdependence among the parameters (Klein 1974, p. 332).

The heavy data requirements and complex nonlinear equations which generally accompany such techniques encourage the search for simpler alternatives.

Coen and Hickman (1970) use a two-step procedure to estimate a two factor Cobb-Douglas production model. First they perform an independent regression on the labor demand equation using a single equation technique. The estimates from this regression imply a set of parameter values for the Cobb-Douglas production function which are then imposed in the estimation of the investment demand equation. Thus, the parameters of the production function are determined implicitly from one of the factor demand equations and the other factor demand equation is constrained so that its parameters are also consistent with the implicitly determined production function parameters. Coen and Hickman find that this two-step procedure produces results that are "virtually the same as those resulting from joint nonlinear estimation (p. 296)."

The issue of which factor demand equation to use to obtain the implicit production function parameters was resolved by Coen and Hickman by simply choosing the one that produced the most reasonable estimates. In applying this procedure to the fifty-one regions of ECESIS it is almost certain that ambiguous cases would arise with this decision rule.

An alternative approach is to first estimate the parameters of the production function directly. Then estimate each of the factor demand equations, constraining their parameters to be consistent with those of the production function. While this procedure avoids the ambiguous decision rule of the Coen and Hickman two-step procedure, it introduces added complexities in having to estimate the production relation directly.

Assume an underlying Cobb-Douglas production function relating manufacturing output to capital and labor inputs in long-run equilibrium,

$$(3.1.1) \qquad Q^{\circ} = A(L^{\circ})^{\alpha}(K^{\circ})^{\beta}\exp(\gamma T),$$

where Q°, K°, L° are equilibrium levels of output, capital stocks and labor and T is a productivity trend.

For an expected output of Q°, profit maximizing firms will hire factors of production up to the point where marginal revenue products equal the factor prices. Assuming the production relation of (3.1.1) and imperfect local demand markets, the implicit desired factor input functions are:

$$(3.1.2a) \qquad L^{\circ} = \alpha Q^{\circ}P(1-1/\xi)/w,$$

$$(3.1.2b) \qquad K^{\circ} = \beta Q^{\circ}P(1-1/\xi)/r.$$

Where P is the output price; w is the money wage rate; r is the nominal user cost of capital; $P(1-1/\xi)$ is marginal revenue; and ξ is the elasticity of demand.

The remainder of this chapter concerns the the specification and estimation of the production function. Special attention is given to the problems of directly estimating production relations. An iterative estimation procedure that simultaneously determines the production function parameters and the regional capacity utilization rates is developed to cope with these problems.

The specification and estimation of the factor demand equations is the subject of Chapter Four.

3.2 SPECIFICATION AND ESTIMATION PROCEDURE

The production technology used in this study in assumed to be in the form of the Cobb-Douglas production function. The Cobb-Douglas function is easy to use and its properties are well known. Any number of more complex functions could have been chosen but in regional analysis, where limitations and reliability of data are severe, the particular form chosen for the production function becomes a secondary issue.

The decision to estimate the production function directly and constrain the parameters of the factor demand equations accordingly raises a difficult issue. The production function, as noted by Coen and Hickman (1970), is a relationship among variables at equilibrium. Thus, for the Cobb-Douglas production function,

$$(3.2.1) \qquad Q^{\circ} = A(L^{\circ})^{\alpha}(K^{\circ})^{\beta},$$

Q° is the long-run equilibrium level of output and L° and K° are the equilibrium levels of labor and capital inputs, respectively.[1] Usually the economy is not at equilibrium so that these variables cannot be directly observed. Presumably, at equilibrium capital and labor inputs are fully utilized. At all other points the observed quantities of capital and labor inputs are not the relevant values for the production function.

Capital stocks are difficult to adjust quickly so that at any point in time existing capital stock may be utilized in the production process at some rate, say υ_k. Labor inputs, on the other hand, are measured in terms of manhours and may be adjusted quickly through hires and layoffs and length of work week adjustments. It is reasonable to assume then, for annual data, that observed labor inputs are fully utilized.

---

[1] Time and region subscripts are dropped to simplify notation.

Actual output (Q) would then be related to observed inputs L and K as,

(3.2.2) $$Q = AL^{\alpha}(\upsilon_k K)^{\beta}.$$

Available labor inputs, however, may be greater than labor inputs actually hired. Nonzero unemployment rates attest to this observation. Even in a fairly localized area, one industry may have an excess supply of workers while other industries in the same area experience a labor shortage. As firms hire and layoff workers the firms tend to accumulate a pool of "attached" workers who have invested enough resources in their employment decisions that they are willing to wait out periods of unemployment rather than incur the costs of new job search and possible relocation (Haltiwanger 1980). Denote this potential level of labor inputs as LF. Then the utilization rate of labor is,

$$\upsilon_l = L/LF.$$

If all available inputs were fully utilized then the maximum or capacity output (QC) that could be produced would be,

(3.2.3) $$QC = A \cdot LF^{\alpha} K^{\beta}.$$

Dividing (3.2.2) by (3.2.3) gives the capacity output rate (υ_q),

(3.2.4) $\upsilon_q = Q/QC = (\upsilon_l)^{\alpha}(\upsilon_k)^{\beta}.$

The parameters of interest are A, α and β; but υ_l and υ_k are also unknown and vary both by region and time. Thus if there are T observations on Q, K and L in region r then there are T+3 unknown parameters to estimate in equation (3.2.2). Some method of reducing the number of unknown parameters must be used in order to proceed with the estimation.

Klein and Preston (1967) make the assumption that labor and capital are utilized at the same rate ($\upsilon_k=\upsilon_l$). This implies,

(3.2.5) $\upsilon_q = (\upsilon_l)^{\alpha+\beta}.$

If Q were total output for an entire regional economy then υ_l could be measured by one minus the regional unemployment rate. However, if Q represents output for only a particular industry then such specific unemployment rates are not available. In the latter case, some independent estimate of labor capacity must be made with which to estimate υ_l. Once the estimates for $\upsilon_l(=\upsilon_k)$ are made the production function (3.2.2) may be directly estimated.

Although Klein and Preston find this approach to be quite successful, there is some question over the empirical validity of assumption (3.2.5) (See DeLeeuw (1979), Phillips (1963) and Klein and Long (1973)).

An alternative approach is to assume that the utilization rate of capital is equal to the output capacity rate ($\upsilon_k=\upsilon_q$). In this case, equation (3.2.4) implies,

$$\upsilon_q = \upsilon_k = (\upsilon_l)^{\alpha/(1-\beta)}. \qquad (3.2.6)$$

Only in the case of constant returns to scale are assumptions (3.2.5) and (3.2.6) equivalent.

Either of two approaches may now be used. An independent estimate of υ_l may again be made. In this case, however, equation (3.2.2) cannot be directly estimated using a linear method since υ_k is a function of not only υ_l but also of the parameters α and β. Substituting (3.2.6) into (3.2.2) and using υ_l = L/LF yields,

$$Q = AL^{\alpha/(1-\beta)}LF^{(1-\beta)/\alpha\beta}K^{\beta}. \qquad (3.2.7)$$

This expression could be estimated using nonlinear techniques but the likely high collinearity among L, LF and K does not portend success.

The other alternative is to make use of some independent measure of the output capacity rate υ_q. As in the case of assumption (3.2.5), if an independent estimate of υ_q exists then equation (3.2.2) may be estimated directly.

Several estimates of output capacity utilization rates are available at the national level (See DeLeeuw (1979), Perry (1973) and Phillips (1963)). Unfortunately, none of these series are available at the subnational level.[2] It would be possible at the state level to use the trend-through-peaks method used in the Wharton index. The sample period of output data available at the state level, however, is quite short. Typically only one undisputed peak is observed in the period 1958 to 1975. Also, the problem remains with this method of extrapolating the capacity rates beyond the sample period for forecasting exercises.

There is an increased tendency to use the production function itself to derive a measure of capacity output. Klein and Su (1979) develop a model in which a production function approach is tied to the Wharton Index to forecast capacity rates. A variation of this approach, not relying upon an independently available capacity index, will be used here. Assumption (3.2.6) ($\upsilon_k=\upsilon_q$) will be used and an iterative procedure will be developed to estimate a variant of equation (3.2.7).

---

[2] The Bureau of Census state level capacity measures based on an establishment survey are only recently available and do not provide a sufficient time series.

First note that even if υ_k is known, it is not a trivial task to estimate equation (3.2.2). High collinearity among the independent variables often makes the estimates of α and β unreliable. Marginal efficiency arguments may be used to avoid this problem (See Klein (1974) and Klein and Preston (1967)). Cost minimizing behavior implies that marginal revenue products are equal to factor prices. In the context of the Cobb-Douglas production function with imperfect demand markets this implies,

$$(wL)/(PQ) = \alpha(1 - 1/\xi),$$

$$(rK)/(PQ) = \beta(1 - 1/\xi),$$

where w and r are the money wage rate and the user cost of capital,[3] P is the price of output and ξ is the elasticity of demand. The ratio of these two equilibrium conditions may be used to estimate the ratio β/α.

$$(3.2.8) \qquad (\beta/\alpha)^{+} = (1/T)\Sigma_t[(r_tK_t)/(w_tL_t)].$$

Where T is the number of observations and the superscript $^{+}$ denotes the estimated ratio.

Using (3.2.8) and assuming that υ_k is known, the production function could be estimated in the form,

$$(3.2.9) \qquad \log(Q) = \log(A)+\alpha\{\log(L)+[(\beta/\alpha)^{+}]\log(\upsilon_kK)\},$$

---

[3] The estimation of r is discussed in Chapter Four.

to estimate A and α. Once α is known, β can be calculated from the product of $(\beta/\alpha)^{+}$ and the estimate of α. This particular two-step procedure, unlike that of Coen and Hickman, is used to circumvent the problem of multicollinearity.

But, υ_k is not known. Using assumption (3.2.6), υ_k is shown to be a function of υ_l and α and β. The first step is to make an independent estimate of υ_l.

Using a simplified version of a method outlined by Klein and Su, capacity manufacturing labor inputs for a region may be estimated as,

$$(3.2.10) \quad LF_t = (EM/POP)^c{}_t POP_t H^c \cdot 52wk/yr,$$

where $(EM/POP)^c{}_t$ is the peak ratio of manufacturing employment to total population, POP_t is the current population in the region, and H^c is the peak hours worked per week.

Rather than substitute (3.2.6) into (3.2.2) and estimate using a nonlinear method, equation (3.2.9) may be estimated with an iterative procedure as follows. The sth iteration parameters are estimated from,

$$Q = A(s)[L \cdot K^{(\beta/\alpha)^{+}} \upsilon_q(s-1)^{(\beta/\alpha)^{+}}]^{\alpha(s)}.$$

The sth iteration capacity output is then calculated as,

$$QC(s) = A(s)[LF \cdot K^{(\beta/\alpha)+}]^{\alpha(s)}.$$

Which implies,

$$\upsilon_q(s) = \upsilon_1^{\alpha(s)}\upsilon_q(s-1)^{\alpha(s)(\beta/\alpha)+}.$$

These three equations are iterated until A(s), $\alpha(s)$ and $\upsilon_q(s)$ converge.[4]

For a given initial vector $\upsilon_q(0)$, $\upsilon_q(s)$ may be written as,

$$\upsilon_q(s) = \upsilon_1^{v} \cdot \upsilon_q(0)^{w},$$

where,

$$v = \{\alpha(s)+\sum_{i=1}^{s-1}\alpha(i)[(\beta/\alpha)^{+}]^{i+1}\Pi^{s}_{j=i+1}\alpha(j)\},$$

and

$$w = \{[(\beta/\alpha)^{+}]^{s}\Pi^{s}_{i=1}\alpha(i)\}.$$

The iterative process is stable and will converge if:

(i) $0 < \upsilon_q(0)_t < 1$; $\forall$ t = 1,...,T

(ii) $0 < (\beta/\alpha)^{+} < 1$

(iii) $\alpha(s) > 0$; $\forall$ s.

---

[4] Recall that $\upsilon_q(s)$ is a T×1 vector.

The initial point $\upsilon_q(0)$ is taken to be the Federal Reserve Boards' national level estimate of the manufacturing capacity utilization rate.

3.3 DATA

Before examining the results of the estimations, the data used in the regressions will be briefly examined.

The production function is specified as net of material inputs. Accordingly, output (Q) is measured as manufacturing value added. These data are available at the state level on an annual basis from the Annual Survey of Manufactures.

State manufacturing employment, on a number of jobs basis, is available from the Bureau of Labor Statistics. The same source provides estimates of average length of work week enabling construction of labor inputs in terms of manhours.

Manufacturing labor force (LF), in manhours, is constructed via equation (3.2.10). The peak hours per week (H^c) is simply taken to be the highest value observed over the historical time period 1958 to 1975. The peak manufacturing employment to population ratio, $(EM/POP)^c$, is calculated as the highest historical value with the constrainc that this value can be no more than ten percent above the actual observed ratio. The latter constraint is required because over the sample period some fast growing states managed to increase the size of their manufacturing sectors fivefold.

The estimation of capital stocks is more complex. Manufacturing capital stocks at current dollar gross book value are available for the states from the 1958 and 1977 U.S. Census of Manufactures and various Annual Survey of Manufactures (ASM). The appropriate series to use in the production function, however, is the constant dollar net value of capital stock. The Survey of Current Business provides estimates of total U.S. fixed nonresidential business capital of nonfinancial corporations in both current and constant dollars and in both gross and net values. Using these values, the 1957 and 1976 state current dollar gross value capital stocks of states are converted to constant dollar net values. The technique keeps the relative values among states constant but changes the absolute level of capital stocks.

Having done this for the two endpoint years of 1957 and 1976, a perpetual inventory method constrained to hit these two endpoints may be used to estimate the intermediate years. Assuming a geometric rate of capital depreciation (δ), capital stock is determined as,

(3.2.11) $K_t = (1 - \delta)K_{t-1} + GI_t$,

where K is constant dollar net capital stock and GI is constant dollar gross investment. With the initial value (K_{57}) and the terminal value (K_{76}) known, this equation may be transformed into a Tth order difference equation in $(1-\delta)$.

$$K_{76} = \sum_i (1-\delta)^i GI_{76-i} + (1-\delta)^{20} K_0.$$

After this difference equation is solved for δ, equation (3.2.11) may be used to calculate the intermediate values of the constant dollar net capital stock for each state.

State manufacturing current dollar gross investment data are available from the ASM. These data are deflated to 1972 dollars using the U.S. nonresidential gross private domestic investment deflator.

The depreciation rates resulting from this process are given in Table 3.3.1.

TABLE 3.3.1

DEPRECIATION RATES

STATE	δ	STATE	δ
ALABAMA	10.4	MONTANA	10.4
ALASKA	12.2	NEBRASKA	10.8
ARÍZONA	11.1	NEVADA	10.3
ARKANSAS	11.1	NEW HAMPSHIRE	12.3
CALIFORNIA	12.2	NEW JERSEY	12.5
COLORADO	12.7	NEW MEXICO	15.2
CONNECTICUT	11.9	NEW YORK	13.5
DELAWARE	10.0	NORTH CAROLINA	11.6
DIST. OF COLUMBIA	11.0	NORTH DAKOTA	8.7
FLORIDA	12.6	OHIO	11.2
GEORGIA	11.3	OKLAHOMA	12.5
HAWAII	9.5	OREGON	11.7
IDAHO	7.5	PENNSYLVANIA	10.5
ILLINOIS	11.4	RHODE ISLAND	12.6
INDIANA	10.2	SOUTH CAROLINA	10.3
IOWA	11.2	SOUTH DAKOTA	12.4
KANSAS	10.4	TENNESSEE	10.5
KENTUCKY	10.6	TEXAS	11.0
LOUISIANA	9.9	UTAH	9.0
MAINE	15.4	VERMONT	12.5
MARYLAND	10.4	VIRGINIA	11.7
MASSACHUSETTS	13.3	WASHINGTON	10.4
MICHIGAN	14.3	WEST VIRGINIA	10.2
MINNESOTA	12.6	WISCONSIN	11.4
MISSISSIPPI	10.4	WYOMING	9.1
MISSOURI	11.0		

The rates range from a high of 15.4% in Maine to a low of 7.5% in Idaho. A high depreciation rate might result from an old capital stock or a capital stock mix that is high in quickly depreciating equipment and low in the longer lived structures component.

The geographic distribution of the depreciation rates is displayed in Figure 3.3.1. Some observations are worth noting about this figure. First, five of the states with high depreciation rates include California, Arizona, Colorado, New Mexico and Florida. These are among the fastest growing states in the country. These are also states which are leaders in attracting new high technology industries. Many of these industries, for instance, the microelectronics industry centered in the silicon valley area of California, are very capital intensive. But this new capital is equipment oriented and by its high technology nature it also depreciates quickly.

This scenario is in direct contrast to the New England area, also displaying high depreciation rates, where the capital stock is typically old and concentrated in more stagnant industries. Here capital is operating at marginal efficiency and must be frequently overhauled to maintain steady production.

The manufacturing intensive Great Lakes states have a varied distribution of depreciation rates. Steel production is at the heart of Indiana's manufacturing industry and the capital in use is heavily structure oriented and old; much older than the seventeen years allowed for tax depreciation of structures. These two factors combined give Indiana the quite low depreciation rate of 10.2%. Michigan, on the

FIGURE 3.3.1

SPATIAL DISTRIBUTION OF DEPRECIATION RATES

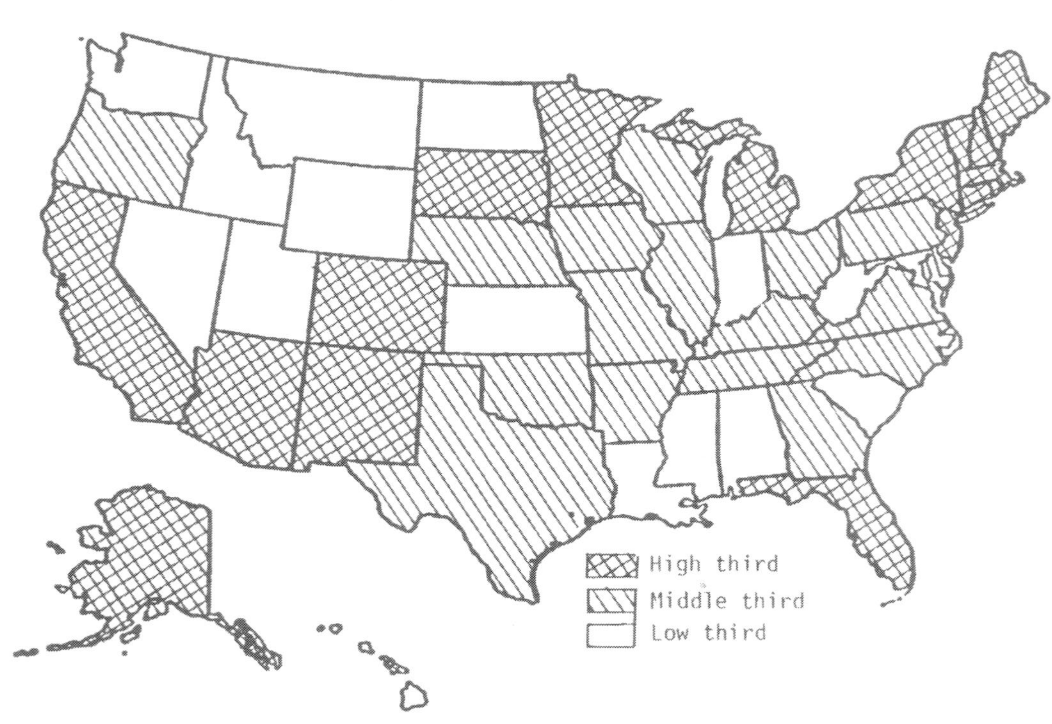

other hand, has a high depreciation rate (14.3%). Frequent retooling of equipment in the dominating auto industry may account for this.

In a region as small as a state, technological advances can have a sizable impact on the production process. For example, the impacts of the introduction of high technologies associated with the electronics industry is clearly visible in some of the Southwestern states. In an attempt to capture this influence, a productivity trend variable (T) has been added to the production function. More than a simple time trend, T represents the average growth of labor productivity in the state over the sample period.

$$T = [(1+i)^{t-57}/(1+i)^{15}]\cdot 100,$$

where,

$$(1+i) = \exp\{[\log(APL_{75}/APL_{58})]/17\},$$

and APL_t is the average product of labor in period t.

The average rates of productivity growth are given in Table 3.3.2.

TABLE 3.3.2

AVERAGE PRODUCTIVITY GROWTH RATES

STATE	%	STATE	%
ALABAMA	3.4	MONTANA	2.7
ALASKA	3.6	NEBRASKA	4.1
ARIZONA	3.9	NEVADA	1.4
ARKANSAS	4.2	NEW HAMPSHIRE	4.0
CALIFORNIA	2.9	NEW JERSEY	2.7
COLORADO	2.7	NEW MEXICO	2.8
CONNECTICUT	3.3	NEW YORK	3.6
DELAWARE	3.1	NORTH CAROLINA	3.6
DIST. OF COLUMBIA	4.6	NORTH DAKOTA	1.9
FLORIDA	3.5	OHIO	3.2
GEORGIA	4.0	OKLAHOMA	3.2
HAWAII	5.6	OREGON	3.3
IDAHO	3.6	PENNSYLVANIA	3.3
ILLINOIS	3.3	RHODE ISLAND	3.1
INDIANA	2.9	SOUTH CAROLINA	3.7
IOWA	3.8	SOUTH DAKOTA	2.3
KANSAS	3.5	TENNESSEE	3.1
KENTUCKY	3.0	TEXAS	3.7
LOUISIANA	5.7	UTAH	1.3
MAINE	3.5	VERMONT	3.4
MARYLAND	3.1	VIRGINIA	2.7
MASSACHUSETTS	3.5	WASHINGTON	3.7
MICHIGAN	3.3	WEST VIRGINIA	2.9
MINNESOTA	2.8	WISCONSIN	3.4
MISSISSIPPI	4.3	WYOMING	5.1
MISSOURI	3.3		

The average growth of productivity in the U.S. over the sample period was 3.3%. Both the Great Lakes states and the Mid-Atlantic states experienced below average productivity growth while the Southeastern states experienced productivity growth well above the national average. It is also interesting to note that, contrary to popular belief, the New England states managed to keep slightly ahead of the U.S. average productivity growth.

3.4 ESTIMATION RESULTS

Including the productivity trend, T, makes the final specification for the production function,

$$Q = A \cdot L^{\alpha}(\upsilon_k K)^{\beta}\exp(\gamma T)\exp(u).$$

The complete results from the iterative estimation procedure are given in Appendix 3.1 at the end of this chapter. The procedure converged in all but three states; Hawaii, Nevada and Tennessee. Hawaii has a relatively small manufacturing sector but the problem that occurred with that state sheds some light on the mechanics of the iterative process. Real manufacturing value added in Hawaii increased by over 65% from 1973 to 1974. This was due almost entirely to the severe sugar shortage of that year.[5] This large one year increase has the impact of setting capacity utilization in 1974 to one, forcing the capacity rate in other years to be lower than they would normally be set. As the number of iterations increase, the 1974 observation becomes relatively more important with υ_k in other years slowly drifting to

---

[5] Food and kindred products (SIC 20) are included in manufacturing output. Real value will increase due to the price rise because sugar products are a small part of the price index which is used to deflate SIC 20.

lower values.

A similar problem occurs in Tennessee where in 1964 there was a 69% increase in output. In this case the cause is almost certainly a data reporting error.

Manufacturing output in Nevada increased by a factor of five over the sample period. This high growth, from essentially zero to something still very small, has the same impact as a data outlier; later years get disproportionate weight in the iterative procedure.

In addition to these three states, two other states (Idaho and Montana) had similar but less serious estimation problems. Four states (Hawaii, Idaho, Montana and Tennessee) were re-estimated using the assumption that the capacity utilization rate was equal to the Federal Reserve Board (FRB) series (i.e., $\upsilon_q(0)$). Finally, the parameters for the Nevada production function were set at the values; A=1, γ=1 and α=.7274. The latter coefficient being determined by the capital to labor ratio $(\beta/\alpha)^*$ and the additional assumption of constant returns to scale.

The states where the iterative procedure broke down are states, with the exception of Tennessee, where the manufacturing sectors are small.[6] The procedure tended to work very well in most other states. The estimates of α were all positive and significant at the one percent level and the estimates of γ were all positive and, in most cases, significant at the one percent level.

The state level capacity utilization (CU) rates estimated from the iterative procedure appear to be quite reasonable. Figure 3.4.1 displays the FRB CU rate ($\upsilon_q(0)$) along with rates from three diverse states.

California has had a fast growing economy with above average CU rates. Except for the 1970-71 recession which coincided with a severe cutback in the aeronautics industry, the California CU rate has also been fairly stable. This is in contrast to the CU rate for Michigan. Dominated by the highly cyclical auto industry, Michigan's manufacturing sector has followed the general trend of the U.S. economy but with much greater amplitude. New York's CU rate shows a general downward trend with an incomplete recovery from the 1970-'71 recession. The estimated CU rates for these three states, with quite different manufacturing sectors, are very much like one would expect a priori.

---

[6] A data outlier was also associated with each of the problem states.

FIGURE 3.4.1

SELECTED CU RATES

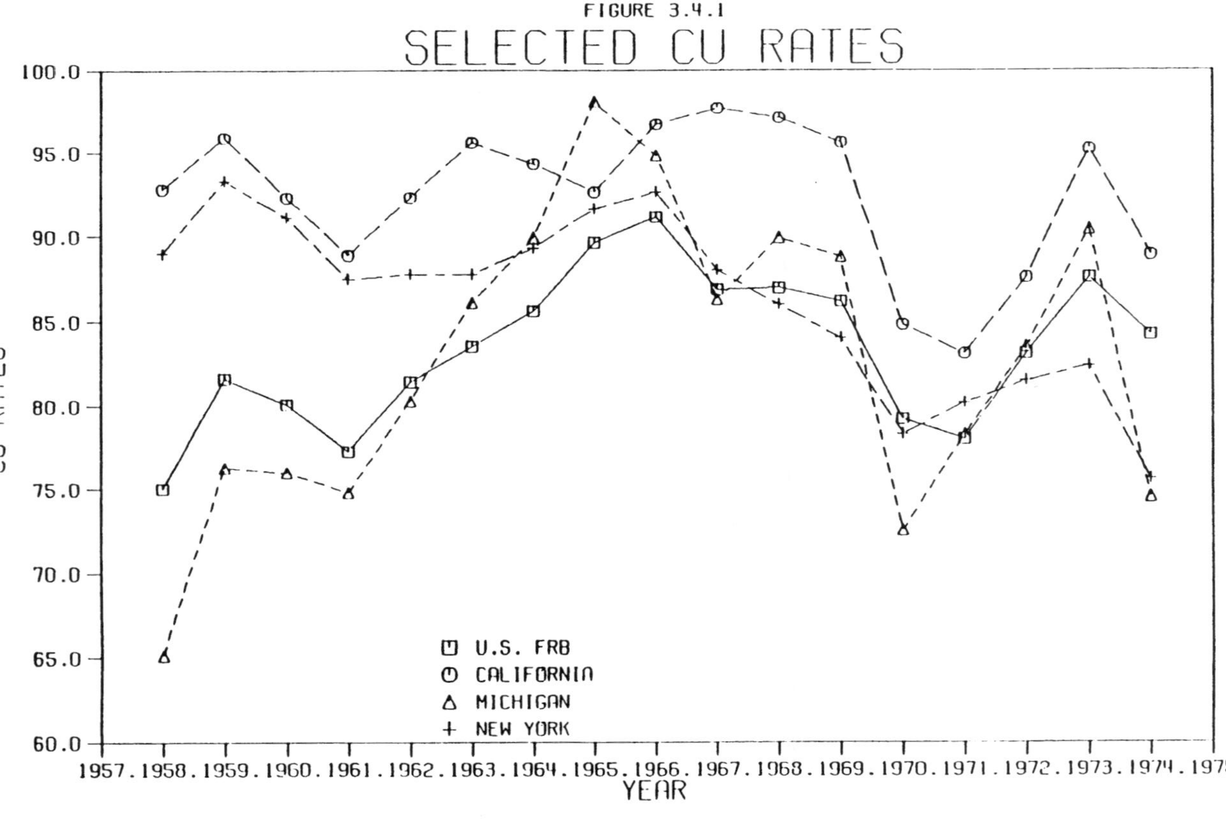

There appears to be a general tendency for the iterative procedure to overstate the CU rate at the peak production year. This is evident in Figure 3.4.2 comparing the U.S. FRB CU rate with the U.S. CU rate implied by the estimated state CU rates. The two plots are similar except that the FRB CU rate is uniformly lower than the U.S. CU rate resulting from the estimation procedure.

Multiplying the capital to labor ratio $(\beta/\alpha)^{*}$, estimated independently via expression (3.2.8), by the estimate of α yields the estimated value for β. The sum of α and β give the estimated returns to scale which are reported in Table 3.4.1.

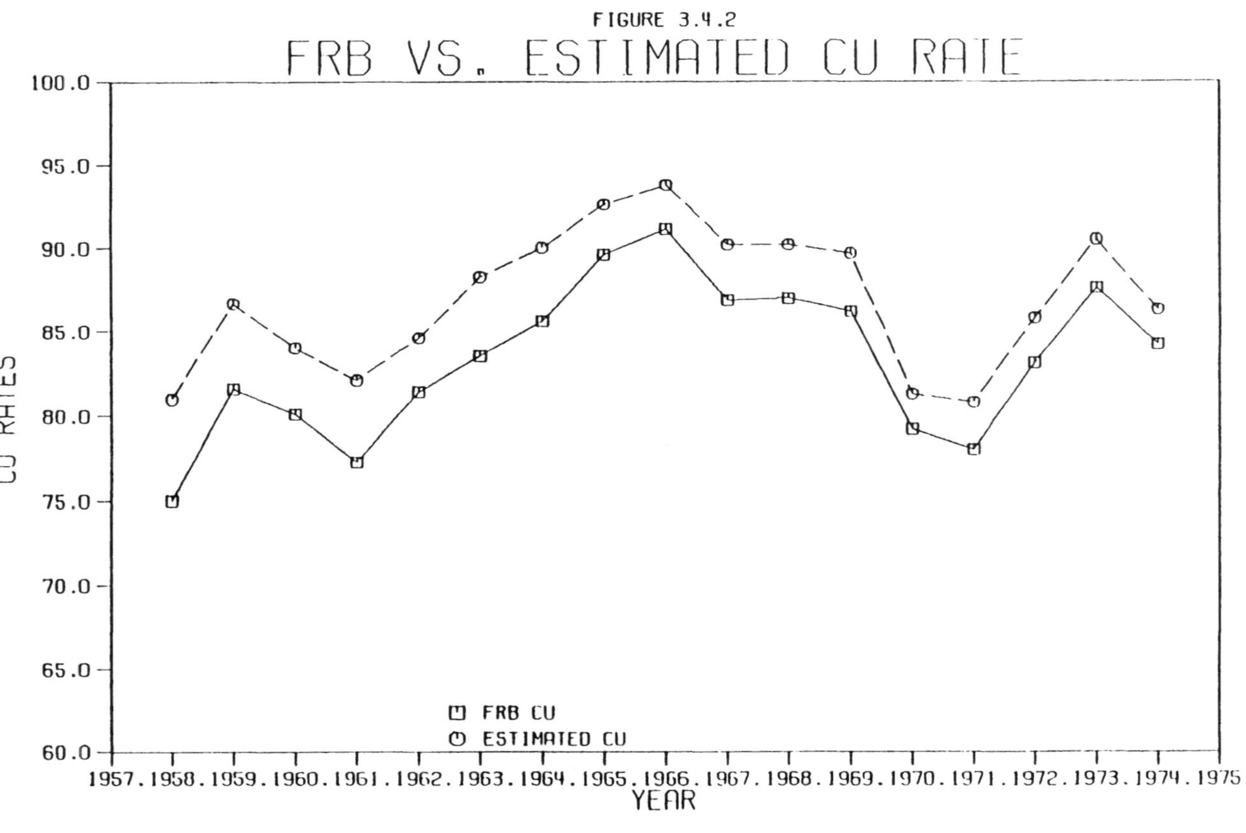
FIGURE 3.4.2
FRB VS. ESTIMATED CU RATE
CU RATES
100.0
95.0
90.0
85.0
80.0
75.0
70.0
65.0
60.0
1957. 1958. 1959. 1960. 1961. 1962. 1963. 1964. 1965. 1966. 1967. 1968. 1969. 1970. 1971. 1972. 1973. 1974. 1975.
YEAR
FRB CU
ESTIMATED CU

TABLE 3.4.1

RETURNS TO SCALE

STATE	$\alpha+\beta$	STATE	$\alpha+\beta$
ALABAMA	1.660	MONTANA	1.642
ALASKA	1.427	NEBRASKA	1.206
ARIZONA	0.892	NEVADA	1.000
ARKANSAS	1.637	NEW HAMPSHIRE	1.081
CALIFORNIA	1.058	NEW JERSEY	1.419
COLORADO	0.720	NEW MEXICO	1.044
CONNECTICUT	1.385	NEW YORK	1.323
DELAWARE	1.755	NORTH CAROLINA	0.982
DIST. OF COLUMBIA	0.879	NORTH DAKOTA	1.377
FLORIDA	1.194	OHIO	1.040
GEORGIA	1.190	OKLAHOMA	1.121
HAWAII	0.869	OREGON	1.285
IDAHO	0.934	PENNSYLVANIA	1.240
ILLINOIS	1.114	RHODE ISLAND	1.534
INDIANA	1.047	SOUTH CAROLINA	1.373
IOWA	1.201	SOUTH DAKOTA	1.615
KANSAS	0.954	TENNESSEE	1.133
KENTUCKY	1.360	TEXAS	1.175
LOUISIANA	0.959	UTAH	1.251
MAINE	0.811	VERMONT	1.281
MARYLAND	1.258	VIRGINIA	1.327
MASSACHUSETTS	1.331	WASHINGTON	0.993
MICHIGAN	1.227	WEST VIRGINIA	1.500
MINNESOTA	0.963	WISCONSIN	1.168
MISSISSIPPI	1.369	WYOMING	1.386
MISSOURI	1.057		

In most cases the estimations implied increasing returns to scale. There is no apparent significance to the spatial distribution of these values. The largest of the manufacturing states, however, display moderate levels of increasing returns. The extreme values tend to arise in states with relatively small manufacturing sectors.

The elasticity of demand may be calculated from,

$$\xi = \alpha/(\alpha - \Omega),$$

where,

$$\Omega = 1/T[\textstyle\sum_t (wL)/(PQ)],$$

is the estimated wage share for the region. The higher the elasticity, the more competitive is the industry in that region. The nature of the marginal conditions of the Cobb-Douglas production function impose the restriction that the elasticity of demand be greater than one.[7] This observation is verified empirically by the elasticities listed in Table 3.4.2.

[7] A profit maximizing monopolist will not operate at a point where demand elasticity is less than one.

TABLE 3.4.2

ELASTICITY OF DEMAND

STATE	ξ	STATE	ξ
ALABAMA	1.68	MONTANA	1.79
ALASKA	1.95	NEBRASKA	1.82
ARIZONA	3.79	NEVADA	2.53
ARKANSAS	1.55	NEW HAMPSHIRE	2.62
CALIFORNIA	2.55	NEW JERSEY	1.78
COLORADO	5.89	NEW MEXICO	3.66
CONNECTICUT	1.95	NEW YORK	1.93
DELAWARE	2.07	NORTH CAROLINA	2.49
DIST. OF COLUMBIA	3.79	NORTH DAKOTA	1.77
FLORIDA	2.15	OHIO	2.76
GEORGIA	2.04	OKLAHOMA	2.46
HAWAII	5.32	OREGON	2.06
IDAHO	3.05	PENNSYLVANIA	2.32
ILLINOIS	2.32	RHODE ISLAND	1.72
INDIANA	2.83	SOUTH CAROLINA	1.95
IOWA	1.81	SOUTH DAKOTA	1.54
KANSAS	2.45	TENNESSEE	2.11
KENTUCKY	1.59	TEXAS	2.05
LOUISIANA	3.24	UTAH	1.93
MAINE	6.79	VERMONT	1.98
MARYLAND	1.94	VIRGINIA	1.84
MASSACHUSETTS	1.69	WASHINGTON	2.96
MICHIGAN	2.35	WEST VIRGINIA	1.80
MINNESOTA	2.68	WISCONSIN	2.13
MISSISSIPPI	1.88	WYOMING	2.62
MISSOURI	2.32		

The Mid-Atlantic and New England states have fairly low elasticities and the Western and Mountain states have fairly high elasticities. Maine and Utah are the exceptions. Defense expenditures, generally on a cost-plus basis, may have some influence in the Northeastern states. The Great Lakes states have higher than average elasticities indicating a competitive climate. Analysis of trade flows indicate that competition in this region is primarily with other states in the same region.

Estimation of production relations is a difficult affair. This is particularly true at the state level where data are scarce and sometimes unreliable. The assumption of a Cobb-Douglas technology simplifies matters a great deal. Many problems remain and have been discussed in this section. The iterative procedure developed to simultaneously estimate the production function parameters and the capacity utilization rates has been quite successful. Areas where further effort would be most profitable include tests with alternative production functions and region specific functions.

APPENDIX 3.1

PRODUCTION FUNCTION ESTIMATION RESULTS

The equation estimated is,

$$\log(Q) = \log(A) + \alpha[\log(L)+\log(\upsilon_k K)(\beta/\alpha)^{*}] + \gamma T + u.$$

Section 3.2 describes the variables and the iterative technique used to estimate this equation. The estimation sample period is 1958 to 1974.

The first three columns after the state name give the estimated values for log(A), α and γ. The t-statistics are reported directly below these estimates. The critical point for the 5% two-tailed test of log(A) is 2.145. For α and γ the one-tailed t-test critical point is 1.761. The fourth column reports the adjusted coefficient of determination with the Durbin-Watson statistic directly below. The uncertainty region for the D-W test is .9 to 1.4. The number of iterations required until convergence (.01% convergence tolerance) is given in column five with the capital to labor ratio, estimated from equation (3.2.8), reported directly below this.

Hawaii, Idaho, Montana, and Tennessee were estimated assuming that $\upsilon_k=\upsilon_q(0)$. This assumption eliminates the need for the iterative procedure. The Federal Reserve Board's national manufacturing capacity utilization rate is used for

$\upsilon_q(0)$.

Nevada coefficients were chosen using a nonregression ad hoc method. See text for further details.

STATE	log(A)	α	γ	$\bar{R}^2$/D-W	#I/(β/α)
ALABAMA	-2.961 3.83	1.203 11.85	-.059 0.28	.99 0.85	14 .380
ALASKA	-0.027 0.05	0.983 5.15	0.440 1.01	.97 2.03	12 .452
ARIZONA	1.070 1.63	0.737 4.690	1.490 3.530	.99 1.69	6 .211
ARKANSAS	-2.447 3.75	1.227 11.59	0.181 0.78	.99 1.24	14 .334
CALIFORNIA	0.226 0.22	0.887 7.66	1.362 11.12	.99 0.81	6 .192
COLORADO	2.044 1.84	0.580 2.67	1.512 3.09	.99 1.28	5 .242
CONNECTICUT	-1.852 3.31	1.164 16.87	1.075 20.99	.99 1.03	6 .190
DELAWARE	-3.290 4.76	1.367 11.82	1.080 7.41	.98 1.25	9 .283
DIST. OF COLUMBIA	1.550 2.13	0.735 5.06	1.046 13.78	.94 1.57	6 .195
FLORIDA	-0.424 0.64	0.937 9.37	0.856 3.85	.99 1.75	8 .274
GEORGIA	-0.518 0.37	0.937 5.13	0.870 2.96	.98 0.58	7 .271
HAWAII	0.909 0.33	0.568 1.40	1.308 10.07	.88 1.10	n.a. .530
IDAHO	0.798 0.57	0.638 2.41	1.196 2.03	.97 0.97	n.a. .464

ILLINOIS	-0.064 0.07	0.897 9.43	1.087 14.51	.99 0.69	5 .241
INDIANA	0.401 0.51	0.781 9.01	1.011 7.31	.99 0.64	6 .341
IOWA	-0.181 0.21	0.940 7.58	0.883 5.46	.99 0.85	7 .278
KANSAS	1.034 1.54	0.753 7.45	1.184 9.79	.99 1.09	8 .267
KENTUCKY	-0.811 0.93	1.024 7.66	0.360 1.12	.99 1.49	11 .328
LOUISIANA	1.031 0.93	0.577 5.14	0.641 3.14	.98 0.73	10 .663
MAINE	1.336 2.29	0.636 7.58	1.323 26.53	.99 1.44	5 .275
MARYLAND	-1.034 0.71	0.971 5.69	1.179 19.53	.97 1.04	14 .296
MASSACHUSETTS	-1.781 1.13	1.139 6.29	1.353 21.04	.97 0.53	7 .168
MICHIGAN	-0.751 1.05	1.102 12.71	0.936 10.01	.98 0.80	6 .213
MINNESOTA	0.938 1.37	0.807 7.64	1.313 7.60	.99 1.42	6 .193
MISSISSIPPI	-1.300 2.15	1.049 10.62	0.557 2.55	.99 1.33	9 .305
MISSOURI	0.386 0.52	0.880 9.23	1.200 14.87	.99 1.30	3 .202
MONTANA	-2.090 1.14	1.055 3.37	0.56 1.24	.93 1.50	n.a. .556
NEBRASKA	-0.325 0.28	0.943 4.80	1.158 4.99	.99 1.00	7 .279
NEVADA	0.0 n.a.	0.727 n.a.	1.00 n.a.	n.a. n.a.	n.a. .375
NEW HAMPSHIRE	0.074 0.10	0.907 7.68	1.233 18.73	.99 1.40	10 .191

NEW JERSEY	-2.470 1.81	1.163 7.77	1.236 15.75	.98 0.91	8 .220
NEW MEXICO	0.09 0.19	0.850 5.89	1.414 4.81	.97 1.90	6 .228
NEW YORK	-1.922 1.34	1.143 7.84	1.336 21.41	.97 0.64	7 .158
NORTH CAROLINA	0.696 1.08	0.766 9.34	1.116 7.00	.99 1.25	8 .282
NORTH DAKOTA	-1.907 4.62	0.997 4.30	2.473 2.94	.97 1.43	13 .381
OHIO	0.541 0.57	0.823 8.44	1.032 10.84	.99 0.65	6 .264
OKLAHOMA	0.087 0.08	0.880 4.34	0.994 2.37	.99 1.83	7 .273
OREGON	-0.841 0.71	0.978 5.73	0.847 3.35	.99 0.84	8 .314
PENNSYLVANIA	-1.343 1.38	0.976 10.24	1.137 19.34	.99 0.78	5 .271
RHODE ISLAND	-2.449 2.80	1.298 9.65	1.255 20.36	.98 0.94	7 .181
SOUTH CAROLINA	-1.478 1.40	1.108 7.15	0.365 1.22	.99 0.66	9 .349
SOUTH DAKOTA	-1.419 1.35	1.321 4.13	0.923 1.91	.95 1.76	9 .222
TENNESSEE	-0.78 0.02	0.863 2.02	0.828 0.86	.90 1.80	n.a. .313
TEXAS	0.826 0.59	0.934 4.69	1.026 3.44	.98 0.56	7 .462
UTAH	-0.990 1.21	0.944 5.39	1.542 3.17	.94 1.13	7 .326
VERMONT	-0.449 1.03	1.034 11.76	0.890 8.51	.98 0.97	5 .239
VIRGINIA	-1.072 1.19	1.027 8.06	0.486 1.83	.99 0.50	9 .292

WASHINGTON	0.885 0.88	0.762 6.11	1.097 8.59	.95 1.22	5 .303
WEST VIRGINIA	-2.112 2.36	1.004 9.63	0.607 5.31	.97 0.67	11 .494
WISCONSIN	-0.329 0.39	0.954 9.32	1.054 14.10	.99 0.87	5 .225
WYOMING	-1.336 1.66	0.793 6.35	1.27 18.04	.96 1.71	15 .748

CHAPTER FOUR: FACTOR DEMANDS

4.1 DEMAND FOR CAPITAL INPUTS

4.1.1 REVIEW OF REGIONAL INVESTMENT MODELS

Interest in regional macroeconometric modeling has lagged somewhat behind that of its national counterpart. It is reasonable, therefore, that the first attempts at modeling regional investment functions reflected the developments of national level Investment functions. An early example is the investment functions for regions of Canada by Guccione and Gillen (1972). Following the specification suggestions of Klein (1969), Guccione and Gillen transplant a Jorgenson style national investment function into a regional setting. In their paper, regional gross investment is determined as a function of output, lagged capital stock and lagged gross investment. Due to data limitations, the function is respecified to eliminate explicit reference to capital stocks. Also, Guccione and Gillen specified their investment functions to be related to national output rather than regional output. The final specification for regional gross investment is,

$$(4.1.1) \quad GI_r = b_0 + b_1 Q_{us} + b_2 GI_{r,t-1} + b_3 GI_{r,t-2} + u_r,$$

where GI_r is gross investment in region r and Q_{us} is a function of national output.

As expected, given the lag structure, the functions fit the data fairly well. Nevertheless, the specification may be criticized for containing little region specific information.

Since this early attempt regional economists have expended considerable effort on the task of developing a regional investment equation that is distinctly regional.

In a later paper, Guccione and Gillen (1974) modify their function to include region specific output and capital prices. Although this specification more accurately follows the theory of Jorgenson and the suggestions made by Klein (1969) the individual regions still behave as if in isolation.

Borrowing an idea from international capital flow theory, Engle (1974) develops an investment model that does allow for interregional competition. Engle speculates that investment at the regional level is the result of a two-step process. The decision of how much to invest in total is first made at the national level using conventional marginal efficiency arguments. Then the decision of the spatial allocation of investment is made on the basis of region specific data. The idea is appealing on several accounts. The fluidity of assets markets make the determination of interest rates a national phenomena, lending justification to the first step in the decision process. Existing and well established national macroeconometric models may be relied upon for estimates of the level of investment. Also, the allocation problem may be resolved in a number of ways, adding flexibility to the model specification.

The specification chosen by Engle was,

$$(4.1.2) \qquad GI_r = b_0 + b_1 r_r / r* + b_2 GI_{us},$$

where GI_r, GI_{us} are gross investment in region r and the U.S., and r_r and $r*$ are the marginal value product of capital in region r and in some alternative location.

An equation similar to (4.1.2) was estimated for each of the states in the ECESIS model. Gross profits divided by capital stock was used as an estimate for r with the U.S. value being used for r*. The estimation results were not good. The coefficient for the profit rate ratios (b_1) was significantly (5%) positive in only four states (Connecticut, Massachusetts, New Jersey, Texas); b_1 was significantly negative in seven states (Colorado, Kentucky, Maine, Maryland, New Hampshire, Virginia, Washington). On the other hand, total U.S. gross investment was significant with the correct sign in all but five states (District of Columbia, Hawaii, New Mexico, South Dakota, Wyoming). The $\bar{R}^2$ from these equations are quite variable but generally fall in the 40 to 90 percent range.

Several different variations of the alternative opportunities variables were tried with virtually no affect on the results. In every case U.S. gross investment is clearly the dominant variable. In Massachusetts, Engle's example state, the simple correlation between GI_r and GI_{us} is 93%. There is little variation left for the relative profit rates to explain. Also, the reasonably good $\bar{R}^2$'s are due to the use of gross investment rather than net investment. Gross investment is far less variable than net investment due to the inclusion of the large and fairly stable depreciation charges in gross investment. Ultimately, it is net investment that is of interest.

As noted in Chapter Three, a complete model will specify a production technology as well as factor demand equations. Equation (4.1.2) will not be theoretically or empirically consistent with the type of production relations generally specified in econometric models.

Crow (1979) recognizes the appeal of Engle's two-step determination process and also the theoretical weaknesses of the approach. Working directly from the factor demand equations implied by a specific production function Crow develops a system that avoids the inconsistencies implicit in Engle's model. Briefly, and in simplified form, Crow's approach is to specify a production function and derive the implicit desired factor input equations.

(4.1.3) $Q^{\circ} = f(K^{\circ}, L^{\circ})$,

(4.1.4) $K^{\circ} = k(Q^{\circ}, r, w)$,

(4.1.5) $L^{\circ} = l(Q^{\circ}, r, w)$.

Where Q°, K°, L° are desired output, capital and labor inputs and r and w are the prices of capital and labor.

Renormalizing equation (4.1.4) for Q° converts the capital input equation into a desired output equation.

(4.1.6) $Q^{\circ} = k^{-1}(K^{\circ}, r, w)$.

A simple adjustment process converts desired output to actual output.

(4.1.7) $Q/Q_{-1} = g(Q^{\circ}/Q_{-1})$.

Next, the regions share of gross investment is determined as a function of relative profit rates, output, tax rates, etc.

(4.1.8) GI_{r}/GI_{us}=i(local variables/national variables).

This extension of an Engle's type investment equation, along with the assumption that desired and actual capital stocks are equal, yields K° as an input to equation (4.1.6).

This set of equations is logically consistent even though it uses an investment function very much like that of Engle's. Crow has taken advantage of his freedom to normalize equations in order to avoid the inconsistency problem.

A drawback of this procedure is that the conventional output demand equation of econometric models is replaced by a desired output equation based on desired capital stocks (4.1.6) and an output adjustment equation (4.1.7). This implies that output at the regional level is primarily determined by supply conditions rather than demand conditions.

In this study, attempts to estimate investment functions of the type (4.1.8) have met with little success. Both logit and simple share equations regressed on a large array of regional variables failed to produce an empirically reasonable investment function. Combined with the results of the estimation of Engle's investment equation (4.1.2), this indicates that when estimating regional investment in a top-down model the key explanatory variable is national investment (GI_{us}). When GI_{us} is included as an independent variable it overpowers other explanatory variables. When the equations are specified in ratio form, the results are weak and unstable.

The poor results obtained with the Engle and Crow specifications indicate that some variant of the Guccione and Gillen specification will be the most robust across diverse regions. In keeping with the design features of ECESIS, the investment equations should be bottom-up specifications and maintain consistency with the production function. Also, because of severe limitations with regional investment data, the specifications must be as simple as possible.

4.1.2 SPECIFICATION OF INVESTMENT EQUATION

Typically capital expansion programs are large in scale and require implementation over several periods. Thus, the level of investment devoted to capital expansion in any given period is a function of expansion decisions made over several previous periods as well as new plans initiated in the current period. Let b_i be the proportion of investment projects initiated in period t and completed in period t+i. Then at each time t the level of investment for capital expansion (I_t = net investment) is a weighted average of the level of projects initiated in all previous periods,

$$I_t = b_0 IN_t + b_1 IN_{t-1} + b_2 IN/r_{-2} + \cdots,$$

where IN_t is the level of projects started in period t.[1] Using more compact notation,

(4.1.9) $$I_t = B(\ell)IN_t,$$

where $B(\ell) = b_0 + b_1\ell + b_2\ell^2 + \cdots$ is a power series in the lag operator ℓ.

The backlog of uncompleted projects in period t is equal to the sum of the uncompleted portions of all past projects already started,

$$IN_t + (1-b_0)IN_{t-1} + (1-b_0-b_1)IN_{t-2} + \cdots.$$

Or using the lag operator notation,

$$[(1-\ell\cdot B(\ell))/(1-\ell)]IN_t.$$

In order to achieve equilibrium, this backlog of uncompleted projects must equal the difference between desired capital stock and actual capital stock (i.e., the level of capital stock at the beginning of the period).

(4.1.10) $$K^\circ_t-K_{t-1} = [(1-\ell\cdot B(\ell))/(1-\ell)]\ IN_t.$$

Using (4.1.9), rewrite (4.1.10) as,

(4.1.11) $$(1-\ell)B(\ell)(K^\circ_t-K_{t-1}) = [1-\ell B(\ell)]I_t.$$

---

[1] An important assumption here is than the b's depend only on the length of the interval (i) and not upon the time period t. See Jorgenson (1965). This section closely parallels Jorgenson's exposition.

Now let a_i be the proportion of investment goods acquired in period t and replaced in period t+i. Then replacement investment in period t would be,

(4.1.12) $IR_t = A(\ell)GI_t$,

where $A(\ell) = a_0 + a_1\ell + a_2\ell^2 + \cdots$ is a power series in the lag operator ℓ.

Capital stock in period t is the sum of all past investments minus replacement,

$$K_t = \sum_i (GI_{t-i} - IR_{t-i}) = (GI_t - IR_t)/(1-\ell),$$

(4.1.13) or, solving for gross investment,

$$GI_t = (1-\ell)K_t + IR_t.$$

Since,

(4.1.14) $I_t = (1-\ell)K_t$,

equations (4.1.11) through (4.1.14) combine to yield,

(4.1.15) $GI_t = [(1-\ell)B(\ell)][(1-\ell B(\ell))(1-A(\ell))]^{-1}(K^\circ_t - K_{t-1})$.

Recalling that the Cobb-Douglas production technology implies,

(4.1.16) $K^\circ_t = \beta Q^\circ_t P_t(1-1/\xi)/r_t$,

and assuming that the complex lag structure of (4.1.15) may

be approximated by the ratio of two finite polynomials in ℓ, $\Phi(\ell)/\Theta(\ell)$, the gross investment equation may be written as,

$$(4.1.17) \qquad \Theta(\ell)GI_t = \Phi(\ell)[\beta Q^\circ{}_t P_t(1-1/\xi)/r_t - K_{t-1}].$$

Note that every variable in expression (4.1.17) may be region specific. Annual manufacturing capital stock data exist for each of the fifty states and the District of Columbia. The user cost of capital (r) depends upon local tax rates and investment incentives. Data limitations force the output price to be set at the national level, but the elasticity of demand (ξ) is a state specific variable. Output (Q) is determined as a function of demand in every state weighted by interstate trade flows.[2] Thus, equation (4.1.17) represents a theoretically consistent factor demand equation with not only a good deal of regional specific input but also regional interdependencies.

4.1.3 DATA

Manufacturing gross investment data are available at the state level from the U.S. Bureau of the Census' Annual Survey of Manufactures (ASM). Assuming a fixed rate of economic depreciation (δ), net investment is easily calculated.

---

[2] See Chapter Two.

Desired capital stock (K°) is a function of several parameters. Manufacturing value added for each state is obtained from the ASA. The parameter β and the elasticity of demand (ξ) are obtained from the estimation of the production function. The user cost of capital (r) is a more elusive variable. In the following paragraphs some theoretical observations are made concerning the estimation of r; concluding with the empirical realities and limitations of estimating r.

The nominal user cost of capital services (r) is not the cost of new capital equipment but rather the cost that industry would attribute to using its entire stock of capital--including all vintages.

Due to the assumption made in ECESIS of imperfect demand markets, it is not valid in this instance to estimate the cost of capital as gross profits divided by the capital stock. An expression for the user cost may be derived, however, under the hypothesis that firms attempt to maximize net worth subject to assumptions on tax arrangements and production constraints. In the simplest case, net worth (NW) is defined as the discounted sum of revenue less current and capital account expenses.

(4.1.18) $NW = \int e^{-ft}(PQ - wL - qGI)dt,$

where q is the cost of new investment goods and f is the financing rate. Net worth is maximized subject to two constraints. First, output and inputs are constrained by some production relation, say,

$$F(Q, L, K) = 0.$$

Second, capital stock may only grow at the rate of gross investment less replacement capital. Assuming a geometric distribution of replacements and a continuous time model, this condition may be written as

$$dK/dt = GI - \delta K.$$

The constrained maximization can be written as the Lagrangean expression,

$$\max \Lambda = \int\{e^{-ft}(PQ-wL-GI)+\lambda_0 F(Q,L,K)+\lambda_1(dK/dt-GI+\delta K)\}dt.$$

Solving the first-order conditions for this maximization implies that the user cost of capital is equal to the current cost of investment goods times the sum of the finance rate and the capital depreciation rate,

$$(4.1.19) \qquad r = q(f + \delta).$$

Hendershott and Hu (1980a), using a more realistic set of assumptions, derive a somewhat more complicated expression.

Let τ_1 and τ_2 be the income tax rate and the property tax rate, respectively, and let μ be the effective rate of the investment tax credit. The proportion of net investment that is debt financed will be designated as σ. Assume that debt financing charges, depreciation and property taxes may be deducted from the income tax base. Let the depreciation rate allowed for tax purposes in period t be d_t.

Given this added complexity, the appropriate discount rate now becomes the after-tax average financing rate (f_a),

$$f_a = (1 - \tau_1)\sigma \cdot i + (1 - \sigma)e_a. \tag{4.1.20}$$

Where i is the interest rate on debt and e_a is the after-tax return on equity.

In addition to the tax rates, investment credit rates and loan-to-value ratio discussed above, Hendershott and Hu also allow a constant rate of capital appreciation (ρ) and the existence of secondary markets for capital goods. Assume that a capital good is held N years and that Ψ is the cost, as a percent of the market price, of selling the capital good in the secondary market. Finally, the discrete-time, finite-life version of (4.1.19), incorporating all of the above assumptions, is derived as,

$$r = q[(G-\mu)(r_a-\rho+\delta)/D - \tau_1\delta + (1-\tau_1)\tau_2 - \tau_1(d^{+}-\delta)]/(1-\tau_1). \tag{4.1.21}$$

Where:

$$G = 1 - (1-\Psi)(1+\rho-\delta)^N/(1+f_a)^N,$$

$$D = 1 - (1+\rho-d)^N/(1+f_a)^N,$$

$$d^+ = [(f_a-\rho+\delta)/D]\Sigma^N[d_t/(1+f_a)^t].$$

Many of the variables in (4.1.21) are specific to a particular region. Feldstein and Poterba (1980) have shown that the effective tax rates τ_1 and τ_2 are substantially influenced by state and local taxes. Unfortunately, it is beyond the scope of this study to collect such detailed tax information from each of the states. Thus, only the national level effective tax rates, investment credits and finance rates are used. The depreciation rate (δ) remains state specific.

Estimates for the national level user cost of capital for equipment and for structures are given in Hendershott and Hu (1980b). These two series are averaged[3] to get a user cost for equipment and structures combined.

[3] The weights used are suggested by Hendershott and Hu (1980a).

4.1.4 ESTIMATION RESULTS

The problem remains to specify the lag structure of the gross investment equation given by (4.1.17). Procedures commonly used for time series analysis are not reliable with so few observations. Thus, embracing the principle that the simplest design that works is the best design, it is assumed that gross investment is a simple weighted average of past desired to actual capital stock discrepancies. Assuming the weights to be geometrically declining gives,

$$GI_t = a_0 + a_1 \sum_i w^i (K^\circ_{t-i} - K_{t-1-i}).$$

Or, in lag operator notation,

$$GI_t = a_0 + (1-w\ell)^{-1} a_1 (K^\circ_t - K_{t-1}).$$

Transforming this expression to an easily estimable form gives the gross investment function,

$$(4.1.22) \qquad GI_t = b_0 + b_1 GI_{t-1} + b_2 (K^\circ_t - K_{t-1}).$$

The complete estimation results are given in Appendix 4.1.

In light of the severe data problems, the estimation results are generally reasonable. Two states, New Mexico and Oklahoma, are estimated with the restriction that $b_1=1$. Wyoming is estimated with the restriction $b_1=0$. The data for Washington D. C. are so erratic that a simple average is used to estimate gross investment in that region. The equation tends to perform very well in the large manufacturing states where the data base is large and data errors are likely to be relatively less severe. This lends support to the idea that the equation is sound in theory but undone by data problems.

The average lags for the gross investment equations[4] are reported in Table 4.1.1. Over half of the average lag values lie between one and four years. Most of the low values for average lag occur in states with small manufacturing sectors. In Colorado and South Carolina b_1 is so close to one that the average lag becomes very large. These are the same states where the estimations are least reliable.

---

[4] Calculated as $b_1/(1-b_1)$. The calculation is not appropriate in D. C., New Mexico, Oklahoma, and Wyoming.

TABLE 4.1.1

AVERAGE LAGS

STATE	lag(yrs)	STATE	lag(yrs)
ALABAMA	2.16	MONTANA	0.06
ALASKA	0.22	NEBRASKA	0.92
ARIZONA	3.76	NEVADA	0.34
ARKANSAS	3.46	NEW HAMPSHIRE	1.83
CALIFORNIA	4.15	NEW JERSEY	2.11
COLORADO	332.	NEW MEXICO	n.a.
CONNECTICUT	2.22	NEW YORK	6.58
DELAWARE	0.94	NORTH CAROLINA	4.99
DIST. OF COLUMBIA	n.a.	NORTH DAKOTA	0.47
FLORIDA	1.86	OHIO	3.33
GEORGIA	12.3	OKLAHOMA	n.a.
HAWAII	0.61	OREGON	2.09
IDAHO	1.10	PENNSYLVANIA	3.29
ILLINOIS	4.35	RHODE ISLAND	1.51
INDIANA	3.39	SOUTH CAROLINA	18.6
IOWA	3.83	SOUTH DAKOTA	0.60
KANSAS	1.77	TENNESSEE	11.4
KENTUCKY	3.03	TEXAS	3.65
LOUISIANA	5.80	UTAH	1.69
MAINE	1.00	VERMONT	2.83
MARYLAND	0.66	VIRGINIA	5.37
MASSACHUSETTS	1.68	WASHINGTON	2.69
MICHIGAN	1.70	WEST VIRGINIA	0.95
MINNESOTA	6.09	WISCONSIN	2.55
MISSISSIPPI	1.31	WYOMING	n.a.
MISSOURI	2.51		

The investment equation is difficult to estimate in any model and this is especially so in regional models. As noted above there is a considerable amount of data work that must be done. Much of these data at the state level are suspect. Investment is difficult to classify spatially when many firms are multistate in scope. The result is an investment series that is quite volatile. Many of these problems could be disguised by using moving averages of the original series or other transformations.

The investment function is an important part of any econometric model. For the purposes of ECESIS this specification is probably adequate but clearly major improvements are possible. Ideally, the investment equation, like all the equations in the model, should be custom-tailored to each state. The payoffs from specialization of the investment equation may be higher than for other equations due to the volatile nature of investment. One possibility is to use a specification like (4.1.17) for the large manufacturing states and a simple share equation for the remaining states. This issue will have to be left to a subsequent study.

4.2 DEMAND FOR LABOR INPUTS

4.2.1 MANUFACTURING EMPLOYMENT

The desired level of labor inputs (L°) based on profit maximizing behavior and a Cobb-Douglas production function was given in Chapter Two as,

(4.2.1) $$L^\circ = \alpha Q^\circ P(1 - 1/\xi)/w.$$

Renormalizing to solve for nominal output yields the aggregate supply curve derived in Chapter Two,

$$(4.2.2) \qquad PQ^{\circ} = wL^{\circ}[\alpha(1 - 1/\xi)]^{-1}.$$

An expression similar to (4.2.1) is used in most macroeconometric models.

Assuming that there are some costs and frictions involved in adapting to desired levels of inputs, the level of actual labor inputs may be determined by a partial adjustment model.

$$(4.2.3) \qquad L/L_{-1} = \lambda(L^{\circ}/L_{-1})^{\gamma}; \; 0<\gamma<1.$$

Labor inputs, measured in millions of manhours, are constructed from employment and hours per week data available from the Bureau of Labor Statistics. The wage rate (w) is nominal average earnings per employee per hour.

Since α and ξ in (4.2.1) are estimated from the production function, (4.2.3) may be estimated directly. Using data over the sample period 1958 to 1974 from the state of Indiana, (4.2.3) is estimated in log form as,

$$(4.2.4) \qquad [\log(L)-\log(L_{-1})] = .005 + .693[\log(L^{\circ})-\log(L_{-1})]$$

$$(.77) \quad (8.80)$$

$$\bar{R}^2 = .84 \qquad D\text{-}W = 1.46$$

The adjustment rate of .693 indicates that the Indiana manufacturing sector responds quite quickly to changes in desired labor inputs. Rewriting (4.2.4) as,

$$(4.2.5) \qquad \log(L) = .005 + .693\log(L^{\circ}) + .307\log(L_{-1}),$$

indicates an average lag of .307/(1-.307)=.443 years. This rapid adjustment process lends support to the hypothesis that labor is near full utilization during most periods.

The labor demand equation estimated in the unconstrained form of (4.2.5) for Indiana yields,

$$(4.2.6) \qquad \log(L) = \underset{(1.33)}{.509} + \underset{(7.91)}{.653}\log(L^{\circ}) + \underset{(4.26)}{.277}\log(L_{-1})$$

$$\bar{R}^2 = .95 \qquad D\text{-}H = .78$$

The estimated adjustment rate from (4.2.6) is not significantly different from that estimated in (4.2.4). For states with small manufacturing sectors and less reliable estimates of α and ξ, the latter specification is quite useful.

The production function estimates for Indiana give α=.7807 and ξ=2.8336, implying $\alpha(1-1/\xi)$=.5052. Thus, (4.2.6) could be rewritten as,

$$(4.2.7) \qquad \log(L) = .064 + .653\log[QP/w] + .277\log(L_{-1}).$$

The similarity of the constrained and unconstrained estimation results are consistent with the findings of Coen and Hickman (1970) that the labor demand equation gives estimation results that are quite consistent with the implied production function.

If labor inputs are measured in terms of jobs (E) rather than manhours (w is then wages per person per year), the unconstrained estimation (4.2.7) yields,

$$\text{(4.2.8)} \quad \log(E) = \underset{(.20)}{-.072} + \underset{(6.63)}{.574}\log[QP/w] + \underset{(4.42)}{.377}\log(E_{-1})$$

$$\bar{R}^2 = .96 \qquad D\text{-}H = -.12$$

This adjustment rate (.574) is slower than when the equation is estimated in terms of manhours (.653) indicating that firms, faced with uncertainty as to the duration of demand fluctuations, are more likely to adjust labor inputs by varying overtime than by incurring the costs of hiring and firing employees. The average lag associated with (4.2.8) is .605 years, one-third longer than when the equation is measured in man hours.

Equation (4.2.6), using manhours, is estimated for all fifty-one regions in ECESIS. The complete estimation results are presented in Appendix 4.2. Table 4.2.1 reports the adjustment rates for each of the regions.

TABLE 4.2.1

LABOR ADJUSTMENT RATES (γ)

STATE	γ(%)	STATE	γ(%)
ALABAMA	54	MONTANA	12
ALASKA	44	NEBRASKA	41
ARIZONA	43	NEVADA	18
ARKANSAS	79	NEW HAMPSHIRE	53
CALIFORNIA	51	NEW JERSEY	54
COLORADO	48	NEW MEXICO	35
CONNECTICUT	55	NEW YORK	63
DELAWARE	30	NORTH CAROLINA	93
DIST. OF COLUMBIA	42	NORTH DAKOTA	24
FLORIDA	58	OHIO	71
GEORGIA	34	OKLAHOMA	31
HAWAII	09	OREGON	47
IDAHO	17	PENNSYLVANIA	53
ILLINOIS	59	RHODE ISLAND	44
INDIANA	65	SOUTH CAROLINA	40
IOWA	54	SOUTH DAKOTA	37
KANSAS	68	TENNESSEE	12
KENTUCKY	49	TEXAS	39
LOUISIANA	09	UTAH	26
MAINE	33	VERMONT	56
MARYLAND	58	VIRGINIA	52
MASSACHUSETTS	66	WASHINGTON	53
MICHIGAN	67	WEST VIRGINIA	28
MINNESOTA	68	WISCONSIN	68
MISSISSIPPI	57	WYOMING	14
MISSOURI	63		

The labor adjustment rate was not significantly different from zero in five states: Hawaii, Louisiana, Montana, Tennessee and Wyoming. With the exception of Tennessee, these states have small manufacturing sectors.

The spatial distribution of the adjustment rates is shown in Figure 4.2.1. The ˙ndustrial and high growth regions of the country show rapid adjustments to desired labor inputs.

Manufacturing employment is determined from labor inputs from the identity,

(4.2.9) $EM = L/(MHR \cdot 52/1000)$,

where MHR is average hours worked per week per manufacturing employee and EM is measured in units of thousands of jobs.

4.2.2 NONMANUFACTURING EMPLOYMENT

Since no output variable is determined for the nonmanufacturing sector, nonmanufacturing employment (ENM) is determined from a reduced-form specification. Demand in the nonmanufacturing sector, which is dominated by the trade, services and government sectors, is more localized than demand for manufactured goods. This fact may be used to compensate for the lack of a nonmanufacturing interstate trade matrix. Assuming that closer markets have more impact on the local nonmanufacturing sector than distant markets, the matrix of distances between population centroids of states may serve as the nonmanufacturing trade matrix. Using the population in state j (POP_j) as a proxy for the market size in that state, an interregional demand variable

FIGURE 4.2.1

SPATIAL DISTRIBUTION OF LABOR ADJUSTMENT RATES

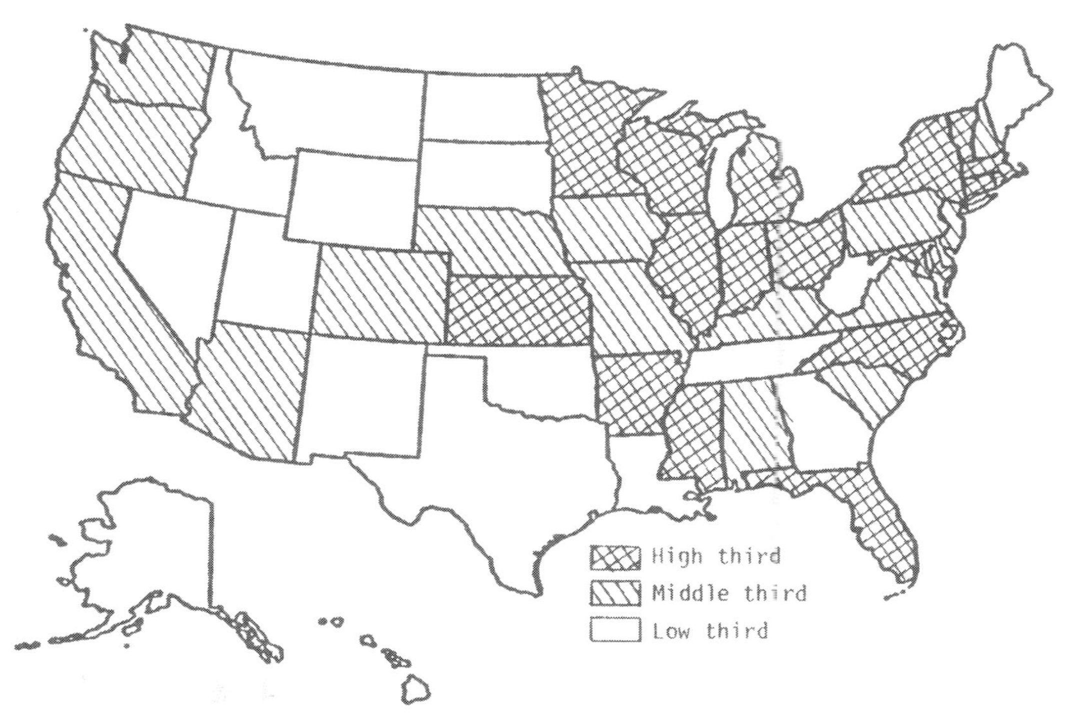

may be constructed as,

$$\Sigma_j d_{ij}^{-1} \cdot POP_j .$$

Most regional econometric models, either explicitly or implicitly, incorporate some form of the economic-base hypothesis in their specification. In its simplest form, this theory divides the local economy into two producing sectors. Goods sold outside the region are called "basic" and goods sold within the region are called "nonbasic". The principal assumptions underlying this theory (Glickman 1977) are that regional growth begins in the basic sector and then extends into the nonbasic sector, and that a stable relationship exists between the basic and nonbasic sectors.

Determining which sectors are basic is a serious problem in implementing economic-base models (Gerking and Isserman 1980). In the simple disaggregation scheme of the ECESIS model, the manufacturing sector is regarded as the basic sector with the nonmanufacturing sector treated as nonbasic. The economic-base theory is implemented by making nonmanufacturing employment a function of manufacturing employment.

Labor costs are also taken into account by using the real nonmanufacturing wage (WNM/CPI).

In some states lagged nonmanufacturing employment was also used as an explanatory variable. This makes the final specification for ENM,

$$(4.2.10) \quad ENM_i = a_0 + a_1 ENM_{i,-1} + a_2(\sum_j d_{ij}^{-1} \cdot POP_j) + a_3 EM_i + a_4(WNM_i/CPI_i).$$

The complete estimation results for this equation are included in Appendix 4.3. Table 4.2.2 gives the elasticity of nonmanufacturing employment with respect to manufacturing employment, as computed at the mean, for each of the states.

TABLE 4.2.2

ELASTICITY OF ENM W.R.T. EM

STATE	ELAS	STATE	ELAS
ALABAMA	0.66	MONTANA	n.a.
ALASKA	0.70	NEBRASKA	0.37
ARIZONA	0.62	NEVADA	0.36
ARKANSAS	0.58	NEW HAMPSHIRE	0.36
CALIFORNIA	0.23	NEW JERSEY	0.15
COLORADO	0.90	NEW MEXICO	0.32
CONNECTICUT	0.11	NEW YORK	0.21
DELAWARE	0.12	NORTH CAROLINA	1.10
DIST. OF COLUMBIA	0.13	NORTH DAKOTA	0.24
FLORIDA	1.10	OHIO	0.47
GEORGIA	1.11	OKLAHOMA	0.27
HAWAII	0.68	OREGON	0.69
IDAHO	0.83	PENNSYLVANIA	0.16
ILLINOIS	0.20	RHODE ISLAND	0.19
INDIANA	0.46	SOUTH CAROLINA	1.53
IOWA	0.28	SOUTH DAKOTA	0.38
KANSAS	0.22	TENNESSEE	0.86
KENTUCKY	0.27	TEXAS	0.64
LOUISIANA	0.64	UTAH	0.21
MAINE	n.a.	VERMONT	0.03
MARYLAND	0.15	VIRGINIA	1.62
MASSACHUSETTS	0.26	WASHINGTON	0.21
MICHIGAN	0.22	WEST VIRGINIA	0.08
MINNESOTA	0.13	WISCONSIN	0.28
MISSISSIPPI	0.88	WYOMING	0.70
MISSOURI	0.21		

Those states whose elasticity is greater than one-half are highlighted in Figure 4.2.2. This figure indicates the important role that the manufacturing sector has played in the rapid growth of the Southeastern and Southwestern states.

FIGURE 4.2.2

SPATIAL DISTRIBUTION OF ECONOMIC-BASE PARAMETERS

Total state employment, in thousands of persons, is determined from the identity,

(4.2.11) ET = EM + ENM + EOTHER,

where EOTHER includes agricultural employment and a conversion factor to account for multiple job holders in EM and ENM.

APPENDIX 4.1

INVESTMENT EQUATION ESTIMATION RESULTS

The specification estimated is,

$$GI_t = b_0 + b_1 GI_{t-1} + b_2(K^\circ_t - K_{t-1}) + u_t.$$

Columns one through three in the table below give the estimated coefficients for b_0, b_1 and b_2 with their t-statistics listed directly below. The next column gives the adjusted coefficient of determination with the Durbin-h statistic reported directly below that. The Durbin-Watson statistic is reported for the states: New Mexico, Oklahoma, and Wyoming. A question mark indicates that the Durbin-h cannot be computed. The critical point for the t-tests at the 5% level is 2.145 for the two-tailed test on the constant (b_0) and 1.76 for the one-tailed tests on b_1 and b_2. Serial correlation in the errors would be indicated when the absolute value of the Durbin-h statistic is over 1.96. The sample period of the estimation is 1958 to 1974.

STATE	b_0	b_1	b_2	$\bar{R}^2$/D-H
ALABAMA	99.58 1.34	.684 3.30	.118 3.16	.66 2.42
ALASKA	11.54 3.64	.181 0.77	.162 3.97	.81 0.84

ARIZONA	18.95 1.63	.790 5.99	.132 2.28	.87 -1.30
ARKANSAS	37.04 1.47	.776 3.85	.056 1.39	.77 -0.07
CALIFORNIA	296.68 1.78	.806 7.07	.065 3.28	.86 0.35
COLORADO	9.69 0.54	.997 8.54	.048 0.65	.84 -1.67
CONNECTICUT	104.73 2.39	.689 5.61	.071 3.40	.78 0.36
DELAWARE	42.05 2.37	.484 2.34	.061 2.13	.53 1.46
DIST. OF COLUMBIA	19.11 n.a.	0.0 n.a.	0.0 n.a.	n.a. n.a.
FLORIDA	115.18 1.46	.650 2.35	.082 1.54	.73 ?
GEORGIA	41.34 0.93	.925 8.02	.060 1.82	.87 -2.46
HAWAII	21.81 2.23	.377 1.47	.006 0.21	.01 ?
IDAHO	25.94 2.31	.524 2.63	.118 2.86	.56 -1.66
ILLINOIS	254.32 2.25	.813 10.0	.062 4.49	.91 0.72
INDIANA	198.61 1.66	.772 6.49	.076 3.27	.78 0.85
IOWA	53.68 1.32	.793 4.35	.072 2.04	.76 -1.25
KANSAS	49.20 2.45	.639 4.31	.116 3.95	.83 -0.10
KENTUCKY	66.34 2.11	.752 7.01	.111 3.69	.85 -0.67
LOUISIANA	63.96 1.15	.853 7.80	.118 3.48	.83 -1.66

MAINE	52.77 2.53	.501 2.59	.103 2.17	.54 -1.30
MARYLAND	166.48 2.60	.399 1.85	.074 1.98	.28 3.02
MASSACHUSETTS	182.62 2.41	.627 3.95	.076 2.47	.66 -0.44
MICHIGAN	496.63 2.25	.630 3.73	.089 2.97	.74 -1.26
MINNESOTA	45.82 1.13	.859 4.79	.031 0.95	.82 0.83
MISSISSIPPI	73.55 2.08	.568 2.98	.102 1.42	.42 -0.83
MISSOURI	98.06 1.97	.715 4.51	.044 1.92	.81 -0.87
MONTANA	40.58 3.74	.056 0.22	.182 3.14	.49 ?
NEBRASKA	37.34 3.11	.478 3.10	.083 4.08	.76 -0.64
NEVADA	9.57 2.68	.254 1.04	.114 1.65	.14 ?
NEW HAMPSHIRE	22.82 1.91	.647 3.73	.098 1.52	.52 -2.48
NEW JERSEY	266.16 2.11	.678 4.34	.044 2.22	.71 -0.59
NEW MEXICO	-0.47 0.09	1.00 n.a.	.211 1.96	.15 1.85
NEW YORK	209.77 1.33	.868 7.25	.032 1.58	.83 0.57
NORTH CAROLINA	109.76 2.07	.833 9.50	.090 2.51	.90 -0.88
NORTH DAKOTA	6.94 2.74	.319 1.41	.087 2.65	.45 0.80
OHIO	332.41 1.95	.769 7.26	.079 4.50	.84 0.34

OKLAHOMA	7.00 1.27	1.00 n.a.	.050 2.43	.23 2.27
OREGON	79.38 2.34	.676 4.61	.065 2.26	.68 0.13
PENNSYLVANIA	332.32 2.01	.767 6.86	.049 3.26	.82 1.00
RHODE ISLAND	30.23 2.86	.601 4.16	.064 2.78	.76 -1.28
SOUTH CAROLINA	32.49 0.91	.949 9.33	.065 1.91	.88 0.39
SOUTH DAKOTA	8.20 3.91	.376 2.44	.153 4.32	.71 -1.12
TENNESSEE	45.76 0.80	.919 7.22	.049 1.84	.81 -0.31
TEXAS	238.29 1.14	.785 4.66	.127 3.33	.75 1.35
UTAH	21.77 1.12	.628 1.17	.055 1.30	.26 ?
VERMONT	9.61 1.34	.739 4.17	.088 1.53	.55 0.88
VIRGINIA	56.10 1.51	.843 8.05	.101 3.45	.91 -0.71
WASHINGTON	83.27 1.53	.729 4.49	.080 1.85	.64 1.28
WEST VIRGINIA	110.24 2.83	.487 3.17	.067 2.92	.49 0.72
WISCONSIN	127.37 2.26	.718 5.87	.096 4.84	.85 0.45
WYOMING	12.85 9.65	0.0 n.a.	.029 1.51	.07 2.16

APPENDIX 4.2

LABOR DEMAND EQUATION ESTIMATION RESULTS

The specification estimated is,

$$\log(L_t) = b_0 + b_1\log(L^\circ{}_t) + b_2\log(L_{t-1}) + u_t.$$

Columns one through three in the table below give the estimated coefficients for b_0, b_1 and b_2 with their t-statistics reported directly below the estimates. The critical value for the t-tests at the five percent level are 2.16 for the two-tailed test on the constant term and 1.771 for the one-tailed tests on b_1 and b_2. Column four gives the adjusted coefficient of determination with the Durbin-h statistic reported directly below that. A question mark indicates that the Durbin-h could not be computed. Using a five percent test, serial correlation in the error terms is indicated if the absolute value of the Durbin-h statistic is greater than 1.96. The sample period of the estimations is 1958 to 1974.

STATE	b_0	b_1	b_2	$\bar{R}^2$/D-H
ALABAMA	.572 2.59	.541 5.13	.371 3.11	.98 0.57
ALASKA	.572 2.25	.444 2.17	.353 1.45	.84 ?
ARIZONA	.695 3.57	.425 3.88	.444 3.33	.98 0.62

ARKANSAS	.281 2.96	.786 8.46	.166 1.79	.99 -0.49
CALIFORNIA	1.85 3.93	.512 6.62	.259 2.54	.94 2.23
COLORADO	-.15 0.54	.482 3.19	.551 3.98	.97 1.81
CONNECTICUT	1.25 4.56	.550 14.1	.267 5.38	.97 1.41
DELAWARE	1.24 5.31	.303 7.60	.443 6.23	.97 0.95
DIST. OF COLUMBIA	-.62 2.30	.423 4.18	.741 6.26	.95 -0.94
FLORIDA	.213 1.04	.583 4.48	.387 3.15	.98 -0.17
GEORGIA	.429 1.22	.338 3.09	.601 5.57	.96 1.47
HAWAII	2.75 4.57	.033 0.50	.266 1.69	.11 1.90
IDAHO	.365 1.41	.167 2.24	.754 6.50	.96 -0.52
ILLINOIS	1.16 3.04	.588 11.1	.267 4.26	.96 0.32
INDIANA	.509 1.33	.653 7.91	.277 3.46	.95 0.81
IOWA	.278 1.30	.538 10.1	.419 6.61	.98 1.73
KANSAS	1.35 3.73	.675 8.27	.087 0.73	.95 0.36
KENTUCKY	-.08 0.40	.486 4.79	.531 5.39	.98 -0.74
LOUISIANA	.561 1.28	.086 0.90	.821 5.59	.93 1.84
MAINE	.921 1.22	.326 2.39	.505 3.02	.70 3.50

MARYLAND	-.78 1.14	.575 6.11	.549 5.56	.88 -0.61
MASSACHUSETTS	-.14 0.17	.659 6.73	.360 3.29	.86 3.60
MICHIGAN	-.09 0.15	.670 8.50	.340 4.67	.93 2.03
MINNESOTA	-.32 1.08	.677 5.89	.374 3.66	.97 -0.64
MISSISSIPPI	.758 3.25	.571 4.46	.301 1.97	.98 0.88
MISSOURI	.214 0.48	.628 6.21	.341 3.58	.94 0.96
MONTANA	.774 1.72	.122 1.08	.679 3.89	.77 1.01
NEBRASKA	1.45 4.19	.414 4.07	.304 1.93	.96 2.25
NEVADA	-.17 0.82	.184 1.09	.895 5.67	.94 0.27
NEW HAMPSHIRE	.798 1.39	.532 5.69	.316 2.97	.81 1.08
NEW JERSEY	.691 1.58	.537 9.32	.370 5.85	.94 0.26
NEW MEXICO	.910 2.21	.345 3.51	.416 2.07	.95 -0.81
NEW YORK	-1.1 1.36	.624 5.47	.507 4.00	.90 3.29
NORTH CAROLINA	-.25 1.04	.926 6.22	.110 0.83	.99 1.99
NORTH DAKOTA	.164 .049	.240 2.12	.713 3.31	.93 4.93
OHIO	.290 .064	.714 9.65	.249 3.47	.95 0.73
OKLAHOMA	-.03 0.15	.309 2.17	.703 4.66	.97 0.13

OREGON	.407 1.75	.466 7.91	.466 6.48	.98 0.47
PENNSYLVANIA	2.22 3.80	.527 7.10	.196 1.87	.91 0.11
RHODE ISLAND	.862 1.86	.436 8.91	.407 5.24	.89 1.00
SOUTH CAROLINA	.290 1.28	.401 4.39	.557 6.52	.98 0.88
SOUTH DAKOTA	.402 1.04	.365 3.31	.528 3.34	.84 -0.27
TENNESSEE	.380 1.15	.124 1.65	.824 10.6	.96 -0.15
TEXAS	.004 0.02	.390 5.19	.612 7.58	.99 -0.15
UTAH	.499 1.11	.255 1.88	.643 4.28	.85 3.31
VERMONT	-.02 0.04	.561 6.05	.445 4.72	.89 1.19
VIRGINIA	-.35 1.24	.517 5.09	.539 6.71	.98 0.83
WASHINGTON	.629 .072	.530 3.70	.369 2.30	.73 2.09
WEST VIRGINIA	1.59 3.27	.283 5.55	.432 4.26	.87 1.34
WISCONSIN	.495 1.14	.681 9.31	.249 3.07	.94 0.77
WYOMING	.942 1.55	.141 1.37	.516 1.99	.40 ?

APPENDIX 4.3

NONMANUFACTURING EMPLOYMENT EQUATION ESTIMATION RESULTS

The specification estimated is,

$$ENM_t = b_0 + b_1 ENM_{t-1} + b_2 DPOP_t + b_3 EM_t + b_4 WNM_t/CPI_t + u_t,$$

where $DPOP = \sum_j d_{ij}^{-1} POP_j$, as explained in the text of Section 3.4. Various coefficients in several states are constrained to zero.

Columns one through five give the estimates of the parameters with their t-statistics reported directly below. The critical values of the t-tests vary from state to state as the number of degrees of freedom change. The estimations are based on seventeen observations; 1958 to 1974. Column six reports the adjusted coefficient of determination with the Durbin statistic (either the Durbin-h or Durbin-Watson, whichever is appropriate) reported below that.

STATE	b_0	b_1	b_2	b_3	b_4	$\bar{R}^2$/D
ALABAMA	-765.13 3.78	0 -	0.265 4.76	1.452 3.77	-88.44 3.65	.98 0.93
ALASKA	-105.79 2.04	0 -	0.044 2.75	7.406 3.13	-3.20 0.71	.95 1.87
ARIZONA	-419.38 0.85	0 -	0.227 1.36	3.224 1.66	-62.50 1.25	.89 0.33
ARKANSAS	-104.91 0.99	0 -	0.063 2.31	1.336 7.18	-15.60 2.00	.99 1.84

CALIFORNIA	-5121.17 8.85	0 -	2.200 13.9	0.718 1.85	-505.1 4.24	.99 0.86
COLORADO	-647.48 3.03	0 -	0.225 1.88	4.683 6.13	-34.73 0.94	.98 1.09
CONNECTICUT	-227.36 2.42	.942 16.8	0.016 1.51	0.159 2.26	0 -	.99 -.45
DELAWARE	-95.26 2.93	.761 11.4	0.017 4.39	0.236 1.25	-11.32 3.48	.99 0.71
DIST. OF COLUMBIA	-729.25 8.62	0 -	0.084 9.13	3.478 1.99	-20.80 3.63	.97 0.93
FLORIDA	-2002.27 1.53	0 -	0.738 2.26	6.203 2.85	-323.6 2.59	.96 0.45
GEORGIA	-2752.03 6.95	0 -	0.704 7.47	2.541 3.29	-242.1 4.34	.98 0.87
HAWAII	-784.13 6.95	0 -	0.227 11.2	6.119 1.81	-34.83 3.59	.98 0.80
IDAHO	18.35 0.29	0 -	0.051 1.36	3.596 3.44	-25.25 2.69	.98 1.21
ILLINOIS	-1301.37 4.02	.776 12.7	0.235 2.45	0.414 5.74	-39.47 0.96	.99 1.67
INDIANA	-2118.40 14.13	0 -	0.477 14.0	0.698 3.55	-158.9 5.24	.99 1.01
IOWA	-321.32 3.21	.621 6.73	0.111 2.67	0.753 5.84	-33.59 2.03	.99 1.70
KANSAS	-608.11 4.80	0 -	0.253 3.66	0.815 2.19	-41.17 1.40	.95 0.29
KENTUCKY	-298.97 1.96	.631 4.60	0.082 2.44	0.719 2.15	-28.31 2.26	.99 -.07
LOUISIANA	-698.25 4.27	.408 2.43	0.204 3.98	3.028 2.68	-61.69 2.95	.99 0.70
MAINE	-266.56 5.11	0 -	0.121 9.44	0 -	-56.41 3.66	.94 1.05
MARYLAND	-764.47 2.42	.905 13.5	0.075 1.78	0.502 1.26	-21.51 0.84	.99 -.62

MASSACHUSETTS	-916.09 4.94	.894 14.0	0.062 3.00	0.552 4.68	0 -	.99 -1.2
MICHIGAN	-635.65 1.44	.880 10.8	0.081 0.84	0.352 3.94	-13.76 0.43	.99 0.68
MINNESOTA	-418.48 1.51	.790 6.85	0.139 1.40	0.415 2.19	-27.82 1.23	.99 0.27
MISSISSIPPI	-37.90 0.31	0 -	0.065 2.36	1.944 8.52	-39.68 4.27	.99 1.13
MISSOURI	-605.63 2.94	.734 8.07	0.144 2.24	0.558 3.50	-21.74 1.24	.99 1.05
MONTANA	-95.34 2.64	0 -	0.092 7.76	0 -	-18.96 2.10	.92 0.43
NEBRASKA	-540.27 4.34	0 -	0.231 4.24	1.786 2.26	-51.31 2.36	.96 0.32
NEVADA	-327.80 21.39	0 -	.0073 11.2	7.510 7.56	-2.63 0.79	.99 1.45
NEW HAMPSHIRE	-654.83 13.18	0 -	0.123 10.0	0.581 1.31	-73.63 5.16	.96 1.28
NEW JERSEY	-314.51 2.75	.990 32.6	0.010 0.80	0.276 3.55	0 -	.99 -.22
NEW MEXICO	-75.57 2.09	0 -	0.081 7.78	3.991 9.75	-13.19 1.73	.99 1.00
NEW YORK	-2088.30 5.22	.955 13.1	0.111 2.00	0.570 5.51	0 -	.99 -.90
NORTH CAROLINA	-1193.18 3.41	0 -	0.259 3.45	1.601 6.98	-108.1 3.23	.99 0.74
NORTH DAKOTA	-116.13 4.19	0 -	0.065 4.99	3.753 6.12	-7.37 1.80	.99 1.23
OHIO	-5390.40 15.91	0 -	1.148 12.3	0.772 2.95	-401.9 5.30	.97 1.01
OKLAHOMA	-27.54 0.41	.578 4.39	0.056 2.16	1.366 3.99	-20.88 2.96	.99 0.14
OREGON	-630.08 9.08	0 -	0.204 8.01	2.001 6.39	-29.98 1.74	.99 0.94

PENNSYLVANIA	-1049.31 4.70	.875 14.4	0.090 2.51	0.275 2.52	0 -	.99 -.33
RHODE ISLAND	-385.68 9.48	0 -	0.042 8.54	0.320 1.17	-3.98 0.79	.97 0.34
SOUTH CAROLINA	-518.12 1.26	0 -	0.128 1.59	2.217 2.94	-79.51 3.94	.96 0.55
SOUTH DAKOTA	-95.96 5.32	0 -	0.052 3.80	3.663 7.53	-7.54 1.05	.99 1.97
TENNESSEE	-1387.78 2.92	0 -	0.432 4.05	1.639 3.23	-182.8 3.23	.97 0.76
TEXAS	-3178.61 3.55	0 -	1.445 4.57	2.612 4.41	-370.2 3.06	.98 0.50
UTAH	-306.12 6.01	0 -	0.194 9.08	1.052 2.04	-50.07 3.24	.98 0.84
VERMONT	-329.30 7.58	0 -	0.055 6.11	0.065 0.12	-9.50 1.54	.92 0.35
VIRGINIA	-1230.83 1.80	0 -	0.277 2.40	4.800 4.18	-210.4 5.63	.98 1.22
WASHINGTON	-446.45 3.87	.687 6.86	0.173 3.07	0.653 5.04	-33.62 1.96	.99 1.24
WEST VIRGINIA	-207.98 5.02	.831 12.5	0.028 4.83	0.225 0.75	0 -	.99 1.18
WISCONSIN	-2466.80 13.82	0 -	0.618 6.63	0.519 1.30	-133.3 2.17	.97 0.55
WYOMING	-156.71 6.73	0 -	0.047 2.29	8.971 3.36	-1.75 0.17	.90 1.50

CHAPTER FIVE: WAGES AND INCOME

5.1 INTRODUCTION

This chapter presents the wage and income equations of the ECESIS model. Section 2 first reviews several regional wage models and then derives and gives the estimation results of the ECESIS wage model. The leading region-leading sector approach used is found to be quite robust and simple to use. The state personal income accounts are presented in Section 3. These are closely related to the wage equations because of the dominance of wage income in the accounts. Specification and estimations of the other endogenous income items are also presented in this section.

5.2 WAGES

5.2.1 REVIEW OF REGIONAL WAGE MODELS

The determination of wage rates is a central issue in the specification of regional econometric models. Following Klein (1969), wage rates in early regional models were specified as a function of national wage and price trends. This specification is useful for single region or top-down models, but is not adequate for multiregion bottom-up models like ECESIS. For the latter, the wage rate issue must be faced squarely at the regional level.

The regional Phillips curve and wage diffusion hypotheses currently dominate regional wage specifications. Quite naturally, the Phillips hypothesis has been carried over to models of regional wage rate determination. Empirical tests of this hypothesis have had mixed results. As a consequence, wage diffusion or transmission mechanisms have received increased attention from modelers. Most variations of this hypothesis argue that institutional arrangements exist between regions that lead to uniform movements of wage rates (Hart and MacKay 1977).

Institutional arrangements that force regional wage rates to move together may be the result of a quite simple process. Gerking and Weirick (1983) find that when occupation, skill and demographic characteristics of workers are taken into account there are only minor differences in regional wage rates. Observed regional wage disparities may simply be the result of aggregating over different industry and demographic groups. If this is indeed true then any wage increase for a particular type worker will quickly spread to all regions. The impact on average wages in a particular region depends upon the relative number of that type worker in the region. Empirically this process will be captured by the wage diffusion model. It is also evident from this discussion that the national wage rate should be a good explanatory variable for regional wage rates. However, it does not follow that a national wage rate "determines" regional wages. Rather, wage changes in any particular region may diffuse quickly to other regions to maintain implicitly established wage relativities among labor groups.

The wage transmission and regional Phillips hypotheses are not mutually exclusive theories. The wage rate in a region may be sensitive to both the local labor market conditions and the wage rates in surrounding and competing regions.

The wage rate specifications of Glickman (1977) are typical of those used in single region models, where the regional wage rate is determined as a function of the national wage rate and local unemployment. The assumption of an exogenous national wage rate is a reasonable one when considering a single region. The assumption of the stability of local Phillips curves, however, is not as easily accepted.

Recent studies involving the regional Phillips hypothesis have had ambiguous results. Most of the studies specify wages as a function of local unemployment, inflation and sometimes a wage transmission variable. Marcis and Reed

(1974) use Zellner's three-stage least squares seemingly unrelated regressions estimator (SUR) to estimate equations of the form,[1]

$$(5.2.1) \qquad W^{\circ}_{i} = a_0 + a_1(1/UR_i) + a_2UR^{\circ}_{i} + a_3P^{\circ}_{i} + a_4W*_{i,-2},$$

where W°_{i}, UR°_{i} and P°_{i} represent the percentage changes in wages, unemployment rates and prices in region I; $1/UR_i$ is the inverse of the unemployment rate and $W*_{i,-2}$ is a wage difference variable (lagged two periods) to measure intraregional feedback. The spatial units in the study are five SMSA's.

Marcis and Reed find that, while the SUR estimators are more efficient than OLS estimates, the increased efficiency did not change the interpretation of the statistical results. In neither the OLS nor SUR estimations were 1/UR or UR° found to be significant. In both estimation procedures, however, the inflation rate (P°) and the wage feedback variable (W*) were found to be highly significant.

Several earlier studies finding no relationship between wage rates and unemployment rates have been criticized for not using simultaneous equations estimation techniques. The finding of Marcis and Reed that simultaneous equation

---

[1] Time subscripts are dropped throughout.

techniques did not yield significantly different results from single equation methods is important in rebutting these criticisms.

Similar results were obtained in a later study of urban areas by Reed and Hutchinson (1976). In this case the urban areas were divided into 'leaders' and 'followers'. Using the same notation as above, the specification used for 'leading' urban areas was,

$$(5.2.2) \qquad W^{\circ}_{i} = f_{i}[(UR_{i})^{-\alpha}, UR^{\circ}_{i}, P^{\circ}_{i}]$$

For the 'following' urban areas the specification tested was

$$(5.2.3) \qquad W^{\circ}_{j} = f_{j}[(UR_{j})^{-\alpha}, UR^{\circ}_{j}, P^{\circ}_{j}, W*_{j}],$$

where $W*_{j}$ is a rather complicated variable measuring wage transmission across regions.

The model was estimated with ordinary least squares using quarterly data. As in the previous study, Reed and Hutchinson find $UR^{-\alpha}$ and UR° to be insignificant while P° and $W*$ are highly significant.

Santomero and Seater (1978) noted in their review article that the Phillips hypothesis seems to fair better when quarterly data are used rather than annual data. Rubin (1979) tests this hypothesis using monthly, quarterly and annual data on twenty-two urban areas. Three models are estimated using OLS:

(5.2.4) $W^{\circ}_{i} = a_0 + a_1(1/UR_i) + a_2P^{\circ}_{i,-1},$

(5.2.5) $W^{\circ}_{i} = a_0 + a_1(1/UR_i) + a_2P^{\circ}_{i,-1} + a_3W^{\circ}_{us},$

(5.2.6) $W^{\circ}_{i} = a_0 + a_1(1/UR_i) + a_2P^{\circ}_{i,-1} + a_3P^{\circ}_{us},$

where W°_{us} and P°_{us} are the rate of change of national money wages and national consumer prices, respectively.

Rubin finds that the use of monthly, quarterly or annual data make little difference in the models. In no case does he find 1/UR to be significant.

An interesting aspect of Rubin's study is that he finds that the inclusion of W°_{us} or P°_{us} in the equation has no effect on the significance of 1/UR. Previous studies finding 1/UR insignificant have been criticized for specification bias due to omitting either W°_{us} or P°_{us}.

Hart and MacKay (1977) attempt to estimate the regional earnings structure of the U.K. by using several variations of a leading region approach. They conclude that,

> earnings increases may be transmitted across regions even where potential mobility, and hence the competitive pressures on employers, is limited. Wage increases in one region, through the institutional mechanisms we have discussed, will lead to similar increases elsewhere. Systematic and persistent differences in unemployment appear to have very little impact on this process (pg. 280).

Izraeli and Kellman (1979), on the other hand, are fairly successful in identifying independent Phillips curves for separate urban labor markets. The specifications tested were,

$$(5.2.7) \qquad W^{\circ}_{i} = a_0 + a_1 P^{\circ}_{i,-2} + a_2 UR^{\circ}_{i} + a_3(1/UR_i)$$

$$(5.2.8) \qquad W^{\circ}_{i} = a_0 + a_1 P^{\circ}_{i} + a_2 UR^{\circ}_{i} + a_3(1/UR_i).$$

Notably absent is a wage spillover or wage transmission variable like those used by Rubin (1979), Reed and Hutchinson (1976) and Marcis and Reed (1974). Izraeli and Kellman argue, "[s]uch an effect is not consistent with our theoretical model. ... To be sure these [local labor] markets are interconnected with many linkages. However, basically, local conditions are primarily responsible for explaining variations in local rates of wage inflation (pg. 378)."

Equations (5.2.7) and (5.2.8) were estimated for twenty-one SMSA's using annual data from 1961 to 1977. The results indicate that the price inflation variable (P°_{i}) is much more significant if lagged two periods than if used concurrently. The inverse unemployment rate ($1/UR_i$) is generally significant but with the incorrect (negative) sign. However, the rate of change of the unemployment rate is generally significant with the correct sign. Izraeli and

Kellman conclude, like Mathur (1976), that there is support for significant local area Phillips curves.

Equation (5.2.8) used by Izraeli and Kellman is very similar to (5.2.1) used by Marcis and Reed. The sample period and some of the SMSA's used in the estimations are identical; the results, however, are quite different. Rees and Hamilton (1967) noting similar anomalies in studies done at the national level concluded,

> Our final caution is that we have been astounded by how many very different Phillips curves can be constructed on reasonable assumptions from the same body of data. The nature of the relationship between wage changes and unemployment is highly sensitive to the exact choice of the other variables that enter the regression and to the forms of all the variables (pg. 70).

The studies reviewed so far have assumed that the wage rate and unemployment rate should be negatively related. Reza (1978), however, claims that for urban areas the relationship between these two variables should be positive. He argues that high unemployment areas should also have high productivity rates due to low job turnover rates, thus employers can afford to pay more. Using cross section data for SMSA's, Reza finds some support for his hypothesis.

The ambiguous results of previous studies on the effects of local labor market conditions on regional wages and the necessity of treating national wages as exogenous make the Glickman style single region wage specifications inadequate for a multiregion bottom-up model.

In a multiregion top-down model, Milne, Glickman, and Adams (1980) specify wages using local Phillips curves and wage transmission variables. Wages in a region are determined as a function of the local labor market and of the wages in surrounding regions. The results of studies using wage transmission variables have been less ambiguous than those of the local Phillips curves. The underpinning of most wage transmission specifications is the earnings-spread hypothesis (Hart and MacKay 1977). Most versions of the earnings-spread hypothesis identify a group of regions as wage rate leaders with other regions following their example. The obvious problem is how to identify the leading regions.

Using U.S. states, Brechling (1973), attempted to identify leading states according to (i) low unemployment rates and (ii) high wage rates. Brechling found no support for picking leading states on the basis of unemployment rates and limited success using wage levels.

Hart and MacKay (1977) using U.K. regions required a leading region to be in the top third of the wage earnings hierarchy and the bottom third of the unemployment rate hierarchy for each and every year of the sample period.

The states in the relevant third of each hierarchy are listed in Table 5.2.1. There is no intersection between the high wage and low unemployment states; thus, the Hart and MacKay rule is not particularly useful in this case.

TABLE 5.2.1

HART & MACKAY RULE APPLIED TO U.S. STATES

HIGH WAGE STATES: CONSISTENTLY IN TOP THIRD, 1958-1978	LOW UNEMPLOYMENT STATES: CONSISTENTLY IN BOTTOM THIRD, 1958-1978
ALASKA	IOWA
CALIFORNIA	NEBRASKA
CONNECTICUT	SOUTH DAKOTA
DELAWARE	VIRGINIA
DISTRICT OF COLUMBIA	
ILLINOIS	
INDIANA	
MICHIGAN	
NEW JERSEY	
NEW YORK	
OHIO	
WASHINGTON	

Table 5.2.1 also indicates why Brechling had little success identifying leading states via the low unemployment rate rule. The states identified by this criterion are: Iowa, Nebraska, South Dakota and Virginia. These are not likely to be the states that are setting the trends in wage rate determination.

Further evidence that the unemployment rate is a poor criterion for identifying wage leaders is indicated in Figure 5.2.1. Time series plots of the unemployment rates of three states and the U.S. are shown. Michigan is a high wage state, Mississippi is a low wage state, Indiana is an average wage state and the U.S. is the national average rate. Unemployment rates are quite volatile and there is apparently no uniform ranking even between states with extreme wage rate differences.

The relativities among wage rates, on the other hand, are much more stable as indicated in Figure 5.2.2, where the manufacturing wage rates for the same three states and the U.S. are plotted. In the case of wages, the ranking is uniform throughout the sample period.[2]

While the rankings based on manufacturing wage rates are fairly stable, they are not without problems. Washington D.C., for example, is identified as a leader even though only three percent of its income is due to manufacturing. Ideally, any ranking should take into account the size of the sector in determining which states are leaders.

---

[2] The wage rate is average earnings per manufacturing employee per annum. The wage rate could be put into hourly terms using BLS data on average hours worked per week but the variation in hours worked per week is not very large for annual data.

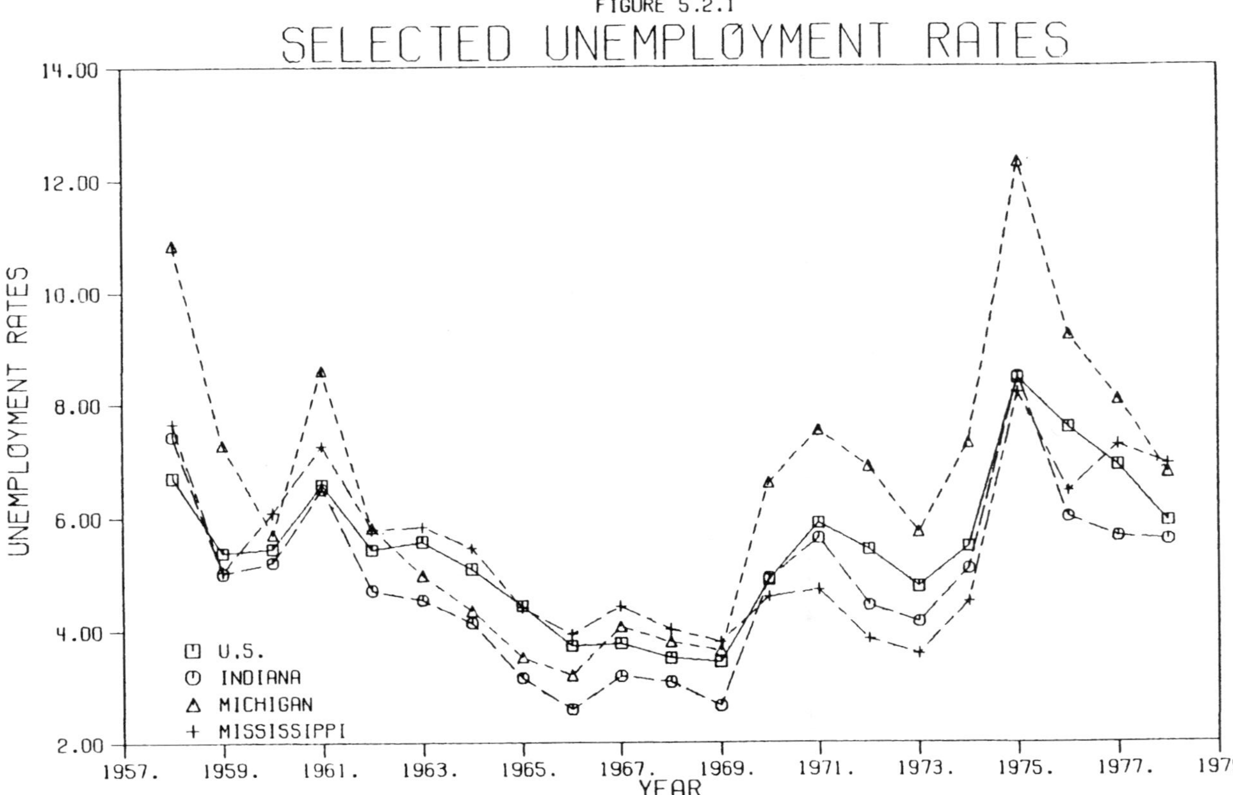
FIGURE 5.2.1
SELECTED UNEMPLØYMENT RATES
UNEMPLØYMENT RATES
14.00
12.00
10.00
8.00
6.00
4.00
2.00
U.S.
INDIANA
MICHIGAN
MISSISSIPPI
1957.
1959.
1961.
1963.
1965.
1967.
1969.
1971.
1973.
1975.
1977.
1979.
YEAR

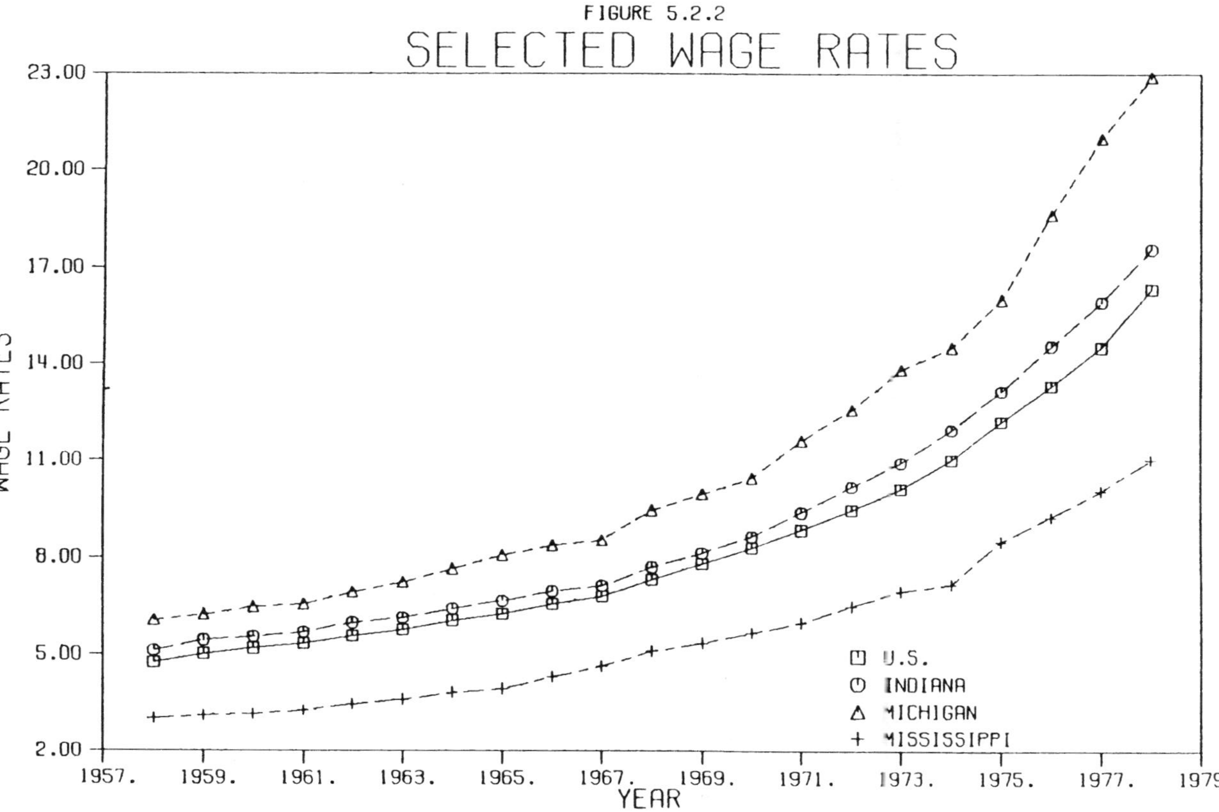
FIGURE 5.2.2
SELECTED WAGE RATES
WAGE RATES
23.00
20.00
17.00
14.00
11.00
8.00
5.00
2.00
1957.
1959.
1961.
1963.
1965.
1967.
1969.
1971.
1973.
1975.
1977.
1979.
YEAR
U.S.
INDIANA
MICHIGAN
MISSISSIPPI

Other techniques that have been used to identify leading regions are population size (Reed and Hutchinson 1976), wage elasticity (Milne 1980) and key industry groups (Eckstein and Wilson 1962).

The key-group approach consists of identifying certain key industries (i.e., auto and steel) and then choosing the leading states as those states with high concentrations of the key industries. Obviously the problem now becomes one of identifying key industries. Mehra (1976) reports,

> These key industries now compromise the majority of the manufacturing sector. Wage movements in these industries are highly correlated but there is no evidence that there are one or two "key bargains" that are setting the pattern of bargaining.

Any ranking procedure will be artificial and in a highly aggregated model it is likely, as Mehra claims, that every state has some claims to be a leading state by one or another criterion.

This brief survey indicates the dilemma faced by multiregion model builders. The evidence on local labor market effects on wages is ambiguous and, while they tend to work well, wage transmission variables are difficult to define and construct with any consistency across regions. This circumstance is reflected in the Ballard, Gustely, and Wendling (1980) multiregion bottom-up model. In their model wages in some states are modeled using the local Phillips curve hypothesis, other states rely on wage differentials and employment growth and some small states use the U.S. wage rate as the determinant variable. It is also worth noting that the hypotheses discussed above will have to be carefully re-examined in light of new data from 1981 to 1984. This interesting period may change some of the above results dramatically.

5.2.2 THE ECESIS MODEL OF WAGES

In ECESIS both a regional and sectoral wage diffusion process is assumed. The impetus for wage changes initially arises in a leading sector of a leading region and then diffuses through other economic sectors and to other regions. Considerable support has been found for the sectoral diffusion approach (Behman 1964, Eckstein and Wilson 1962, Milne 1980) and the previous subsection indicates support for the regional diffusion process.

The leading sector in ECESIS is taken to be the manufacturing sector with the aggregated nonmanufacturing sector serving as the following sector. The regions are the fifty states of the U.S. plus Washington D.C.

The problem of choosing leading regions is resolved by allowing all regions to have some impact on the manufacturing wage transmission variable.

Define:

(5.2.9) $W^*_i = \sum_j\{(1/d_{ij})\cdot RMS_j\cdot S_i\}WM_j$,

and

(5.2.10) $RMS_j = (YM_j/YTLPR_j)/(YM_{us}/YTLPR_{us})$.

Where d_{ij} is the distance between 1970 population centroids of states i and j; RMS_j is the size of the manufacturing sector of state j relative to the U.S.; S_i is a scaling factor (equal to the mean distance from state i to all other states) to keep the dimension of W* comparable to that of WM; WM_j is the manufacturing wage rate in state j; YM_j and YM_{us} are the manufacturing income of state j and the U.S.; and $YTLPR_j$ and $YTLPR_{us}$ are total personal income of state j and the U.S.[3]

Every state's manufacturing wage has some influence on W^*_i but closer states and states with large manufacturing sectors have more influence. Consider, for example, W^*_i for the state of Virginia. Manufacturing wages in D.C. and Michigan are about the same level ($12,605 and $13,830 for 1973 respectively). Over forty percent of Michigan's income, however, is due to manufacturing compared to three percent for D.C. The wage transmission variable should

---

[3] Income data are from the Bureau of Economic Analysis state personal income accounts. Employment data are from the Bureau of Labor Statistics (BLS).

reflect the fact that Michigan, from sheer size, is an influential state in the determination of Virginia's manufacturing wages. This is accomplished by the RMS_j term, which is equal to 1.64 for Michigan and .12 for D.C.

On the other hand, measuring from 1970 population centroids, it is 481 miles from Michigan to Virginia and only 104 miles from D.C. to Virginia. The net effect is that for 1973 the term in brackets in (5.2.9) is equal to .067 for Michigan and .022 for D.C. (S_i=1007 for Virginia).

The wage transmission variable defined in (5.2.9) has the desirable properties that every state's manufacturing wage has some influence on Virginia's manufacturing wage but nearby and heavily industrialized states have greater impact than others. In the example above, D.C. has a high wage and is quite close to Virginia but the manufacturing sector in D.C. is so small that Michigan's huge manufacturing economy has three times the impact on Virginia that does D.C.'s.

This wage transmission variable is quite flexible. If the industry mix in a state changes so will its influence on the wages of other states. California, for example, is much less dominant in the early seventies than it was in the early sixties due to a relative decline in the size of its manufacturing sector and relatively slow wage increases in recent years.

The wage transmission variable enters the manufacturing wage equation with a one period lag to reflect the gradual wage adjustment process.

Other factors which influence a state's manufacturing wage include the local industry's ability to substitute for scarce resources and the local inflation rate. The local consumer price index captures inflationary effects while the ratio of manufacturing employment to working age population (EM/P1864) and manufacturing capacity utilization rate (CU) capture the effects of factor market tightness. The employment to population ratio is used in lieu of the unemployment rate because the former is industry specific and the latter is volatile and unreliable in simulation experiments (see Chapter Six).

An industry's response to wage demands will partially depend upon whether that industry can substitute other factors of production for expensive labor. When the capacity utilization rate is high, firms are less able to make that substitution and wage increases subsequently should be greater.

Estimated in log linear form, the final specification for the manufacturing wage equation is

$$(5.2.11) \qquad \log(WM_i) = a_0 + a_1\log(W^*_i)_{-1} + a_2\log(EM_i/P1864_i)_{-1} + a_3\log(CU_i)$$

$$+ a_4 \log(CPI_i)_{-1}.$$

All coefficients are expected to be positive. The complete estimation results for this equation are given in Appendix 5.1.

The wage transmission variable is significant in nearly all cases. The capacity utilization rate and employment to population ratio variables are often not significant or only marginally significant, indicating that local labor market conditions often may not have a sizable impact on the local manufacturing wage rate.

The nonmanufacturing wage (WNM) is assumed to be primarily determined by what happens to the leading manufacturing wage in the same region. Presumably, the nonmanufacturing sector, which is dominated by the service and trade sectors, is more localized than the manufacturing sector so that the nonmanufacturing employment to working age population ratio should play a more important role in this sector.

The final specification for the nonmanufacturing wage equation is

$$(5.2.12) \qquad \log(WNM_i) = a_0 + a_1 \log(WM_i) + a_2 \log(ENM_i/P1864_i)_{-1}.$$

All coefficients are expected to be positive. The complete estimation results are given in Appendix 5.2.

As expected, the employment to population ratio variable is generally more significant than in the manufacturing wage equation. This suggests that local labor market conditions are indeed more important in determining local trade and service sector wages than in the manufacturing sector where wage negotiations are often national in scope.

The variables WM and WNM are average earnings per worker and are measured in units of thousands of current dollars per worker per year. In some instances an hourly wage rate is desirable. The manufacturing nominal hourly wage rate (WMH) is determined from the identity

(5.2.13) $WMH = WM/(MHR \cdot 52/1000)$,

where MHR is hours worked per manufacturing employee per week. MHR is from the Bureau of Labor Statistics and is exogenous to ECESIS.

The real (1972 dollars) manufacturing hourly wage rate (MMH72) is calculated from

(5.2.14) $WMH72 = (WMH/CPI) \cdot 100$.

Total average earnings (WT) is calculated from

(5.2.15) $WT = (YM + YNM)/(EM + ENM)$,

where YM and YNM are manufacturing income and nonmanufacturing income; both are measured in millions of current dollars.

The identity

(5.2.16) $WT72 = (WT/CPI)\cdot 100$,

is used to calculate total real average earnings.

5.3 INCOME EQUATIONS

Because of the lack of subnational final demand data, personal income accounts play an important role in regional models. Table 5.3.1 shows the level of disaggregation of the personal income accounts in ECESIS.

TABLE 5.3.1

ECESIS PERSONAL INCOME ACCOUNTS

YM	Manufacturing wage and salary disbursements and other labor income
+ YNM	Nonmanufacturing wage and salary disbursements and other labor income
+ YPROP	Nonfarm proprietors' income
+ YFARM	Farm income
= YTLPR	Total labor and proprietors' income by place of work
- YSIC	Personal contributions for social insurance by place of work
+ YRA	Residence adjustment
+ YDIR	Dividend, interest, and rental income
+ YTP	Transfer payments
= YT	Personal income by place of residence

Manufacturing includes both durable and nondurable goods. Nonmanufacturing consists of: agricultural services, forestry, fisheries and other; mining; construction; transportation and public utilities; wholesale trade; retail trade; finance, insurance, and real estate; services; and government and government enterprises. Farm income includes farm proprietors' income.

All income variables are from the Bureau of Economic Analysis and are measured in millions of current dollars.

YRA and YFARM are exogenous to ECESIS; YM, YNM, YTLPR, and YT are calculated by identity; and YPROP, YSIC, YDIR, and YTP are calculated by stochastic equation.

Manufacturing and nonmanufacturing income are calculated from the identities

(5.3.1) $YM = WM \cdot EM$,

(5.3.2) $YNM = WNM \cdot ENM$,

where WM and WNM are manufacturing and nonmanufacturing average earnings in thousands of dollars, and EM and ENM are manufacturing and nonmanufacturing employment in thousands of jobs.[4]

Nonfarm proprietors' income measures the net business earnings of owners of unincorporated nonfarm enterprises. The size of the market and the general level of economic activity of the region are the most likely determinants of this variable. YPROP is estimated for each state by

(5.3.3) $YPROP = a_0 + a_1 YT + a_2 PTOT$,

where YT is total state personal income and PTOT is total state population in thousands of persons. The coefficients a_1 and a_2 are expected to be positive. The complete

[4] Average earnings is actually calculated from the income and employment data but (5.3.1) and (5.3.2) are used in the model.

estimation results for YPROP are given in Appendix 5.3.

Total labor and proprietors' income is calculated from the identity

(5.3.4) YTLPR = YM + YNM + YPROP + YFARM.

Social insurance contributions are estimated in rate form as a function of the exogenous U.S. social insurance contribution rate,

(5.3.5) $YSIC/YTLPR = a_0 + a_1 USSICR$,

where USSICR=USYSIC/USYTLPR for the estimation period of 1958 to 1974. The estimation results for (5.3.5) are given in Appendix 5.4. For simulation purposes, (5.3.5) is normalized to solve for YSIC directly.

Dividend, interest and rental income (YDIR) is modelled as a function of gross manufacturing profits (MGP), the U.S. prime interest rate (PR) and the consumer price index (CPI). Since property income is relatively stable over time, the dependent variable lagged one period is used to capture the slow adjustment process. Gross manufacturing profits are calculated as

(5.3.6) MGP = PQ - YM,

where PQ is manufacturing value added in millions of current dollars. To remove some of its volatility, a two period moving average of gross profits is used in the YDIR equation. The final specification for YDIR is

$$(5.3.7) \qquad YDIR = a_0 + a_1 YDIR_{-1} + a_2(MGP+MGP_{-1})/2 + a_3 PR + a_4 CPI.$$

All coefficients should be positive with a_1 less than one. The estimation results are given in Appendix 5.5.

Transfer payments are receipts of persons from government and business (excluding government interest) for which no services are rendered currently. There are over fifty separate series included in the transfer payments data[5] which is the fastest growing of all the personal income data series.

Over eighty percent of transfer payments are from the federal government and these are dominated by social insurance benefits; particularly Old Age, Survivors and Disability Insurance. State and local government transfer payments are split between social insurance benefits and direct public assistance. Business transfer payments are dominated by consumer bad debts and corporate gifts to nonprofit institutions.

---

[5] See Bureau of Economic Analysis (July 1976) for details on this and the other personal income series.

Transfer payments are estimated in per capita form as a function of per capita income (YT/PTOT), proportion of the state population sixty-five years and over (P65/PTOT), and the share of the population unemployed (U/PTOT),

$$(5.3.8) \qquad YTP/PTOT = a_0 + a_1(YT/PTOT) + a_2(P65/PTOT) + a_3(U/PTOT).$$

All coefficients should be positive. Appendix 5.6 gives the estimation results. Surprisingly, the coefficient a_2 was generally not significantly positive. Since most state populations became steadily older over the estimation period, some of the effects of a_2 were probably picked up by the per capita income variable which is also highly trended. The unemployment variable was generally significantly positive even though unemployment benefits account for less than five percent of all transfer payments. This probably reflects the irregular pattern of this variable. For simulation purposes, (5.3.8) is normalized to solve for YTP.

Total state personal income by place of residence (YT) is calculated from the identity

$$(5.3.9) \qquad YT = YTLPR - YSIC + YRA + YDIR + YTP.$$

Any real income variables needed in the model are calculated by dividing the nominal variable by the CPI (base year 1972) and appending the suffix "72" to the variable name.

APPENDIX 5.1

MANUFACTURING WAGE EQUATION

The specification estimated is

$$\log(WM) = a_0 + a_1\log(W^*)_{-1} + a_2\log(EM/P1864)_{-1}$$
$$+ a_3\log(CU) + a_4\log(CPI)_{-1}.$$

The estimation sample period is 1959 to 1974. All slope coefficients are expected to be positive.

The first five columns after the state names in the table below give the estimated coefficients a_0 to a_4 with their t-statistics reported directly below. Using a five percent significance level, the critical value for the two-tailed test on a_0 is 2.201; the critical value for the one-tailed tests on the slope parameters is 1.796.

The last column reports the squared coefficient of multiple correlation corrected for degrees of freedom and the Durbin-Watson statistic below that. The uncertainty range for the D-W test is .64 to 1.80.

STATE	a_0	a_1	a_2	a_3	a_4	$\bar{R}^2$/D-W
ALABAMA	.098 0.16	.718 3.62	.135 0.82	.210 1.51	.091 0.40	.99 2.28
ALASKA	1.150 1.71	.726 12.0	.040 0.21	.022 0.24	0 –	.96 1.77

ARIZONA	-.886 2.59	.603 8.66	.107 2.87	0 -	.464 4.20	.99 2.92
ARKANSAS	-2.740 3.37	.117 0.34	.490 2.01	.022 0.09	1.181 3.31	.99 1.66
CALIFORNIA	.683 3.96	.926 30.0	.162 1.62	.072 0.76	0 -	.99 1.55
COLORADO	-1.359 2.70	.686 8.36	.058 0.61	.152 1.93	.508 3.50	.99 3.41
CONNECTICUT	-2.260 5.00	1.046 12.0	.093 1.68	.099 2.17	.264 1.51	.99 2.14
DELAWARE	-2.833 6.50	.684 5.88	0 -	0 -	.666 3.56	.99 2.16
DIST. OF COLUMBIA	-2.842 7.86	1.102 9.51	.137 2.58	.040 0.60	.429 2.35	.99 2.42
FLORIDA	.955 3.75	.874 34.1	.365 4.35	0 -	0 -	.99 1.98
GEORGIA	.164 0.66	.973 34.0	.375 3.42	.154 2.36	0 -	.99 2.33
HAWAII	-2.250 1.01	.986 1.94	0 -	.277 0.95	.527 0.66	.98 1.29
IDAHO	.216 2.21	.869 15.6	0 -	0 -	0 -	.94 0.76
ILLINOIS	-3.157 5.16	.484 4.35	.127 1.83	.088 1.50	.964 4.55	.99 2.59
INDIANA	-3.030 3.89	.415 2.40	.096 1.07	.142 2.10	.964 3.22	.99 2.88
IOWA	-2.415 4.28	.470 3.61	.247 2.96	.039 0.62	.880 4.17	.99 2.25
KANSAS	-.782 0.81	.624 3.89	0 -	.084 0.46	.334 1.11	.99 2.00
KENTUCKY	-2.890 6.07	.516 3.22	.013 0.11	.041 0.44	.831 4.21	.99 1.82
LOUISIANA	-.023 0.04	.756 5.80	.286 2.02	.114 1.40	.256 1.14	.99 2.28

MAINE	-3.041 5.12	.634 5.07	.088 1.56	.169 2.07	.742 3.30	.99 3.46
MARYLAND	-1.499 4.71	1.426 11.2	.563 3.81	.217 2.42	.102 0.85	.99 2.71
MASSACHUSETTS	-1.750 2.89	1.177 12.1	.077 0.54	.092 0.60	.026 0.12	.99 1.25
MICHIGAN	-4.265 2.36	.344 0.98	.135 0.99	.270 2.59	1.344 2.08	.99 2.21
MINNESOTA	-1.360 3.53	.631 8.30	.173 4.36	.000 0.00	.547 4.23	.99 2.99
MISSISSIPPI	.688 0.87	.659 2.84	.508 2.75	.010 0.11	.116 0.40	.99 2.23
MISSOURI	-.615 0.84	.773 5.69	.274 2.96	.104 1.14	.322 1.28	.99 2.64
MONTANA	-2.934 3.08	.178 0.75	.175 0.70	.310 2.03	1.172 3.08	.99 1.98
NEBRASKA	-2.208 3.75	.397 3.24	.132 2.42	.169 1.93	.826 4.16	.99 3.03
NEVADA	.537 14.6	.793 47.9	0 -	.074 0.89	0 -	.99 1.72
NEW HAMPSHIRE	-2.763 4.83	1.055 10.0	.180 1.94	.120 1.43	.372 1.69	.99 2.08
NEW JERSEY	-1.817 6.45	1.004 15.4	.185 2.21	0 -	.237 2.14	.99 1.98
NEW MEXICO	.932 1.47	.492 8.05	.002 0.01	.009 0.08	0 -	.94 1.39
NEW YORK	-2.501 6.34	.905 14.8	.285 3.59	.055 0.61	.533 3.69	.99 2.12
NORTH CAROLINA	-.829 1.52	.643 3.44	.570 3.07	.233 1.01	.413 1.79	.99 2.56
NORTH DAKOTA	2.036 2.32	.637 5.12	.384 2.15	.244 2.77	0 -	.97 2.21
OHIO	-2.266 3.89	.593 4.79	.083 0.95	.173 2.40	.689 3.13	.99 2.61

OKLAHOMA	1.280 2.88	.675 9.98	.286 2.35	.153 1.57	0 –	.99 2.28
OREGON	-2.109 1.99	.599 3.60	.259 0.94	.097 0.89	.768 2.54	.99 2.87
PENNSYLVANIA	-3.690 7.57	.464 4.07	.112 1.50	.196 3.67	1.035 5.40	.99 2.71
RHODE ISLAND	-1.815 15.5	1.140 45.8	.144 1.44	0 –	0 –	.99 0.85
SOUTH CAROLINA	-1.223 1.38	.455 1.00	.753 1.74	.158 0.79	.692 1.18	.99 2.26
SOUTH DAKOTA	.109 0.07	.545 2.58	.269 1.23	0 –	.340 0.92	.98 1.95
TENNESSEE	-2.799 3.89	.207 1.08	.408 3.68	.127 1.16	1.114 3.73	.99 2.15
TEXAS	-.854 1.93	.480 5.37	.276 4.56	.104 1.67	.590 3.93	.99 2.29
UTAH	-.590 0.89	.502 4.24	.170 2.15	.064 1.07	.446 2.11	.99 2.65
VERMONT	-2.476 2.48	.998 4.52	.275 2.24	0 –	.458 1.13	.99 1.17
VIRGINIA	-1.285 2.65	.620 3.08	.457 2.73	.204 1.76	.554 2.08	.99 2.76
WASHINGTON	-.926 0.90	.896 5.21	.183 2.19	.033 0.40	.357 1.06	.99 3.06
WEST VIRGINIA	-2.093 3.02	.489 2.57	.229 1.75	.039 0.66	.781 2.41	.99 2.37
WISCONSIN	-1.799 2.56	.693 5.26	.160 1.35	.060 0.70	.570 2.23	.99 2.07
WYOMING	.957 1.41	.723 13.7	.100 0.43	.232 1.87	0 –	.95 2.35

APPENDIX 5.2

NONMANUFACTURING WAGE EQUATION

The specification estimated is

$$\log(WNM) = a_0 + a_1\log(WM) + a_2\log(ENM/P1864)_{-1}.$$

The estimation sample period is 1959 to 1974. All slope coefficients are expected to be positive.

The first three columns after the state names in the table below give the estimated coefficients for a_0, a_1 and a_2 with their t-statistics reported directly below. Using a five percent significance level, the critical value for the two-tailed test on a_0 is 2.160; the critical value for the one-tailed tests on a_1 and a_2 is 1.771.

The last column reports the squared coefficient of multiple correlation adjusted for degrees of freedom and the Durbin-Watson statistic below that. The uncertainty range for the D-W test is .86 to 1.40.

STATE	a_0	a_1	a_2	$\bar{R}^2$/D-W
ALABAMA	.566 0.77	.882 6.09	.258 0.58	.99 0.65
ALASKA	1.643 5.49	.614 7.31	.598 4.33	.99 1.71
ARIZONA	.182 0.84	.935 17.6	.082 0.60	.99 1.36

ARKANSAS	.398 17.7	.850 58.1	0 -	.99 1.07
CALIFORNIA	.199 9.21	.891 86.0	0 -	.99 0.77
COLORADO	.427 0.92	.860 8.71	.269 0.71	.99 1.28
CONNECTICUT	.808 3.37	.704 13.4	.273 1.91	.99 1.73
DELAWARE	.900 1.52	.639 4.60	.494 1.46	.99 1.20
DIST. OF COLUMBIA	-.202 2.73	1.060 26.3	.170 1.43	.99 0.85
FLORIDA	1.071 3.83	.693 8.91	.599 3.38	.99 1.05
GEORGIA	1.044 5.52	.690 14.5	.333 2.91	.99 1.08
HAWAII	.880 3.32	.709 8.84	.170 0.93	.99 1.01
IDAHO	2.652 4.62	.286 2.07	1.544 4.18	.97 1.14
ILLINOIS	.477 5.07	.826 41.9	.223 3.24	.99 1.94
INDIANA	1.193 8.34	.613 19.8	.589 7.14	.99 1.19
IOWA	.397 4.16	.755 32.9	.098 1.71	.99 1.89
KANSAS	.561 1.67	.883 11.5	.480 2.18	.99 0.56
KENTUCKY	2.165 6.59	.447 5.93	1.056 5.95	.99 1.44
LOUISIANA	.622 2.68	.783 15.4	.309 1.96	.99 0.59
MAINE	.950 6.48	.659 18.4	.231 2.60	.99 2.13

MARYLAND	1.130 2.35	.646 5.13	.474 1.74	.99 0.71
MASSACHUSETTS	.152 7.79	.915 89.0	0 –	.99 1.23
MICHIGAN	.797 5.07	.726 24.0	.429 4.75	.99 1.62
MINNESOTA	.476 3.92	.797 27.3	.249 3.04	.99 1.49
MISSISSIPPI	.653 0.93	.748 4.27	.055 0.15	.99 1.01
MISSOURI	.082 5.09	.925 110.	0 –	.99 1.09
MONTANA	.101 2.15	.914 36.6	0 –	.99 1.50
NEBRASKA	.199 0.89	.907 15.5	.135 0.87	.99 1.44
NEVADA	.002 0.05	.998 61.6	0 –	.99 1.66
NEW HAMPSHIRE	.494 38.5	.760 101.	0 –	.99 1.34
NEW JERSEY	.377 0.82	.842 8.08	.087 0.33	.99 1.46
NEW MEXICO	-.193 0.24	1.266 5.36	.288 0.52	.93 0.72
NEW YORK	.202 1.83	.917 39.0	.050 0.58	.99 1.21
NORTH CAROLINA	.484 34.4	.848 96.0	0 –	.99 1.32
NORTH DAKOTA	1.493 1.38	.573 1.93	.855 1.28	.95 0.94
OHIO	1.329 3.20	.615 7.24	.730 2.91	.99 0.34
OKLAHOMA	.523 1.09	.890 8.78	.393 1.17	.99 0.58

OREGON	.532 2.56	.728 15.2	.070 0.50	.99 2.02
PENNSYLVANIA	.986 3.51	.750 13.1	.600 3.32	.99 0.62
RHODE ISLAND	.284 7.12	.926 40.8	0 –	.99 1.05
SOUTH CAROLINA	.855 1.66	.752 6.22	.197 0.72	.99 0.67
SOUTH DAKOTA	.395 0.95	.840 7.31	.251 1.00	.99 1.72
TENNESSEE	1.102 3.51	.709 9.35	.509 2.83	.99 1.15
TEXAS	.152 0.93	.944 24.4	.130 1.21	.99 1.25
UTAH	.078 0.26	.996 12.9	.240 1.03	.99 1.08
VERMONT	2.298 4.66	.374 3.56	1.297 3.86	.99 1.04
VIRGINIA	.523 0.78	.835 4.82	.006 0.02	.99 0.78
WASHINGTON	.384 2.00	.795 22.9	.038 0.27	.99 2.08
WEST VIRGINIA	.829 2.14	.822 10.3	.637 2.71	.99 1.26
WISCONSIN	.339 3.56	.792 35.3	.109 1.97	.99 1.33
WYOMING	1.053 1.61	.797 4.72	1.114 2.07	.96 1.88

APPENDIX 5.3

NONFARM PROPRIETORS' INCOME EQUATION

The specification estimated is

$$YPROP = a_0 + a_1 YT + a_2 PTOT.$$

The estimation sample period is 1958 to 1974. Coefficients a_1 and a_2 are expected to be positive.

The first three columns after the state manes in the table below give the estimated coefficients for a_0, a_1 and a_2 with their t-statistics reported directly below. Using a five percent significance level, the critical value for the two-tailed test on a_0 is 2.145; the critical value for the one-tailed tests on a_1 and a_2 is 1.761.

The last column reports the squared coefficient of multiple correlation adjusted for degrees of freedom and the Durbin-Watson statistic below that. The uncertainty range for the D-W test is .90 to 1.40.

STATE	a_0	a_1	a_2	$\bar{R}^2$/D-W
ALABAMA	-271.447 1.01	.031 10.3	.180 2.12	.97 1.62
ALASKA	3.715 0.21	.029 4.92	.120 1.38	.97 1.29
ARIZONA	-22.069 0.19	.018 1.81	.180 1.78	.92 0.86

ARKANSAS	-59.670 0.30	.045 8.39	.131 1.13	.98 2.00
CALIFORNIA	-749.248 0.83	.022 4.78	.255 3.93	.97 1.45
COLORADO	108.109 1.18	.034 7.08	.115 1.92	.99 1.80
CONNECTICUT	-707.471 3.26	.009 1.84	.495 5.21	.95 1.30
DELAWARE	-47.900 2.51	.012 3.79	.251 5.16	.98 1.27
DIST. OF COLUMBIA	-153.861 1.22	.019 4.51	.334 2.20	.56 0.87
FLORIDA	34.707 0.07	.027 2.50	.146 1.26	.93 1.76
GEORGIA	-765.191 1.35	.019 2.04	.327 2.11	.92 1.37
HAWAII	-96.242 1.58	.013 2.02	.295 2.77	.97 1.19
IDAHO	74.500 12.1	.053 18.2	0 –	.95 0.61
ILLINOIS	-3778.476 3.11	.008 1.88	.577 4.50	.92 1.33
INDIANA	-1394.308 2.78	.022 4.35	.430 3.70	.98 1.60
IOWA	482.292 20.1	.041 15.5	0 –	.94 0.72
KANSAS	284.232 14.8	.047 18.1	0 –	.95 1.06
KENTUCKY	-947.360 1.60	.033 4.58	.426 2.08	.97 0.84
LOUISIANA	-386.893 1.63	.025 5.50	.237 3.02	.97 1.22
MAINE	51.387 14.2	.057 44.6	0 –	.99 1.21

MARYLAND	-417.658 3.16	.017 5.37	.280 5.94	.98 1.73
MASSACHUSETTS	-2227.410 4.47	.015 3.80	.578 5.59	.97 1.12
MICHIGAN	1171.635 12.8	.026 8.81	0 -	.83 0.37
MINNESOTA	-608.334 130	.014 2.35	.355 2.43	.93 0.88
MISSISSIPPI	146.674 18.8	.050 31.8	0 -	.98 1.67
MISSOURI	-735.424 1.09	.024 3.77	.324 1.93	.96 1.18
MONTANA	57.157 0.45	.059 12.5	.004 0.02	.97 1.70
NEBRASKA	186.001 0.72	.048 10.4	.003 0.02	.96 1.18
NEVADA	35.860 2.41	.028 4.36	.067 1.17	.94 1.33
NEW HAMPSHIRE	-114.691 1.47	.013 1.12	.358 2.40	.94 1.64
NEW JERSEY	-1105.830 2.75	.015 4.13	.358 4.97	.97 0.73
NEW MEXICO	55.881 1.10	.031 8.92	.055 0.93	.98 2.06
NEW YORK	-11381.54 4.46	.007 1.65	.870 5.50	.92 0.76
NORTH CAROLINA	-636.245 1.02	.024 3.27	.257 1.76	.95 1.36
NORTH DAKOTA	87.910 20.9	.034 15.9	0 -	.94 0.92
OHIO	-6161.059 5.01	.004 0.88	.804 6.01	.95 1.15
OKLAHOMA	216.158 12.4	.051 21.5	0 -	.97 1.88

OREGON	-273.441 1.35	.027 3.12	.363 2.80	.97 0.93
PENNSYLVANIA	-5837.196 2.51	.024 5.71	.660 3.12	.94 0.75
RHODE ISLAND	-64.570 0.54	.032 5.39	.167 1.11	.96 0.65
SOUTH CAROLINA	-689.265 1.54	.019 2.10	.390 1.96	.95 1.20
SOUTH DAKOTA	74.361 16.1	.047 19.7	0 -	.96 1.54
TENNESSEE	-35.527 0.09	.043 8.08	.123 1.09	.98 0.97
TEXAS	296.839 0.32	.044 6.38	.096 0.89	.98 1.69
UTAH	-20.491 0.36	.027 4.37	.152 2.07	.97 1.09
VERMONT	-155.767 1.86	.008 0.52	.595 2.45	.97 1.30
VIRGINIA	-572.628 2.71	.020 6.63	.255 4.52	.99 1.32
WASHINGTON	113.698 .025	.023 2.12	.164 0.91	.88 0.49
WEST VIRGINIA	96.592 8.85	.043 18.5	0 -	.96 1.14
WISCONSIN	-932.383 2.07	.006 1.11	.441 3.58	.92 0.99
WYOMING	27.129 4.88	.064 13.0	0 -	.91 1.52

APPENDIX 5.4

SOCIAL INSURANCE CONTRIBUTION EQUATION

The specification estimated is

$$YSIC/YTLPR = a_0 + a_1 USSICR.$$

The estimation sample period is 1958 to 1974. Coefficient a_1 is expected to be positive.

The first two columns after the state names in the table below give the estimated coefficients for a_0 and a_1 with their t-statistics reported directly below. Using a five percent significance level, the critical value for the two-tailed test for a_0 is 2.131; the critical value for the one-tailed test on a_1 is 1.753.

The last column reports the squared coefficient of multiple correlation adjusted for degrees of freedom and the Durbin-Watson statistic below that. The uncertainty range for the D-W test is 1.01 to 1.25.

STATE	a_0	a_1	$\bar{R}^2$/D-W
ALABAMA	-.0014 1.82	1.087 51.95	.99 1.01
ALASKA	-.0013 .033	1.059 10.11	.86 0.77
ARIZONA	.0004 0.38	.996 35.32	.99 0.93

ARKANSAS	-.0027 2.09	1.074 31.00	.98 1.18
CALIFORNIA	.0028 2.64	1.024 36.35	.99 1.86
COLORADO	.0023 3.61	.904 54.34	.99 0.58
CONNECTICUT	-.0052 3.69	1.072 28.87	.98 2.38
DELAWARE	-.0084 4.29	1.089 21.15	.97 0.84
DIST. OF COLUMBIA	.0206 23.8	.705 30.87	.98 1.67
FLORIDA	-.0005 0.46	1.014 34.43	.99 1.70
GEORGIA	-.0005 0.34	1.016 25.00	.97 1.81
HAWAII	.0052 5.96	.963 41.64	.99 1.57
IDAHO	-.0005 0.17	1.010 11.80	.90 0.72
ILLINOIS	-.0012 2.79	.984 89.11	.99 1.73
INDIANA	-.0028 3.20	.995 42.43	.99 2.28
IOWA	-.0012 0.71	.997 21.97	.97 1.98
KANSAS	-.0015 0.74	1.047 19.12	.96 1.47
KENTUCKY	-.0028 5.53	1.042 78.99	.99 1.28
LOUISIANA	-.0016 3.26	.966 76.08	.99 1.26
MAINE	.0009 1.02	.987 40.33	.99 2.01

MARYLAND	.0042 6.06	.952 51.71	.99 1.78
MASSACHUSETTS	.0016 3.09	.906 68.07	.99 2.04
MICHIGAN	-.0026 3.47	.982 49.10	.99 1.36
MINNESOTA	-.0010 0.94	1.007 34.67	.99 1.56
MISSISSIPPI	-.0054 4.65	1.114 36.21	.99 1.27
MISSOURI	-.0010 0.85	.997 33.63	.99 1.54
MONTANA	.0057 2.71	.946 16.92	.95 1.12
NEBRASKA	.0009 0.49	.988 21.19	.97 1.92
NEVADA	-.0023 1.22	.951 19.09	.96 0.83
NEW HAMPSHIRE	-.0037 2.12	1.146 25.12	.98 1.71
NEW JERSEY	-.0031 4.21	1.096 56.18	.99 1.61
NEW MEXICO	-.0011 1.06	1.032 39.13	.99 1.33
NEW YORK	.0034 3.62	.890 35.46	.99 0.98
NORTH CAROLINA	-.0047 5.72	1.112 51.41	.99 1.56
NORTH DAKOTA	.0064 1.31	.779 6.10	.69 1.21
OHIO	-.0007 1.67	.984 90.49	.99 1.91
OKLAHOMA	-.0014 1.14	1.061 33.53	.99 1.42

OREGON	-.0054 6.75	1.178 55.65	.99 2.21
PENNSYLVANIA	-.0015 2.18	1.063 59.97	.99 1.80
RHODE ISLAND	.0027 1.61	1.102 24.50	.97 1.50
SOUTH CAROLINA	-.0036 3.34	1.104 38.91	.99 1.25
SOUTH DAKOTA	.0013 0.41	.901 10.83	.88 2.42
TENNESSEE	-.0040 6.13	1.117 65.17	.99 0.91
TEXAS	.0014 2.96	.943 78.06	.99 1.98
UTAH	.0011 0.78	1.080 28.43	.98 0.43
VERMONT	-.0015 0.89	1.017 22.38	.97 1.27
VIRGINIA	.0021 5.03	.984 90.15	.99 1.27
WASHINGTON	-.0018 1.34	1.080 31.04	.98 0.60
WEST VIRGINIA	-.0042 3.98	1.130 40.84	.99 2.10
WISCONSIN	-.0035 10.2	1.086 119.3	.99 1.90
WYOMING	-.0034 2.69	1.122 33.60	.99 0.86

APPENDIX 5.5

DIVIDEND, INTEREST AND RENTAL INCOME EQUATION

The specification estimated is

$$YDIR = a_0 + a_1 YDIR_{-1} + a_2(MGP+MGP_{-1})/2$$
$$+ a_3 PR + a_4 CPI.$$

The estimation sample period is 1959 to 1974. All slope coefficients are expected to be positive.

The first five columns after the state names in the table below give the estimated coefficients for a_0 to a_4 with their t-statistics reported directly below. Using a five percent significance level, the critical value for the two-tailed test on a_0 is 2.201; the critical value for the one-tailed tests on the slope coefficients is 1.796.

The last column reports the squared coefficient of multiple correlation adjusted for degrees of freedom and the Durbin-H statistic below that. In some cases the Durbin-H is undefined. Using a five percent test, significant autocorrelation is indicated when the absolute value of D-H is greater than 1.96.

STATE	a_0	a_1	a_2	a_3	a_4	$\bar{R}^2$/D-H
ALABAMA	-163.124 2.54	.751 5.88	.069 1.40	9.099 1.29	3.323 1.98	.99 0.84

ALASKA	-59.349 2.00	.414 1.74	.360 4.57	1.307 1.27	.649 1.56	.99 4.17
ARIZONA	-472.196 3.57	.648 5.87	.163 3.36	0 -	8.502 3.53	.99 0.94
ARKANSAS	-38.959 1.35	.690 4.22	.158 1.99	17.609 2.63	0 -	.99 3.52
CALIFORNIA	-2558.63 3.07	.739 6.76	.067 0.83	100.59 1.67	50.661 2.68	.99 1.82
COLORADO	-415.678 4.34	.546 5.07	.329 3.46	3.859 0.89	7.700 3.44	.99 -1.66
CONNECTICUT	-844.323 7.44	.516 7.57	.271 7.72	0 -	13.411 6.36	.99 -.71
DELAWARE	-36.636 1.71	.551 2.36	.103 1.64	3.951 1.64	2.044 1.85	.99 3.02
DIST. OF COLUMBIA	-90.238 3.14	.399 2.44	1.53 2.60	1.581 0.37	1.960 1.81	.98 1.85
FLORIDA	-919.243 0.60	.984 2.93	.220 0.85	0 -	13.195 0.43	.99 ?
GEORGIA	-240.741 2.14	.871 15.2	.070 3.92	12.666 2.75	3.902 1.48	.99 -2.57
HAWAII	-111.777 2.63	.773 9.82	.182 3.08	6.118 2.58	1.546 2.10	.99 0.44
IDAHO	-100.720 2.01	.969 5.51	0 -	0 -	1.753 1.50	.99 -.62
ILLINOIS	-1636.97 4.69	.584 5.96	.186 3.68	0 -	29.079 3.75	.99 1.93
INDIANA	-782.126 5.77	.586 6.92	.104 4.28	6.449 0.65	13.596 4.41	.99 0.09
IOWA	-487.675 2.06	.517 2.55	.248 2.35	0 -	9.100 1.75	.99 2.94
KANSAS	-522.279 2.73	.694 1.66	.033 0.11	15.162 1.00	9.940 2.07	.99 ?
KENTUCKY	-491.180 4.39	.446 2.16	.090 1.63	7.824 1.15	10.765 3.56	.99 2.87

LOUISIANA	-407.319 3.02	.837 7.16	0 -	0 -	9.448 2.67	.99 2.90
MAINE	-29.642 0.61	.667 5.44	.302 3.07	0 -	.279 0.23	.99 0.83
MARYLAND	-270.427 2.75	.873 11.8	.176 2.37	0 -	2.942 1.29	.99 0.34
MASSACHUSETTS	-383.027 1.55	.727 4.75	.202 1.45	280315 1.01	3.470 0.71	.99 0.00
MICHIGAN	-774.613 3.07	.783 9.20	.068 2.70	22.516 1.25	13.331 2.40	.99 -.26
MINNESOTA	-673.106 4.53	.304 2.12	.327 3.80	0 -	13.607 3.97	.99 0.49
MISSISSIPPI	-205.051 2.81	.768 6.72	0 -	5.899 1.32	4.478 2.30	.99 0.34
MISSOURI	-615.400 2.85	.450 1.84	.248 1.60	17.007 1.07	11.669 2.09	.99 8.00
MONTANA	-80.292 3.40	.531 6.43	.717 8.62	1.649 0.85	1.312 2.18	.99 0.32
NEBRASKA	-240.035 2.23	.926 8.31	0 -	0 -	4.552 1.97	.99 0.04
NEVADA	-158.125 3.00	.521 2.53	.773 2.08	0 -	2.558 2.50	.98 2.68
NEW HAMPSHIRE	-116.016 2.78	.583 4.49	.180 2.27	5.986 2.49	1.855 1.92	.99 0.94
NEW JERSEY	-1247.59 2.20	.670 3.16	.160 1.31	3.668 0.11	16.564 2.06	.99 1.81
NEW MEXICO	-162.339 2.12	.770 4.57	.066 0.34	0 -	3.361 2.08	.99 -1.25
NEW YORK	-2179.27 2.33	.543 2.12	.367 1.30	80.906 0.71	31.106 1.85	.99. ?
NORTH CAROLINA	-156.879 0.33	.534 2.13	.182 1.23	19.879 1.97	1.375 0.13	.99 ?
NORTH DAKOTA	-34.528 0.15	.894 3.02	.621 0.61	0 -	.564 0.15	.96 ?

OHIO	-754.299 2.29	.785 7.99	.083 2.22	0 -	14.152 1.67	.99 -2.13
OKLAHOMA	-250.867 1.13	.717 5.59	.259 1.81	8.160 0.95	5.304 1.02	.99 -.02
OREGON	-211.504 1.74	.947 9.63	.001 0.04	8.701 2.07	3.394 1.27	.99 -.76
PENNSYLVANIA	-1024.94 4.07	.710 7.94	.108 3.05	0 -	21.076 3.33	.99 2.18
RHODE ISLAND	-95.104 2.43	.843 6.30	.010 0.15	.778 0.19	1.822 1.99	.99 1.07
SOUTH CAROLINA	-324.318 4.37	.430 4.04	.152 6.60	4.438 1.53	5.989 3.57	.99 -.66
SOUTH DAKOTA	-122.489 2.46	.837 5.86	0 -	0 -	2.461 2.28	.99 3.24
TENNESSEE	-465.508 4.11	.784 7.97	.029 1.98	0 -	9.685 3.67	.99 -1.22
TEXAS	-2833.11 3.80	.519 2.99	.158 2.43	0 -	59.104 3.35	.99 4.03
UTAH	-157.931 3.67	.772 6.19	0 -	0 -	3.126 3.20	.99 0.76
VERMONT	-101.408 2.00	.578 1.94	.187 1.33	0 -	1.795 1.92	.98 ?
VIRGINIA	-592.310 4.22	.655 6.46	.182 2.63	0 -	10.295 3.33	.99 0.92
WASHINGTON	-596.045 2.76	.796 5.84	0 -	14.962 1.41	11.273 2.20	.99 0.98
WEST VIRGINIA	-346.157 8.05	.242 1.84	.129 4.60	0 -	7.979 7.46	.99 0.92
WISCONSIN	-736.053 4.51	.479 3.33	.180 2.96	0 -	13.995 3.45	.99 1.47
WYOMING	-129.835 2.50	.374 1.38	.592 3.17	1.506 0.94	2.801 2.19	.99 ?

APPENDIX 5.6

TRANSFER PAYMENTS EQUATION

The specification estimated is

$$YTP/PTOT = a_0 + a_1(YT/PTOT) + a_2(P65/PTOT) + a_3(U/PTOT).$$

The estimation sample period is 1958 to 1974. All slope coefficients are expected to be positive.

The first four columns after the state names in the table below give the estimated coefficients for a_0, a_1, a_2 and a_3 with their t-statistics reported directly below. Using a five percent significance level, the critical value for the two-tailed test on a_0 is 2.160; the critical value for the one-tailed tests on the slope coefficients is 1.771.

The last column reports the squared coefficient of multiple correlation adjusted for degrees of freedom and the Durbin-Watson statistic below that. The uncertainty range for the D-W test is .90 to 1.40.

STATE	a_0	a_1	a_2	a_3	$\bar{R}^2$/D-W
ALABAMA	-.246 18.8	.174 79.7	0 -	5.002 9.37	.99 1.34
ALASKA	-.661 4.04	.134 6.10	12.415 2.15	4.084 1.04	.88 1.83

ARIZONA	−.273 4.99	.133 13.6	1.597 1.73	2.927 4.33	.99 1.40
ARKANSAS	−.352 4.83	.168 26.9	1.511 2.00	4.954 6.66	.99 2.10
CALIFORNIA	−1.195 4.81	.139 18.4	10.476 3.36	3.977 7.58	.99 1.43
COLORADO	−.189 1.11	.130 24.4	.515 0.30	1.214 1.34	.99 1.91
CONNECTICUT	−1.088 10.1	.118 71.3	8.577 7.29	3.637 13.5	.99 2.35
DELAWARE	−.537 5.73	.113 49.6	3.534 2.76	4.279 9.01	.99 1.89
DIST. OF COLUMBIA	−.525 1.92	.243 10.7	.135 0.04	5.734 1.40	.98 0.93
FLORIDA	−.249 3.70	.171 17.2	.268 0.39	2.675 4.52	.99 1.32
GEORGIA	−.596 1.65	.110 5.42	6.152 1.12	3.524 4.07	.99 1.78
HAWAII	−.341 1.47	.091 3.32	2.769 0.44	6.700 5.00	.98 0.49
IDAHO	−.274 1.32	.132 19.3	1.182 0.50	3.153 2.65	.99 1.30
ILLINOIS	−.719 2.93	.128 42.1	4.350 1.71	5.953 8.62	.99 1.63
INDIANA	−.854 3.98	.122 64.1	6.670 2.99	4.105 11.4	.99 2.22
IOWA	−.182 7.28	.125 27.7	0 −	6.262 3.30	.98 2.00
KANSAS	−.171 14.0	.130 56.6	0 −	2.965 3.87	.99 1.60
KENTUCKY	−.185 7.94	.163 33.7	0 −	3.005 3.68	.99 0.97
LOUISIANA	−.230 15.4	.150 56.3	0 −	5.146 8.13	.99 1.42

MAINE	-.301 1.02	.190 29.4	.221 0.09	3.964 3.22	.99 1.18
MARYLAND	-.351 2.03	.121 20.6	1.538 0.59	5.304 7.52	.99 1.32
MASSACHUSETTS	-.291 20.3	.145 31.3	0 -	6.647 7.79	.99 0.79
MICHIGAN	-1.026 3.30	.120 18.8	9.200 2.46	4.996 7.12	.99 1.51
MINNESOTA	-.192 8.97	.131 41.0	0 -	3.671 3.97	.99 2.26
MISSISSIPPI	-.225 1.45	.179 9.98	.239 0.12	4.680 5.01	.99 2.05
MISSOURI	-.279 0.80	.143 18.4	.533 0.17	6.051 6.00	.99 0.87
MONTANA	-.589 1.25	.132 17.0	4.740 0.94	2.239 1.67	.98 2.26
NEBRASKA	-.115 9.38	.126 33.0	0 -	0 -	.99 1.96
NEVADA	-.468 10.4	.110 24.1	3.465 3.69	4.803 5.96	.99 1.18
NEW HAMPSHIRE	-.363 3.59	.148 48.6	1.126 1.36	5.063 15.5	.99 2.33
NEW JERSEY	-.709 4.00	.119 21.3	4.632 2.23	5.891 17.0	.99 1.69
NEW MEXICO	-.264 31.0	.186 40.3	0 -	2.796 3.67	.99 0.83
NEW YORK	-.392 20.8	.169 49.1	0 -	5.837 6.52	.99 0.73
NORTH CAROLINA	-.162 8.27	.125 36.8	0 -	2.948 4.32	.99 1.52
NORTH DAKOTA	-.550 3.72	.067 6.84	6.158 3.63	0 -	.96 1.42
OHIO	-1.346 5.07	.125 25.5	12.241 4.07	3.331 7.17	.99 1.18

OKLAHOMA	-.188 11.8	.162 72.3	0 -	3.273 3.96	.99 2.03
OREGON	-.319 1.06	.147 21.9	.591 0.20	5.535 8.22	.99 1.23
PENNSYLVANIA	-.850 4.62	.176 24.6	4.839 2.54	4.366 14.0	.99 1.44
RHODE ISLAND	-1.139 3.98	.170 17.3	7.481 2.64	5.579 8.08	.99 1.12
SOUTH CAROLINA	-.181 6.67	.133 32.1	0 -	4.327 3.27	.98 0.46
SOUTH DAKOTA	-.272 1.57	.119 9.90	1.877 1.08	0 -	.96 2.13
TENNESSEE	-.275 1.78	.150 13.3	.773 0.40	3.805 7.55	.99 1.49
TEXAS	-.205 20.5	.135 89.5	0 -	2.990 7.93	.99 1.70
UTAH	-.181 17.6	.155 42.7	0 -	0 -	.99 0.41
VERMONT	-.531 1.78	.173 16.5	2.010 0.86	5.316 4.51	.98 0.74
VIRGINIA	-.270 2.00	.130 17.1	.576 0.28	6.754 11.6	.99 1.76
WASHINGTON	-.918 4.01	.154 27.0	6.147 2.64	5.382 6.66	.99 0.74
WEST VIRGINIA	-.310 10.5	.235 35.9	0 -	2.702 4.77	.99 1.14
WISCONSIN	-.228 23.0	.126 39.9	0 -	7.732 8.10	.99 1.63
WYOMING	-.261 2.80	.116 25.8	1.501 1.49	1.669 1.50	.99 0.97

CHAPTER SIX: LABOR FORCE AND UNEMPLOYMENT

6.1 INTRODUCTION

The labor market is the key link between the economic and demographic variables of a model. Population (POP), employment (E), labor force (LF), the labor force participation rate (ρ), the unemployment rate (UR) and the wage rate (W) are the principal variables in the labor market. How best to model these variables, which are not all independent of one another, in a consistent manner within the context of a multiregion model is the subject of this chapter.

Section 2 examines the consistency problem. Among the conclusions drawn are that the unemployment rate should be modelled as an identity and the labor force participation rates should be modelled as behavioral equations. The specifications, data and estimation results of the labor force participation rate equations are discussed in Section 3. The complete estimation results are presented in Appendices 6.1 to 6.4 at the end of this chapter.

6.2 LABOR MARKET MODELLING STRATEGIES

As shown in Chapter Five, wages in ECESIS are determined by a wage transmission and Phillips hypothesis model. Thus, in conjunction with labor demand and supply functions and conventional economic theory, the wage rate, labor force, employment and unemployment may all be determined simultaneously. This approach, shown in Figure 6.2.1, is typical of econometric models. Excluding the wage rate, the other five labor market variables (POP, E, LF, ρ, UR) are related by two identities. It is up to the model builder to decide which variables will be determined stochastically and which by identity. The ten possible alternatives are listed in Table 6.2.1.

FIGURE 6.2.1

LABOR MARKET WITH PREDETERMINED WAGE RATE

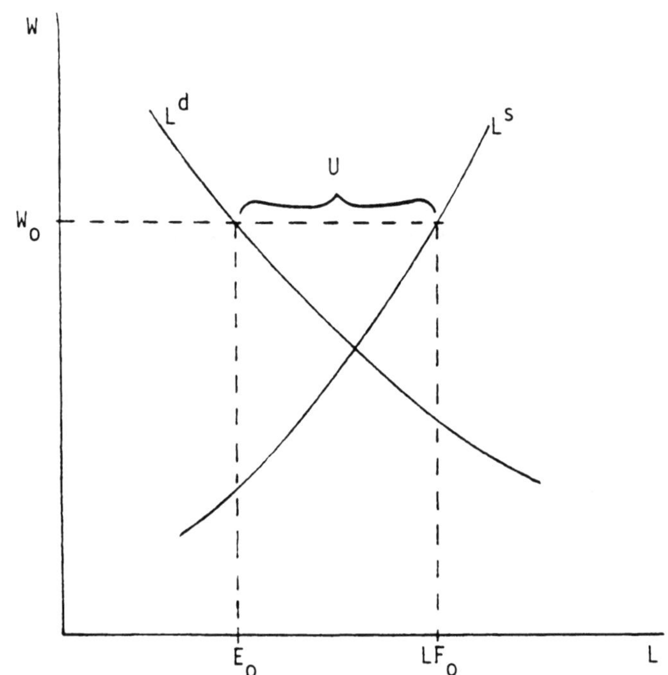

TABLE 6.2.1

ALTERNATIVE LABOR MARKET MODELLING STRATEGIES

E - Employment
POP - Population
LF - Labor force
ρ - Labor force participation rate
UR - Unemployment rate

CASE	STOCHASTIC VARIABLES	RESIDUAL VARIABLES
1	E,POP,LF	ρ,UR
2	E,POP,ρ	LF,UR
3	E,POP,UR	LF,ρ
4	E,LF,ρ	POP,UR
5	E,LF,UR	POP,ρ
6	E,ρ,UR	POP,LF
7	POP,LF,ρ	E,UR
8	POP,LF,UR	E,ρ
9	POP,ρ,UR	E,LF
10	LF,ρ,UR	E,POP

In a purely demand driven model, case five for example, population is determined by an equation like

(6.2.1) $$POP = LF/\rho,$$

or,

(6.2.2) $$POP = E/(\rho(1-UR)).$$

Alternatively, in a completely supply driven model, like case eight, employment would be determined from an equation like

(6.2.3) $$E = LF(1-UR).$$

Equations (6.2.1) and (6.2.2) make little sense in the context of a model like ECESIS which has an elaborate demographic model. Similarly determining employment from an identity like (6.2.3) is not satisfactory within the context of an economic model. Given that ECESIS has both an employment sector (see Chapter Four) and a population sector (see Chapter Eight), cases four through ten in Table 6.2.1 may be ruled out as possible modelling strategies. The remaining cases embrace both demand and supply elements and are the cases most commonly used by model builders.[1]

Cases one and two use the identity

(6.2.4) $UR = 1 - E/LF$

to determine the unemployment rate. Since E and LF are approximately the same order of magnitude, (6.2.4) may lead to large forecasting errors for UR. For example, if E is overestimated by one percent and LF is underestimated by one percent, then UR will be underestimated by approximately twenty percent. Such large errors may lead to severe simulation problems with a model where UR plays a key role (Ledent 1981). Case three avoids this problem by

---

[1] Often the supply aspects of the labor market are compromised because the key population variable is left exogenous to the model. See Adams, Brooking, Glickman (1975); Chang (1976); Jefferson (1978); Puffer and Williams (1967); Moody and Puffer (1969); Hall and Licari (1974); Klein (1969); Chau (1970); and Ghali and Renaud (1975).

determining UR stochastically, and thus is preferred by many model builders (Adams, Brookings, and Glickman 1975; Chang 1976; Jefferson 1978; Glickman 1972, 1977; Klein and Glickman 1973; and Rubin and Erickson 1980). Case three, however, determines both ρ and LF by identity and cannot provide the age-sex specific detail for the labor force that ECESIS requires.

When ρ is determined by the identity

(6.2.5) $\rho = LF/POP$,

as in cases one and three, it is subject to the same forecasting error problems as UR when determined by (6.2.4). Case two seems to be the best choice for a modelling strategy for the ECESIS labor market variables. The participation rates are determined stochastically so that the age-sex detail may be modelled specifically.[2] Both E and POP are determined stochastically to allow for both demand and supply side effects. The population submodel is the subject of the next two chapters. Chapter Four examined the employment equations. The unemployment rate is determined by identity (6.2.4) and thus is quite volatile. To compensate for this, employment to population ratios are used whenever possible in the model in place of the

---

[2] The Bureau of Labor Statistics also chooses this option when making labor force projections. See Ryscavage (1979).

unemployment rate. This isolates the model from the adverse affects of volatile UR projections. Using case two, the labor force is determined from the identity

(6.2.6) $LF = \rho \cdot POP.$

Other than POP, which is discussed in Chapter Eight, only the labor force participation rate remains to be determined. This is the subject of the next section.

6.3 LABOR FORCE PARTICIPATION RATE EQUATIONS

6.3.1 DATA

There is considerable evidence that labor force participation rates should be modelled on an age-sex specific basis (Tella 1965; Land and Pampel 1980; Stolzenberg and Waite 1977). Figure 6.3.1 demonstrates the very different trends in male and female participation rates in recent years.

The population age groups used in ECESIS are: 0-4, 5-17, 18-44, 45-64, and 65+. Unfortunately, labor force data at the state level are not available with this age detail with sex disaggregation. To alleviate this problem, a special labor force data set was constructed for the ECESIS model.

FIGURE 6.3.1
LABOR FORCE PARTICIPATION RATES

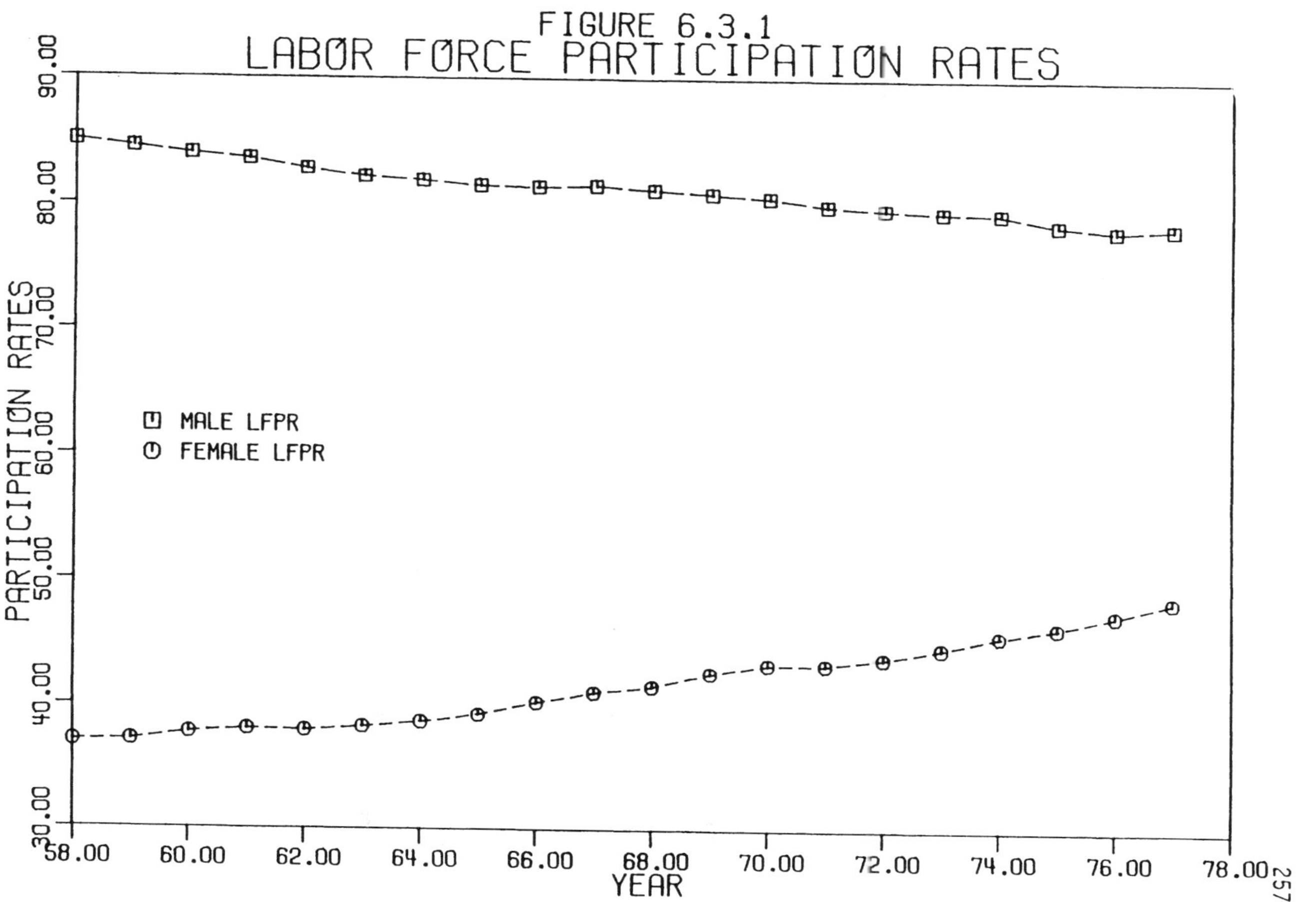

The following notation will be useful. Denote the labor force for age group a and sex group s in state i as ${}^{a}LF_{i}^{s}$, where:

a = 1 : 0–4 years
= 2 : 5–17 years
= 3 : 18–44 years
= 4 : 45–64 years
= 5 : 65+ years

and,

s = 1 : male
= 2 : female.

Thus, ${}^{3}LF_{i}^{1}$ denotes the 18–44 year old male labor force for state i. The total labor force for state i is simply denoted as LF_i. Time subscripts are omitted throughout.

Annual time series data on total state labor force and age-sex specific U.S. labor force (${}^{a}LF_{us}^{s}$) are readily available. For a given year, these data may serve as the margins of a matrix with age-sex groups along the columns and states along the rows.

...	LF_1
...	...
$^aLF_i^s$	LF_i
...	...
...	LF_{51}
$^2LF_{us}^1 \ldots {}^aLF_{us}^s \ldots {}^5LF_{us}^2$	LF_{us}

The individual elements of the matrix are $^aLF_i^s$. The row sums equal $^aLF_{us}^s$ and the column sums equal LF_i. The final row and final column both sum to the total U.S. labor force (LF_{us}). It is the internal elements of the matrix that are missing and that must be constructed.

Estimates of the $^aLF_i^s$ may be obtained from the Social Security Administration's Continuous Work History Sample (U.S. Department of Commerce 1976). The CWHS is a longitudinal file that follows one percent of all workers in the Social Security System over a period of years.[3] Workers unemployed for over twelve months and workers not covered by the Social Security System are excluded from this data base. Enough demographic information is available for these workers to construct estimates of the cell elements of the

[3] Originally the CWHS files were to be used to construct interstate migration data for ECESIS. The data, however, proved to be unreliable for this purpose (see Chapter Eight).

matrix. The CWHS data are used to get initial estimates of the ${}^{a}LF_i^{s}$'s then a RAS adjustment procedure is used to adjust the cell elements so that the rows and columns add to the margin constraints. This procedure is repeated for each of the years from 1958 to 1975.

Legal problems have prevented use of the CWHS files beyond the 1975 data. Thus, a time series of LF can be constructed by this method only for the period 1958 to 1975. Data beyond 1975 must be forecast.[4]

Given ${}^{a}LF_i^{s}$ and the age-sex population data (see Chapter Eight), the age-sex specific labor force participation rates may be generated from

$$(6.3.1) \qquad {}^{a}\rho_i^{s} = {}^{a}LF_i^{s}/{}^{a}POP_i^{s}.$$

This does not completely solve the data problems associated with estimating the participation rate equations. Age-sex specific participation rates should ideally be modelled as functions of age-sex specific independent variables. The participation rate of 18-44 year old females, for example, should be a function of the wage rate that 18-44 year old females receive. Virtually none of the variables that would be used in modelling participation

[4] This is partially the reason why the estimation period for most equations in ECESIS is 1958 to 1974.

rates, however, have age-sex disaggregation at the state level. Nor are there adequate data sets like the CWHS with which to estimate these values. The participation rates must be modelled as functions of aggregate data.

6.3.2 SPECIFICATION AND ESTIMATION

Given the precarious nature of the data, the total labor force participation rate for state i (ρ_i) is modelled as a function of aggregate data and then each age-sex specific rate is modelled in the form of a ratio with the total rate.

Standard economic theory says that the labor force participation rate should be directly related to wages and inversely related to nonlabor income. Often an opportunity or competition variable is also included in the specification (Tella 1964). Nonlabor income is measured as total dividend, interest and rental income per working age person (YDIR/P1864). This variable is lagged one year. Total real average earnings (WT72) are used for wages. Various opportunity type variables were tried in the specification with little success.

Several studies (Lucas and Rapping 1969; Wachter 1972, 1974; Simler and Tella 1980) have found that the inflation rate has significant influence on the labor force participation rate. As the inflation rate increases, so does its variability (Foster 1978), thus workers become more uncertain about their future earning prospects. This uncertainty affects both labor and nonlabor income so the net effect of the inflation rate on ρ is an empirical question. Simler and Tella (1980) find a positive relationship between the inflation rate and ρ indicating that, during inflationary periods, workers reduce their expectations about future real nonlabor income by more than they reduce their expectations about future real wage rates.

The final specification for the total labor force participation rate is

$$(6.3.2) \quad \rho_i = a_0 + a_1(YDIR_i/P1864_i)_{-1} + a_2WT72_i + a_3CPI_i^{\circ},$$

where CPI° is the percentage change in the consumer price index. The complete estimation results are presented in Appendix 6.1. The coefficients a_2 and a_3 are significantly positive in nearly all states. Surprisingly, a_1 is significantly negative in only about one-half of the states.

The total labor force is then calculated from

$$(6.3.3) \quad LF_i = \rho_i \cdot PTOT_i,$$

where $PTOT_i$ is the total population of state i.

The age-sex specific labor force participation rates are estimated as a ratio with ρ_i.

The participation rates for both males and females in the age groups 5-17 years[5] and sixty-five and over are taken as exogenous.

The participation rate ratios of 18-44 and 45-64 year old males is modelled as a Koyck lag on the per capita nonlabor income variable,

$$(6.3.4) \quad {}^{a}\rho_i{}^{1}/\rho_i = a_0 + a_1({}^{a}\rho_i{}^{1}/\rho_i)_{-1} + a_2(YDIR_i/P1864_i)_{-1}; \ a=3,4.$$

The complete estimation results for these equations are presented in Appendices 6.2 and 6.3.

The 18-44 year old female labor force participation rate ratio is modelled as a Koyck lag on the general fertility rate ($BRATE_i$),[6]

$$(6.3.5) \quad {}^{3}\rho_i{}^{2}/\rho_i = a_0 + a_1({}^{3}\rho_i{}^{2}/\rho_i)_{-1} + a_2 BRATE_i.$$

Land and Pampel (1980) argue that a_2 should not be significantly different from zero while Cramer (1980) argues

---

[5] The 5-17 labor force group is a result of the ECESIS age disaggregation. In this group, only persons sixteen and seventeen years old may be counted in the labor force.

[6] BRATE is defined as total births over the the female population aged 18 to 44 (an approximation for fecund females).

that a_2 should be significantly negative. The complete estimation results for (6.3.5) are given in Appendix 6.4. The coefficient a_2 is found to be significantly negative in about three-quarters of the states.

Since the total participation rate is determined stochastically, one of the age-sex rates must be determined by identity. The participation rate of 45 to 64 year old females is chosen for this role. First, age-sex labor forces are calculated from

$$(6.3.6) \qquad {}^{a}LF_i{}^{s} = {}^{a}\rho_i{}^{s} \cdot {}^{a}POP_i{}^{s},$$

for all a and s except the a=4 and s=2 combination. Then the labor force for 45 to 64 year old females is calculated from

$$(6.3.7) \qquad {}^{4}LF_i{}^{2} = LF_i - \Sigma_a \Sigma_s {}^{a}LF_i{}^{s}, \ (a \neq 4, s \neq 2).$$

The labor force participation rate for 45 to 64 year old females is calculated from

$$(6.3.8) \qquad {}^{4}\rho_i{}^{2} = {}^{4}LF_i{}^{2} / {}^{4}POP_i{}^{2}.$$

Finally, the unemployment rate for state i is calculated from

$$(6.3.9) \qquad UR_i = (LF_i - ET_i)/LF_i,$$

where ET_i is total employment in state i.

APPENDIX 6.1

TOTAL LABOR FORCE PARTICIPATION RATE

The specification estimated is

$$\rho_i = a_0 + a_1(YDIR_i/P1864_i)_{-1} + a_2WT72_i + a_3CPI^{\circ}.$$

The estimation sample period is 1959 to 1974. Coefficient a_1 should be negative and coefficient a_2 should be positive. Coefficient a_3 could be negative or positive but is expected to be positive in most cases.

The first four columns in the table below give the estimated coefficients a_0, a_1, a_2 and a_3 with their t-statistics reported directly below. Using a five percent significance level, the critical value for the two-tailed tests on a_0 and a_3 is 2.179; the critical value for the one-tailed tests on a_1 and a_2 is 1.782.

The last column reports the squared coefficient of multiple correlation corrected for degrees of freedom and the Durbin- Watson statistic below that. The uncertainty range for the D-W test is .75 to 1.59.

STATE	a_0	a_1	a_2	a_3	$\bar{R}^2$/D-W
ALABAMA	.140 1.44	-.218 1.45	.043 1.98	.0037 2.69	.80 0.94
ALASKA	.174 0.77	0 -	.010 0.51	.0109 3.47	.57 0.93

ARIZONA	.207 2.92	0 –	.013 1.53	.0092 4.31	.78 0.45
ARKANSAS	.112 4.29	–.039 2.11	.037 7.34	.0033 4.31	.97 2.05
CALIFORNIA	.318 5.64	0 –	.006 0.95	.0075 5.89	.79 0.66
COLORADO	.350 11.8	–.237 4.40	.031 3.58	.0081 9.53	.91 1.62
CONNECTICUT	.437 30.1	–.011 0.81	0 –	.0056 5.16	.75 1.06
DELAWARE	.349 6.92	–.049 2.31	.014 2.38	.0025 1.99	.75 1.03
DIST. OF COLUMBIA	.484 31.7	–.008 0.42	.001 0.66	–.002 2.58	.42 2.09
FLORIDA	.329 10.7	0 –	.003 0.69	.0065 5.22	.84 0.70
GEORGIA	.225 7.74	0 –	.018 4.73	.0051 3.78	.90 0.61
HAWAII	.203 2.27	–.074 0.67	.025 1.21	.0102 4.55	.83 0.90
IDAHO	.201 3.28	0 –	.025 3.21	.0027 2.40	.75 1.10
ILLINOIS	.296 12.4	–.060 3.73	.021 4.82	.0036 5.22	.91 1.53
INDIANA	.252 4.69	–.033 0.73	.021 2.11	.0046 5.28	.94 0.97
IOWA	.160 3.06	–.026 0.94	.037 3.68	.0029 2.46	.91 1.10
KANSAS	.312 7.05	0 –	.011 1.83	.0053 4.30	.82 1.01
KENTUCKY	.168 3.70	0 –	.022 3.77	.0049 3.14	.88 0.98
LOUISIANA	.238 3.89	–.098 1.00	.022 1.43	.0027 1.91	.54 1.16

MAINE	.333 7.63	0 –	.006 0.92	.0059 5.47	.83 0.60
MARYLAND	.245 6.59	–.336 4.51	.048 4.59	.0072 6.92	.89 1.30
MASSACHUSETTS	.394 23.9	–.093 5.45	.015 3.68	.0048 9.02	.90 1.32
MICHIGAN	.334 19.3	–.097 4.06	.015 4.29	.0040 6.49	.88 1.86
MINNESOTA	.287 5.24	–.151 2.10	.033 2.41	.0054 3.44	.65 0.99
MISSISSIPPI	.226 5.72	0 –	.015 2.63	.0046 3.06	.82 0.66
MISSOURI	.348 15.7	–.071 2.17	.015 2.61	.0037 4.45	.78 1.70
MONTANA	.249 3.02	–.016 0.37	.016 1.30	.0081 3.60	.77 0.84
NEBRASKA	.342 4.33	–.047 1.22	.016 1.04	.0066 3.16	.57 0.67
NEVADA	.181 2.38	–.100 1.13	.030 2.82	.0141 5.43	.86 1.02
NEW HAMPSHIRE	.512 29.6	–.118 5.38	0 –	.0066 5.93	.70 2.11
NEW JERSEY	.157 4.11	–.207 6.09	.053 6.48	.0064 8.06	.92 1.91
NEW MEXICO	.260 2.46	0 –	.009 0.69	.0049 4.37	.65 0.65
NEW YORK	.360 19.8	–.064 4.03	.013 3.40	.0025 4.20	.77 1.37
NORTH CAROLINA	.132 1.92	–.189 1.69	.049 2.84	.0060 4.13	.94 1.28
NORTH DAKOTA	.372 7.58	–.070 2.08	.009 0.98	.0076 2.55	.21 1.15
OHIO	.187 1.70	–.216 1.61	.044 1.74	.0078 4.56	.77 1.02

OKLAHOMA	.336 4.32	-.003 0.04	.005 0.35	.0047 2.68	.66 0.73
OREGON	.151 2.73	-.041 0.79	.036 3.02	.0043 4.39	.96 1.17
PENNSYLVANIA	.257 6.87	-.194 4.32	.037 4.16	.0039 4.90	.86 0.87
RHODE ISLAND	.377 ?.??	0 -	0 -	.0005 ?.??	.?? ?.??
SOUTH CAROLINA	.263 6.29	0 -	.017 2.86	.0015 0.78	.65 0.83
SOUTH DAKOTA	.001 0.01	-.131 3.41	.071 3.49	.0106 5.03	.78 1.27
TENNESSEE	.250 7.59	0 -	.018 3.87	.0042 3.24	.89 0.68
TEXAS	.169 3.64	-.053 0.98	.030 2.91	.0049 3.15	.91 0.96
UTAH	.191 2.92	-.062 1.04	.031 2.40	.0039 3.20	.71 1.55
VERMONT	.362 21.5	-.003 0.16	.006 1.58	.0036 4.53	.88 1.01
VIRGINIA	.239 3.96	0 -	.014 1.83	.0077 3.66	.78 0.59
WASHINGTON	.285 11.1	0 -	.012 4.28	.0031 3.99	.89 1.07
WEST VIRGINIA	.219 5.64	-.100 1.98	.021 2.88	.0028 2.91	.75 1.34
WISCONSIN	.089 1.15	-.274 3.30	.068 3.90	.0077 4.26	.81 1.24
WYOMING	.270 2.91	-.046 1.35	.023 1.73	.0016 0.67	.08 2.03

APPENDIX 6.2

LFPR FOR 18-44 YEAR OLD MALES

The specification estimated is

$$^{3}\rho_i{}^{1}/\rho_i = a_0 + a_1({}^{3}\rho_i{}^{1}/\rho_i)_{-1} + a_2(YDIR_i/P1864_i)_{-1}.$$

The estimation sample period is 1959 to 1974. Coefficient a_1 should be positive and coefficient a_2 should be negative.

The first three columns in the table below give the estimated coefficients a_0, a_1 and a_2 with their t-statistics reported directly below. Using a five percent significance level, the critical value for the two-tailed test on a_0 is 2.160; the critical value for the one-tailed tests on a_1 and a_2 is 1.771.

The last column reports the squared coefficient of multiple correlation corrected for degrees of freedom and the Durbin- H statistic below that. Using a five percent test, significant autocorrelation is indicated when the absolute value of D-H is greater than 1.96. A '?' appears in those cases where the D-H is undefined.

STATE	a_0	a_1	a_2	$\bar{R}^2$/D-H
ALABAMA	1.823 3.16	.422 2.28	-.921 3.36	.97 3.36
ALASKA	.864 2.91	.460 2.56	0 -	.27 3.65

ARIZONA	.918 1.66	.643 3.05	-.181 1.33	.74 1.30
ARKANSAS	1.835 2.37	.365 1.38	-.576 2.34	.92 ?
CALIFORNIA	.264 0.75	.922 7.22	-.114 1.07	.91 0.33
COLORADO	1.141 1.88	.649 3.33	-.413 2.02	.91 0.00
CONNECTICUT	.885 2.97	.659 5.39	-.149 3.47	.92 -2.06
DELAWARE	.059 0.23	.960 7.48	0 -	.79 -2.17
DIST. OF COLUMBIA	.440 1.09	.841 4.87	-.096 0.35	.61 2.21
FLORIDA	1.434 3.09	.432 2.28	-.180 2.75	.73 3.92
GEORGIA	2.715 3.39	.043 0.15	-1.022 3.41	.98 ?
HAWAII	1.624 3.15	.103 0.37	-.250 2.14	.39 ?
IDAHO	2.431 2.91	.149 0.51	-.771 2.85	.89 ?
ILLINOIS	.304 1.39	.909 10.5	-.119 2.74	.95 0.38
INDIANA	.373 1.49	.888 10.1	-.193 2.45	.98 -.49
IOWA	.780 2.95	.731 7.01	-.200 4.08	.93 -2.05
KANSAS	.718 1.68	.729 4.73	-.176 1.52	.91 0.30
KENTUCKY	2.011 4.40	.338 2.20	-.779 4.57	.95 2.13
LOUISIANA	.580 2.30	.848 11.7	-.271 3.01	.99 -.25

MAINE	.633 1.57	.740 4.07	-.118 2.06	.69 -.50
MARYLAND	.427 1.54	.861 8.50	-.192 1.97	.95 -.61
MASSACHUSETTS	.277 1.15	.902 7.81	-.098 2.36	.85 0.27
MICHIGAN	.349 1.83	.901 13.4	-.170 3.16	.98 -.73
MINNESOTA	.385 1.94	.928 14.5	-.269 3.99	.98 -.27
MISSISSIPPI	2.533 5.97	.189 1.38	-1.312 6.24	.98 -.81
MISSOURI	.698 3.56	.804 11.3	-.304 5.57	.97 -.88
MONTANA	1.040 1.95	.624 3.13	-.266 1.93	.77 0.07
NEBRASKA	.786 1.66	.690 3.57	-.132 1.93	.86 0.57
NEVADA	2.275 4.74	.066 0.32	-.630 3.61	.56 -.25
NEW HAMPSHIRE	1.416 3.10	.378 1.77	-.263 3.03	.63 -.04
NEW JERSEY	.740 3.52	.714 8.31	-.187 4.37	.98 -.83
NEW MEXICO	.685 1.44	.760 4.07	-.213 1.79	.73 -1.05
NEW YORK	.136 0.63	.984 9.29	-.101 3.61	.86 0.09
NORTH CAROLINA	1.410 3.73	.483 3.46	-.639 3.91	.98 1.37
NORTH DAKOTA	1.861 3.01	.246 0.98	-.265 2.69	.67 ?
OHIO	.239 1.52	.950 17.6	-.156 3.70	.99 -.88

OKLAHOMA	1.688 3.69	.402 2.45	-.464 3.90	.96 -1.75
OREGON	1.713 2.72	.419 1.96	-.501 2.67	.90 1.08
PENNSYLVANIA	1.127 6.62	.578 8.75	-.287 7.35	.99 -1.66
RHODE ISLAND	1.011 2.76	.537 3.07	-.286 2.38	.72 0.78
SOUTH CAROLINA	1.773 3.66	.370 2.16	-1.009 3.80	.98 2.42
SOUTH DAKOTA	1.264 2.83	.463 2.31	-.170 2.73	.61 -1.97
TENNESSEE	1.679 3.67	.436 2.81	-.701 3.86	.97 0.74
TEXAS	.759 2.13	.728 5.53	-.181 2.49	.97 -1.91
UTAH	.844 1.42	.695 3.48	-.263 1.14	.87 0.37
VERMONT	2.059 3.07	.217 0.90	-.412 2.20	.63 2.57
VIRGINIA	1.074 5.68	.590 7.82	-.419 6.42	.99 0.00
WASHINGTON	.700 2.19	.758 6.43	-.229 2.56	.95 0.25
WEST VIRGINIA	1.566 3.45	.499 3.38	-.597 3.47	.93 1.31
WISCONSIN	.428 2.38	.912 13.9	-.267 4.75	.97 -.70
WYOMING	1.121 2.06	.531 2.42	-.142 1.51	.65 1.29

APPENDIX 6.3

LFPR FOR 45-64 YEAR OLD MALES

The specification estimated is

$$^{4}\rho_i{}^{1}/\rho_i = a_0 + a_1(^{4}\rho_i{}^{1}/\rho_i)_{-1} + a_2(YDIR_i/P1864_i)_{-1}.$$

The estimation sample period is 1959 to 1974. Coefficient a_1 should be positive and coefficient a_2 should be negative.

The first three columns in the table below give the estimated coefficients a_0, a_1 and a_2 with their t-statistics reported directly below. Using a five percent significance level, the critical value for the two-tailed test on a_0 is 2.160; the critical value for the one-tailed tests on a_1 and a_2 is 1.771.

The last column reports the squared coefficient of multiple correlation corrected for degrees of freedom and the Durbin- H statistic below that. Using a five percent test, significant autocorrelation is indicated when the absolute value of D-H is greater than 1.96. A '?' appears in those cases where the D-H is undefined.

STATE	a_0	a_1	a_2	$\bar{R}^2$/D-H
ALABAMA	.216 0.70	.964 9.49	-.281 2.14	.96 -1.18
ALASKA	.314 0.69	.866 5.21	0 -	.64 -.51

ARIZONA	2.488 2.76	.328 1.48	-1.096 2.47	.89 3.72
ARKANSAS	.264 0.71	.924 6.90	-.209 1.43	.90 -.64
CALIFORNIA	.116 0.44	1.05 15.4	-.253 1.95	.97 -1.16
COLORADO	.033 0.09	1.01 9.46	-.089 0.61	.95 0.24
CONNECTICUT	.502 1.91	.845 7.86	-.136 2.98	.87 -1.42
DELAWARE	.233 0.61	1.092 11.4	-.306 1.37	.90 -1.65
DIST. OF COLUMBIA	1.188 2.21	.639 3.73	-.459 1.96	.75 0.52
FLORIDA	1.217 2.14	.622 3.61	-.325 1.96	.80 3.37
GEORGIA	-.152 0.26	1.10 4.98	-.148 0.86	.86 -2.69
HAWAII	.500 0.99	.846 6.25	-.260 0.96	.92 -.24
IDAHO	1.442 2.21	.582 2.88	-.733 2.40	.86 -1.46
ILLINOIS	.704 1.90	.742 4.65	-.157 3.18	.82 1.35
INDIANA	.625 1.77	.811 6.38	-.285 2.81	.95 -.56
IOWA	.411 1.22	.856 5.96	-.148 2.21	.91 -.12
KANSAS	.149 0.41	.992 7.08	-.150 1.74	.92 -.68
KENTUCKY	-.039 0.10	1.05 8.43	-.172 1.01	.95 -.07
LOUISIANA	.088 0.25	1.00 9.74	-.159 1.14	.93 -.42

MAINE	1.075 2.13	.635 3.53	-.432 2.39	.90 -1.30
MARYLAND	.415 1.78	.934 12.3	-.349 3.24	.96 -.57
MASSACHUSETTS	.332 1.39	.905 9.86	-.180 2.55	.96 0.95
MICHIGAN	.765 2.36	.821 8.26	-.412 3.57	.95 1.57
MINNESOTA	.676 2.22	.792 6.55	-.294 3.64	.92 -.41
MISSISSIPPI	.419 0.97	.906 6.17	-.423 2.06	.88 -.69
MISSOURI	.571 1.82	.791 5.93	-.150 2.40	.83 0.05
MONTANA	.726 1.21	.786 3.98	-.310 1.47	.84 -2.35
NEBRASKA	.240 0.54	.906 4.02	.069 1.09	.53 -1.06
NEVADA	.352 0.57	.885 5.13	-.165 0.43	.69 1.52
NEW HAMPSHIRE	.339 0.59	.879 4.44	-.140 0.66	.88 -.43
NEW JERSEY	.242 2.34	.963 23.6	-.207 7.53	.99 -.51
NEW MEXICO	.618 0.88	.814 4.05	-.323 0.96	.86 1.08
NEW YORK	.186 0.70	.938 8.69	-.063 1.52	.94 0.02
NORTH CAROLINA	-.059 0.19	1.03 8.98	-.070 0.59	.97 0.11
NORTH DAKOTA	.053 0.13	.959 4.71	0 -	.59 1.34
OHIO	1.620 2.34	.497 2.05	-.461 2.42	.56 -1.72

OKLAHOMA	.279 0.65	.918 6.32	-.147 1.06	.95 0.37
OREGON	1.170 1.87	.640 3.26	-.531 2.02	.94 0.58
PENNSYLVANIA	0.533 3.01	.864 13.9	-.288 5.05	.97 0.50
RHODE ISLAND	-.062 0.22	1.07 10.4	-.141 1.20	.91 -1.07
SOUTH CAROLINA	.267 0.57	.922 5.67	-.232 1.06	.87 0.37
SOUTH DAKOTA	.850 1.49	.642 2.68	-.226 1.50	.77 0.14
TENNESSEE	-.142 0.39	1.10 7.83	-.155 1.69	.92 -.05
TEXAS	.086 0.23	1.00 7.88	-.122 1.32	.95 -1.74
UTAH	.028 0.06	1.02 9.35	-.183 0.52	.95 -1.02
VERMONT	.923 2.26	.747 5.17	-.418 2.74	.80 0.51
VIRGINIA	-.101 0.26	1.05 8.14	-.070 0.44	.95 -.30
WASHINGTON	.325 1.24	.931 10.5	-.207 2.53	.97 0.28
WEST VIRGINIA	.464 1.31	.905 8.97	-.408 2.29	.96 0.07
WISCONSIN	-.035 0.11	1.04 9.92	-.087 0.83	.96 1.01
WYOMING	2.046 2.90	.232 0.87	-.508 2.69	.69 ?

APPENDIX 6.4

LFPR FOR 18-44 YEAR OLD FEMALES

The specification estimated is

$$^{3}\rho_i{}^{2}/\rho_i = a_0 + a_1({}^{3}\rho_i{}^{2}/\rho_i)_{-1} + a_2 BRATE_i .$$

The estimation sample period is 1959 to 1974. Coefficient a_1 should be positive and coefficient a_2 should be negative.

The first three columns in the table below give the estimated coefficients a_0, a_1 and a_2 with their t-statistics reported directly below. Using a five percent significance level, the critical value for the two-tailed test on a_0 is 2.160; the critical value for the one-tailed tests on a_1 and a_2 is 1.771.

The last column reports the squared coefficient of multiple correlation corrected for degrees of freedom and the Durbin- H statistic below that. Using a five percent test, significant autocorrelation is indicated when the absolute value of D-H is greater than 1.96. A '?' appears in those cases where the D-H is undefined.

STATE	a_0	a_1	a_2	$\bar{R}^2$/D-H
ALABAMA	.403 1.41	.761 4.08	-.967 1.49	.90 -1.38
ALASKA	.892 3.30	.274 1.26	0 -	.04 3.24

ARIZONA	.947 2.16	.464 1.85	-2.425 2.01	.92 ?
ARKANSAS	.498 2.04	.776 6.02	-1.723 2.19	.95 -1.00
CALIFORNIA	.779 3.71	.529 3.89	-2.183 4.02	.98 0.17
COLORADO	.745 2.17	.500 2.20	-1.497 1.82	.86 0.53
CONNECTICUT	.957 3.15	.280 1.19	-1.804 3.20	.92 3.91
DELAWARE	.690 2.16	.498 2.18	-.971 1.43	.63 -0.20
DIST. OF COLUMBIA	.289 1.17	.811 5.38	-.297 0.46	.84 0.73
FLORIDA	.149 0.80	.928 8.85	-.385 0.63	.95 0.99
GEORGIA	1.523 3.96	.082 0.34	-3.389 4.32	.93 4.25
HAWAII	.672 1.69	.549 2.21	-.237 0.37	.28 -0.89
IDAHO	.299 0.80	.858 4.23	-.863 0.75	.91 -2.46
ILLINOIS	.477 2.00	.686 4.29	-1.004 1.80	.95 2.00
INDIANA	.824 2.78	.504 2.73	-2.242 2.74	.96 -0.06
IOWA	.616 1.85	.614 2.92	-1.052 1.67	.95 -1.89
KANSAS	.461 2.42	.749 6.62	-1.379 2.40	.98 -0.87
KENTUCKY	1.236 3.44	.177 0.75	-2.256 2.94	.88 -1.09
LOUISIANA	.359 1.37	.762 3.96	-.749 1.46	.89 0.72

MAINE	.918 2.65	.443 2.00	-2.086 2.66	.90 2.33
MARYLAND	.510 2.28	.630 3.93	-.718 1.73	.93 0.10
MASSACHUSETTS	.647 1.89	.569 2.38	-1.302 2.01	.94 -0.14
MICHIGAN	.456 2.08	.707 4.92	-1.039 1.88	.97 0.12
MINNESOTA	.395 1.22	.759 3.72	-.705 1.11	.93 3.22
MISSISSIPPI	.440 1.43	.755 4.00	-.787 1.35	.77 1.89
MISSOURI	.651 2.88	.576 3.81	-1.211 2.79	.94 0.53
MONTANA	1.372 3.01	.220 0.82	-3.411 2.93	.87 ?
NEBRASKA	.461 1.19	.709 3.01	-.754 0.85	.89 -1.25
NEVADA	.799 2.72	.605 3.56	-3.105 2.80	.84 0.98
NEW HAMPSHIRE	.735 3.04	.515 3.28	-1.329 2.17	.82 0.05
NEW JERSEY	.521 1.55	.700 3.17	-1.833 1.81	.96 -0.64
NEW MEXICO	.597 1.37	.647 2.53	-1.014 1.13	.88 ?
NEW YORK	.231 1.04	.856 5.76	-.606 0.97	.95 0.45
NORTH CAROLINA	.742 2.04	.548 2.46	-1.377 1.87	.91 0.48
NORTH DAKOTA	.611 1.42	.667 3.08	-1.129 0.95	.84 2.20
OHIO	.525 1.62	.640 2.78	-1.230 1.59	.95 1.18

OKLAHOMA	.368 1.58	.821 5.99	-1.337 1.73	.94 -1.79
OREGON	.162 0.67	.877 5.92	-.033 0.05	.95 -1.04
PENNSYLVANIA	.422 1.80	.686 4.04	-.694 1.29	.90 -1.12
RHODE ISLAND	1.332 3.43	.193 0.77	-3.118 3.65	.86 ?
SOUTH CAROLINA	.327 1.07	.830 4.17	-.881 1.43	.81 -1.85
SOUTH DAKOTA	1.117 2.05	.365 1.23	-1.962 1.62	.80 ?
TENNESSEE	.332 1.10	.800 3.86	-.771 1.33	.88 -.032
TEXAS	.639 2.82	.631 4.53	-1.749 2.91	.98 -0.34
UTAH	1.230 4.06	.262 1.59	-2.322 2.93	.90 -0.96
VERMONT	.061 0.51	.954 8.68	0 -	.83 0.02
VIRGINIA	.688 2.04	.586 2.79	-1.657 2.04	.94 -1.95
WASHINGTON	.777 1.83	.467 1.55	-1.424 1.81	.84 ?
WEST VIRGINIA	.448 1.19	.709 2.59	-1.302 1.20	.77 ?
WISCONSIN	.734 2.97	.533 3.32	-1.388 2.82	.97 1.85
WYOMING	1.012 2.02	.339 1.14	-1.846 1.29	.44 ?

CHAPTER SEVEN: POPULATION PROJECTION TECHNIQUES

7.1 INTRODUCTION

In this chapter the various technologies available for projecting future population trends are discussed. These approaches may be categorized as naive approaches (extrapolation, ratio, land use), economic-base approaches and cohort-component approaches. Special attention will be given to the Bureau of Economic Analysis (BEA) economic-base model and the Bureau of the Census cohort-component model. In the final section of this chapter, the cohort-component method is extended from a single to a multiregion framework.

Many readers will be familiar with the material in this chapter and can quickly skim over it before moving on to Chapter Eight which describes the demographic accounts model used in ECESIS. Readers not familiar with demographic techniques should find this review useful for understanding some of the unique features of the ECESIS demographic model.

7.2 NAIVE METHODS

Under this heading the ratio, land use and extrapolation techniques will be discussed. The title naive refers not to the accuracy or mechanical complexity of these methods but rather to the amount of available information that the methods take advantage of.

7.2.1 RATIO

The ratio method assumes the existence of a population projection for some parent region. The population of a subregion is then calculated as a share of the parent region's projected population. For example, assume that the 1980 Census showed that the population of California was ten percent of the total U.S. population and that the Census Bureau had projected the 1985 U.S. population to be 250 million. A simple application of the ratio method would project the 1985 population of California to be twenty five million persons.

Various levels of sophistication may be used in order to project the ratios. The advantages of the method lie in its simplicity and parsimonious use of data. The ratio method is best suited for fairly small subregions where additional information is typically unavailable (Irwin 1972).

7.2.2 LAND USE

Land use techniques generally rely on assumptions about the maximum feasible population of an area. These assumptions may be based on local zoning ordinances, maximum housing density, average family size, etc. Once the relationship between population and ,say, housing density is established, new information on household construction may be used to project future population. As the local population approaches its maximum feasible level then growth in the area must slow down.

This approach is often quite useful for city and small area planners. The larger the region involved, the less useful are the land use techniques since land uses are more variable and substitutions of uses more prevalent in more aggregate areas.

7.2.3 EXTRAPOLATION

Mathematical extrapolation techniques range from simple arithmetic and geometric projections to sophisticated time-series methods.

Consider a model that projects next periods population by applying the most recently observed population growth rate to the current periods population.

$$(7.2.1) \qquad P_{t+1} = (P_t/P_{t-1}) \cdot P_t = g \cdot P_t$$

Rogers (1968) refers to the term g as the population "growth multiplier". Equation (7.2.1) is parsimonious with the data and may be used to produce projections well into the future. The method is naive, however, because it makes no use of other available data. For example, g may be decomposed into crude birth, death and net migration rates and these rates may be projected individually. This is the basis of the interregional components of change model which will be discussed later in this chapter. The remainder of this subsection is concerned with those methods that rely only on previous population figures.

Equation (7.2.1) may be modified to incorporate more information by estimating g via a simple regression model,

$$(7.2.2) \qquad P_t = b_0 + b_1 P_{t-1} + e_t,$$

where b_0 and b_1 are parameters to be estimated and e_t is a white noise series.

The most general specification in the class of models represented by (7.2.2) is the autoregressive integrated moving average (ARIMA) process. The general ARIMA model is written as,

$$(7.2.3) \qquad \Phi(\mathcal{L})(1-\mathcal{L})^d P_t = \Theta_0 + \Theta(\mathcal{L}) e_t.$$

ℓ is the lag operator such that, $\ell x_t = x_{t-1}$, $\ell^2 x_t = x_{t-2}$, etc. θ_0 is a constant and $\Phi(\ell)$ and $\theta(\ell)$ are p^{th} and q^{th} order polynomials in ℓ. I.e.,

$$\theta(\ell) = 1 + \theta_1 \ell + \theta_2 \ell^2 + \cdots + \theta_q \ell^q.$$

The term $(1-\ell)^d$ represents a dth order difference. Equation (7.2.3) is denoted as an ARIMA(p,d,q) model.

Voss, Palit, Kale and Krebs (1981) have estimated ARIMA(1,1,0) models for each of the states in the U.S. The ARIMA(1,1,0) model may be written as,

$$(7.2.4) \qquad P_t = \theta_0 + (1+\Phi)P_{t-1} - \Phi P_{t-2} + e_t,$$

or,

$$P_t = b_0 + b_1 P_{t-1} + b_2 P_{t-2} + e_t.$$

Equation (7.2.4) may be estimated using simple least squares with the restriction that $b_1 + b_2 = 1$. This model is simple and easy to use and after extensive evaluation Voss et al. (1981) conclude that "... this strategy produces population forecasts at least as reliable as more traditional demographic models (p. 53)."

The ARIMA technique is powerful and simple to use. Like all naive techniques, ARIMA models may be criticized for their lack of attention to demographic theory and the highly aggregated nature of their forecasts.

7.3 ECONOMIC-BASE METHODS

Economic-base population projection techniques are based on the assumption that economic variables play a key role in the determination of demographic variables. Early work by Sjaastad (1962) and Lowry (1966) has led to a particular emphasis of this relationship in the area of migration. Many studies (see Greenwood 1975) indicate that migration in and out of a region is influenced by relative employment opportunities in that and other regions. Since migration is the most volatile of the components in the basic demographic equation, economic variables must play an important role in regional population variations.

The most widely known economic-base population projection model is the one used by the U.S. Bureau of Economic Analysis to project regional populations (Friedenberg, Bretzfelder, Johnson, and Trott 1980). In the BEA model, which is also used to project income and employment, population is divided into three broad age groups: pre-labor pool (ages 0-14), labor pool (ages 15-64), and post-labor pool (ages 65 and over). The labor pool population in each state is projected as follows. The ratio of the state's labor pool population to total employment in the state is calculated as a percent of the same ratio for the nation as a whole. This compound ratio is projected on the basis of its historical trend. Next this projected ratio is multiplied with the nation's labor pool population to employment ratio (determined independently) to obtain the projected labor pool population to employment ratio for the state. This ratio is in turn multiplied by the projected employment for the state (determined in a previous step independently of population) to obtain the projected labor pool population for the state.

Given state level birth and death rates, last periods labor pool population and this periods projected labor pool population, the net migration of the labor pool population may be determined from the basic demographic equation,

$$NM = P - P_{-1} + D,$$

where NM is net migration, P is population and D is deaths.[1]

The pre-labor pool population projection is based on this net migration of the labor pool population (parents). The post-labor pool population is projected on the basis of the state's historical trend. Finally, the population groups are constrained to add up across states to the national population projections made by the Census Bureau.

The BEA technique is extremely simple and parsimonious with data requirements. The population projections are based entirely on the employment projections which are

---

[1] There are no births into the labor force age groups.

arrived at by an independent procedure. This has the advantage of capturing the influences of economic variables on interstate population movements. On the other hand, virtually none of the detailed accounting information available for demographic techniques is used in the BEA approach.

An attempt to incorporate more demographic information into the projection technique without introducing a large demographic accounts model was made by Ballard, Gustely and Wendling (1980) in the National Regional Impact Evaluation System (NRIES). Starting from the basic demographic equation for a region,

$$P_t = P_{t-1} + B_t - D_t + NM_t,$$

Ballard et al. make use of the fact that births and deaths are primarily functions of the size of the population and that net migration is primarily a function of employment and income in the region relative to the U.S. as a whole. Thus, working age population may be determined from the regression,

$$P_t = b_0 + b_1 P_{t-1} + b_2 E_t + b_3 Y_t + e_t,$$

where E and Y are some functions of employment and income. Other age groups take more account of demographic data and less of economic data. While the NRIES specifications certainly make more use of demographic information than the BEA model, the approach is still open to the criticism of making little use of available detailed demographic accounting information.

7.4 SINGLE REGION COHORT-COMPONENT METHODS

Demographers have an advantage over most other social scientists in that they are able to devise a very elaborate demographic accounting system. After all, people are born, they get older in a predictable way, they move around and they die. Unfortunately, not all of this process is well documented--particularly population movements. The cohort-component method attempts to make maximum use of this accounting structure and the available demographic data.

Once again, the basic demographic equation for a region is,

$$P = P_{-1} + B - D + NM,$$

where P is current population, P_{-1} is last periods population, B is total births during the period, D is total deaths during the period, and NM is the difference between the number of people moving into the region (inmigrants) and the number of people moving out of the region (outmigrants) during the period. The components of change of a region's population are births, deaths and net migration,

$$\Delta P = P - P_{-1} = B - D + NM.$$

The cohort-component method estimates the components of change for specific population subgroups and applies those changes to that subgroup as it moves through time. For example, white males aged 30 to 34 years in 1980 may be identified as a particular cohort. By the year 1985, all members of this cohort will be either white males aged 35 to 39 years or they will have died. Generally the time interval for the projection period is equal to the age width of the cohorts. Thus with cohorts spanning five year age groups projections will be made for five year intervals. In this way the entire cohort is aged to the next age group each period.

The U.S. Bureau of the Census state level population projection model (U. S. Bureau of the Census 1979, #796) is an excellent example of a single region cohort-component model. The Census model disaggregates state populations by five year age groups, sex and two race groups. The projections are done for five year intervals starting from the most recent decennial census. The state projections are dependent upon the national population projections for such values as national fertility and survival rates and total

U.S. population (see Long 1981).

The most recent population projections released by the Census were made in 1977 (#796). The first stage in the projection process is to multiply the end of last periods population in each cohort by a survival rate for that particular cohort to obtain a survived state population. The survival rates are calculated by forming the ratio of actual deaths in a state for some recent historical period to deaths predicted for that state by applying national survival rates to the state's population. These ratios are assumed to approach one linearly by the year 2020. The product of this ratio and the projected national survival rate is the projected survival rate for that state. A final adjustment is made to ensure that the sum of deaths in each state equals the projected national deaths. The survived state population is then disaggregated into three subgroups: state military population, state college population, and state civilian noncollege (CNC) population. The special military and college populations are treated separately because of the substantially different migration rates attributable to these groups (Long 1983).

The survived state CNC population may now either join the military, enroll in college, migrate to another state or remain in the same state. Similarly, the military and college populations may remain in their special groups, leave the group and move to another state or leave the group and remain in the same state. Interstate migration of the military and college populations in determined by historical data and is assumed to remain constant throughout the projection period. The state CNC population is migrated via a two-step procedure. Outmigration rates by age, race and sex are calculated from historical data and are assumed to remain constant. These outmigration rates are applied to the survived CNC population of each state to obtain a migrant "pool". The number of inmigrants allocated back to each state is a fixed proportion, determined from the most recently available historical data, of the total migrant pool. Individuals leaving the military or college populations during the period are assumed to migrate in the same proportion as the state CNC population.

Since the rates are age, race and sex specific, the projected net migration of a state is dependent upon the population distribution of all of the states. If a state's population is growing faster than average its contribution to the migrant pool becomes proportionally larger over time. That state's share of inmigrants, however, is a constant proportion. Thus, there is a tendency for this method to project converging net migration rates over time.

After each of the special population groups has been migrated they are added up again to obtain a survived-migrated state population. The youngest cohort is determined from the number of births during the period. Fertility rates are extrapolated in a similar fashion to survival rates. The ratio of state births to total U.S. births is calculated for some historical period. These ratios are assumed to linearly approach unity by the year 2020. The product of these ratios and the previously projected U.S. fertility rates determine the state's projected fertility rates. As with deaths, the sum of the births across all states is constrained to equal total births projected for the U.S. Finally, net immigrants to the U.S. are allocated to the states according to an historical pattern.

The cohort-component model is a powerful forecasting tool because it exploits to the fullest the basic demographic accounting relationships. The Census model is a fairly complete version of a cohort-component model. Unlike the BEA model, however, the Census model makes very little use of economic data that may help to explain some demographic trends and improve the accuracy of the projections. The BEA model omits demographic accounts data in an attempt to keep the model as small and simple as possible. The Census decision to use a pure demographic approach is also the result of policy.

The Census Bureau uses a conservative approach to its projections. For example, fertility and survival rates are not projected on the basis of an existing long historical time-series, but rather on the most recent observation alone. When there is doubt concerning the trend of a rate, that rate is simply held constant. Typically the Census Bureau will provide three or more projection series reflecting different fertility, mortality and migration assumptions. None of these projections is deemed more likely than another. This approach is appropriate given the Census Bureau's philosophy concerning projections. The latest state projections released by the Census include the proviso, "... series in this report are projections or extensions of recent trends, rather than forecasts of population levels expected to occur. ... Relatively minor changes in economic, social, or demographic conditions in any State can cause actual population change to deviate from the projected trends (U.S. Bureau of the Census 1977, #796, p. 3)." The Census Bureau sees its role as one of data collection and dissemination--not explanation or forecasting.

7.5 INTERREGIONAL COHORT-COMPONENT METHODS

A major weakness of the single region cohort-component model is that there is no mechanism built into the system to force consistency across all of the regions. The multiregion cohort-component model addresses this problem by simultaneously determining the demographic variables of each region and accounting for all constraints to the system (Stone 1971; Rogers 1968 and 1975; McMillen and Land 1980; McMillen 1980).

Denote the population of region r in age group a at time period t as,[2]

$$P(r,a,t),\ r=1,\ldots,R;\ a=1,\ldots,A.$$

For region r, P(r,a,t) for a=2,...,A-1 may be determined by,

$$(7.5.1)\quad P(r,a,t) = s(r,a-1,t)\cdot P(r,a-1,t-1) + NM(r,a,t),$$

where s(r,a-1,t) is the survival rate of age group a-1 in region r during the period t-1 to t, and NM(r,a,t) is the number of net migrants into region r of age group a during the period t-1 to t.[3] The first term on the right-hand-side of (7.5.1) represents the number of people in region r who survived during the time period to move into the next older age group.

The first (a=1) and last (a=A) age groups require special attention. The only way to enter the first age group is to

---

[2] Sex and race detail could easily be added.

[3] Expression (7.5.1) assumes that the interval a to a-1 is equal to the interval t to t-1 so that the entire cohort is moved into the next age group during the time interval.

be born during the time period. Let $b(r,a,t)$ denote the crude birth rate of people in age group a in region r at time t. Then,

$$(7.5.2)\quad P(r,1,t) = \textstyle\sum_a b(r,a,t)\cdot P(r,a,t-1) + NM(r,1,t).$$

The last term in (7.5.2) represents the net inmigration of infants into region r during the period t-1 to t. The last age group must be open ended, thus two survival terms are required.

$$(7.5.3)\quad P(r,A,t) = s(r,A-1,t)\cdot P(r,A-1,t-1) + s(r,A,t)\cdot P(r,A,t-1) + NM(r,A,t).$$

The expressions (7.5.1)-(7.5.3) may be written more concisely using matrix notation. Let $S(r,t)$ be the AxA survival matrix of region r in period t. Then,

$$(7.5.4)\quad S(r,t)=\begin{bmatrix} b(r,1,r) & b(r,2,t) & \cdots & b(r,A-1,t) & b(r,A,t) \\ s(r,1,t) & 0 & \cdots & 0 & 0 \\ 0 & s(r,2,t) & \cdots & 0 & 0 \\ \cdot & \cdot & \cdots & \cdot & \cdot \\ \cdot & \cdot & \cdots & \cdot & \cdot \\ 0 & 0 & \cdots & 0 & 0 \\ 0 & 0 & \cdots & s(r,A-1,t) & s(r,A,t) \end{bmatrix}$$

Let $P(r,*,t)$ denote the Ax1 vector of populations in the

various age groups in region r at time t, and let NM(r,*,r) denote the AX1 vector of net inmigrants for region r during the interval from t-1 to t. Expressions (7.5.1)-(7.5.3) may be summarized as,

$$(7.5.5) \quad P(r,*,t) = S(r,t)\cdot P(r,*,t-1) + NM(r,*,t).$$

For example, a system with three age groups (A=3) would be,

$$\begin{bmatrix} P(r,1,t) \\ P(r,2,t) \\ P(r,3,t) \end{bmatrix} = \begin{bmatrix} b(r,1,t) & b(r,2,t) & b(r,3,t) \\ s(r,1,t) & 0 & 0 \\ 0 & s(r,2,t) & s(r,3,t) \end{bmatrix} \begin{bmatrix} P(r,1,t-1) \\ P(r,2,t-1) \\ P(r,3,t-1) \end{bmatrix} + \begin{bmatrix} NM(r,1,t) \\ NM(r,2,t) \\ NM(r,3,t) \end{bmatrix}$$

The multiregion cohort-component model may be derived by simply "stacking" the single region models of (7.5.5) for each of the R regions. Let,

$$(7.5.6) \quad P(*,*,t) = \begin{bmatrix} P(1,*,t) \\ P(2,*,t) \\ \cdot \\ \cdot \\ P(R,*,t) \end{bmatrix}, \text{ and}$$

$$NM(*,*,t) = \begin{bmatrix} NM(1,*,t) \\ NM(2,*,t) \\ \cdot \\ \cdot \\ NM(R,*,t) \end{bmatrix}$$

denote the RAX1 vectors of populations and net migrations for all of the age groups in all of the R regions. Let,

(7.5.7)
$$S(*,t) = \begin{bmatrix} S(1,t) & 0 & \dots & 0 \\ 0 & S(2,t) & \dots & 0 \\ \cdot & \cdot & \dots & \cdot \\ 0 & 0 & \dots & S(R,t) \end{bmatrix}$$

denote the RA×RA block diagonal matrix of survival rates. The diagonal elements of S(*,t) are simply the A×A S(r,t) survival matrices of (7.5.4). The entire multiregion system may be written as,

(7.5.8) $P(*,*,t) = S(*,t) \cdot P(*,*,t-1) + NM(*,*,t).$

Since S(*,t) is block diagonal, the only interaction among the regions occurs in the vector of net migrants, NM(*,*,t). In order to make (7.5.8) truly interregional, this vector must be incorporated into the multiregion survival matrix S(*,t). Let, M(s,r,a,t), denote the number of people who move from region s to region r during the period t-1 to t and who end up in age group a. The population "at risk" of making this move is P(s,a-1,t-1). thus the migration rate from region s to region r for age group a is defined as,[4]

(7.5.9) $m(s,r,a,t) = M(s,r,a,t)/P(s,a-1,t-1)$.

The vector of inmigrants from s to r for all groups may be written in matrix notation as,

$$\begin{bmatrix} M(s,r,1,t) \\ M(s,r,2,t) \\ \cdot \\ M(s,r,A-1,t) \\ M(s,r,A,t) \end{bmatrix} = \begin{bmatrix} 0 & 0 & \cdots & 0 & 0 \\ m(s,r,2,t) & 0 & \cdots & 0 & 0 \\ \cdot & \cdot & \cdots & \cdot & \cdot \\ 0 & 0 & \cdots & 0 & 0 \\ 0 & 0 & \cdots & m(s,r,A,t) & m(s,r,A,t) \end{bmatrix} \times \begin{bmatrix} P(s,1,t-1) \\ P(s,2,t-1) \\ \cdot \\ P(s,A-1,t-1) \\ P(s,A,t-1) \end{bmatrix}$$

Or using compact notation,

(7.5.10) $M(s,r,*,t) = m(s,r,*,t) \cdot P(s,*,t-1)$,

---

[4] Clearly something different must be done for migration of infants. This will be discussed later.

where $M(s,r,*,t)$ and $P(s,*,t-1)$ are the $A\times1$ vectors of migrants from s to r and population of region s, and $m(s,r,*,t)$ is the $A\times A$ matrix with migration rates from s to r along the lower principal diagonal and zeros elsewhere.

Total inmigration (by age groups) for region r would be,

$$\sum_s M(s,r,*,t) = \sum_s m(s,r,*,t)\cdot P(s,*,t-1).$$

Similarly, total outmigration by age from region r would be,

$$(7.5.11)\quad \sum_s M(r,s,*,t) = \sum_s m(r,s,*,t)\cdot P(r,*,t-1).$$

Define the $RA\times RA$ matrix of migration rates as,

$$(7.5.12)\quad m(*,*,*,t)=\begin{bmatrix} 0 & m(2,1,*,t) & m(3,1,*,t) & \dots & m(R,1,*,t) \\ m(1,2,*,t) & 0 & m(3,2,*,t) & \dots & m(R,2,*,t) \\ . & . & . & . & . \\ . & . & . & . & . \\ m(1,R,*,t) & m(2,R,*,t) & m(3,R,*,t) & \dots & 0 \end{bmatrix}$$

Adding the survivorship matrix of (7.5.7) to the migration matrix of (7.5.12) yields the overall $RA\times RA$ population growth matrix operator G,

$$(7.5.13)\quad G(t) = \begin{bmatrix} S(1,t) & m(2,1,*,t) & \dots & m(R,1,*,t) \\ m(1,2,*,t) & S(2,t) & \dots & m(R,2,*,t) \\ . & . & . & . \\ . & . & . & . \\ m(1,R,*,t) & m(2,R,*,t) & \dots & S(R,t) \end{bmatrix}$$

The final form of the interregional cohort-component model, using condensed notation, is,

(7.5.14) $P(*,*,t) = G(t)\cdot P(*,*,t-1)$.

The unknowns in (7.5.14) are the various birth, death and migration rates that are embedded in the growth matrix G(t). As with the simple components of change model, the easiest method of projecting population using (7.5.14) is to assume fixed rates and use the most recently observed historical rates in the matrix G(t). Thus,

$$P(*,*,t+1) = G(t)\cdot P(*,*,t).$$

The major emphasis of economic-demographic analysis is to find more sophisticated methods for predicting these crucial rates.

The basic system (7.5.14) may be an open or closed system depending upon whether deaths are recorded at the beginning of the next period or at the beginning of the current period (McMillen and Land 1980; Land and McMillen 1981). Also, this framework has more general applications in social accounting (McMillen 1980, Chapt. 6).

CHAPTER EIGHT: THE DEMOGRAPHIC MODEL

8.1 INTRODUCTION

The core of the ECESIS demographic model is an interregional cohort-component accounts model. In principle, demographic accounting is similar to double-entry bookkeeping; for a given period, total debits must equal total credits. The units of account are people and debits are outflows from the population and credits are inflows into the population.

Recall that the basic demographic equation is,

$$(8.1.1) \qquad P_{i,t} = P_{i,t-1} + B_{i,t} - D_{i,t} + I_{i,t} - O_{i,t},$$

where $P_{i,t}$ is population in period t in region i, $P_{i,t-1}$ is population in region i at the end of period t-1, and $B_{i,t}$, $D_{i,t}$, $I_{i,t}$ and $O_{i,t}$ are births, deaths, inmigrants and outmigrants during period t for region i. The accounting framework can be emphasized by rearranging (8.1.1) as,

$$(8.1.2) \qquad P_{i,t-1} + B_{i,t} + I_{i,t} = P_{i,t} + D_{i,t} + O_{i,t},$$

where the left-hand-side represents inflows (credits) and the right-hand-side represents outflows (debits).

When gross in- and outmigrant flows are further disaggregated by specific origins and destinations, the accounts model enters the class of interregional demographic accounts models.

The process is complicated, but essentially unchanged, when age, sex and racial detail are added to the populations.

Interregional cohort-component demographic accounts models follow a population cohort (specific age, sex and race group) through time and spatial location.

The components of change (births, deaths and migration), loosely referred to as "state" changes, are the key elements to be modelled. The system may be an "open" or a "closed" accounting system depending on whether the beginning period population undergoes state changes before or after deaths are recorded (Land and McMillen 1981; McMillen and Land 1980; McMillen 1980).

The accounts model is not self-contained. Fertility, mortality and migration rates required to model the state changes must be provided for the accounting model. The determination of these rates is considered in the next chapter. The remainder of this chapter provides a detailed description of the ECESIS interregional cohort-component demographic accounts model.

8.2 A VERBAL DESCRIPTION

Implementing the type of double-entry accounting model described in the introduction is not simply a matter of collecting and reorganizing existing census and vital statistics data. Current data collection and administration techniques produce data that are inconsistent with the double entry accounting concept; outflows do not equal inflows. The demographic model used in ECESIS is a variation of the spatial accounting framework developed by Rees and Wilson (1977). This technique recognizes and corrects inconsistancies in demographic data.

Migration statistics often do not include individuals who are born during the time period. For example, migration questions that ask, "Where did you live X years ago?" cannot include those of age under X. This deficiency can be corrected by estimating infant migrants. Infant migrants that inmigrate and survive are added to the inmigration total in ECESIS and infants migrants that outmigrate are added to the outmigration total whether they survive or not.

Death statistics are inflated by the inclusion of deaths to inmigrants. Since the beginning period population is changed in the basic equation by subtracting deaths occurring to those people in the region at the beginning of the period, deaths of inmigrants must be estimated and subtracted from the actual death statistics. Deaths to inmigrants born during the period should also be subtracted from total deaths. Similarly, outmigration statistics only include those migrants who have survived until the end of the period. The number of outmigrants who die before the end of the period must be estimated and added to the outmigration statistics. To illustrate, a person who moves from New York to Florida and then dies during the period incorrectly appears as a loss of population to Florida rather than to New York. The procedures used in ECESIS assign such deaths correctly.

The modified accounting equation is,

$$POP_{i,t}=POP_{i,t-1}+B_{i,t}-(D_{i,t}-ID_{i,t}-IBD_{i,t})$$
$$+(I_{i,t}+IB_{i,t})-(O_{i,t}+OB_{i,t}+OBD_{i,t}+OD_{i,t}),$$

where $IB_{i,t}$ is the number of inmigrants to i born during the period (t-1,t), $OB_{i,t}$ is the outmigrants from i born during the period, $ID_{i,t}$ is the inmigrants to i who die before t, $OD_{i,t}$ is outmigrants from i who die before t, $IBD_{i,t}$ is inmigrants to i born during the period who die before t, $OBD_{i,t}$ is outmigrants from i born during the period who die before t, and the remaining variables are defined as before. No data are available on the terms, IB, OB, ID, OD, IBD, and OBD. Therefore, these so-called minor flows must be estimated for each age-sex group.

For many states, the magnitude of the minor flows is likely to be small. For particular states and age groups, however, the effects may be significant. For example, seven percent of Florida's population over 65 in 1976 had moved there during the previous year. Given data on death rates, the implication is that over three percent of all deaths in the over 65 age group represents deaths to inmigrants.

An important feature of the demographic accounts in ECESIS is the calculation of appropriate populations for use in calculating and applying the fertility, mortality and migration rates. In historical use with existing data on actual births and deaths, the demographic accounts compute accurate rates by dividing by an appropriate population. For projections, given demographic rates (either from a model or from rates calculated by using the accounts historically), these rates are applied to the appropriate population to obtain correctly defined projections of births, deaths, migration and minor flows.

The "appropriate population" for the computation of rates in the historical mode and the application of rates in the projection mode is defined as the at-risk population. It may be thought of as including anyone in the state at any time during the period multiplied by the fraction of the time period for which that person was in the state. For example, the at-risk population for deaths is estimated by including all surviving stayers, ½ of surviving outmigrants, ½ of surviving inmigrants, ¼ of nonsurviving inmigrants, ¼ of nonsurviving outmigrants, and ½ of nonmoving nonsurvivors. Since the population is disaggregated by age in ECESIS care must be taken to account not only for individuals remaining in the same age group during the period (using the factions above), but also for individuals entering and leaving the age group during the period (in both cases, by assuming that they change age groups halfway through the period).

As another example, the population at-risk of giving birth in a state should include women of childbearing age who migrate into a state. Migrating women who survive will appear, on average, in the at-risk population of both the origin and destination states for half of the time period. Migrating women who survive and are aged into a nonchild-bearing age group are at-risk of giving birth in the destination region for one fourth of the time period.

At-risk coefficients may be thought of as the product of three separate coefficients: (1) the proportion of the time period which the individual was alive, (2) the proportion of the time alive spent in a given age group, and (3) the proportion of time alive in an age group which is spent in a given region. Special care must be taken in computing at-risk populations for the first and last age groups since individuals cannot age into the first age group or out of the last age group.

Population in ECESIS is disaggregated by sex and by the age groups: 0-4, 5-17, 18-44, 45-64, and 65 and over. Since ECESIS is an annual model and the age groups are broader than one year, the number of persons leaving and entering each age group must be estimated for each year. No population data are available by single year of age at the state level so U.S. population totals by sex for single year age groups are used to determine the proportion of individuals changing age groups during the year. These proportions are applied evenly to all states.

Migration in ECESIS is determined by a modified Markov model (see Chapter Nine for a complete description). Each age-sex group is modelled separately with the labor force age groups modelled as a function of the relative economic attractivity of a region. Potential migrants weigh all possible destinations and choose the best of the alternative opportunities.

The version of the Rees-Wilson model used in ECESIS is modified to use gross in- and outmigration totals rather than place-to-place flows. This change economizes data requirements without sacrificing the detail of information available from the model.

Births are estimated by applying the 1975 state birth rates to the population at-risk of giving birth. State level births are then disaggregated by sex by applying the observed national sex ratio (51.33 percent males) to all states. State births (sex disaggregated) are then proportionally adjusted to be consistent with actual U.S. male and female births during the projection period. Thus, the 1975 rates are used as a base to calculate births in other years, but proportional adjustment of the resulting births serves to capture changing birth rates on both state and national levels.

Deaths are estimated by applying the observed 1975 age-sex specific state death rates to the at-risk population in each state. Like births, these figures are then proportionally adjusted to be consistent with U.S. male and female deaths. Because deaths are age-sex disaggregated and national controls are only sex disaggregated, this adjustment must be carried out in two steps. First, the difference between the estimated national total and and the control is allocated for each sex to states in proportion to the state's share of national deaths. Next, the age-sex disaggregated deaths within each state are adjusted to conform with the new state level deaths for each sex by allocating the numbers from the first step to age groups in proportion to the state age group's share of total deaths in the state.

Finally, net foreign immigration is added to the population by assuming a constant 400,000 immigrants per year. Immigrants are allocated to states based on the state of intended residence of immigrants in 1972 and 1973 according to data provided by the Immigration and Naturalization Services. The intended residence is used in ECESIS, rather than the residence observed as much as five years later by the census, because immigrants revise their plans in part on the basis of economic opportunities. Their reaction to those opportunities is modelled endogenously using the migration equations.

8.3 A MATHEMATICAL DESCRIPTION

The following step by step description illustrates the ECESIS version of the Rees and Wilson spatial demographic accounting approach. The procedure uses an iterative algorithm that continues until some prespecified level of convergence in the population flows is achieved. Any values that are unknown in the first iteration are set to zero and then updated in subsequent iterations. For ease of comparison, the notation of Rees and Wilson has been adopted for this section. Table 8.3.1 summarizes this notation; for simplicity the subscript for sex is omitted.

TABLE 8.3.1

DEMOGRAPHIC ACCOUNTS NOTATION

NOTATION	DESCRIPTION
K	capital k's represent final or actual population counts
k	small k's represent at-risk populations
$K_{s-1,s}^{ii}$	number of people in region i and age group s-1 at time t who are in region i and age group s at time t+1
$K_{s-1,s}^{id(i)}$	number of people in region i and age group s-1 at time t who die in region i in age group s
$K_{s-1,s}^{ij}$	number of people in region i and in age group s-1 at time t who migrate to region j and survive to age group s at time t+1
$K_{s-1,s}^{id(j)}$	number of people in region i and in age group s-1 at time t who migrate to region j and die in age group s before time t+1
$K_{rs}^{b(i)i}$	number of births in region i during (t,t+1) which survive to age group s in region i at t+1 and whose mothers are in age group r at time t
$K_{rs}^{b(i)j}$	number of births in region i during (t,t+1) which migrate to j and survive to age group s and are born to mothers in age group r at time t
$K_{rs}^{b(i)d(i)}$	number of births in region i to mothers in age group r at time t which die in region i in age group s before t+1
$K_{rs}^{b(i)d(j)}$	number of births in region i to mothers in age group r at time t which migrate to j and die there in age group s before t+1

TABLE 8.3.1 (Continued)

DEMOGRAPHIC ACCOUNTS NOTATION

NOTATION	DESCRIPTION
K_{r*}^{i*}	total population in region i and in age group r at time t
K_{*r}^{*i}	total population in region i and in age group r at time t+1
δ_{*s}^{*i}	death rate to age group s in region i during (t,t+1)
β_{*s}^{*i}	birth rate in region i during (t,t+1) to mothers age s at time of birth
k_{*s}^{di}	number of people at-risk of dying in region i and age group s at time t+1
k_{*s}^{bi}	number of people in age group s at-risk of giving birth in region i at time t+1

STEP 1: INITIAL VALUES

The procedure starts with beginning period population (K_{t*}^{i*}), death rates (δ_{*s}^{*i}), birth rates (β_{*s}^{*i}), inmigration ($\sum_j K_{*s}^{ij}$) and outmigration ($\sum_j K_{*s}^{ji}$), for each age and sex group by state.[1]

---

[1] The determination of the birth and death rates and in- and outmigration are discussed in the next chapter.

STEP 2: DISAGGREGATE MIGRANTS

Separate in- and outmigrants into those who change age groups during the year and those who do not.

(S2.1) $\Sigma_j K_{rs}{}^{ij} = q_{rs}\Sigma_j K_{*s}{}^{ij}$

(S2.2) $\Sigma_j K_{rs}{}^{ji} = q_{rs}\Sigma_j K_{*s}{}^{ji}$; r=s-1,s; s=1,...5.

The proportion of people in age group s at time t+1 who are in age group r at time t is given by q_{rs}.

(S2.3) $q_{rs} = K_{rs}{}^{**}/K_{*s}{}^{**}$,

where ** denotes the U.S. population. The proportion of individuals 0-4 at time t+1 who were born during the year (t,t+1) is denoted by coefficient q_{01}. This coefficient is applied to available migration data for the 0-4 age group to obtain an estimate of the migration of infants.

STEP 3: COMPUTE AT-RISK POPULATIONS

The population at-risk of dying in region i is,

(S3.1) $k_{*s}{}^{di} = k_{s-1,s}{}^{di} + k_{ss}{}^{di}$; s=1,...,5.

Where the first term on the right is the at-risk population which changes age groups during the period. This term is calculated as,

$$(S3.2)\quad k_{s-1,s}^{di} = \theta_1 K_{s-1,s}^{ii} + \theta_2 K_{s-1,s}^{id(i)} + \theta_3 \Sigma_j K_{s-1,s}^{ij} + \theta_4 \Sigma_j K_{s-1,s}^{id(j)} + \theta_5 \Sigma_j K_{s-1,s}^{ji} + \theta_6 \Sigma_j K_{s-1,s}^{jd(i)};\quad s=2,\ldots,5.$$

The first two terms on the right-hand-side of the equation represent the number of people in region i and age group s-1 at time t who survive and remain in region i in age group s or who die in age group s in region i before period t+1. The next two terms represent outmigrants from region i who age from age group s-1 to age group s and either survive or die in region j. The final two terms are similarly defined for inmigrants to region i who change age groups during the period.

The second term on the right side of (S3.1) represents the population at-risk of dying in region i which begin the period in age group s. This term may be calculated as,

$$(S3.3)\quad k_{ss}^{di} = \theta_{27} K_{ss}^{ii} + \theta_{28} \Sigma_j K_{ss}^{ij} + \theta_{29} \Sigma_j K_{ss}^{ji} + \theta_8 K_{ss}^{id(i)} + \theta_{11} \Sigma_j K_{ss}^{id(j)} + \theta_{13} \Sigma_j K_{ss}^{jd(i)} + \theta_7 K_{s,s+1}^{ii} + \theta_{10} \Sigma_j K_{s,s+1}^{ij} + \theta_{15} \Sigma_j K_{s,s+}^{ji} + \theta_9 K_{s,s+1}^{id(i)} + \theta_{12} \Sigma_j K_{s,s+1}^{id(j)} + \theta_{14} \Sigma_j K_{s,s+1}^{jd(i)};\quad s=1,\ldots,4.$$

This expression consists of those people who are in age group s at time t and spend at least part of the period in region i. This group in turn may be divided into those people who survive until period t+1--the first three terms of (S3.3)--and those people who do not survive until period t+1--the fourth through sixth terms of (S3.3). In addition, those people who age from age group s to age group s+1 during the period spend at least part of the period in age group s and thus are at-risk of dying during the period while in age group s. The seventh through ninth terms of (S3.3) represent the portion of this latter group who survive to period t+1 while the tenth through twelfth terms represent those who do not survive until period t+1. Note that each set of three terms includes people who start in region i at time t and remain there until time t+1 and those people who migrate out of and into region i. All of these people spend some portion of the period (t,t+1) in age group s and in region i and are thus part of the population at-risk of dying in age group s and region i. Since all of these groups spend varying amounts of time in the at-risk group, they must be weighted accordingly. The θ's in (S3.2) and (S3.3) represent the proportion of the time period spent alive in age group s in region i. Following Rees and Wilson, it is convenient to divide this coefficient into three components:

ψ_1 - the proportion of the time period which the individual was alive,

ψ_2 - the proportion of the time alive which was spent in age group s,

ψ_3 - proportion of time alive in age group s which is spent in region i.

The θ's are the products of these three components. Table 8.3.2 details the ψ and θ coefficients and shows to which term each θ applies.

TABLE 8.3.2

Coefficients for Computation of At-Risk Populations

θ_i	Coefficient of	ψ_1	ψ_2	ψ_3	θ
θ_1	$K_{s-1,s}{}^{ii}$	1	.5	1	.5
θ_2	$K_{s-1,s}{}^{id(i)}$	.5	.5	1	.25
θ_3	$\sum_j K_{s-1,s}{}^{ij}$	1	.5	.5	.25
θ_4	$\sum_j K_{s-1,s}{}^{id(j)}$	.5	.5	.5	.125
θ_5	$\sum_j K_{s-1,s}{}^{ji}$	1	.5	.5	.25
θ_6	$\sum_j K_{s-1\,s}{}^{jd(i)}$	.5	.5	.5	.125
θ_7	$K_{s,s+1}{}^{ii}$	1	.5	1	.5
θ_8	$K_{ss}{}^{id(i)}$	.5	1	1	.5
θ_9	$K_{s,s+1}{}^{id(i)}$	.5	.5	1	.25
θ_{10}	$\sum_j K_{s,s+1}{}^{ij}$	1	.5	.5	.25
θ_{11}	$\sum_j K_{ss}{}^{id(j)}$	.5	1	.5	.25
θ_{12}	$\sum_j K_{s,s+1}{}^{id(j)}$	.5	.5	.5	.125
θ_{13}	$\sum_j K_{ss}{}^{jd(i)}$	.5	1	.5	.25
θ_{14}	$\sum_j K_{s,s+1}{}^{jd(i)}$	.5	.5	.5	.125
θ_{15}	$\sum_j K_{s,s+1}{}^{ji}$	1	.5	.5	.25
θ_{16}	$K_{*1}{}^{b(i)i}$	.5	1	1	.5
θ_{17}	$K_{*1}{}^{b(i)d(i)}$	.25	1	1	.25
θ_{18}	$\sum_j K_{*1}{}^{b(i)j}$	.5	1	.5	.25
θ_{19}	$\sum_j K_{*1}{}^{b(i)d(j)}$	.25	1	.5	.125
θ_{20}	$\sum_j K_{*1}{}^{b(j)i}$	.5	1	.5	.25
θ_{21}	$\sum_j K_{*1}{}^{b(j)d(i)}$	.25	1	.5	.125

TABLE 8.3.2 (Continued)

Coefficients for Computation of At-Risk Populations

θ_i	Coefficient of	ψ_1	ψ_2	ψ_3	θ
θ_{22}	$K_{55}^{id(i)}$	.5	1	1	.5
θ_{23}	$\sum_j K_{55}^{ij}$	1	1	.5	.5
θ_{24}	$\sum_j K_{55}^{id(j)}$	.5	1	.5	.25
θ_{25}	$\sum_j K_{55}^{ji}$	1	1	.5	.5
θ_{26}	$\sum_j K_{55}^{jd(i)}$	.5	1	.5	.25
θ_{27}	K_{ss}^{ii}	1	1	1	1
θ_{28}	$\sum_j K_{ss}^{ij}$	1	1	.5	.5
θ_{29}	$\sum_j K_{ss}^{ji}$	1	1	.5	.5
θ_{30}	K_{55}^{ii}	1	1	1	1

Individuals that are born during the period (t,t+1) and are at-risk of dying in region i while in age group 1 must be handled separately from (S3.2).

$$(S3.4)\quad k_{01}^{di} = \theta_{16}K_{*1}^{b(i)i} + \theta_{17}K_{*1}^{b(i)d(i)} + \theta_{18}\sum_j K_{*1}^{b(i)j} + \theta_{19}\sum_j K_{*1}^{b(i)d(j)} + \theta_{20}\sum_j K_{*1}^{b(j)i} + \theta_{21}\sum_j K_{*1}^{b(j)d(i)}$$

This group consists of individuals born in region i and who either survive or die in region i at t+1--the first two terms of (S3.4)--plus individuals born in region i but who migrate to another region and either survive or die in that region at t+1--the third and fourth terms--plus individuals who are born in some other region but migrate into region i where they either survive or not at time t+1--the last two terms.

The fifth age group, individuals 65 and over, must also be treated separately since this is an opened-ended group. The number of people at-risk of dying in region i while in age group five is,

$$(S3.5)\quad k_{55}^{di} = \theta_{30}K_{55}^{ii} + \theta_{23}\Sigma_j K_{55}^{ij} + \theta_{25}\Sigma_j K_{55}^{ji} + \theta_{22}K_{55}^{id(i)} + \theta_{24}\Sigma_j K_{55}^{id(j)} + \theta_{26}\Sigma_j K_{55}^{jd(i)}$$

This expression is similar to (S3.3) except that the possibility of aging to a new age group is excluded.

In ECESIS, the child bearing group is restricted to females in the third age group (18-44 years). Thus, the population at-risk of giving birth includes females who age from age group two into age group three during the period (t,t+1) and females who are already in age group three at time t.

$$(S3.6)\quad k_{*3}^{bi} = k_{23}^{bi} + k_{33}^{bi}$$

The first term on the right is computed as,

$$(S3.7)\quad k_{23}^{bi} = \theta_1 K_{23}^{ii} + \theta_2 K_{23}^{id(i)} + \theta_3 \textstyle\sum_j K_{23}^{ij} + \theta_4 \sum_j K_{23}^{id(j)} + \theta_5 \sum_j K_{23}^{ji} + \theta_6 \sum_j K_{23}^{jd(i)}.$$

The first two terms represent individuals who are in region i at time t and either die or remain in region i. The third and fourth terms represent individuals who migrate out of region i during the period and the last two terms represent individuals who migrate into region i during the period.

The second term on the right side of (S3.6) is computed as,

$$(S3.8)\quad k_{33}^{bi} = \theta_{27} K_{33}^{ii} + \theta_{28} \textstyle\sum_j K_{33}^{ij} + \theta_{29} \sum_j K_{33}^{ji} + \theta_8 K_{33}^{id(i)} + \theta_{11} \sum_j K_{33}^{id(j)} + \theta_{13} \sum_j K_{33}^{jd(i)} + \theta_7 K_{34}^{ii} + \theta_{10} \sum_j K_{34}^{ij} + \theta_{15} \sum_j K_{34}^{ji} + \theta_9 K_{34}^{id(i)} + \theta_{12} \sum_j K_{34}^{id(j)} + \theta_{14} \sum_j K_{34}^{jd(i)}.$$

The terms in this expression may be interpreted analogously to those in (S3.3).

STEP 4: COMPUTE TOTAL BIRTHS AND TOTAL DEATHS

Total deaths to age group s in region i during the period (t,t+1) is,

$$(S4.1)\quad K_{*s}^{*d(i)} = \delta_{*s}^{*i} \cdot k_{*s}^{di}.$$

Total births in region i during the period (t,t+1) is,

$$\text{(S4.2)}\quad K_{\star 3}^{b(i)\star} = \beta_{\star 3}^{\star i} \cdot k_{\star 3}^{bi}.$$

Births are divided into males and females by assigning 51.33 percent of all births to be males.

Total births and total deaths are summed across all regions and constrained to be consistent with the national estimates and projections of the U.S. Bureau of the Census.

STEP 5: COMPUTE MAJOR FLOWS

First, estimate the number of people in age group one and in region i at time t who die in region i at time t+1. This total consists of persons already in region i and in age group one at time t who die before t+1 and also of persons born in region i during the period and who die before time t+1.

$$\text{(S5.1)}\quad K_{\star 1}^{id(i)} + K_{\star 1}^{b(i)d(i)} = K_{\star 1}^{\star d(i)} - \sum_j \sum_r K_{r1}^{jd(i)} - \sum_j K_{31}^{b(j)d(i)};\ r=0,1.$$

The first term on the right is total deaths in region i of persons in age group one (calculated in step 4). The second and third terms on the right subtract the number of individuals who inmigrate into region i and then die in age group one.

Next, the two terms on the left-hand-side are separated. The number of births in region i during the period which die before period t+1 is,

(S5.2) $K_{*1}^{b(i)d(i)} = c_{01}(K_{*1}^{id(i)} + K_{*1}^{b(i)d(i)})$,

where c_{01} is defined according to (S5.2). The remaining left hand term of (S5.1) is calculated as,

(S5.3) $K_{*1}^{id(i)} = (1-c_{01})(K_{*1}^{id(i)} + K_{*1}^{b(i)d(i)})$.

Disaggregating by initial age groups,

(S5.4) $K_{r1}^{id(i)} = c_{r1}(K_{*1}^{id(i)} + K_{*1}^{b(i)d(i)})$; $r=0,1$.

To calculate the number of individuals in region i who die in region i in other age groups use,

(S5.5) $K_{*s}^{id(i)} = K_{*s}^{*d(i)} - \sum_j\sum_r K_{rs}^{jd(i)}$;

$r=s-1,s;\ s=2,\ldots,5$.

(S5.6) $K_{rs}^{id(i)} = c_{rs}K_{*s}^{id(i)}$; $r=s-1,s;\ s=2,\ldots,5$.

Where,

$$c_{rs} = K_{rs}^{d*}/K_{*s}^{d*},$$

and the other terms have similar interpretations as those discussed above.

Next estimate the number of births in region i during the period (t,t+1) which survive to period t+1.

$$(S5.7)\quad K_{31}{}^{b(i)i} = K_{31}{}^{b(i)*} - K_{31}{}^{b(i)d(i)} - \sum_j K_{31}{}^{b(i)j} - \sum_j K_{31}{}^{b(i)d(j)}.$$

The first term on the right is total births in region i (estimated in step 4). From this is subtracted births in region i which do not survive, births in region i which survive but migrate out of the region, and births in region i which migrate out and do not survive.

The number of people in other age groups in region i who survive to period t+1 in region i is,

$$(S5.8)\quad K_{r*}{}^{ii} = K_{r*}{}^{i*} - \sum_s K_{rs}{}^{id(i)} - \sum_j \sum_s K_{rs}{}^{ij} - \sum_j \sum_s K_{rs}{}^{id(j)};\ r=s-1,s;\ s=2,3,4,5.$$

The first term on the right is the total population in region i and in age group r at time t (given in step 1). From this is subtracted: the number of people in region i at time t who die in region i before time t+1, the number of surviving outmigrants from region i, and the number of outmigrants from region i who do not survive until time t+1.

Finally, the number of people in region i and age group r at time t who are in region i and age group s at time t+1 is,

(S5.9) $K_{rs}^{ii} = p_{rs}K_{r*}^{ii}$; $r=s-1,s$; $s=1,...,5$.

Where,

(S5.10) $p_{rs} = K_{rs}^{**}/K_{r*}^{**}$,

is the proportion of people who were in age group r at time t and who are in age group s at time t+1. This ratio is based on annual U.S. population data.

STEP 6: CALCULATE MINOR FLOWS

The population at-risk of outmigrating and dying is,

(S6.1) $$\sum_j k_{*s}^{id(j)} = \theta_3\sum_j K_{s-1,s}^{ij} + \theta_4\sum_j K_{s-1,s}^{id(j)} + \theta_{10}\sum_j K_{s,s+1}^{ij} + \theta_{28}\sum_j K_{ss}^{ij} + \theta_{12}\sum_j K_{s,s+1}^{id(j)} + \theta_{11}\sum_j K_{ss}^{id(j)};\ s=2,3,4.$$

This expression must be slightly modified for the first and last age groups. For the first age group (s=1) the population at-risk of outmigrating and dying is,

(S6.2) $$\sum_j k_{*1}^{id(j)} = \theta_{28}\sum_j K_{11}^{ij} + \theta_{10}\sum_j K_{12}^{ij} + \theta_{11}\sum_j K_{11}^{id(j)} + \theta_{12}\sum_j K_{12}^{id(j)} + \theta_{18}\sum_j K_{01}^{b(i)j} + \theta_{19}\sum_j K_{01}^{b(i)d(j)}.$$

For the last age group the expression becomes,

(S6.3) $$\sum_j k_{*5}^{id(j)} = \theta_3\sum_j K_{45}^{ij} + \theta_4\sum_j K_{45}^{id(j)} + \theta_{28}\sum_j K_{55}^{ij} + \theta_{11}\sum_j K_{55}^{id(j)}.$$

The total number of persons who outmigrate from region i and die elsewhere during the period is,

(S6.4) $\sum_j K_{*s}^{id(j)} = \delta_{*s}^{*i} \cdot (\sum_j k_{*s}^{id(j)})$; s=1,...,5.

There are similar expressions for individuals who inmigrate and die.

The above formulations assume that migrants take on the death rate of the region that they migrate to. ECESIS improves upon this simple assumption by assuming that the death rate of migrants is a weighted average of the death rate at the origin and the death rate at the destination. Initially assume that inmigrants take on the death rate of the destination region,

(S6.5) $\sum_j K_{*s}^{jd(i)} = \delta_{*s}^{*i} \cdot (\sum_j k_{*s}^{jd(i)})$; s=1,...,5.

Equations (S6.1) - (S6.5) must be solved simultaneously. Because of the initial simplifying assumption concerning death rates, total deaths to inmigrants will not equal total deaths to outmigrants,

$$\sum_i \sum_j K_{*s}^{id(j)} \neq \sum_i \sum_j K_{*s}^{jd(i)}; \text{ s=1,...,5.}$$

To enforce this identity the difference,

(S6.6) $D = \sum_i \sum_j K_{*s}^{id(j)} - \sum_i \sum_j K_{*s}^{jd(i)}$; s=1,...,5,

is allocated to each state after it has been multiplied by

its share of the national total of inmigrants and outmigrants who die,

(S6.7) $\sum_j K_{*s}{}^{id(j)} = \sum_j K_{*s}{}^{id(j)}$

$- .5(D(\sum_j K_{*s}{}^{id(j)} / \sum_i \sum_j K_{*s}{}^{id(j)}))$; s=1,...,5

(S6.8) $\sum_{j*s}{}^{jd(i)} = \sum_j K_{*s}{}^{jd(i)}$

$- .5(D(\sum_j K_{*s}{}^{jd(i)} / \sum_i \sum_j K_{*s}{}^{jd(i)}))$; s=1,...,5

STEP 7: COMPUTE NEW POPULATION IN REGION I

For age group one the period t+1 population is,

(S7.1) $K_{*1}{}^{*i} = \sum_r K_{r1}{}^{ii} + \sum_j \sum_r K_{r1}{}^{ji}$

$+ K_{31}{}^{b(i)i} + \sum_j K_{31}{}^{b(j)i}$; r=0,1.

For the other age groups,

(S7.2) $K_{*s}{}^{*i} = \sum_r K_{rs}{}^{ii} + \sum_j \sum_r K_{rs}{}^{ji}$; r=s-1,s; s=2,3,4,5.

(S7.3) $K_{rs}{}^{*i} = q_{rs} \cdot K_{*s}{}^{*i}$; r=s-1,s; s=1,...,5.

where q_{rs} is defined in (S2.3).

This completes the first iteration of the demographic model. Subsequent iterations begin at step 3 and go through step 7. The iterations continue until convergence is achieved in the calculation of the minor flows.

Although the description of the ECESIS demographic model is rather tedious, it is essentially the same as the Rogers multiregional cohort-component model of Section 7.5. The principle enhancements are a more accurate calculation of the various at-risk populations and the inclusion of various minor flows into the basic demographic equation to account for short-comings in the currently available demographic data. The matrix approach described in Section 7.5 would still be valid (if not very clumsy) with these modifications.

Elaborate as the ECESIS demographic accounts framework is, it is still only an accounting system. The birth, death and migration rates that the system uses must be determined elsewhere. The following chapter describes how these rates are determined in the ECESIS model.

CHAPTER NINE: FERTILITY, MORTALITY AND MIGRATION

9.1 INTRODUCTION

The previous chapter outlined the accounting framework used in the ECESIS demographic model. The accounting system takes as given state level fertility and mortality rates and state-to-state migration flows. This chapter describes how each of these variables is determined in ECESIS.

To avoid confusion, in this section the term "fertility rate" will refer to births per thousand females in the age group 18-44 years. This rate is not disaggregated by race. A "crude birth rate" further aggregates by sex. The "mortality rate" refers to deaths per age-sex cohort. Again, there is no race disaggregation.

9.2 FERTILITY RATES

Economists have begun to analyze fertility using the same framework that they have traditionally used to analyze goods. The "price" of bearing and raising children consists of direct costs such as food, clothing, health care, etc., and indirect costs such as the opportunity cost of (typically) the mother's time. Several studies have found the expected negative relationship between female wages and the fertility rate (Cain and Dooley 1976; Cain and Weininger 1973; DeFronzo 1976; DeTray 1973; Butz and Ward 1979). Continuing the analogy, the income effect on the fertility rate should be positive as suggested by Malthus. In fact, there tends to be a negative relationship between income and fertility. The simple correlation, however, fails to account for the influence of other variables. Becker and Lewis (1973), Easterlin (1976), and Leibenstein (1975,1976) have presented arguments showing that the income effect on fertility may be offset by the effect of income on other variables which also affect fertility.

Two theories currently dominate research on the economic effects on fertility. The first, proposed by Easterlin (1973), focuses on relative cohort size and the resulting relative income measures. The second, proposed by Butz and Ward (1979), is a countercyclical model of fertility focussing on prices.

Easterlin asserts that a small cohort following a large cohort will have a set of relative economic advantages. Resources, from educational goods to jobs, will be distributed among fewer individuals. The labor supply effects will result in relatively higher income for the smaller cohorts. These higher income levels will be associated with higher fertility levels--a relationship that was first hypothesized by Malthus.

Butz and Ward, on the other hand, focus on price effects and suggest that fertility runs counter to economic cycles. In an expanding economy, female wages increase and thus so does the associated price of having children. When the economy is contracting and the excess supply of labor drives the cost of labor down, the cost, in terms of lost wages, of having children decreases and fertility increases. This negative relationship has been observed using both female wages and female labor force participation (e.g., Cain and Dooley 1976, DeFronzo 1976; Anker 1978). O'Connel (1983) suggests that the countercyclical fertility theory may be more robust for fertility downswings than upswings. During the 1980-82 recession, for example, fertility rates decreased implying procyclical behavior.

Other factors included in models of fertility include education (Anker 1978), race, ethnic or religious groups (Cain and Weininger 1973), the divorce rate (Ahlburg 1981), and the median age at marriage (Rindfuss and Bumpass 1976). It should be noted that these models are primarily national level models and for the most part the logic has not been extended to the subnational level; although Ahlburg (1982) and Isserman (1982) do address the subnational issue.

There have been several attempts to model fertility with national time-series data (Butz and Ward 1979; Gregory, Campbell, and Cheng 1972; Wachter 1975; Redwood 1982; Ahlburg 1982). Several of these studies use complex simultaneous models of fertility, marriage and labor force participation. All of the studies incorporate data that are not available annually for states. Given the paucity of data available at the state level, it is doubtful that reliable time-series models of state fertility will be forthcoming soon (Isserman 1982).

An alternative strategy is to forecast state fertility based on a national fertility model (Redwood 1982; Ahlburg 1982). Such top-down approaches are common in regional modelling. The disadvantage of this approach, in the context of ECESIS, is that an additional level of linkages to a national model would have to be supplied.

To avoid this additional complexity, state fertility in ECESIS will be modelled with a mechanical method similar to the one used by the U.S. Bureau of the Census in their state level population projection model. The general fertility rate in a state is calculated as the number of live births per thousand females aged 18 to 44. The ratio of the state's and the nation's general fertility rate is determined for a base year. The Census Bureau assumes that these ratios will approach one (linearly) in the year 2020.

This assumption of converging fertility rates appeared to be quite reasonable over the decades of the fifties and sixties. The late sixties and seventies, however, have shown a dramatic divergence of state fertility rates (Isserman 1982; Alonso 1980). Two alternative approaches for updating the ratios are incorporated in the ECESIS model.

The first alternative is simply that the ratios will remain constant. The second alternative is that the ratios will be forecast using a simple autoregressive model. In both cases, the ratios are multiplied by the Series II national fertility rate projected by the U.S. Bureau of the Census (U. S. Bureau of the Census, 1977, #704) to get the projected state rate. The sum of births across all states are constrained to be consistent with the total U.S. births projected by Series II.

While this method of forecasting state fertility appears to be crude, it is sadly the current state of the art. There is little prospect for achieving at the state level the kind of success for forecasting fertility that has been achieved at the national level.

9.3 MORTALITY RATES

Mortality rates are also subject to scrutiny by economists (Rodgers 1979; MacMahon, Kovar and Feldman 1972; Grossman and Jacobowitz 1981). Local mortality rates may be assumed to depend upon per capita income and other economic factors of the locality. The U.S., however, is a relatively mobile and affluent society. There are not great variations in mortality rates across regions within the U.S. What variations do occur are largely explained by the age, sex and racial compositions of the regions. Thus, state mortality rates are treated as exogenous in ECESIS. The projected state mortality rates are forced to be consistent with national mortality rates projected by the U.S. Bureau of the Census (#704). This adjustment procedure is described in Chapter Eight.

9.4 MIGRATION RATES

Migration is the largest and most volatile component in the change of a state's population. Therefore, accurate state level population projections depend critically upon accurate migration forecasts. This presents a difficult modelling assignment because of the paucity of information available on interstate migration. This section provides a brief review of the current theories on migration, a discussion of available interstate migration data sets, and a description of the method used in the ECESIS model to estimate migration.

9.4.1 MIGRATION THEORY

Since the seminal article of Sjaastad (1962), the human capital theory of migration has dominated the literature.[1] Essentially, migration is treated as an investment in human capital. Higher human capital will increase future human productivity and the rewards paid for that productivity. An individual will migrate if the present value of future benefits from the move are greater than the present value of future costs.

The simplest implementation of this theory is to have individuals move in response to simple wage rate differentials (Borts and Stein 1964; Ghali, Akiyama, and Fujiwara 1978; Smith 1974 and 1975). It is assumed that the supply and demand for labor are in equilibrium and that labor supply adjusts to relative wage rates between areas. That is to say, labor migrates from areas of low wages to areas of high wages, with the volume of migration a function of the size of the wage differential.

---

[1] For a good review of the migration literature see Greenwood 1975.

Studies using net migration to test this relationship have shown mixed results. Tarver and Gurley (1965) found a direct relationship between median family income for counties and 1950-60 net migration. Similarly, Sommers and Suits (1973) show a positive relationship between interstate net migration for the 1960-70 period and per capita income. Others have reported either weak (Bass and Alexander 1972; Raymond 1972) or no association (Rutman 1970) using net migration. Other studies have allowed for the decomposition of net migration into flows in and out of a region. Presumably, high wages would attract migrants and low wages would repel migrants. In addition, unemployment is often used to reflect local labor market tightness. In other words, unemployment is the push factor associated with the pull effects of relative income. Thus, unemployment should be positively associated with outmigration and negatively associated with inmigration. Empirical results are again mixed. Some have found the expected relationships (Cebula and Vedder 1973; Sommers and Suits 1973). Others like Beals, Levy, and Moses (1967) and Lowrey (1966) find one or the other relationship, but not both, to apply to their data.

Often, unemployment is used as a proxy for the probability of gaining employment. A complete description of the probability of gaining employment would involve a transition matrix describing all permutations of moves between the states of in and out of the labor force and in and out of employment for each region. Current data are insufficient to determine all cells of this transition matrix so various proxies have been devised. Employment opportunities have been measured by population (Greenwood and Sweetland 1972; Levy and Wadycki 1974; Miller 1973; and Rogers 1967), the employment-to-population ratio (Dahlberg and Holmlund 1978), the growth in employment (Todaro 1969 and 1976; Duffy and Greenwood 1980), and the rate of new hires (Fields 1976 and 1979). Employment competition is generally measured by the level of unemployment. This measure ignores the effects of discouraged workers, the age distribution of the population, and employment induced migration. Blanco (1963) adjusts unemployment to account for some of these factors. More sophisticated approaches, measuring opportunity-to-competition ratios, have been tried by Fields (1976, 1979), Gleave and Cordey-Hayes (1977), Plaut (1981) and Todaro (1969).

Sjaastad's conceptual cost-benefit formulation extended well beyond expected wage rate differentials to include other socio-economic factors and even the psychic costs of a move.

Data from the Annual Housing Surveys indicate that job related reasons are the primary motivation for moving for fifty-one percent of interstate migrants. This figure increases to over sixty-five percent for working males twenty to thirty-four years old and drops to under four percent for females fifty-five years and older (Long and Hansen 1979). Previous studies have found that age, sex, race, education, labor force and employment status, and family characteristics influence the decision to migrate (Greenwood and Gormely 1971; Lichter 1980; Long 1974; Lewis 1977; Lowry 1966; Rogers 1967; Sandell 1977; Long and Hansen 1979).

Less quantifiable factors such as quality of life and regional amenities may also influence the migration decision (Alperovitch, Bergsman and Ehemann 1975; Graves 1980, Graves and Linneman 1979; Clark and Ballard 1980; Lui 1975; Miller 1973; Milne 1981; Haurin 1980). Over fourteen percent of males fifty-five years and older indicate that a change in climate was their primary motivation for moving. Family reasons are the principal reason for moving for over sixty percent of elderly females. In addition, there are special population groups, like the military, college age, and the elderly, for which economic factors are not the primary motives for migration. Long (1983) shows that the conventional economic model does not apply to either the military or the college population, particularly when applied to those persons migrating and either entering or remaining in the special population. Similarly, McMillen (1983) and Smith and Fishkind (1980) show that the distinct behavior of elderly migrants suggests that there too a different model applies.

While the economic motivation for moves is certainly the largest, it does not cover all possibilities. However, the figures for economic motivation could be somewhat understated. A person may desire to move primarily for a change in climate but economic conditions may dictate whether that move is possible or which of several alternatives will be the final destination.

Many specifications for migration models are variations of the gravity concept (Ledent 1982; Plane and Rogerson 1982). In general terms,

$$M_{ij} = C \cdot A_i^{\alpha} \cdot A_j^{\beta} / d_{ij}^{\gamma},$$

where M_{ij} is the number of migrants from region i to region j, A_i and A_j are attractors for regions i and j, d_{ij} is the distance between i and j, and C, α, β and γ are parameters to be estimated. The attractors may be single variables or groups of variables. Examples are population, labor force, unemployment and wage rates (Lowry 1966; Rogers 1967). While such models are generally estimated using cross-section data, some pooled data have been used (Duffy and Greenwood 1980).

Opportunity costs or alternative opportunities is also an important concept in migration modelling. Since the cost of acquiring and taking advantage of information on alternative opportunities is likely to increase with distance, gravity models are often argued to capture this concept implicitly (Levy and Wadycki 1974; Wadycki 1979; Feder 1979 and 1980). As Feder (1979) demonstrates, the alternative opportunities concept implies that the relative attractiveness of all regions is affected by a change in opportunities in any region.

9.4.2 MIGRATION DATA

Even this short discussion of migration theories indicates how complex an issue internal migration is. Empirical evaluation of such complex theories requires detailed and accurate data. Bilsborrow and Akin (1982) have identified several criteria by which a data set may be evaluated for its usefulness in analyzing migration:

(1) Identification of migrants over space and time.

(2) An adequate sample of migrants.

(3) Micro-level data for individuals and households.

(4) The use of a longitudinal or specially designed single-round survey.

(5) The collection of detailed socio-economic information for each person in the household.

(6) Data for community or areal units, in both origin and destination area.

(7) Information on intentions and attitudes.

(8) Data on modelling the decision process within multi-person decision units.

(9) Moving costs.

Bilsborrow and Akin consider items (1) to (6) to be minimum data requirements while items (7) to (9) will be necessary to develop the next generation of migration models.

Below, eight migration data sets are appraised in light of these criteria.[2]

DECENNIAL CENSUS. The decennial census provides detailed demographic and socio-economic data for a very large sample of migrants for the periods 1955 to 1960, 1965 to 1970 and 1975 to 1980. However, the samples do not provide longitudinal data nor are they consistent across the three time periods. The data are based on responses to the question: "Did this person live in this house five years ago?" No attempt is made to gather information on multiple moves during the five year period nor on individuals who moved away and then returned. Thus the data set is not very

[2] More detailed descriptions of most of these data sets may be found in Bilsborrow and Akin (1982), Isserman, Plane and McMillen (1982), McMillen and Long (1981), and Wetrogan and Engles (1982).

useful for studying annual migration patterns. No information pertaining to items (7) to (9) is collected.

CURRENT POPULATION SURVEY. The Current Population Survey (CPS) has been carried out every month since 1948 by the Bureau of the Census. The primary use of the CPS is to provide monthly employment and unemployment estimates to the Bureau of Labor Statistics. The sample is large (currently 55,000 households) and contains detailed demographic and socio-economic information on the respondents. It is the March supplement of the CPS that identifies migrants. From 1948 to 1971 the question asked was: "Were you living at this residence one year ago?" However, in 1972 the question dropped its annual orientation and the reference point became 1970. In 1976 the reference point became 1975 and in 1981 the reference point changed again to 1980. This change of reference points has seriously hampered the usefulness of the CPS in analyzing migration. Further, to insure confidentiality, origin and destination of migrants are not identified beyond the nine census regions. The data set has limited longitudinal information since a household may be included for a maximum of sixteen months.

RESIDUAL NET MIGRATION. Net migration data may be calculated as a residual from the decennial census data and the annual state population estimates using the basic equation of population change.

$$NM = P - P_{-1} - B + D$$

Any errors in the estimates of the right-hand-side variables or inconsistencies in the procedures used to get P and P_{-1} are transferred directly to the net migration estimate. The magnitude of this error is not trivial. In approximately half of the states the errors in the population estimates are larger than the magnitudes of the net migration estimates (Isserman, Plane, Rogerson, and Beaumont 1981). No demographic or socio-economic information can be obtained for the net migrants nor can gross migration flows be retrieved from these estimates.

SURVEY OF INCOME AND EDUCATION. The Survey of Income and Education interviewed approximately 150,000 households between April and July of 1976. The survey is rich in demographic and socio-economic information and also collects this information for each member of the household. The survey identifies the origin and destination of migrants only to the state level, collects no retrospective information and is not longitudinal. Its usefulness for migration studies is limited.

NATIONAL LONGITUDINAL SURVEY OF LABOR MARKET EXPERIENCE. This survey is a joint venture of the Center for Human Resource Research of Ohio State University (1981), the Bureau of the Census and the U.S. Department of Labor. The survey is longitudinal but some years are skipped or shortened questionaires are used. Detailed demographic and socio-economic data for heads of households are available but little information on other household members is collected. Origin and destination data on migrants is very limited and the sample size is too small to analyze gross migration flows.

MICHIGAN PANEL SURVEY OF INCOME DYNAMICS. This is a longitudinal survey conducted annually since 1968 by the Survey Research Center of the University of Michigan. The survey contains detailed demographic and socio-economic data on the household head and over the years has added similar data on other household members. Extensive income, tax and area data are available as well as intentions and attitudinal data. The small sample size, 5000 families, precludes place-to-place migration analysis. However, a household's movements over a long period of time may be analyzed. Several researchers have found this a valuable data source for migration analysis (DaVanzo 1976 and 1981; Akin, Guilkey, and Sickles 1979; Duncan and Newman 1975).

CONTINUOUS WORK HISTORY SAMPLE. The Continuous Work History Sample (CWHS) is a longitudinal one percent sample of all persons with a social security number who have worked in covered employment during the year. Detailed place-to-place migration flow matrices may be tabulated with some demographic and socio-economic information available for the workers. Individuals are located by place of employment rather than place of residence so local moves or job changes within the area may be erroneously reported. Data on non-covered workers are not available nor is any household information available. Several researchers have used the CWHS for migration studies (Clark and Ballard 1980; Duffy and Greenwood 1980; Plane and Isserman 1983; Smith and Slater 1981) but recent work indicates that gross reporting errors may lead to large over-estimates of migration in the CWHS (Isserman, Plane, Rogerson and Beaumont 1981; Renshaw 1978; McMillen and Long 1981). The CWHS is available annually since 1958 but the 1976 Tax Reform Act and the transfer of the data to the Internal Revenue Service have led to no new tabulations being released since 1975.

INTERNAL REVENUE SERVICE DATA. Since General Revenue Sharing funds have been allocated on the basis of population estimates, the Census Bureau has been authorized to estimate migration using Internal Revenue Service (IRS) income tax returns. Migrants are identified by matching returns from year to year and comparing addresses of filers. While the coverage of the data set is impressive (90 million returns plus information on dependents), little demographic or socio-economic information on filers is available. The Bureau of the Census is planning to match the IRS data to a ten percent sample of the Social Security File data so that more detailed individual information may be obtained. This data source has great potential but budget cuts are slowing development. Presently one year matches with no age detail are available for the years 1975-76, 1976-77, and 1978-79.

Of all these data sets, the Panel Survey of Income Dynamics is the best suited to study internal migration. The small sample size, however, precludes the use of this data set to study place-to-place flows--the goal of ECESIS. There are 2550 state-to-state migrant flows to be estimated in ECESIS. Even the CPS, with over 50,000 respondents, leads to too sparse a migration matrix. Of the other large surveys, the decennial census is excluded because of its dependence on five year periods and the CWHS is excluded because of large reporting errors in the data set. This leaves the IRS data with which to examine migration within the ECESIS model.

9.4.3 THE ECESIS MIGRATION MODEL

The procedure developed to estimate migration in the ECESIS model is called the Generalized Destination Weighted (GDW) model. The GDW model is a merger of the gravity and Markov model approaches (Plane and Rogerson 1982; Plane 1982). The simple gravity model may be written,

(9.4.1) $M_{ij}(t) = C \cdot A_i(t)^{\alpha} \cdot A_j(t)^{\beta} d_{ij}^{-\gamma}$; $i,j=1,\ldots,R$.

Where A_i and A_j are attractiveness measures of regions i and j in period t, d_{ij} is the distance between regions i and j, $M_{ij}(t)$ is the migration flow in period t and C, α, β, and γ are parameters (greater than zero) to be estimated. In the purest form of the gravity model, α and β are 1.0, γ is 2.0, the A's are regional populations in period t and the model is "calibrated" by adjusting the constant C.

A fixed transition matrix Markov model estimates migration from,

(9.4.2) $M_{ij}(t) = P_i(t-1) \cdot p_{ij}(b)$; $i,j=1,\ldots,R$.

Where $P_i(t-1)$ is the population in region i at the beginning of period t that survives until the end of period t, and $p_{ij}(b)$ is the Markov transmission matrix defined for some base period b,

$$p_{ij}(b) = M_{ij}(b)/P_i(b-1).$$

To be a well-defined Markov matrix, the rows of p_{ij} must sum to one,

$$\Sigma_j M_{ij}(b) = P_i(b-1).$$

This is the reason that P_i is restricted to those individuals who survive the period.

Conceptually, (9.4.1) and (9.4.2) are quite similar. The p_{ij} should be a better weighting factor than d_{ij} so one would expect the Markov model to dominate on that account. On the other hand, the gravity model allows attractiveness measures for both the origin and destination while the Markov model only has origin attractors. As region j becomes more attractive relative to all other regions in period t as compared to the base period, migration into region j should increase. The Markov model may be extended to capture this effect by adding a relative attractiveness variable for region j.

$$(9.4.3) \quad M_{ij} = P_i(t-1)\cdot p_{ij}(b)\frac{[A_j(t)/\Sigma_j A_j(t)]}{[A_j(b)/\Sigma_j A_j(b)]}\,; \qquad i,j=1,\ldots,R.$$

The condition,

$$\Sigma_j M_{ij}(t) = P_i(t-1),$$

is imposed by dividing the left-hand-side of (9.4.3) by $P_i(t-1)$ and the right-hand-side by $\Sigma_k M_{ik}(t)$ and substituting for the latter from (9.4.3),

$$(9.4.4) \quad \frac{M_{ij}(t)}{P_i(t-1)} = \frac{M_{ij}(b)[A_j(t)/A_j(b)]}{\Sigma_k M_{ik}(b)[A_k(t)/A_k(b)]}$$

A further refinement to the model is made by allowing the elasticity of migration with respect to attractiveness to differ from unity.[3]

$$(9.4.5)\quad \frac{M_{ij}(t)}{P_i(t-1)} = \frac{M_{ij}(b)[A_j(t)/A_j(b)]^{\gamma}}{\sum_k M_{ik}(b)[A_k(t)/A_k(b)]^{\gamma}}$$

By dividing the numerator and denominator of the right-hand-side by $P_i(b-1)$, the GDW model may be written in the more convenient form,

$$(9.4.6)\quad p_{ij}(t) = p_{ij}(b)[A_j(t)/A_j(b)]^{\gamma}\cdot D_i^{-1},$$

where,

$$D_i = \sum_k p_{ik}(b)[A_k(t)/A_k(b)]^{\gamma}.$$

Given two sets of migration flow matrices, the parameter γ may be estimated using a maximum likelihood estimator minimizing the root mean square error of the transition rates.

In the GDW model all transition rates are interdependent. A change in the relative attractiveness of any region will change all of the transition probabilities. Thus the GDW model is consistent with the alternative opportunities hypothesis.

To illustrate this point, and how the model works in general, consider a simple three region model. The base year flow matrix is given by,

---

[3] Because of the complex denominator, γ is only a close approximation of this elasticity. See Rogerson (1981).

$$M_{ij}(b) = \begin{bmatrix} 400 & 75 & 50 \\ 75 & 625 & 25 \\ 50 & 50 & 150 \end{bmatrix}$$

The row sums are the populations of the regions at the beginning of the period (525, 725, and 250, respectively), and the column sums are the populations of the regions at the end of the period (525, 750, and 225). The base period transition matrix is,

$$p_{ij}(b) = \begin{bmatrix} .762 & .143 & .095 \\ .103 & .862 & .034 \\ .200 & .200 & .600 \end{bmatrix}$$

Now let the relative attractiveness of region three decline while the relative attractiveness of regions one and two remain unchanged,

$$A_j(t)/A_j(b) = 1.,\ 1.,\ .6\ ;\ j=1,2,3.$$

Assuming $\gamma=1$, the new transition matrix becomes,

$$p_{ij}(t) = \begin{bmatrix} .792 & .149 & .059 \\ .105 & .875 & .020 \\ .263 & .263 & .474 \end{bmatrix}$$

The difference in the two transition matrices is,

$$p_{ij}(t) - p_{ij}(b) = \begin{bmatrix} .030 & .006 & -.036 \\ .002 & .013 & -.014 \\ .063 & .063 & -.126 \end{bmatrix}$$

Even though the relative attractiveness of regions one and two was unchanged, the alternative opportunity change in region three created a change in the migration rates between regions one and two.

Before the GDW model can be estimated a measure of destination attractiveness must be determined. In the discussion of migration theories it was observed that different age-sex groups have quite different motives for migration. The ten demographic groups in ECESIS will undoubtedly not respond to the same attractiveness measure. The prime working age groups (18-44 and 45-64) are motivated most strongly by economic conditions (Long and Hansen 1979) so an attractiveness measure for those four age-sex groups is discussed first.

At the micro decision making level, expected wage disparities should be a good measure of attractiveness. Upon aggregation, however, this measure loses much of its appeal. Only the average expected wage of a region is readily observed, not the complete distribution of wages. A better measure of a regions attractiveness for those seeking employment is the ratio of the pool of job opportunities in the region to the pool of competitors for those jobs. Lacking data on job vacancies and turnovers for all fifty states, the pool of employment opportunities in region j is approximated by the number of new jobs created in the region (ΔE_j, where E is employment) plus the number of job turnovers in the region ($s(t)\cdot E_j(t-1)$, where s is the separation rate excluding layoffs). The pool of competitors for those jobs would include those people already unemployed in the region ($U_j(t-1)$) plus those persons turning over jobs ($s(t)\cdot E_j(t-1)$). The destination attractiveness for region j is,

$$(9.4.7) \quad {}^{a}A_j{}^{s}(t) = \frac{\Delta E_j(t)+s(t)\cdot E_j(t-1)}{U_j(t-1)+s(t)\cdot E_j(t-1)} ,$$

age groups (a) = 3,4; sex groups (s) = 1,2.

Since separation rates are not available for all state, the national separation rate is used in (9.4.7).

Using (9.4.7) the GDW model was estimated using the 1975-76 and 1976-77 IRS migration flow matrices. Since these matrices do not have age-sex detail, it was necessary to impose that disaggregation using the age-sex distribution of the 1965-70 decennial census flows and the changing age composition of the states (Plane and Rogerson 1982).

Under the assumption that the γ's do not change, the GDW model was used to forecast migration for 1978-79. When $\gamma=0$, the GDW model reduces to the Markov model given in (9.4.2). Forecasts from the GDW and Markov models were compared to the actual IRS migration data for 1978-79 by computing the mean absolute error in net migration. In each age-sex group the GDW model offers considerable improvement over the Markov model. Table 9.4.1 summarizes these results.

TABLE 9.4.1

COMPARISON OF MARKOV AND GDW MODELS

Group	γ	Improvement with GDW
18-44M	.4265	20%
18-44F	.4817	21%
45-64M	.4977	22%
45-64F	.5340	17%

The destination attractiveness of the first two age groups (0-4 and 5-17) is based on the migration rates of fecund females. The assumption is simply that childrer migrate with their mothers.

$$(9.4.8) \quad {}^{a}A_{j}^{s}(t) = \frac{{}^{3}M_{ij}^{2}(t)}{{}^{3}M_{ij}^{2}(b)} \; ; \; a=1,2; \; s=1,2.$$

Migration of the elderly was modelled with the simple Markov model, assuming $\gamma=0$, or $A_j=1$. Undoubtedly this group does have some economic motivations for moves (Smith and Fishkind 1981; Warnes 1982), however, the special problems associated with the migration of the elderly are not the focus of ECESIS and are treated in a very simple manner.

In order to do historical simulations with the ECESIS model, a special base year migration matrix must be constructed. Information from the 1960 and 1970 decennial censuses, Current Population Surveys, and the changing age and sex compositions of the states are combined to construct this base year matrix. While there is no way to check the accuracy of this matrix, it is possible to "track" the model historically to correct for any errors in this matrix. This process is described in Chapter Ten.

In practice, the base year matrix of the GDW model is updated as the simulation or forecast proceeds. Thus, in year t+1, the base year matrix becomes the transition matrix estimated for year t, and so on. Equation (9.4.6) may be rewritten in its simulation form as,

(9.4.9) $p_{ij}(t) = p_{ij}(t-1)[A_j(t)/A_j(t-1)]^{\gamma} \cdot D_i^{-1}$,

where,

$$D_i = \Sigma_k p_{ik}(t-1)[A_k(t)/A_k(t-1)]^{\gamma}.$$

In the context of the full ECESIS model, the migration component is solved simultaneously with the economic and population models. For a given year, the economic model passes measures of economic attractiveness for each state to the GDW model which calculates interstate migration. The demographic accounts model uses this information to estimate state populations. These updated population figures are then passed to the economic models which produce new estimates of the attractiveness variables. The process iterates until all variables in all states have converged.

CHAPTER TEN: MULTIPLIER TESTS

10.1 INTRODUCTION

In the previous chapters the theory, specification and estimation of the ECESIS model was described. In this and the next two chapters the properties and performance of ECESIS is analyzed. This chapter examines various multipliers of the system.

Multipliers quantify the effects of a change in one variable on other variables in the system. ECESIS is a simultaneous system of nonlinear, dynamic equations coupled with a complex dual-level linkage mechanism. As such, multipliers are difficult to compute. For small linear models the multipliers may be computed analytically; for models like ECESIS an empirical approximation must be used.

This section describes how multipliers are computed for nonlinear systems in general and how they are used in ECESIS in particular. Section 2 describes how the CONTROL solution is constructed. The basic trends of the CONTROL solution are also discussed in that section. The design of the multiplier tests and the multiplier results are described in Section three. That section concludes with a brief discussion of the implications of the multiplier experiments.

Assume that the ith normalized nonlinear equation of an n equation system can be written as

$$(10.1.1) \qquad y_{ti} = f_i(Y_t, Y_{t-1}, \cdots, Y_{t-p}, X_t; \theta_i) + \epsilon_{ti},$$

where Y_t denotes the vector $(y_{t1}, y_{t2}, \ldots, y_{tn})$, Y_{t-j} denotes the jth period lag of the vector Y_t, X_t denotes the vector of exogenous variables $(x_{t1}, x_{t2}, \ldots, x_{tm})$, θ_i is the set of parameters for the ith equation, and ϵ_{ti} is an additive random error. The entire system of n equations can be written as

$$(10.1.2) \qquad Y_t = F(Y_t, Y_{t-1}, \ldots, Y_{t-p}; X_t; \theta) + \epsilon_t.$$

In this system there are n equations in n endogenous variables (y's), each with a maximum lag of p periods, and m exogenous variables (x's).[1] Each of the equations is normalized for a unique endogenous variable. The specifications may be implicit; y_{ti} may appear on the right-hand-side of the ith equation.

For a given set of parameters (θ), random disturbances $(\epsilon_{t+k}, k=1,\ldots,s)$, and a particular set of exogenous data $(X^c_{t+k}, k=1,\ldots,s)$, a control solution for the endogenous

[1] Note that any lagged exogenous variable may simply be redefined as a new exogenous variable.

variables may be computed from (10.1.2) using the Gauss-Seidel method (Klein 1974). Denote this control solution as

(10.1.3) $\{Y^c_{t+k}, X^c_{t+k}\}$, $k=1,\ldots,s$.

Now suppose that the jth exogenous variable is incremented by Δ_j from period t+1 to period t+s. Then a new solution for the endogenous variables can be computed as

$$Y^*_{t+k}=F(Y^*_{t+k},\ldots,Y^*_{t+1},Y_t,\ldots,Y_{t+k-p};X^*_{t+k};\theta)+\epsilon_{t+k},\ k<p$$

where

$$X^*_{t+k}=(x^c_{t+k,1},\ldots,x^*_{t+k,j},\ldots,x^c_{t+k,m}),k=1,\ldots,s.$$

Denote the shocked solution as

(10.1.4) $\{Y^*_{t+k}, X^*_{t+k}\}$, $k=1,\ldots,s$.

The kth period <u>dynamic</u> multiplier of variable y_i is defined as

(10.1.5) $\mu_i(k) = (y^*_{t+k,i}-y^c_{t+k,i})/(x^*_{t+k,j}-x^c_{t+k,j})$,
$k=1,\ldots,s$.

The <u>impact</u> multiplier is defined as $\mu_i(1)$. Impact mulitpliers are particularly useful in dynamic models because they indicate the initial effects of a shock before any complicating dynamic adjustment processes come into play.

The <u>total long-run</u> multiplier is the sum of all the changes in the dynamic multipliers over time. In theory the sum would cover an infinite number of periods. In practice the total long-run multiplier is calculated as

$$(10.1.6) \qquad M_i = \sum_{k=2}^{s}[\mu_i(k)-\mu_i(k-1)].$$

If the horizon of the simulation (s) is long enough and the model is stable, then the dynamic multipliers will approach a constant and (10.1.6) will be a close approximation to the true total long-run multiplier. If the model is unstable then M_i would move toward $\pm\infty$ as s gets large.

Multiplier analysis is a useful tool for describing the properties of a model. For example, one might be suspect of a model whose impact income multiplier with respect to government expenditures was negative. Or, a total long-run multiplier with respect to government expenditures of, say, twenty would also indicate a model with poor simulation properties. Multiplier analysis of a model like ECESIS is particularly important since the linkage mechanisms make it very difficult to predict a priori the sensitivity of the system to exogenous shocks.

10.2 CONTROL DATA

To compute multipliers empirically a control solution is needed to compare to the shocked solution. Constructing the control solution is in itself a complex task. In this section the process of constructing the control solution is first described and then the basic trends of the control solution are examined.

10.2.1 CONSTRUCTING THE CONTROL SOLUTION

The multiplier experiments are run over the historical period 1959 to 1980. ECESIS is "tracked" so that the actual historical data from this period serve as the control solution. Tracking a system simply means adjusting the residual elements ϵ_t in (10.1.2) so that the Gauss-Seidel solution of the system yields the observed data over the period. Normally this could be achieved by setting the ϵ_t's equal to the estimation residuals for each equation. Because of the linkage mechanisms and cross-sectional migration model, the process is somewhat more complicated in ECESIS.

First, each of the fifty-one regional economic models is tracked on a stand-alone basis. Let

(10.2.1) $\{Y^a_t,\ X^a_t\}$, t=1959,...,1980.

denote the set of actual historical data. For each period, compute residuals for each of the endogenous economic variables by solving

(10.2.2) $e_t = Y^a{}_t - F(Y^a{}_t, \ldots, Y^a{}_{t-p}, X^a{}_t; \theta)$.

The e_t should equal the estimation residuals except in those cases where the simulation equation is normalized differently than the estimation equation. Note that actual values are used for all right-hand-side endogenous variables rather than the computed values from other equations. Now solving

$$Y^c{}_t = F(Y^c{}_t, \ldots, Y^c{}_{t-p}, X^a{}_t; \theta) + e_t, \quad t=1959, \ldots, 1980,$$

in a dynamic simulation will yield

$$Y^c{}_t = Y^a{}_t, \quad \forall t=1959, \ldots, 1980.$$

It is not necessary to track the interregional economic output, wage and employment variables since these are deterministic functions of individual state economic variables which have already been tracked to actual historical values.

Tracking the demographic model requires a several step process. Ignoring minor flows and regional subscripts for the moment, the demographic model computes age-sex population from

(10.2.3) $\quad {}^{a}POP^{s}_{t} = {}^{a}POP^{s}_{t-1} + {}^{a}B^{s}_{t} - {}^{a}D^{s}_{t} + {}^{a}IN^{s}_{t} - {}^{a}OUT^{s}_{t},$

where POP, B, D, IN and OUT are population, births, deaths and in- and outmigration. The superscripts refer to specific age-sex groups. In the ECESIS demographic model, the migration model is solved first to determine ${}^{a}IN^{s}$ and ${}^{a}OUT^{s}$. These values are then passed to the demographic accounts model which determines ${}^{a}B^{s}$ and ${}^{a}D^{s}$ and then computes ${}^{a}POP^{s}_{t}$. In- and outmigration are functions of economic model data and the population at-risk of migrating. Since the ECESIS demographic accounts model is a closed system, only the "survived population", as opposed to the previous periods total population, is eligible for the at-risk group. The survived population for year t, ${}^{a}SP^{s}_{t}$, is a by-product of the accounts model and is thus not available to the migration model on the first iteration. Thus, it is not possible to track the demographic model in less than two iterations.

Let Y^{a}_{t} denote the vector of actual values of the economic data, then

$${}^{a}IN^{s}_{t}(1) = g(Y^{a}_{t}, {}^{a}SP^{s}_{t}(1))$$

(10.2.4)

$${}^{a}OUT^{s}_{t}(1) = h(Y^{a}_{t}, {}^{a}SP^{s}_{t}(1))$$

are the first iteration values of in- and outmigration. $SP_{t}(1)$ is the last iteration value of SP from t-1 for t>1959 and is ${}^{a}POP^{s}{}_{1958}$ for t=1959.

The computed values from (10.2.4) are passed to the accounts model where births and deaths are computed as described in Chapter Nine and the first iteration values of population are computed as

$$(10.2.5) \quad {}^{a}POP^{s}{}_{t}(1) = {}^{a}POP^{s}{}_{t-1}+{}^{a}B^{s}{}_{t}(1)-{}^{a}D^{s}{}_{t}(1)+ {}^{a}IN^{s}{}_{t}(1) \ {}^{a}OUT^{s}{}_{t}(1).$$

First iteration values for birth, death and population residuals are computed by subtracting ${}^{a}POP^{s}{}_{t}(1)$, etc., from the actual historical values. A by-product of the accounts model is an updated value for the survived population (${}^{a}SP^{s}{}_{t}(2)$). For the second iteration, ${}^{a}SP^{s}{}_{t}(2)$ is substituted into (10.2.4) to compute ${}^{a}IN^{s}{}_{t}(2)$ and ${}^{a}OUT^{s}{}_{t}(2)$. Since the second iteration values of in- and outmigration are computed from the correct survived population values, residuals for in- and outmigration may now be computed. The revised in- and outmigration values are then passed to the accounts model where second iteration birth, death and population residuals can be computed as described above. Further iterations are not necessary since ${}^{a}SP^{s}{}_{t}(3)={}^{a}SP^{s}{}_{t}(2)$.

A further complication arises because a time-series of ${}^{a}IN^{s}{}_{t}$ and ${}^{a}OUT^{s}{}_{t}$ are not available with which to calculate in- and outmigration residuals.[2] The residuals for the migration model, computed only in the second iteration, are calculated as follows. Define

$$(10.2.6) \quad TR = \Sigma_{a,s}({}^{a}POP^{s}_{t} - {}^{a}POP^{s}_{t-1} - {}^{a}B^{s}_{t} + {}^{a}D^{s}_{t} - {}^{a}IN^{s}_{t}(2) + {}^{a}OUT^{s}_{t}(2)),$$

where actual (or tracked) values are used for ${}^{a}POP^{s}$, ${}^{a}B^{s}$ and ${}^{a}D^{s}$. Then compute the in- and outmigration age-sex specific residuals from

$$(10.2.7) \quad \begin{aligned} {}^{a}RIN^{s}_{t} &= {}^{a}IN^{s}_{t}(2) \times TR/[\Sigma_{a,s}({}^{a}IN^{s}_{t}(2) + {}^{a}OUT^{s}_{t}(2))] \\ {}^{a}ROUT^{s}_{t} &= -{}^{a}OUT^{s}_{t}(2) \times TR/[\Sigma_{a,s}({}^{a}IN^{s}_{t}(2) + {}^{a}OUT^{s}_{t}(2))]. \end{aligned}$$

Note that

$$\Sigma_{a,s}({}^{a}RIN^{s}_{t} - {}^{a}ROUT^{s}_{t}) = TR,$$

so that this procedure simply computes the error induced in the basic demographic equation (10.2.6) by using estimated in- and outmigration values and then distributes that error proportionally across the in- and outmigration estimates.

When all of the residuals are added back to the various equations the entire ECESIS system will track the actual historical data exactly in a dynamic simulation. These same residuals are used in all multiplier tests so that only the

[2] Recall that the migration model is based on cross-sectional data. See Chapter Nine.

impact of the exogenous variable changes will be calculated.

Finally, some of the historical data from 1975 to 1980 are incomplete. In these cases, the missing data are simply projected using an ARIMA model and then constrained to add to national totals. These projected values are then treated as actual data for control solution purposes.

10.2.2 ANALYSIS OF THE CONTROL SOLUTION

The last two decades are often referred to as a period of radical change in regional economic and demographic trends in the United States. More accurately, this period marks the return to a traditional pattern of population deconcentration. Since colonial times, the U.S. population has moved from high- to low-density areas.[3] This basic trend was interrupted during the first half of this century when there was a rapid increase in urbanization. Proximity to industrial centers and economies of scale during this period of rapid industrial expansion bolstered the urbanization phase. Technological advances in communication and transportation facilities, however, have reduced the need for agglomeration. Thus, the past two decades have witnessed an end to the urbanization phase and a return to

[3] See Long (1981) for a detailed discussion of population deconcentration in the U.S.

the previous long-term pattern of population deconcentration.

Figure 10.2.1 shows the most and least densely populated regions in the United States in 1960. On the basis of population density alone, one would predict population movements from the Northeast and East North Central states to the Southern and Western (particularly Mountain) states. And, indeed, this has been the trend over the past two decades. Figures 10.2.2 and 10.2.3 show that the trend started tentatively in the 1960's but by the 1970's there was a steady pattern of migration from the Northeast and East North Central states to the Western and Southern states. The spatial pattern is most dramatically illustrated in Figure 10.2.4. With the exceptions of Vermont, New Hampshire and Maine, all of the states in the North Central and Northeast regions of the U.S. had average population growth rates below the national average of .86 percent over the decade of the 1970's. On the other hand, all of the Mountain states, except Montana, had population growth rates during this period of at least twice the national average.

Other factors, besides population density, have influenced this pattern. The past two decades have witnessed a relative decline in the manufacturing sector of the economy. All of the states in the East North Central

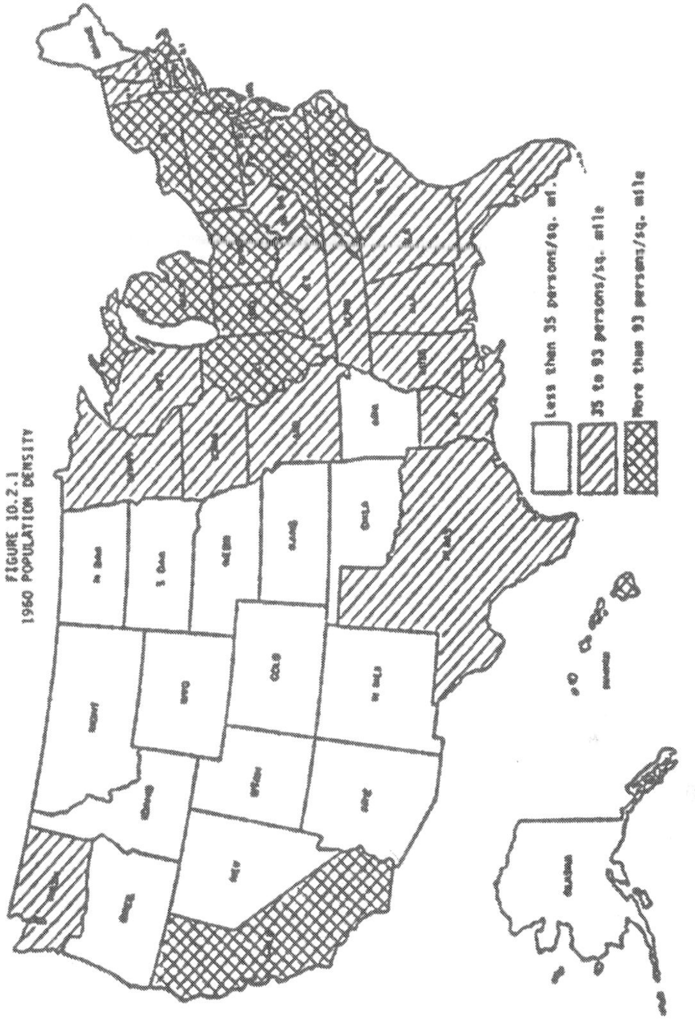

FIGURE 10.2.1
1960 POPULATION DENSITY

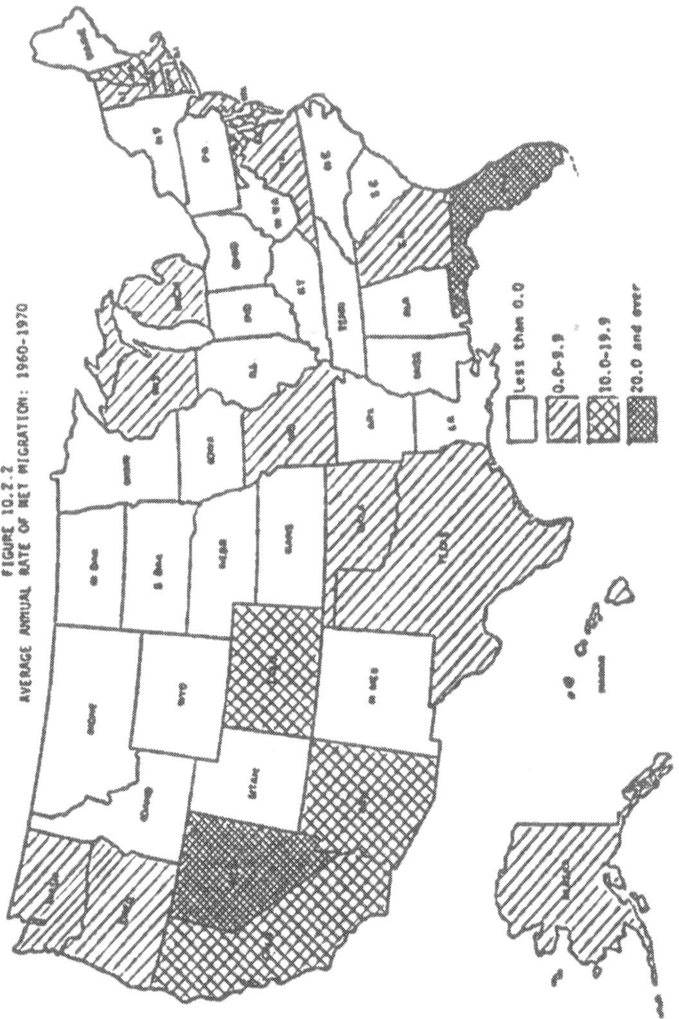

FIGURE 10.2.2
AVERAGE ANNUAL RATE OF NET MIGRATION: 1960-1970

FIGURE 10.2.3
AVERAGE ANNUAL RATE OF NET MIGRATION: 1970-1980

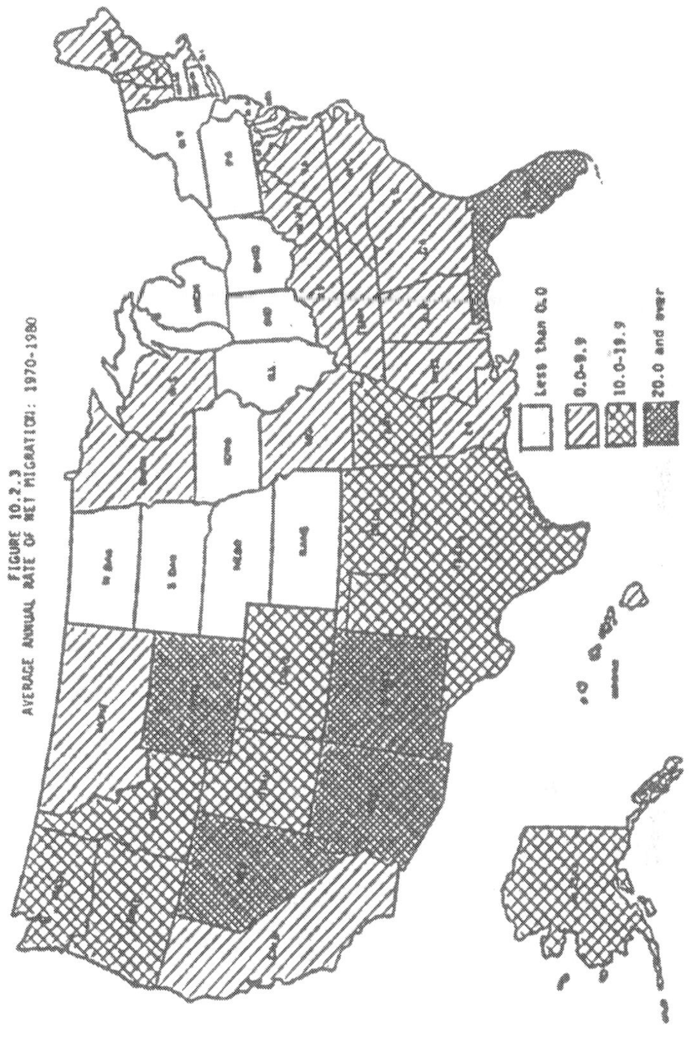

FIGURE 10.2.4
AVERAGE ANNUAL RATE OF POPULATION GROWTH
1970-1979

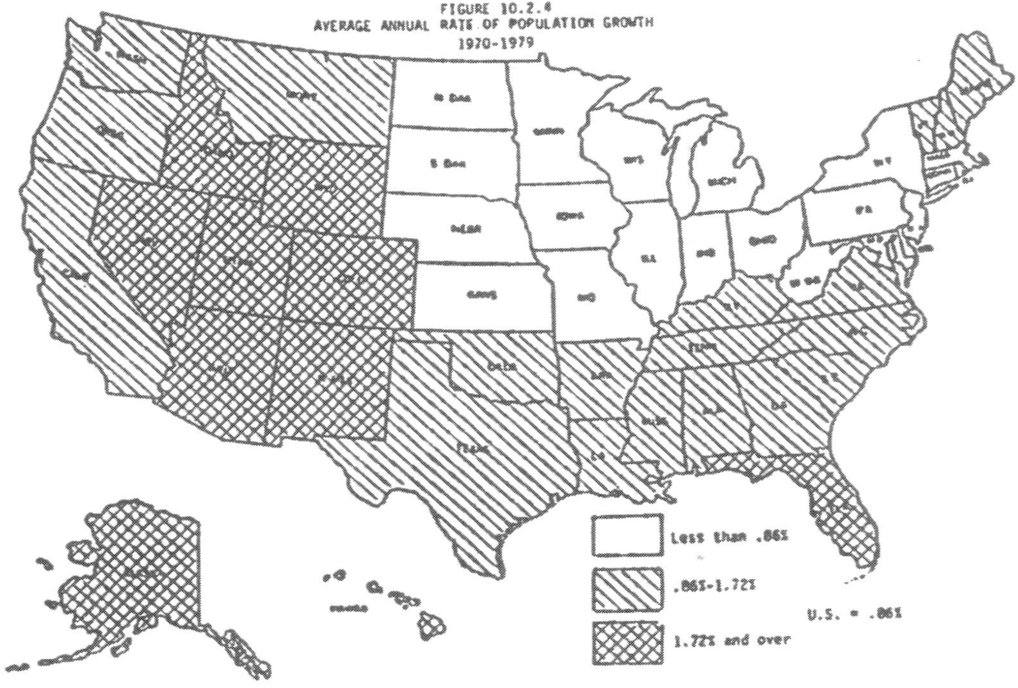

and Northeast regions of the U.S. (except Vermont) had at least one-quarter of total employment in the manufacturing sector. Thirteen of the fifteen states with the largest proportion of employment in the manufacturing sector are in the East North Central and Northeast.[4] During the 1960's manufacturing and nonmanufacturing employment growth were 2.1 and 3.4 percent, respectively. In the 1970's, nonmanufacturing employment growth fell to 2.9 percent while manufacturing employment growth plummetted to under one-half of one percent. The decline in job opportunities in the industrial north induced people to look to the faster growing states for new job opportunities. As seen in Figure 10.2.5, those opportunities were to the west and south.

Even those jobs that were being created in the manufacturing sector were being created mostly outside of the traditional industrial belt. The rate of real gross manufacturing investment in the 1970's was lowest in the East North Central and Northeast regions of the country. Part of this industrial relocation can be explained by the rapid growth in high-technology industries and government and business conditions that favor expansion in the Southern and Western states (Norton and Rees 1979; Markusen and Fastrup 1978; Rones 1980; Rifkin and Barber 1978).

---

[4] The other two states are Delaware and North Carolina.

FIGURE 10.2.5
AVERAGE ANNUAL RATE OF NONMANUFACTURING EMPLOYMENT GROWTH
1970-1979

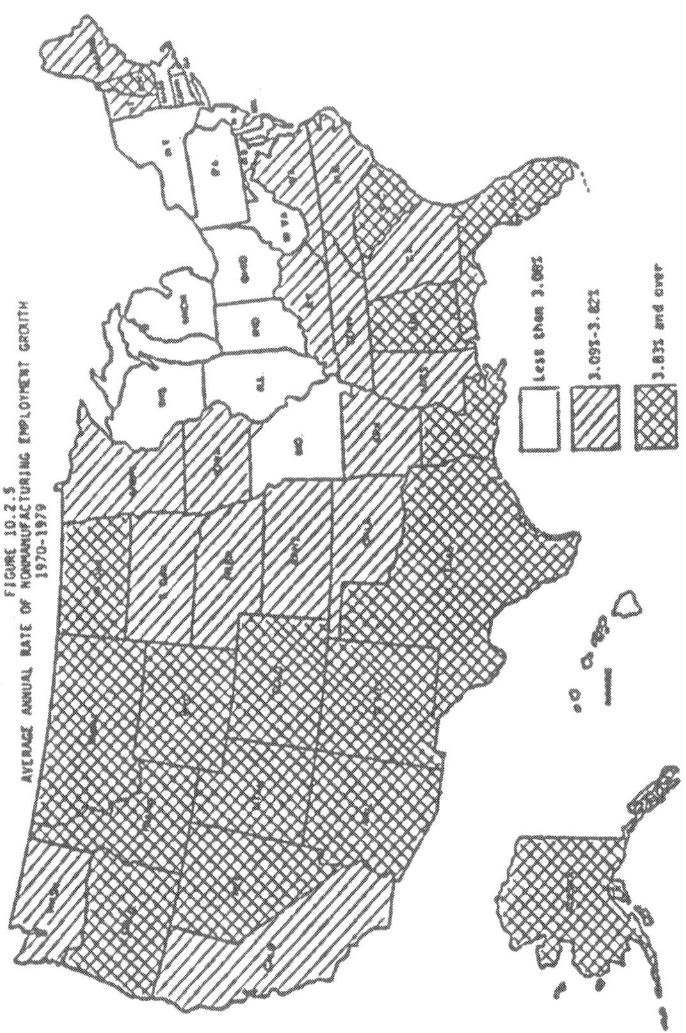

It is against this backdrop of basic trends in the control solution that the multiplier experiments of the following section are run. The trends in the control solution are only of secondary importance for the multiplier experiments. They take on more significance in the simulation experiments of Chapters Eleven and Twelve.

10.3 TEST DESIGN AND RESULTS

Simulations with ECESIS may be run at three different levels. First, level A, the fifty-one state economic models may be run on a stand-alone basis. Each state model behaves independently of the other models. There are no interregional economic linkages and all demographic variables are exogenous at this level. Level B adds the interregional economic linkages to level A. Output, wages and employment in each region are directly affected by economic activity in all other regions. Demographic variables are still treated as exogenous in level B. Finally, level C activates the demographic model and all demographic variables are determined endogenously. Interregional migration flows based on relative regional economic attractiveness create further interregional linkages at level C.

10.3.1 TEST DESIGN

The multiplier experiments are conducted at each of these three levels. The aim is to discover the properties of ECESIS at each of the levels. In particular, does moving from one level to another significantly alter the properties of ECESIS?

The experiment consists of reducing the level of 1959 total personal income in each state by one-half of one percent. This is accomplished by subtracting $.005 \times YT_{1959}$ from the exogenous variable YFARM, total farm income. The same level of the shock is sustained throughout the 1959 to 1980 period. This is a fairly severe shock, amounting to a decline in farm income of about fifteen percent for the U.S. as a whole. It should be noted that farm income is a passive variable in ECESIS in the sense that it does not directly affect any equation except the total income identity. Thus, any exogenous income item could have been used for the purposes of this experiment; residence income adjustment, for instance. There is no special meaning to the reduction in farm income. Also, no other variables are directly shocked. Farm employment, for example, is not reduced along with the income shock. In other words, this shock is generic; many interpretations of the income reduction are possible.

For convenience, the shocked solutions from levels A, B and C are referred to as MULTA, MULTB and MULTC, respectively. Each of these solutions is compared to the control solution described in Section 10.2. Dynamic, impact and long-run multipliers are computed as described in Section 10.1.

10.3.2 TEST RESULTS

Table 10.3.1 provides a convenient summary of the multiplier results for total personal income. Column one lists the MULTA impact income multipliers for each state. They are quite low and similar in magnitude across states, ranging from 1.08 in North Dakota to 1.35 in West Virginia. For the U.S., the impact multiplier is 1.15 and the simple average across the fifty-one regions is 1.18 with a variance of only .0025. Since each state model has essentially the same structure and is shocked by the same percent of income, the similarity of the impact multipliers is not too surprising.

Column two lists the MULTB (endogenous interregional economic linkages) impact income multipliers. These range from 1.06 in Arkansas to 2.16 in North Carolina with a simple average of 1.44 and a variance of .053. The total U.S. multiplier increases to 1.43. Generally, the MULTB

TABLE 10.3.1

IMPACT AND LONG-RUN INCOME MULTIPLIERS

	IMPACT			DYNAMIC		
STATE	MULTA	MULTB	MULTC	MULTA	MULTB	MULTC
UNITED STATES	1.15	1.43	1.43	1.11	2.31	2.07
ALABAMA	1.22	1.78	1.77	1.18	3.16	3.37
ALASKA	1.16	1.59	1.62	1.12	5.18	4.28
ARIZONA	1.15	1.36	1.38	1.11	4.94	5.03
ARKANSAS	1.24	1.06	1.12	1.20	4.01	4.19
CALIFORNIA	1.16	1.39	1.39	1.12	2.77	2.85
COLORADO	1.16	1.82	1.82	1.13	4.21	4.38
CONNECTICUT	1.12	1.39	1.39	1.09	0.35	0.38
DELAWARE	n.a.	n.a.	n.a.	n.a.	n.a.	n.a.
WASHINGTON DC	n.a.	n.a.	n.a.	n.a.	n.a.	n.a.
FLORIDA	1.21	1.60	1.69	1.18	6.52	7.06
GEORGIA	1.12	1.49	1.48	1.09	3.50	2.49
HAWAII	n.a.	n.a.	n.a.	n.a.	n.a.	n.a.
IDAHO	1.19	1.24	1.23	1.15	4.53	3.62
ILLINOIS	1.13	1.30	1.30	1.11	2.68	2.30
INDIANA	1.14	1.53	1.54	1.11	2.59	2.35
IOWA	1.17	1.22	1.21	1.14	3.36	3.23
KANSAS	1.18	1.44	1.43	1.14	2.36	2.41
KENTUCKY	1.21	1.39	1.38	1.19	3.86	4.03
LOUISIANA	1.18	1.42	1.39	1.15	2.74	3.66
MAINE	1.29	1.69	1.67	1.24	2.36	1.83
MARYLAND	1.13	1.54	1.52	1.09	1.46	2.14
MASSACHUSETTS	1.16	1.27	1.27	1.13	1.13	-.30
MICHIGAN	1.14	1.70	1.70	1.11	2.00	0.72
MINNESOTA	1.14	1.28	1.28	1.10	2.93	3.26
MISSISSIPPI	1.27	1.11	1.14	1.22	3.56	4.22
MISSOURI	1.17	1.37	1.37	1.14	2.94	2.89
MONTANA	1.20	1.93	1.95	1.15	2.95	2.68
NEBRASKA	1.18	1.53	1.53	1.14	3.48	3.11
NEVADA	1.13	1.21	1.18	1.10	3.01	3.11
NEW HAMPSHIRE	1.16	1.35	1.34	1.12	2.06	0.78
NEW JERSEY	1.13	1.13	1.13	1.08	0.82	1.76
NEW MEXICO	1.24	1.35	1.33	1.21	2.84	2.82
NEW YORK	1.18	1.30	1.30	1.15	-.96	-1.43
NORTH CAROLINA	1.15	2.16	2.20	1.11	3.14	2.66

TABLE 10.3.1 (cont)

IMPACT AND LONG-RUN INCOME MULTIPLIERS

	IMPACT			DYNAMIC		
STATE	MULTA	MULTB	MULTC	MULTA	MULTB	MULTC
NORTH DAKOTA	1.08	1.30	1.31	1.06	3.23	2.12
OHIO	1.12	1.66	1.66	1.09	2.05	1.95
OKLAHOMA	1.24	1.61	1.59	1.19	4.79	5.05
OREGON	1.18	1.32	1.34	1.13	3.82	3.70
PENNSYLVANIA	1.22	1.64	1.64	1.17	1.91	2.03
RHODE ISLAND	1.21	1.13	1.13	1.18	2.83	2.82
SOUTH CAROLINA	1.15	1.45	1.45	1.11	3.48	3.14
SOUTH DAKOTA	1.17	1.30	1.30	1.13	2.49	2.07
TENNESSEE	1.21	1.54	1.51	1.16	2.86	3.11
TEXAS	1.19	1.55	1.55	1.15	5.82	4.60
UTAH	1.19	1.36	1.35	1.15	2.52	2.62
VERMONT	1.19	1.15	1.14	1.16	1.88	0.78
VIRGINIA	1.14	1.75	1.79	1.11	2.71	0.42
WASHINGTON	1.18	1.23	1.22	1.15	3.48	2.39
WEST VIRGINIA	1.35	1.54	1.52	1.30	2.68	2.47
WISCONSIN	1.12	1.22	1.23	1.09	1.89	2.17
WYOMING	n.a.	n.a.	n.a.	n.a.	n.a.	n.a.
AVERAGE	1.18	1.44	1.44	1.16	2.96	2.71
VARIANCE	.0025	.0527	.0546	.0220	1.771	2.223

impact multipliers are about twenty-five percent higher than their MULTA counterparts. Only in Arkansas, Mississippi, Rhode Island and Vermont do the interregional feedback effects cause a reduction in the impact income multiplier.

Comparing columns two and three shows that there is virtually no change in the impact multipliers when the demographic linkages are activated (MULTC). The U.S. and simple average multipliers are unchanged from MULTB and the variance across states increases only slightly to .055. The greatest change is in Florida, 1.60 to 1.69. As the Florida economy slows due to the negative income shock, net migration into Florida also slows. This relative decline in population feeds back to the state economy increasing the multiplier effect in the fully linked model. This effect is most pronounced in Florida due to the important role of population growth in that state's economy.

Comparison of the impact multipliers across the three levels of linkages does not reveal any major structural changes. This is to be expected since most of the economic and demographic interregional linkages respond to disequilibria over time and would not be expected to have a great impact in the first period of the simulation. The paths of the multiperiod dynamic multipliers over time will better reveal the effects of the varying level of linkages.

The dynamic multipliers from the MULTA simulation indicate that the stand-alone state economic models are essentially static models. The period two dynamic multiplier drops to approximately zero and remains there through to 1980. Thus, the total long-run multipliers are about the same in MULTA as the impact multipliers. Column four of Table 10.3.1 lists the long-run multipliers for MULTA. The fifty-one state average is 1.16 with a variance of .022. Several key variables are exogenous to the states during a level A simulation of ECESIS. Thus, the income shock is not able to filter into the output and employment sectors directly. A "true" stand-alone regional model would be more conscious of within region feedbacks among sectors. This is often done in an ad hoc manner, however, since the key economic linkage variables in ECESIS, trade-weighted income and distance-weighted population and wages, are frequently just replaced with exogenous U.S. level equivalents. ECESIS was designed with interregional and demographic linkages in mind. When those linkages are turned off, the dynamic properties of the state economic models are very simple.

There is a dramatic change in the time path of the dynamic multipliers in the level B simulation. Nearly all of the states follow a damped cyclical pattern of adjustment to the shock. Figure 10.3.1, which plots the MULTA, MULTB and MULTC dynamic multipliers for the total U.S., illustrates the point. Note that it takes a full twenty years to complete just one phase of the cycle.

Figure 10.3.2 shows the change in income from the control solution for each of the three multiplier simulations. Income in MULTA drops by slightly more than the total shock (-$1900. million) and then very slowly and monotonically moves back toward the control solution. In MULTB, income drops steadily until about 1965 before beginning to increase again. By 1973 the recovery falters and another downswing begins. By 1980 another income recovery is about to begin. The cycle is clearly damped but gives all indications of continuing for some time.

The dynamic multiplier and income adjustment paths of most states follow the patterns of Figures 10.3.1 and 10.3.2. Four exceptions are Delaware, District of Columbia, Hawaii and Wyoming which tended to follow explosive cyclical patterns. Consequently, these four state economic models were left exogenous in all of the multiplier experiments. DC, Hawaii and Wyoming all have very small manufacturing sectors, accounting for less than six percent of total personal income. Since the manufacturing sector plays such a key role in ECESIS, it is not surprising that these states do not perform well.

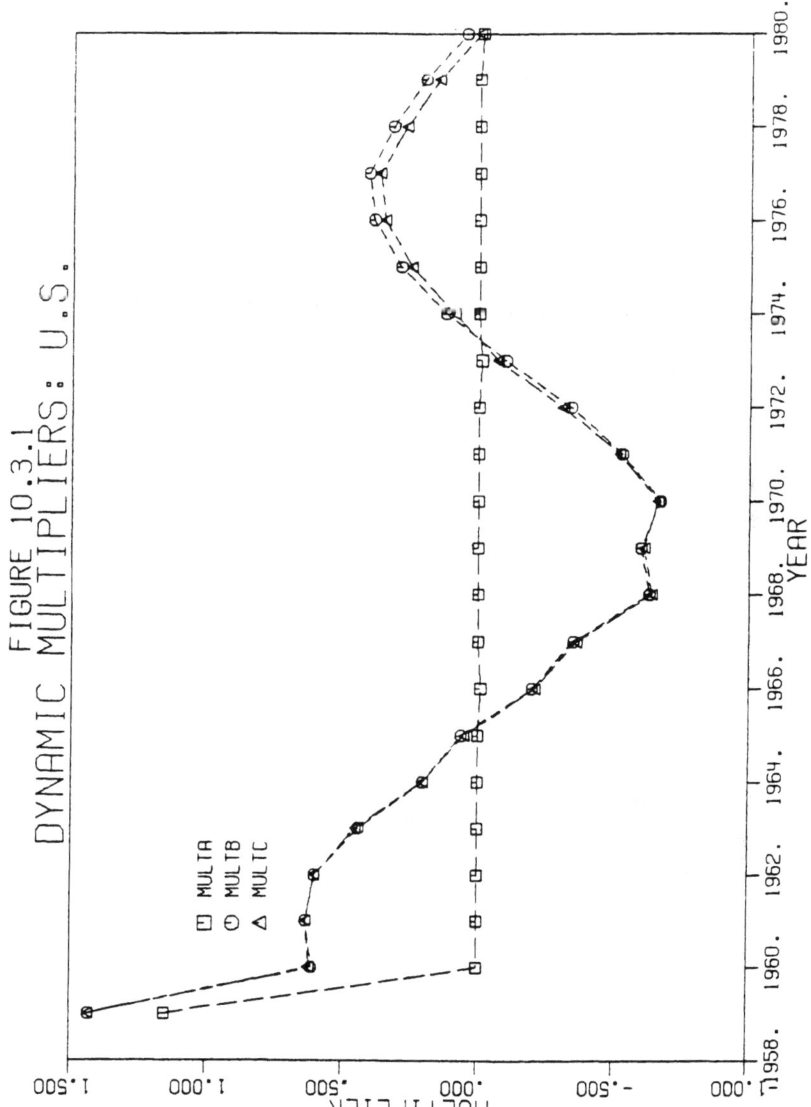

FIGURE 10.3.1
DYNAMIC MULTIPLIERS: U.S.

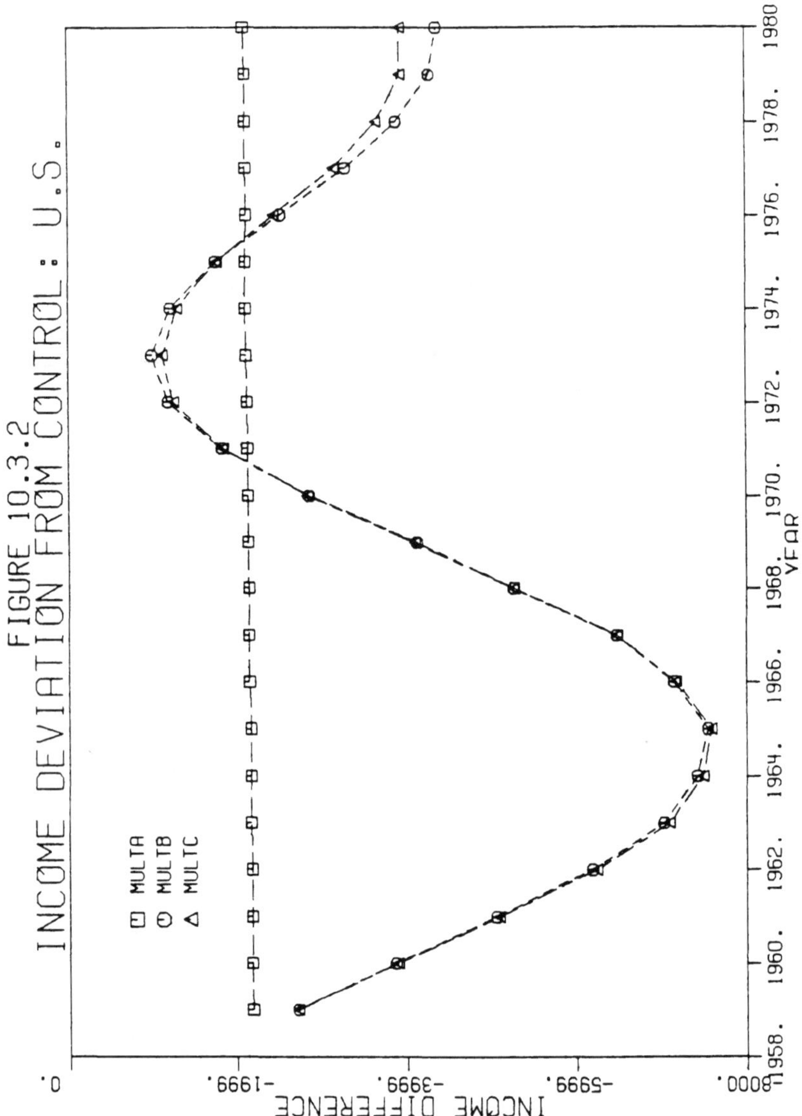

FIGURE 10.3.2
INCOME DEVIATION FROM CONTROL: U.S.

Although they follow the same cyclical pattern, some states fair better than others. Connecticut, New Jersey and New York, for example, enjoy periods when income actually moves above the baseline level. These states have very low capacity utilization rates in the last few years of the control solution.[5] Thus, they are in a very good position to expand output quickly during the upswing of the cycle.

The long-run income multipliers for MULTB are listed in column five of Table 10.3.1. The U.S. multiplier is 2.31 and the fifty-one state average is 2.96; a 150% increase over the MULTA values. The across state variation also increases significantly to 1.77.

The change in model performance from level B to level C is not very great. Figures 10.3.1 and 10.3.2 show that the adjustment paths of MULTB and MULTC are quite similar. The long-run income multipliers, listed in column six of Table 10.3.1, tend to fall by about ten percent but the across state variation increases slightly to 2.22.

The greatest change in adjustment paths occurs in Virginia. As illustrated in Figure 10.3.3, Virginia fairs much better in the MULTC simulation than in MULTB. When population dynamics are endogenous, 15,000 additional

---

[5] Recall that 1975 was a year of severe recession that was particularly hard felt in the Northeast states.

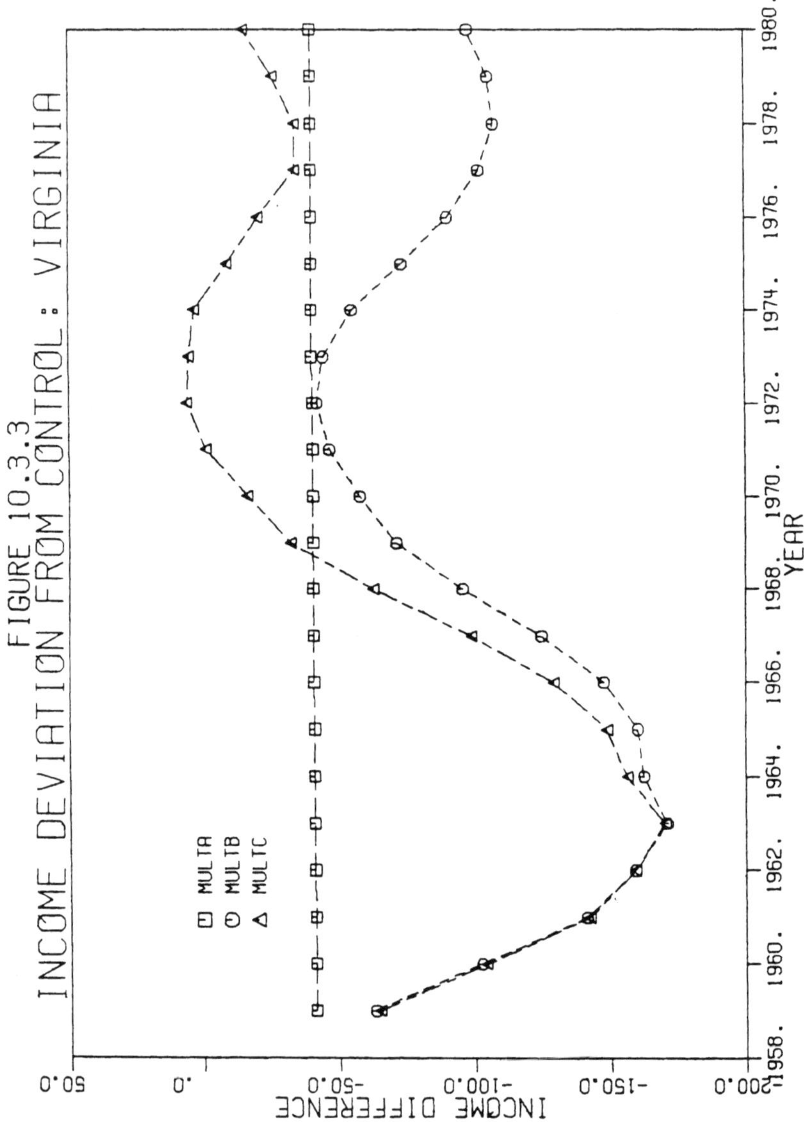

FIGURE 10.3.3
INCOME DEVIATION FROM CONTROL: VIRGINIA

persons move into Virginia during the recovery period from 1963 to 1972. This additional stimulus effect on the Virginia economy makes the MULTC recovery much more pronounced.

Even though the introduction of the demographic linkages does not seem to change the basic properties of the state models, they do significantly influence the state economies. In New York, for example, the economic trough comes in 1965 in response to the income shock. When the demographic linkages are exogenous, income is $850 million below the baseline value in that year. When population is made endogenous, nearly fourteen thousand persons choose to leave New York in 1965 in search of job opportunities in other states less hard hit by the down-turn. As a result, employment falls by five thousand and income falls to $900 million below baseline in 1965. Thus, the economic adjustment cycle in New York is amplified when population dynamics are taken into account. In other states, California, for example, the adjustment cycles are muted when population is made endogenous.

No apparent spatial pattern emerges when the long-run MULTB and MULTC multipliers are compared. However, both the MULTC and MULTB long-run multipliers tend to be the greatest in the Southern states and the smallest in the East North Central, Middle Atlantic and Northeast states. Among the latter, only Rhode Island's MULTC long-run income multiplier is above the simple fifty-one state average.

Multipliers for variables other than total personal income could be analyzed in similar fashion. In general, the income multipliers tell the story quite well. Manufacturing output multipliers follow the same pattern as the income multipliers but the cycles tend to be somewhat more damped. Population multipliers, relevant only in MULTC, tend to be cyclical but quite low and do not follow any particular spatial pattern. This is to be expected in this type of experiment since all regions of the country were similarly shocked. There is no favored region to attract population flows. Individual states, of course, lose or gain population according to their responses to the shock.

The multiplier results are fairly symmetric with either positive or negative income shocks. The positive shocks tended to push some states toward capacity constraints for some years in the early 1960's. This complicates the interpretation of the multipliers so the negative shock was chosen for this analysis.

Clearly the dynamic properties of the ECESIS model change significantly from level A to level C. The most dramatic change occurs when the interregional economic linkages are activated. The cyclical adjustment path of level B is more realistic than the nearly static path of level A. Also, the larger long-run income multipliers for levels B and C are closer to what one might expect a priori. Possibly the adjustment cycles are too long and not damped enough. ECESIS may err on the side of being too sensitive to interregional linkages.

The interregional economic-demographic linkages do not produce dramatically different model properties but do have significant impacts on the state models. The demographic model plays an important role in the ECESIS system.

The overhead costs of moving from level B to level C are very high. Much simpler demographic submodels could have been used to close the ECESIS system. The tests in Chapter Eleven will help determine the influence of various types of demographic models on the ECESIS system.

CHAPTER ELEVEN: ALTERNATIVE DEMOGRAPHIC MODELS

11.1 INTRODUCTION

The ECESIS demographic model is an interregional cohort-component model combined with a modified Markov model using relative economic attractiveness to determine interstate migration. This model is very much "state of the art", but, as seen in Chapters Eight and Nine, it is also very large and complex. The multiplier tests discussed in the previous chapter indicate that the addition of the demographic model to ECESIS does not create major changes in the dynamic properties of the system. The results do indicate, however, that the demographic model has a significant affect on the solution of the system. This chapter examines the question of how sensitive the ECESIS system is to the particular type of demographic model used.

Two issues will be examined. First, what is the impact of varying degrees of economic motivation for the migration decision? Second, is a sophisticated demographic accounts model really necessary in an economic-demographic model? It is not practical to examine these issues in the context of all of the demographic models discussed in Chapter Seven.

Since this research is concerned with interregional economic-demographic models, the naive population projection techniques will not be considered here.[1] Similarly, single region cohort-component models will not be examined. The focus here will be on economic-base models and interregional cohort-component (ICC) models. The latter are typified by the Rees-Wilson procedure, a variant of which is used as the CONTROL version of ECESIS. This demographic model is described in detail in Chapters Eight and Nine. The economic-base model used here is a variation of the Bureau of Economic Analysis (BEA) population projection model described in Section 3 of Chapter Seven. This model completely ignores the complicated aging and components of change accounting that the ICC models use; it provides a good contrasting framework to study the two questions above.

Section 2 describes the CONTROL solution to which the experiments in this chapter are compared. The design of the tests, their rational and mechanical implementation is given in Section 3. Finally, Section 4 summarizes the results of the tests and draws a few conclusions.

---

[1] See Voss, Palit, Kale and Krebs (1981) for a discussion of extrapolative naive models.

11.2 THE CONTROL SOLUTION

The time period for these experiments is from 1981 to 2000. This section describes how the CONTROL solution for that period is constructed.

Chapter Ten gives a brief description of the Gauss-Siedel iterative procedure for solving nonlinear systems like ECESIS. All of the equations in ECESIS are in explicit form, so that the dependent variable in an equation is not directly a function of itself. The values for the s+1 iteration are computed from

$$y_{1t}^{(s+1)} = f_1(y_{2t}^{(s)}, y_{3t}^{(s)}, \ldots, y_{nt}^{(s)}; Y_{t-1}; X_t; \theta_1) + e_{1t}$$

$$(11.2.1) \quad y_{2t}^{(s+1)} = f_2(y_{1t}^{(s+1)}, y_{3t}^{(s)}, \ldots, y_{nt}^{(s)}; Y_{t-1}; X_t; \theta_2) + e_{2t}$$

$$\ldots$$

$$y_{nt}^{(s+1)} = f_n(y_{1t}^{(s+1)}, y_{2t}^{(s+1)}, \ldots, y_{n-1,t}^{(s+1)}; Y_{t-1}; X_t; \theta_n) + e_{nt},$$

where Y_{t-1} is the vector of lagged endogenous variables, X_t is the vector of exogenous variables, θ_i is the vector of parameters for the ith equation and e_{it} is an additive random disturbance term. Since the historical data end in t=1980, special consideration must be given to the initial iterative values for the endogenous variables when t≥1981 ($y_{it}^{(0)}$; t=1981,...,2000). In most cases, the solution is to set

(11.2.2) $y_{it}^{(0)} = y_{i,t-1}$, $\forall i$; $\forall t \geq 1981$.

In addition, values must be provided for the exogenous variables and the residuals for the 1981 to 2000 period.

All of this would be quite routine except for the complex procedure required to compute residuals for the demographic model of ECESIS.[2] The relationships among the residuals and the two-pass algorithm rule out simple extrapolative procedures to obtain the residuals. It is simpler to compute residuals on the basis of extrapolated endogenous variable values. The ideal procedure would be to project values for the endogenous variables for each state economy and the demographic model on a stand-alone basis and use these values for the $y_{it}^{(0)}$, t=1981,...,2000. Time and resource constraints prohibit this procedure. Instead, the economic and demographic data are projected to the year 2000 using a simple autoregressive integrated moving average (ARIMA) model. Next, residual terms are calculated for these data on an individual model basis. This procedure is in lieu of individual model forecasts. No attempt is made at this point to make the projected data consistent with identities and across state restrictions. Using these projected data and calculated residuals as a starting point, the ECESIS model is run in fully linked mode (level C) to

---

[2] See Section 2 of Chapter Ten for the details of this procedure.

produce a CONTROL solution for the period 1981 to 2000.

The CONTROL solution will not be the same as the extrapolated values because the fully linked mode, in resolving all identity, technical and accounting constraints, will require the model to go through several passes before a consistent convergence is achieved. The CONTROL solution, however, is certainly a function of the starting point and that starting point was derived mechanically rather than by considering the particulars of each region.

As a result, the trends of the 1960's and 1970's are more or less extrapolated through to 2000. The North Central and Northeastern states continue their slow decline and the Southern and Western states continue their rapid growth. Many other scenarios are possible. Whether or not this particular one is believable, it is the one that has been imposed in the CONTROL solution. Like all time-series models, ECESIS will project those trends with which it is most familiar. To do otherwise would require "user intervention". In other words, the modeller would have to provide forecasts for particular regions that buck the trends on which the model was estimated. Some evidence suggests that this is precisely what should be done for long-term regional projections. But faced with limited resources and a large model like ECESIS, a mechanical procedure was required.

One advantage of this procedure, other than cost and time savings, is that the CONTROL is relatively smooth. By comparison, the actual historical data for some states are quite volatile--more so than can be comfortably believed. The smooth CONTROL makes the task of comparing the results of the various experiments easier.

Table 11.2.1 shows values for selected variables for the U.S. from the CONTROL solution. The first six columns are percentage growth rates and the last three columns are in levels. No attempt has been made to make these growth rates plausible. They are simply numbers that are internally consistent and in the same ballpark with recent historical values. Regional growth rates do not differ greatly. The regions maintain their relative standings from the 1970's throughout the 1981 to 2000 period.

11.3 DESIGN OF THE TESTS

In an aggregate migration model, it is the "average" person that must be modelled, but people move for many reasons and the priorities that they put on those reasons depend upon the age, sex and socio-economic status of the individual. A key issue for the migration modeller is how much emphasis to place on the economic incentives for moves.

TABLE 11.2.1

SELECTED DATA FROM THE U.S. CONTROL SOLUTION

YT - TOTAL PERSONAL INCOME
WMH - AVERAGE HOURLY MANUFACTURING EARNINGS
CPI72 - CONSUMER PRICE INDEX
PTOT - TOTAL POPULATION
LTOT - TOTAL LABOR FORCE
ET - TOTAL EMPLOYMENT
UR - UNEMPLOYMENT RATE
MCU - MANUFACTURING CAPACITY UTILIZATION RATE
R1844 - 18-44 YEAR OLD LF PARTICIPATION RATE
UNITED STATES

	YT	WMH	CPI72	PTOT	LTOT	ET	UR	MCU	R1844
1981	5.87	4.92	9.81	.88	1.59	1.04	7.60	.80	.79
1982	6.56	6.78	7.00	.95	2.02	-.35	9.75	.78	.80
1983	7.39	5.56	6.00	.96	1.63	1.41	9.99	.80	.81
1984	8.41	5.77	6.00	.96	1.55	2.68	8.99	.82	.82
1985	8.40	5.87	5.62	.95	1.46	2.58	7.99	.84	.82
1986	9.95	5.88	6.41	.94	1.45	2.34	7.18	.86	.83
1987	8.00	6.03	5.99	.92	1.42	1.86	6.78	.88	.84
1988	8.00	6.25	5.02	.90	1.22	1.65	6.38	.89	.84
1989	8.01	6.82	5.00	.88	1.11	1.11	6.38	.89	.85
1990	8.00	6.65	5.00	.85	.95	1.27	6.08	.89	.85
1991	8.00	6.79	4.99	.82	.93	1.14	5.88	.89	.86
1992	8.00	6.97	5.00	.78	.76	.97	5.68	.89	.86
1993	8.00	6.90	5.00	.75	.71	1.03	5.39	.89	.86
1994	8.00	6.90	5.01	.71	.81	1.02	5.19	.89	.86
1995	8.00	6.84	5.00	.68	.87	1.08	5.00	.89	.87
1996	8.00	6.93	4.99	.64	1.00	.99	5.00	.89	.87
1997	8.00	7.02	5.01	.62	.91	.91	5.00	.89	.87
1998	8.00	6.93	4.99	.59	.99	.99	5.00	.89	.88
1999	8.00	6.83	4.99	.57	1.05	1.05	5.00	.89	.88
2000	8.01	6.83	5.02	.56	1.07	1.04	5.02	.89	.88

According to Long and Hansen (1979, pg. 26), "the most commonly cited reasons for moving were either (1) a job transfer or (2) a new job or the search for employment." ECESIS addresses this issue empirically by estimating the elasticity of the migrant's response to economic attractiveness.

Recall that migration in ECESIS is modelled with a modified Markov process,

$$(11.3.1)\quad p_{ij}(t) = p_{ij}(t-1)[A_j(t)/A_j(t-1)]^{\gamma}\cdot D_i^{-1},$$

where

$$p_{ij}(t) = M_{ij}(t)/P_i(t-1),$$
$$D_i = \Sigma_k p_{ik}(t-1)[A_k(t)/A_k(t-1)]^{\gamma}.$$

The term $p_{ij}(t)$ defines the probability of moving from region i to region j during the tth period. The constraint $\Sigma_j p_{ij}(t)=1$ is satisfied by the balancing factor D_i. $M_{ij}(t)$ is the migration flow between regions i and j during period t and $P_i(t-1)$ is the population in region i at the end of period t-1 that survives until the end of period t (the survived population). $A_j(t)$ is the attractiveness of region j and is defined differently according to age-sex groups. For migrants in the labor force age groups, the attraction variable is defined as

$$(11.3.2)\quad A_j(t) = \frac{\Delta ET_j(t)+s(t)\cdot ET_j(t-1)}{U_j(t-1)+s(t)\cdot ET_j(t-1)}$$

where ET is total employment, U is total unemployment, and s is the separation rate excluding layoffs. A separate elasticity (γ) is estimated for each of these age-sex groups; γ ranges from .43 to .53. For persons under labor force age the attraction variable is defined as the migration flow of fecund females with gamma set to one. Elderly migrants are modelled with A_j=1 or equivalently, γ=0.

The simplest way to change the economic incentive for migration in the ECESIS model is to change the value of γ for the labor force age groups. For the CONTROL solution the γ's are approximately one-half. An alternative version of the model is created when all the gammas are set to zero (GAMMA0). This GAMMA0 model is very different from the CONTROL model. When γ=0, D_i=1 and (11.3.1) reduces to the pure fixed transition rate Markov model,

(11.3.3) $p_{ij}(t) = p_{ij}(t-1)$.

In this case, economic incentives play no role in the migration decision; only historical trends matter. GAMMA0 eliminates economic to demographic model feedbacks in the ECESIS system.

Another version of the model is created by setting all of the gammas equal to one (GAMMA1). The GAMMA1 model effectively doubles the migrant's response to economic attractiveness over the CONTROL model.

GAMMA0, CONTROL and GAMMA1 are all variants of the same basic ECESIS demographic model. All retain the demographic accounts model with its complex aging and components of change procedures. Only the economic incentives to migrate are altered. Nonetheless, the conceptual differences among those three variants are considerable. The current state level population projection model of the Bureau of the Census is very much like GAMMA0 with a simpler accounts model. CONTROL and GAMMA1 give progressively more weight to economic incentives to move. Even in GAMMA1, however, previous migration trends play an important role in current migration decisions. The next step in this progression of models is to make the current migration decision completely independent of previous migration patterns and totally dependent upon economic incentives. An entirely different type of demographic model is required to achieve this.

The economic-base model of the U.S. Bureau of Economic Analysis (BEA) suits this purpose. The BEA demographic model (BEAPOP) determines regional population solely on the basis of regional employment growth. The idea is simple. First project economic growth and job creation in a region and then assume that enough people to fill the jobs will migrate to the region. In slow growth regions people will move out. Using the BEA hypothesis, population in state i is determined from

(11.3.4) $PTOT_{i,t} = PTOT_{i,t-1}(ET_{i,t-1}/ET_{i,t-2})$.

The model assumes constant employment to population ratios. In order to achieve the completely post-recursive nature of the BEA procedure, employment growth in BEAPOP is lagged one period. Birth, death, and place-to-place migration flows are not calculated by this model and the formal aging procedure used in the ECESIS demographic model is ignored.

Because the ECESIS economic models expect some age and sex detail, some extensions to the BEA's procedure are made in BEAPOP in order to make comparisons to the other demographic models. Age and sex specific births and deaths are set to the CONTROL solution values and treated as exogenous. Total population is disaggregated into age-sex specific populations as follows. Consider a matrix with the ten age-sex groups of ECESIS along the columns and the fifty-one regions along the rows.

(11.3.5)

.	.
$\cdots {}^{a}POP_{i}{}^{s} \cdots$	$PTOT_{i}$
.	.
$\cdots {}^{a}POP_{us}{}^{s} \cdots$	$PTOT_{us}$

The individual cell elements, ${}^{a}POP_i{}^{s}$, add to total state population ($PTOT_i$) across columns and to total U.S. age-sex specific populations (${}^{a}POP_{us}{}^{s}$) across rows. For each time period, the column totals are determined from (11.3.4) and the row totals are determined by the U.S. population constraints. Given these margins, the cell elements of (11.3.5) can be determined using a simple RAS procedure.[3]

The ECESIS economic models must be slightly modified in order to accommodate the BEAPOP demographic model. Recall from Chapter Six that, excluding wages, there are five key labor market variables that must be determined: population (PTOT), employment (ET), labor force (LF), labor force participation rate (ρ) and unemployment rate (UR). Two of these must be determined by identity. The CONTROL version of ECESIS determines PTOT, ET and ρ by stochastic equation and uses the identities

(11.3.6) $LF = \rho \cdot PTOT$ and $UR = (LF-ET)/LF$

to determine LF and UR. This combination leads to problems in the BEAPOP version of ECESIS. Substituting the LF identity into the UR identity and remembering that PTOT is a function of ET, it can be shown that

(11.3.7) $\xi(UR,ET) = C\cdot[\xi(PTOT,ET)+\xi(\rho,ET)-1]$,

[3] The previous period's values serve as starting points for the cell elements in the RAS procedure.

where C is a constant and $\xi(a,b)$ is the elasticity of a with respect to b. From (11.3.4), $\xi(PTOT,ET)=1$ and, assuming that $\xi(\rho,ET)$ is fairly small, $\xi(UR,ET)$ is approximately zero. In other words, despite the rate of employment growth, the unemployment rate would remain constant. This is particularly troublesome given that the simulations begin in 1981, a year of very high unemployment rates. Clearly then the unemployment rate may be modelled by behavioral equation or by simply making it exogenous but not by identity. The solution taken here is the same one used by the BEA's projection model; the unemployment rate is treated as exogenous and set to the CONTROL solution values. Employment remains determined as before, population is determined from (11.3.4) with age-sex detail added as in (11.3.5) and labor force and the labor force participation rate are determined from the identities

$$\begin{aligned} LF &= ET/(1-UR), \\ \rho &= LF/PTOT. \end{aligned} \tag{11.3.8}$$

No age-sex detail is added to the labor force figures. This approach reduces the demographic to economic feedbacks of the system. Of course, the point of the BEA's, and thus BEAPOP's, model design is to determine regional population on the basis of regional economic conditions and to allow no simultaneous feedbacks.

Given exogenous births (B) and deaths (D) and population from (11.3.4), net migration (NM) for each region can be computed from

(11.3.9) $NM = PTOT - PTOT_{-1} - B + D.$

Since PTOT is completely determined by employment, net migration is also completely determined by local employment. If employment in a region increases then people will migrate into that area to fill those jobs. No weight at all is given to traditional migration trends. Thus, BEAPOP is an extreme case of the GAMMA versions of ECESIS; the polar opposite of GAMMA0.

The simple RAS aging procedure, exogenous births and deaths, and implicit net migration determination of BEAPOP are extremely simple compared to the apparatus carried around by the demographic model in the CONTROL version of ECESIS. Comparing the simulations of the two versions will help indicate whether the additional complexity of demographic accounts models is worthwhile.

Initially there was one other experiment to be considered in this group of tests. Assuming that the demographic accounts model is a useful tool, is the migration model an unnecessary appendage to that system? In other words, even the simple fixed rate Markov migration model of GAMMA0 is quite complex and data intensive. Could the migration model be eliminated entirely? The simplest way to test this is to set net migration for each state equal to zero for each forecast year. This NONET scenario is commonly used at the Bureau of the Census because net migration estimates are so volatile and difficult to project.

Technical problems prevented the completion of this experiment. The problems encountered, however, provide some useful information on the mechanics of the ECESIS model. The demographic model of the CONTROL version of ECESIS is based on the Rees and Wilson demographic accounts model. As described in Chapter Eight, this procedure calculates minor population flows, which as the name suggests, are small in magnitude. These minor flows, however, are a mechanically crucial part of the Rees-Wilson algorithm. If net migration is assumed to be zero, the minor flow calculations break down and the Rees-Wilson demographic model cannot be solved. This is the proverbial tail wagging the dog. Elaborate as the Rees-Wilson demographic accounts model is, one must wonder at its extreme sensitivity to the calculation of seemingly minor variables. This suggests that the Rees-Wilson ediface rests on shaky foundations. Further discussion is contained in the conclusions of Chapter One.

11.4 TEST RESULTS

In terms of economic incentives for interstate migration, the various versions of ECESIS may be ranked in the order: GAMMA0, CONTROL, GAMMA1 and BEAPOP. Economic factors have no affect on the migrants' decisions to move in GAMMA0--only historical trends (the initial Markov transition matrix) affect their decisions. In the CONTROL version the elasticity of the migrants' response to economic attractiveness is estimated to minimize the root mean square prediction error of the migration transition rates. Historical migration trends still play a significant role in this version. GAMMA1 sets the elasticities estimated in CONTROL to one--essentially doubling the elasticity response. Still, past trends affect the migrants' decisions. The same demographic accounts model is used in all of the GAMMA0, CONTROL and GAMMA1 versions; only the economic impact on migration changes. BEAPOP is an entirely different type of demographic model. There is no formal accounting model and the migration decision is completely determined by economic factors. Historical trends have no bearing on the migrants' decisions.

In general, as the economic motivation for migrants increases, the "efficiency" of migration also increases. As migrants pay less attention to previously established migration patterns and more attention to economic opportunities, the U.S. economy as a whole benefits. The figures in Table 11.4.1 help to illustrate this point. It shows changes in total employment, real personal income and the unemployment rate as the degree of economic motivation for migration is increased. For example, in 1995, the CONTROL solution shows increased employment of 85.19 thousand persons, increased real income of $764.3 million and an unemployment rate that is .064 points lower than in the GAMMA0 solution. Continuing to move across the table, the GAMMA1 solution shows an increase in employment of 119.75 thousand persons over the CONTROL solution. At the next level (BEAPOP), employment increases even further--1140.69 thousand persons over the GAMMA1 solution. At each stage of increased economic motivation for migration, employment increases over the previous stage. It should be noted here that the solution for BEAPOP in the year 2000 failed to converge in the maximum twenty passes. To be safe, the values for BEAPOP are reported only through 1998.

Some states proved to be unstable in the BEAPOP version. Thus, to prevent their unreliable solutions from affecting neighboring states, Arizona, Massachusetts, Nebraska and New Hampshire were left exogenous in the BEAPOP simulation. The District of Columbia, Hawaii and Wyoming are exogenous in all simulations in this section as per the discussion in Chapter Ten. Also, recall that the unemployment rate in

TABLE 11.4.1

NATIONAL LEVEL EFFECTS OF INCREASED ECONOMIC MOTIVATION TO MIGRATE

CNTL - CONTROL SOLUTION
G0 - GAMMA0 SOLUTION
G1 - GAMMA1 SOLUTION
BP - BEAPOP SOLUTION
ET - TOTAL EMPLOYMENT (THOUSANDS)
YT72 - REAL TOTAL PERSONAL INCOME (MILLIONS)
UR - UNEMPLOYMENT RATE (PERCENT)

	CNTL-G0			G1-CNTL			BP-G1	
	ET	YT72	UR	ET	YT72	UR	ET	YT72
1981	-7.50	-16.00	.01	7.44	17.00	-.01	-.50	19.00
1982	-8.56	-57.00	.01	8.31	54.00	-.01	.38	24.00
1983	-8.50	-74.00	.01	7.38	67.00	-.01	5.75	65.00
1984	-6.88	-67.00	.01	6.19	77.00	-.00	14.31	126.00
1985	-3.94	-46.00	.01	4.06	71.00	-.00	34.00	276.00
1986	-.13	-24.00	.01	2.75	73.00	.00	72.87	550.00
1987	3.94	11.00	.00	2.56	66.00	.00	131.38	1049.00
1988	9.06	55.00	-.00	4.75	72.00	.00	207.50	1823.00
1989	14.56	116.00	-.00	8.38	81.00	-.00	298.63	2903.00
1990	19.94	192.00	-.01	18.44	107.00	-.01	397.25	4210.00
1991	24.75	273.00	-.01	33.25	182.00	-.03	503.13	5742.00
1992	30.13	355.00	-.01	52.50	317.00	-.05	622.06	7552.00
1993	42.37	424.00	-.03	74.63	508.00	-.07	759.63	9676.00
1994	60.94	551.00	-.04	97.63	756.00	-.09	931.06	12273.00
1995	85.19	764.00	-.07	119.75	1033.00	-.12	1140.69	15281.00
1996	112.44	1057.00	-.10	139.00	1337.00	-.14	1330.69	17693.00
1997	138.75	1421.00	-.13	153.88	1653.00	-.16	1475.63	18435.00
1998	159.69	1815.00	-.15	162.19	1955.00	-.17	1562.13	15622.00
1999	172.56	2209.00	-.17	157.13	2178.00	-.17		
2000	174.50	2560.00	-.17	132.25	2278.00	-.15		

BEAPOP was set exogenously to the values from CONTROL. Thus the final column is omitted from the BP-CNTL group in Table 11.4.1.

There is an order of magnitude difference in the BEAPOP solution and the other solutions. When economic motives completely determine migration patterns migrants will move to wherever the jobs are located; even if that place is New Jersey. Distance, climate or where friends and family have relocated have no bearing on the decision. This, of course, is very efficient for the economy; regional labor shortages are nonexistent. Recall that the labor force and labor force participation rates are determined by identity in BEAPOP. As employment increases, more people are simply pulled into the labor force.

Even relatively small changes in the elasticity of the migrants' response to economic factors has a significant impact on national employment and real income. As the elasticity increases from zero to one, employment increases by over 300,000, real income increases by $4838 million and the unemployment rate drops by a third of a point by the year 2000.

The pattern displayed in Table 11.4.1 is not too surprising. Certainly, a priori, one would expect increased response to economic incentives to lead to increased economic efficiency. What is surprising is the dramatic difference created by BEAPOP. Clearly, the BEA type population projection model is an entirely different animal from the ECESIS CONTROL model.

Not all regions benefit equally from the more efficient allocation of labor resources. Most of the employment growth takes place in the eastern half of the U.S. Figure 11.4.1 shows those states where the employment changes are either always positive or always negative as you move across Table 11.4.1 for 1998. Moving from GAMMA0 to BEAPOP, employment increases for each version in Indiana while it steadily declines in Oklahoma. Florida is the only state east of the Mississippi River that suffers decreased employment as economic incentives for migration increase.

Historically, Florida has had a high rate of positive net migration. GAMMA0 simply projects this trend to the year 2000 independently of the relative economic growth of Florida. The CONTROL and GAMMA1 experiments reduce this pattern somewhat but still the historical trend plays an important role. The BEAPOP scenario, however, completely ignores Florida's history of inmigration and moves people in and out of Florida solely on the basis of relative economic opportunities in Florida. As a consequence, by 1998, Florida's population is 400,000 persons less under BEAPOP than under GAMMA0. Table 11.4.2 gives a more detailed

FIGURE 11.4.1

EMPLOYMENT CHANGES AS THE ECONOMIC INCENTIVES TO LITIGATE INCREASE: 1990

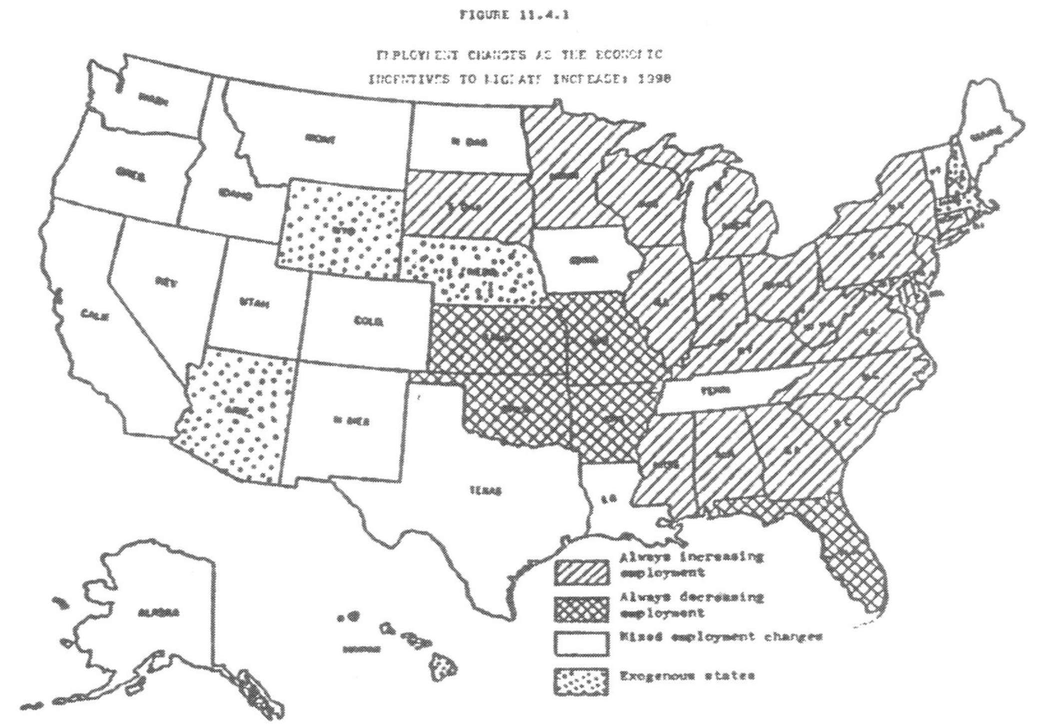

account of the affect of the different versions of the model on Florida. Similar arguments can be made, to a lesser extent, for California and some of the Mountain states.

Florida aside, Kansas, Missouri, Arkansas and Oklahoma suffer the most from the more efficient allocation of labor resources. The East North Central and Middle Atlantic states benefit the most. On the basis of economic factors alone, the Eastern states are fairly attractive. If migrants put sufficient weight on this consideration, there would be less migration out of the region.

The effects of increased economic motivation for migration on the Western states are mixed. These states are already attractive destinations for both economic and noneconomic reasons. The moderate incentive changes in GAMMA0, CONTROL and GAMMA1 show mixed results. Employment drops in all of the Western states, however, when comparing BEAPOP to GAMMA1. In other words, if the high amenities of the Western region are not taken into consideration at all, migrants will prefer the Eastern states. But even if a relatively low weight is given to those noneconomic amenities (GAMMA1), migrants find the Western states as attractive as the Eastern states.

Critics often claim that the BEA's economic and demographic projections overstate growth in the North

TABLE 11.4.2

EFFECTS ON FLORIDA OF INCREASED ECONOMIC MOTIVATION TO MIGRATE

CNTL - CONTROL SOLUTION
G0 - GAMMA0 SOLUTION
G1 - GAMMA1 SOLUTION
BP - BEAPOP SOLUTION
ET - TOTAL EMPLOYMENT (THOUSANDS)
YT72 - REAL TOTAL PERSONAL INCOME (MILLIONS)
PTOT - TOTAL POPULATION (THOUSANDS)

	CNTL-G0			G1-CNTL			BP-G1		
	ET	YT72	PTOT	ET	YT72	PTOT	ET	YT72	PTOT
1981	-.33	-1.86	.41	.42	2.81	.40	-.43	-2.61	-5.19
1982	-.13	-1.83	.43	.34	2.91	.25	-1.61	-9.50	-9.62
1983	-.13	-1.44	.50	.26	2.66	.23	-2.63	-19.07	-16.57
1984	-.07	-1.63	.16	.17	1.78	-.18	-4.26	-30.37	-24.12
1985	-.18	-2.69	-.88	-.11	-.14	-1.23	-6.35	-48.07	-34.43
1986	-.47	-5.42	-2.80	-.61	-4.30	-3.07	-7.79	-58.64	-45.32
1987	-1.04	-9.72	-5.50	-1.27	-9.42	-5.30	-9.14	-65.77	-57.84
1988	-1.85	-16.18	-9.02	-1.94	-15.23	-7.79	-10.26	-69.61	-72.74
1989	-2.90	-24.73	-13.44	-2.91	-24.41	-11.22	-10.91	-64.70	-86.25
1990	-4.18	-35.04	-18.43	-3.84	-34.11	-15.14	-10.88	-50.49	-99.63
1991	-5.69	-47.61	-24.00	-4.76	-43.92	-19.59	-10.35	-25.44	-109.93
1992	-7.88	-68.16	-29.87	-5.68	-53.20	-24.19	-9.29	5.88	-124.93
1993	-9.70	-88.94	-36.57	-6.69	-63.36	-29.61	-7.88	51.41	-137.32
1994	-11.48	-108.38	-43.85	-7.95	-75.14	-35.57	-4.09	124.68	-149.18
1995	-13.21	-127.34	-51.57	-9.45	-88.96	-41.91	2.32	235.74	-158.88
1996	-15.00	-146.80	-59.79	-11.22	-105.91	-48.65	2.51	282.37	-164.27
1997	-16.94	-167.16	-68.21	-13.29	-126.20	-55.49	-24.56	-30.76	-181.71
1998	-19.19	-190.94	-76.79	-15.55	-148.81	-62.18	-116.10	-1248.99	-257.02
1999	-21.80	-218.56	-85.57	-18.06	-175.00	-68.60			
2000	-24.56	-248.25	-94.36	-20.74	-204.19	-74.32			

Central and Northeast states and understate growth in the Southern and Western states. The experiments in this chapter indicate that the implicit migration model assumptions made by the BEA are a probable cause for this bias. Economic motives for migration are certainly important but probably are not the only factors migrants consider. Climate, recreational facilities and family ties are also considered by migrants. Thus, the migration model must model these factors explicitly or give some weight to already established migration trends.

The second issue to be examined in this section is whether the sophisticated demographic accounts model used by ECESIS is really necessary. The BEAPOP model version, in addition to its simple view of the migration decision, used a simple RAS procedure to handle age-sex population disaggregation. No attention is paid to the components of change of population. This is not to say that the basic demographic equation will not hold. Indeed, it is forced to hold since net migration is determined from the identity

$$NM = PTOT - PTOT_{-1} - B + D.$$

What is likely, however, is that some inconsistencies or unlikely patterns may emerge for individual age-sex groups. To isolate the effects of the demographic model, the BEAPOP simulation was rerun using CONTROL values for all of the economic data. In other words, all of the state economic models were treated as exogenous. Comparing the demographic projections from this simulation (BEAPOP-X) to the CONTROL demographic projection will highlight potential problems in the BEA "psuedo" accounts model.

In general, very few problems are encountered because of the lack of a rigorous accounts model. In Florida, for example, by the year 2000, there are 114,000 fewer persons in the BEAPOP-X forecast than in the CONTROL forecast. The RAS procedure distributes this loss proportionally across all age-sex groups. When the changes in the cell elements are large, as in this case, the RAS procedure is quite robust. The cases where consistency problems do arise are where the changes in cell elements are small.

Table 11.4.3 shows the differences between the BEAPOP-X and CONTROL projections for selected demographic variables for the state of Illinois. In the year 1997 the total population projections of the two model versions are very similar; only 20 persons different. But, BEAPOP-X shows 210 fewer males and 230 more females than the CONTROL. Small as these numbers are, it is an unlikely scenario and is representative of the type of errors that may arise when proper demographic accounting is ignored. This result is simply a product of the RAS procedure in BEAPOP-X. Since the cell element changes were very small, they were sensitive to changes induced by larger deviations in other

TABLE 11.4.3

DIFFERENCE IN POPULATION PROJECTIONS FOR BEAPOP-X AND CONTROL
(UNITS ARE THOUSANDS OF PERSONS)

PTOT - TOTAL POPULATION
PMALE - TOTAL MALE POPULATION
PFEM - TOTAL FEMALE POPULATION
P04M - MALE POPULATION AGED 0 TO 4 (ETC)

ILLINOIS

	PTOT	PMALE	PFEM	P04M	P04F	P517M	P517F	P1844M	P1844F	P4564M	P4564F	P65M	P65F
1981	1.21	.59	.62	.04	.04	.11	.11	.27	.26	.10	.12	.06	.09
1982	2.40	1.18	1.22	.10	.09	.23	.22	.54	.52	.20	.22	.11	.17
1983	3.15	1.55	1.60	.14	.13	.29	.28	.71	.68	.26	.28	.15	.22
1984	3.87	1.90	1.96	.18	.17	.36	.34	.86	.83	.32	.35	.19	.28
1985	4.75	2.33	2.42	.22	.21	.44	.41	1.03	1.01	.39	.42	.24	.36
1986	5.38	2.63	2.75	.25	.24	.49	.47	1.15	1.13	.44	.49	.29	.43
1987	5.99	2.91	3.08	.27	.26	.54	.52	1.25	1.25	.50	.55	.35	.51
1988	6.20	2.99	3.21	.27	.26	.55	.52	1.25	1.26	.54	.60	.39	.57
1989	6.64	3.19	3.45	.28	.26	.58	.55	1.31	1.33	.59	.66	.44	.64
1990	6.80	3.26	3.55	.27	.26	.59	.56	1.31	1.35	.62	.69	.47	.69
1991	6.71	3.20	3.51	.26	.24	.58	.55	1.26	1.31	.62	.69	.49	.71
1992	5.42	2.54	2.88	.18	.17	.45	.42	.91	.98	.54	.63	.47	.69
1993	4.44	2.03	2.41	.11	.11	.34	.31	.65	.75	.48	.57	.45	.67
1994	3.33	1.47	1.86	.05	.04	.22	.20	.38	.49	.40	.50	.43	.63
1995	2.40	.99	1.41	-.01	-.01	.11	.09	.15	.27	.33	.44	.41	.61
1996	1.23	.40	.83	-.07	-.07	-.03	-.04	-.12	.02	.25	.36	.38	.56
1997	.02	-.21	.23	-.14	-.14	-.18	-.18	-.38	-.24	.15	.28	.34	.51
1998	-1.11	-.78	-.32	-.20	-.20	-.31	-.31	-.63	-.48	.06	.20	.30	.46
1999	-2.19	-1.34	-.86	-.26	-.25	-.45	-.44	-.87	-.70	-.02	.12	.27	.41
2000	-3.21	-1.86	-1.35	-.32	-.31	-.57	-.56	-1.12	-.92	-.09	.06	.24	.38

cell elements.

Several other problems might arise as a result of the absence of an accounting model. For example, changes in the fertility and mortality rates implied by the BEAPOP-X projection would also be unlikely. In some states the mortality rates of males and females move in opposite directions, for instance. Nonetheless, these problems are not common and involve very small magnitudes. Unless detailed and highly consistent demographic projections are the main goal of an economic-demographic model, complex demographic accounting models appear to buy very little. The bulk and expense of the accounting framework may not be justified in some instances. There is also some evidence that detailed age-sex specific demographic data do not much improve the performance of economic forecasting models (Taylor 1982). Crude population groups with loose accounting links are sufficient for many economic applications. Where detailed demographic data are a valued output of the model, however, simple procedures as in BEAPOP cannot be trusted. In such cases, only the demographic accounts model will ensure consistent and precise demographic projections.

CHAPTER TWELVE: SIMULATION EXPERIMENTS

12.1 INTRODUCTION

Two simulation experiments have been chosen to demonstrate the usefulness of an interregional economic-demographic model of the U.S. in general and the ECESIS model in particular. The first experiment measures the impact of increased Asian immigration to the U.S. The issue is not only how this increased immigration will affect long-term economic growth in the U.S. but also how regional growth patterns will be affected. In terms of the model, this experiment shocks the demographic model and then traces the effects through the demographic to economic linkages to the state models.

The second simulation explores the usefulness of regional policies to stimulate investment in depressed regions. Targeting policies for specific regions may be a cost effective way to stimulate the economy. This experiment relies on the interregional trade linkages to transmit the shock throughout the U.S. Of course, the demographic model also plays a role as the changing economic attractiveness of regions affects internal migration patterns.

Both of these experiments use all of the facilities of ECESIS and could not easily be carried out using models without all of the components of ECESIS. Many such experiments are possible. These two are simply representative of shocks that might occur in different components of the overall model.

12.2 ECONOMIC IMPACTS OF ASIAN IMMIGRATION TO THE U.S.

12.2.1 THE ISSUES

The U.S. is often described as a nation of immigrants. Between 1820 and 1979, in perhaps "the greatest migration in the history of the world" (White 1976, p. 1), nearly 50 million people immigrated to the United States. Most Americans are descendants of immigrants. Nonetheless, there is an increasing cry to limit future immigration. The U.S. is no longer a frontier country able to absorb all newcomers. Many Americans fear the impact of "imported, cheap labor" and of unskilled refugees on their own jobs, wages, taxes, and incomes. Others argue that new immigrants are unwilling to assimilate socially as have other generations of immigrants. Further diversification, they say, will eventually lead to racial and social conflicts and tear the nation's social fabric.

Racial and ethnic attitudes are part of these concerns--particularly since Europe is no longer the source of most immigration. English settlers worried about the uncultured German immigrants in the mid 1800s. At the turn of the century it was the southern and eastern Europeans who drew the ire of "true Americans". Now the Asian immigrant is the subject of scrutiny.

Our nation's awareness of immigration as a social and political issue has been amplified through extensive recent media coverage of illegal Mexican immigration, Southeast Asian boatpeople, and the Cuban and Haitian flotillas. Yet little is known about the impact of immigration. Most studies of immigration concentrate on the qualitative effects but offer little on the quantitative effects of immigration (Greenwood 1979). ECESIS provides a framework for analyzing the economic impacts of immigration at both the national and regional levels. Immigration is an explicit component in ECESIS and the detailed interregional demographic model linked to the state economic models allow immigrants to be tracked as they move throughout the U.S. in response to economic incentives. In turn, the relative economic impacts of differing immigration patterns can also be analyzed. In particular, the impacts of increased Asian immigration to the U.S. will be examined. First, the legislative policies of the U.S. regarding Asian immigration and a brief history of the patterns of Asian immigration to the U.S. will be given. Then a simulation experiment designed to measure the quantitative impacts of Asian immigration will be outlined and the results discussed.

12.2.2 LEGISLATIVE POLICY AND ASIAN IMMIGRATION PATTERNS

The U.S. regards immigration as a privilege, not a right and the particulars of that right are redefined regularly. Immigration Acts and amendments have been passed in 1819, 1847, 1848, 1855, 1875, 1882, 1891, 1903, 1907, 1917, 1921, 1924, 1943, 1946, 1952, 1965, 1976, 1978 and 1981--primarily for the purpose of establishing quotas, who should receive preferential treatment and who is an undesirable.[1] At one time or another criminals, prostitutes, paupers, polygamists, anarchists, drug addicts, sexual deviates, communists, adulterers, lepers, and Asians have been forbidden entry into the U.S. The exclusion for Asians persisted from 1882 to 1965.

In the three decades following 1850 almost 200,000 Chinese entered the U.S. to labor in the gold fields and on the railways. In 1882, under pressure from labor groups, Congress barred Chinese entry to the U.S. Later, with the

---

[1] See the various U.S. Department of Justice documents listed in the Bibliography.

establishment of the Asiatic Barred Zone in 1917, nearly all immigration from Asia and the Pacific Islands was prohibited. In 1943 Congress began to lift the total ban on Asian immigration and establish quotas. The number of immigrants allowed under the quota was 185 for Japan, 105 for China, and 100 each for most other Asian countries. By comparison, the quota for Great Britain was 65,361, for Germany 25,814, and down to about 2000 for the Soviet Union. Under this quota system, allowable immigration from the Principality of Lichtenstein and from the once Free City of Danzig (now Gdansk, Poland) was equal to the immigration allowed from China and India.

Generally, immigrants enter the U.S. under the quota of their birthplace. An exception was made for Asians, however. In 1952 the Asian-Pacific Triangle was established and any person with as much as one-half ancestry from a Triangle nation was assigned to its quota.

Finally in 1965 the national quota system was ended and the Asian-Pacific Triangle provisions abolished. The Eastern Hemisphere was a given a quota of 170,000 with a limit of 20,000 per country and the formerly unrestricted Western Hemisphere was given a quota of 120,000. By 1978 the two quotas were combined to form a worldwide quota of 290,000 with the same 20,000 limit applied to every country. Although that worldwide number was reduced to 270,000 in

1980, another 50,000 places were set aside for the admission of refugess.

The abolition of the old nation-specific quotas in 1965, the present preference system (based on spouses, children, other family members and labor skills), and the changing origins of refugee immigration have had an immense impact on Asian immigration to the U.S. Asia is now the main source of immigration to the U.S., exceeding even Europe and North America. Table 12.2.1 illustrates these changes. During the 1950s 15,700 Asians immigrated per year to the U.S., by 1979 that number had grown to 189,300. Over this period the share of immigrants from Asia has grown from six percent to over forty percent.

TABLE 12.2.1

ANNUAL IMMIGRATION BY CONTINENT OF BIRTH

Place of Birth	Immigrants (thousands)			Share		
	1979	1965	1951-60[a]	1979	1965	1951-60[a]
Worldwide	460.3	296.7	251.6	100.0	100.0	100.0
Asia	189.3	20.7	15.7	41.1	7.0	6.2
North America	157.6	126.7	76.9	34.2	42.7	30.6
Europe	60.8	113.4	149.2	13.2	38.2	59.3
South America	35.3	31.0	7.2	7.7	10.4	2.9
Africa	12.8	3.3	1.7	2.8	1.1	0.7
Oceania	4.5	1.5	0.8	1.0	0.5	0.3

[a] Annual average

Five of the seven main sources of immigration to the U.S. are now Asian countries (Phillippines, Vietnam, Korea, China and Taiwan, India)--the two exceptions are Mexico and Cuba.

When entering the U.S., immigrants indicate their intended place of residence. Table 12.2.2 gives each state's share of total and Asian immigration for 1979. The most frequent destinations for immigrants are New York, California, Illinois, Texas and New Jersey. These five states accounted for thirty-three percent of the U.S. population in 1979 but absorbed sixty-seven percent of the nation's immigrants in that year. Or course immigrants, once here, move from state to state just like all Americans, but immigration is more spatially focussed than the the overall population distribution. The same is true of Asian immigration. Nearly thirty-eight percent of all Asian immigrants list California as the state of their intended residence. Over two-thirds of all Asian immigrants arrive in just six states: California, New York, Illinois, Hawaii, New Jersey and Texas.

TABLE 12.2.2

THE SPATIAL DISTRIBUTION OF IMMIGRATION WITHIN THE UNITED STATES BY STATE: 1979

	TOTAL	ASIAN		TOTAL	ASIAN
Alabama	.2	.2	Montana	.1	.1
Alaska	.1	.2	Nebraska	.2	.3
Arizona	1.1	.6	Nevada	.3	.5
Arkansas	.2	.3	New Hampshire	.2	.1
California	21.6	37.8	New Jersey	6.4	4.5
Colorado	.5	.8	New Mexico	.3	.2
Connecticut	1.8	.8	New York	24.5	11.4
Delaware	.1	.2	North Carolina	.5	.8
Dist. of Columbia	.1	.4	North Dakota	.1	
Florida	5.1	1.6	Ohio	1.8	1.8
Georgia	.5	.9	Oklahoma	.3	.7
Hawaii	1.8	5.1	Oregon	.4	.7
Idaho	.1	.1	Pennsylvania	2.4	2.4
Illinois	6.7	5.4	Rhode Island	.6	.1
Indiana	.6	.7	South Carolina	.3	.4
Iowa	.2	.5	South Dakota	.1	.1
Kansas	.3	.5	Tennessee	.3	.4
Kentucky	.2	.4	Texas	6.6	4.2
Louisiana	.5	.6	Utah	.2	.3
Maine	.2	.1	Vermont	.1	.0
Maryland	1.7	2.3	Virginia	1.6	2.4
Massachusetts	3.3	1.3	Washington	.9	2.3
Michigan	2.4	2.3	West Virginia	.1	.1
Minnesota	.5	1.0	Wisconsin	.5	.6
Mississippi	.1	.2	Wyoming	.1	.1
Missouri	.7	.8			

Since the rate of population change in the U.S. is relatively slow, Asian immigration can have a sizable impact on the population change of some states. Several states, including New York, Illinois, and Pennsylvania, would have lost population in 1979 had not Asian immigrants made up for the net outmigration of residents. For the U.S. as a whole, approximately seven percent of population change is accounted for by Asian immigration. Both in terms as a component of population change and its compact spatial distribution, Asian immigration is an important political and economic issue in the U.S. In the next section, a simulation experiment is designed to determine the regional economic impacts of a further increase in Asian immigration.

12.2.3 SIMULATION DESIGN AND RESULTS

There are many arguments to explain the special attention that Asians have received under U.S. immigration law. Whatever role social and political biases play in these arguments is of interest here only to the extent that these biases manifest themselves in economic arguments. Most economic arguments against immigration are versions in one form or another of what Greenwood (1979) terms the "replacement hypothesis". Briefly, this argument procedes as follows. Increased immigration increases the labor supply. This is doubly true since the majority of immigrants are young adults with high labor force participation rates. Thus, the proportion of immigrants entering the labor force is higher than that for the U.S. population in general. This outward shift in the labor supply curve reduces wages and increases employment. The reduced wage rate decreases the participation rate of "citizen workers" but the new immigrants are willing to work at the lower wage so they displace citizens previously in the labor force.

This argument is powerful in its simplicity and is applied not only to immigrants but to any labor group that may potentially increase the labor force--minority youth, for example. Nonetheless, the argument is deficient on several counts not the least of which is that it completely ignores the labor demand curve. Presumably the newly employed immigrants spend some of their wages. Indeed, it is reasonable to expect that the propensity to consume of the immigrant workers is greater than that of the displaced citizen workers. As immigrants buy goods and services employment demand is increased. The net result of the shifts in the supply and demand curves is uncertain, depending on the relative elasticities of the curves. The results would also be expected to vary both spatially and temporally. In the beginning, supply effects might be expected to dominate with the demand effects coming into play after some adjustment period. Some regions of the country might be more sensitive to labor market shifts than others. As already noted, the spatial distribution of immigrants is far from uniform.

The spatial disaggregation and long projection period (twenty years) of ECESIS allow such factors to be considered. In addition, both the supply and demand effects of population change are modeled in ECESIS. Beginning with the former, immigration leads directly to a change in the labor force through labor force participation rates. This labor supply increase leads to increases in unemployment, because the latter is treated as a residual in the economic models. Capacity output increases, so capacity utilization declines. The decline in capacity utilization and the decrease in the employment-population ratio both tend to decrease wages. The wage decrease, however, may lead to increased manufacturing output through increased demand from other regions because of the lower cost of production. The increased unemployment also leads to increases in transfer income, resulting in increases in both manufacturing and nonmanufacturing output. Thus, even the labor force supply effects have indirect demand effects.

More direct demand effects of immigration occur in ECESIS through the income and output equations. Transfer income, proprietors income, and nonmanufacturing employment increase directly with population. The additional income also induces increases in manufacturing output. These output demand effects are felt both from immigration to the state in question and also indirectly through immigration to other states. The increased demand leads to increases in employment, capacity utilization, and the employment-population ratio, which puts upward pressure on wages.

In short, both the supply and demand effects of immigration have an impact on employment, wages, unemployment, productive capacity and capacity utilization, income, labor force, and migration. These impacts are simultaneous, but not always in the same direction. Which effect dominates is an empirical question whose answer will vary with initial conditions and elasticities in each state and with the extent of immigration. Internal migration in response to changing economic conditions and the linked nature of interregional economic conditions further confound any attempt to identify the economic impact of immigration a priori.

The simulation experiment to estimate the impacts of increased Asian immigration was carried out as follows. Asian immigration was increased by 100,000 annually in each year between 1981 and 2000. The extra immigration was allocated among the states using the 1979 distribution of Asian immigration shown in Table 12.2.2. The immigrants in each state were given the age and sex distribution of total 1979 immigration. Since Asians are not a separate demographic group within the ECESIS model, once located the Asian immigrants take on the same birth, death, labor force participation rates, and internal migration rates as the state's age-sex specific population as a whole. In other words, a twenty-nine year old female Asian immigrant arriving in California looks like any other twenty-nine year old female in California in subsequent years. Later, if this person should move to Iowa, she would assume the birth rate for her age-sex cohort in Iowa.

This creates a minor problem for the demographic accounts model. In ECESIS the total number of U.S. births annually is constrained to totals projected by the Census Bureau. The Census projections are based upon an assumption of 400,000 immigrants per year; thus, the additional 100,000 immigrants should increase the constraints. But since state-to-state migration is endogenous to the system, it is impossible to determine the exact number of additional births due to increased immigration. It would be possible to estimate the number of additional births by repeating the simulation several times and updating the birth constraints at each stage until a consistent solution is achieved. The expense of each simulation makes this impractical. Better would be to simply assume that the immigrants, no matter which state they migrate to, take on the U.S. average birth rate. Using this approximation, 420,000 additional births should be recorded over the entire twenty year forecast period. For mechanical reasons it is not a simple matter to add these births into the system. Essentially the simulation would have to be run twice to incorporate the changes. This was not done. To this extent, the demand effects in the simulation are understated. There is little impact on the labor force by this omission, however, since only about 13,000 of those additional births will have aged to the labor force age groups by the end of the twenty year simulation period--this is in comparison to a total labor force in excess of 137 million by that time.

There are some other limitations of this simulation that are probably more critical than the problem just described. For example, the design of the ECESIS system makes it well-suited for moving people from region to region and industry to industry as incentives dictate. Thus, if the economic incentives are such that a person should leave a manufacturing job in California and take a nonmanufacturing job in North Dakota he will do so--regardless as to whether or not he has the inclination or skills to do so. Generally this will not be too serious a problem since the aggregation of a large number of moves will tend to even things out. But they type of simulation being discussed here may be another matter. Here we have 100,000 new people every year who have no "history". They are simply assigned an economic "personality" according to the needs of the day--needs determined, at least partially, by their arrival. In this regard, the new immigrants are treated somewhat like putty--molded according to the specifications of ECESIS. It is very likely, however, that the skills and cultural backgrounds of the new immigrants would place some limitations on their maleability into the U.S. economic system. One can only speculate as to how serious a problem this is. In any case, there is little that can be done about it within the framework of ECESIS.

For the same reasons as those discussed in the previous chapter, Delaware, District of Columbia, Hawaii and Wyoming were exogenous for this simulation. the simulation results from ASIA are compared to the CONTROL solution for 1981 to 2000 described in Chapter Eleven.

ECESIS is fairly well based in economic theory and, as the results of Chapter Ten indicate, the multipliers of the model are quite reasonable. The model is also dynamic and adjusts to shocks with a partial adjustment mechanism. It takes some time then for impacts to filter through the multilevel linkages of ECESIS.

In the first two to three years of the simulation the supply shocks tend to dominate. The labor force grows at a faster pace than employment so the unemployment rate rises and real wages dip below CONTROL solution levels. Figure 12.2.1 compares ASIA to CONTROL in percentage difference terms for several labor market variables at the national level. There is a very slight decline in the labor force participation rate in the first two years so there is some

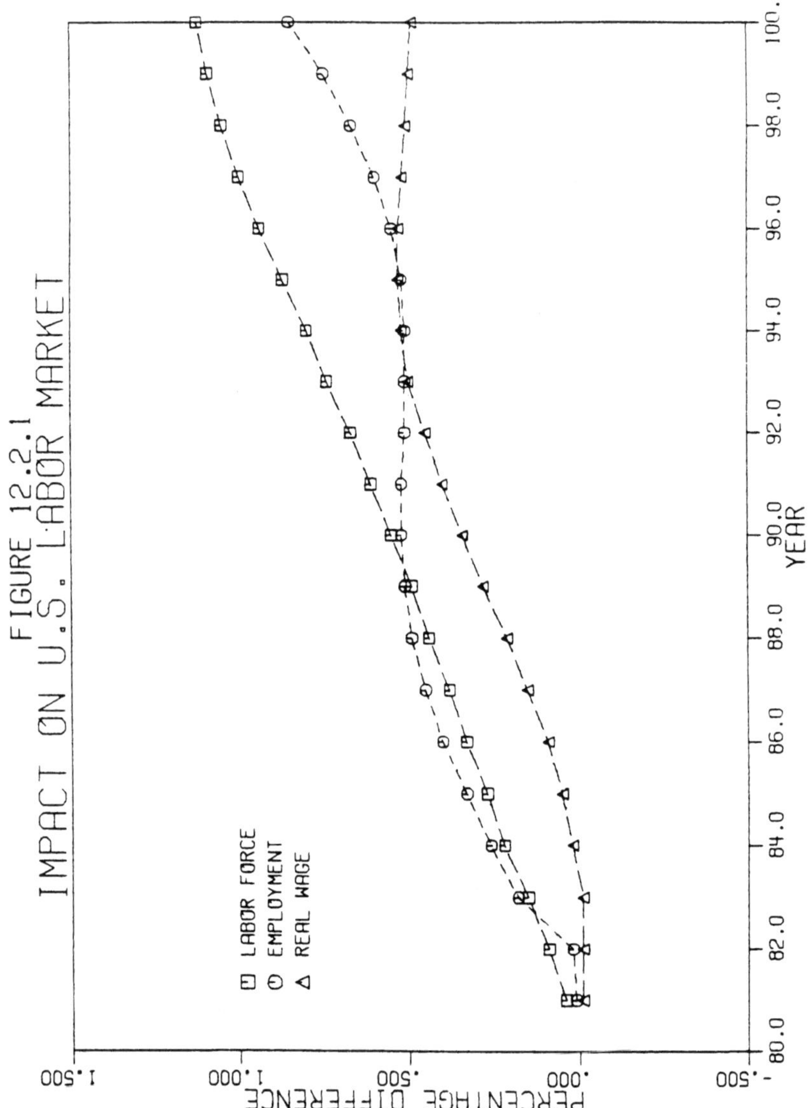
FIGURE 12.2.1
IMPACT ØN U.S. LABØR MARKET
LABØR FØRCE
EMPLØYMENT
REAL WAGE
PERCENTAGE DIFFERENCE
1.500
1.000
.500
.000
-.500
YEAR
80.0
82.0
84.0
86.0
88.0
90.0
92.0
94.0
96.0
98.0
100.0

tendency for domestic workers to drop out of the labor market in the face of lower wages induced by the influx of immigrant workers. The results of these early years of the simulation seem to lend support to the replacement hypothesis. Essentially, these early years verify the static equilibrium results of a labor supply shock which is the basis of the hypothesis.

By the third year of the simulation the supply shocks have fully filtered through the model and demand side adjustments are being felt with considerable strength. From this point up to 1989 the demand side impacts dominate the simulation. Employment growth outpaces the increase in the labor force so the unemployment rate falls and real wages rise above CONTROL levels. This "golden age" cannot last of course. By 1989 employment growth begins to level off and remains fairly stable up to about 1995. Immigration, however, continues at the rate of 100,000 above CONTROL solution so the labor force continues to increase. The unemployment rate begins to increase and the increase in the real wage rates slows and begins to decline by 1996. At about this time the cycle begins to swing the other way and employment again grows at a brisk pace.

The response to the increased immigration is clearly not monotonic. The cyclical properties of ECESIS were examined in the previous two chapters. The manufacturing sector of

ECESIS is probably too sensitive to shocks, leading to exaggerated economic cycles--though still stable. Figure 12.2.2 graphically confirms this. The growth in manufacturing employment peaks in 1987 and begins a long decline reaching a trough in about 1995. The nonmanufacturing sector is much less cyclical and, since it accounts for about two-thirds of total employment, it serves to dampen the effects of the manufacturing sector on the whole economy.

The above discussion suggests that the states with a large industrial base may fare worse in this simulation than other states. Figure 12.2.3 verifies that the manufacturing employment slump is fairly well localized in the East North Central, Middle Atlantic and New England states. As indicated by Figure 12.2.4, the source of the problem seems to lie in the manufacturing wage rate.

As a whole, the East North Central states do not attract many of the new Asian immigrants so the labor force in these states does not increase by much. But these states are called upon to produce much of the nation's additional manufactured output to satisfy the increased demand caused by the the new immigrants in other parts of the country. As a result, tight labor markets develop and drive up wage rates. As has historically been the case, increased employment opportunities in the North Central and Northeast

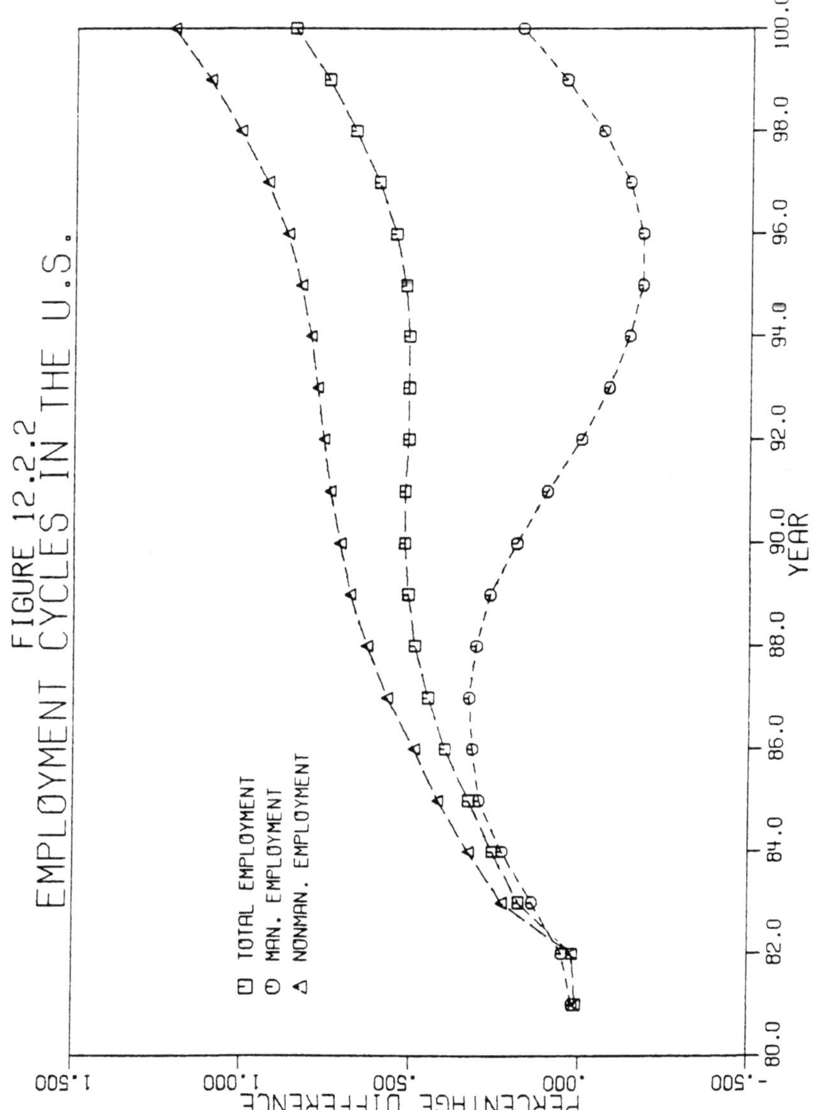

FIGURE 12.2.2
EMPLOYMENT CYCLES IN THE U.S.

PERCENT IMPACT ON MANUFACTURING EMPLOYMENT, 2000

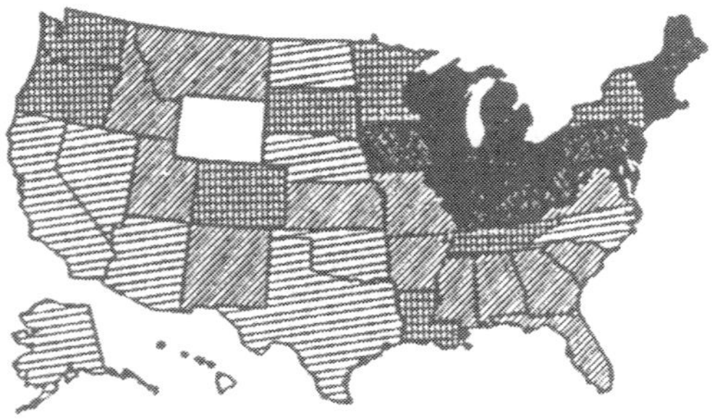

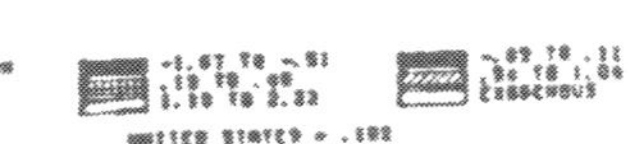

PERCENT IMPACT ON MANUFACTURING WAGE, 2000

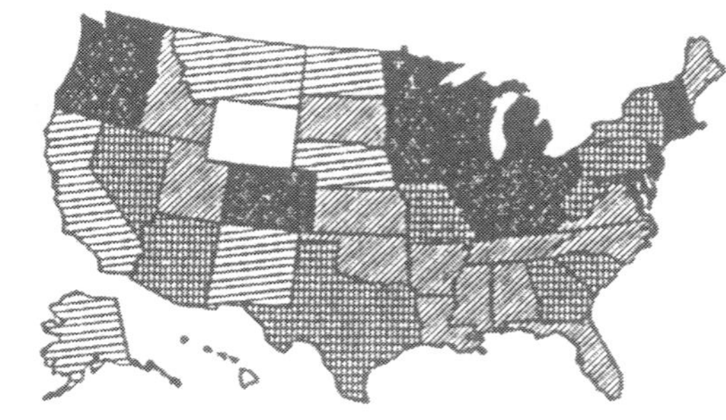

states do not significantly increase migration into those states. Thus, the wage pressure is not easily resolved by attracting new labor. Eventually, the higher wages in this region make their manufactured products less attractive to buyers and cheaper suppliers are found and jobs are lost in the East North Central states. Unfortunately, wage rates in the East North Central states are traditionally slow to adjust downward and the states remain in their relatively uncompetitive position for some time. This, of course, is a "feature" of the ECESIS model. Like all time-series models, it pursues previous trends unless instructed otherwise.

The manufacturing cycle may not be entirely due to an over zealous model, however. Recall that the shock consists of increasing Asian immigration to the U.S. and, as noted earlier, the spatial distribution of these immigrants is far from uniform. California and New York, for instance, attract nearly fifty percent of the new immigrants.

New York provides a particularly interesting example because it is also one of the large industrial states discussed above. Over 11,000 new immigrants arrive in New York each year of this simulation. Thus, New York gets a much larger increment to its labor force than any of the other states in the region. As a result, there is less wage pressure than in surrounding states. By the year 2000, manufacturing wages in New York are .54 percent above

CONTROL--quite comparable to the .49 percent U.S. average but considerably below the .74 percent average of the other East North Central, Middle Atlantic and Northeast states. This comparative advantage makes it much easier for New York to weather the manufacturing cycle.

California is an altogether unique case. Receiving 37,800 additional immigrants annually, it is by far the dominant destination of Asian immigrants. By the last year of the simulation, total employment is 2.65 percent above CONTROL, more than three times the U.S. average increase. But, because the labor force also increased at this fast pace, real wages in California increase by only one-half the average U.S. increase. Output, income, employment and profits are all up in California without a significant increase in the unemployment rate. The negative consequences predicted by the displacement hypothesis, often directed at California, are not apparent.

The impacts of the simulation vary across states. Only the most extreme and interesting examples have been discussed here. In general, the dire consequences predicted by the displacement hypothesis are not apparent; the discouraging aspects coming at the regional level. Asian immigration appears to benefit all regions of the country except the Northeast and North Central industrial states. Apparently the U.S. economy can absorb the present generation of immigrants as well as it did previous generations. There seems to be little merit to recent economic rationales to restrict further immigration. If the limitations of this simulation turn out to be second-order effects then these results should be at least qualitatively accurate.

These simulation results indicate that another dimension could be added to U.S. immigration policy. While traditionally concerned with the origins of immigrants, U.S. Immigration policy might also consider the destinations of immigrants.

12.3 IMPACTS OF REGIONAL STIMULUS POLICIES

12.3.1 ISSUES AND SIMULATION DESIGN

Differences in regional growth rates has been a lingering economic issue in the U.S. for some time. Most recently, the Western and Southern states have enjoyed rapid growth while the North Central and Northeastern states have languished with slow or even negative growth. The recent spurt of growth in high-technology industries located in the Northeast has had some ameliorating effects. Not enough, however, to overcome the basic trends discussed here. Many factors may be cited to account for these growth rate differentials. Manufacturing is the dominant sector in the heavily industrialized North Central and Northeast regions. Historically manufacturing industries have been more sensitive to economic cycles than nonmanufacturing industries. Thus, the sharp economic recessions of the mid 1970s and early 1980s affected the North Central and Northeast regions quite severely. The Western and Southern regions, with their broad base in the service and trade sectors, was more insulated from the recessions and able to recover more quickly. Compounding this, in recent years there has been a relative decline in the importance of the manufacturing industries in the U.S. This structural shift away from manufacturing and into the services, trade and government sectors has benefited the Western and Southern states.

Recent migration patterns have also been a factor. The 1970s saw a dramatic increase in "frost belt" to "sun belt" migration. It is difficult to separate cause and effect but the increased migration to the West and South appears to be greater than would have been induced by the increased economic growth of the regions alone. As per capita incomes and leisure time increase people are more inclined to seek locations with high amenities. Of course, this trend augments the decline of the North Central and Northeast regions.

Obviously for people in the North Central and Northeast regions these trends are not particularly welcome developments. Worse, the trends are well into their second decade and show every indication of persisting for some time to come. The Northeast states are in a somewhat better position than the North Central states, having already initiated the push toward higher growth manufacturing industries. Even this gain may be short-lived, however, as Western and Southern states have begun to aggressively counter with tax breaks and other fringes to attract or keep high-tech firms. The Northeast can ill-afford this kind of competition--to play to aggressively is to lose the advantages of winning the game. It is reasonable to ask, therefore, whether or not some federal policies could be implemented to aid the troubled regions. Region specific policies are difficult to justify politically--even for the populous Northeast. Subsidies to Michigan, for example, would quickly be challenged by the representatives of other states. Instead, indirect or implicit regional subsidies are often used. An import quota on automobiles, for example, clearly benefits Michigan--essentially by taxing all other states. Energy tax credits apply throughout the nation but their greatest impact is in the energy dependent Northeast.

In this simulation experiment the feasibility of a federal policy to stimulate manufacturing investment in the depressed North Central and Northeast regions is examined. The policy may be implemented in any number of politically acceptable ways. An investment tax credit that most directly affects firms in these regions, for example. The central issue is whether or not such a policy will have any long-term effects on regional growth rates.

The experiment is conducted over the period 1981 to 2000 and is compared to the CONTROL solution for that period. The target area for the policy is the East North Central and Middle Atlantic states (Illinois, Indiana, Michigan, New Jersey, New York, Ohio, Pennsylvania and Wisconsin).[2] Specifically the policy is a five year program to reduce the user cost of capital in the target states. In year one (1981) the user cost of capital is reduced by 5.66 percent. The policy is gradually phased out so that in year two the reduction is 4.21 percent; 2.72 percent in year three; 1.19 percent in year four; and back to the CONTROL level in year five or 1985. This policy is designed to subsidize capital development in the targeted states. Presumably this will allow the regions to rebuild their capital stocks and gain a temporary competitive advantage over the rest of the nation.

---

[2] As in previous experiments, Delaware, District of Columbia, Hawaii and Wyoming are exogenous in this simulation experiment.

It is hoped that the capital stock built up during this period will put the target regions in a stronger competitive position after the subsidy is phased out. The result should be long-run regional growth rates that are more equal between regions than without the policy.

12.3.2 SIMULATION RESULTS

As expected, the policy creates a spurt of real gross manufacturing investment in the target states. The peak impact is in 1982 and as the program is phased out investment quickly falls back to the CONTROL levels. Figure 12.3.1 shows the investment pattern for a representative target state. The vertical axis is deviation from CONTROL measured in basis points (100 basis points equals one percent). Since the target states are among the largest producers of manufactured goods in the U.S. their impact on total U.S. manufacturing is considerable. For the U.S. as a whole, real gross manufacturing investment is up by just over one percent in 1982--about $421 million 1972 dollars. Nontarget states also show an increase in investment but the effect is much smaller (less than 50 basis points) and the peak does not occur until about 1988.

As has been witnessed elsewhere with the ECESIS model, the impact generates a cyclical adjustment path. Using real

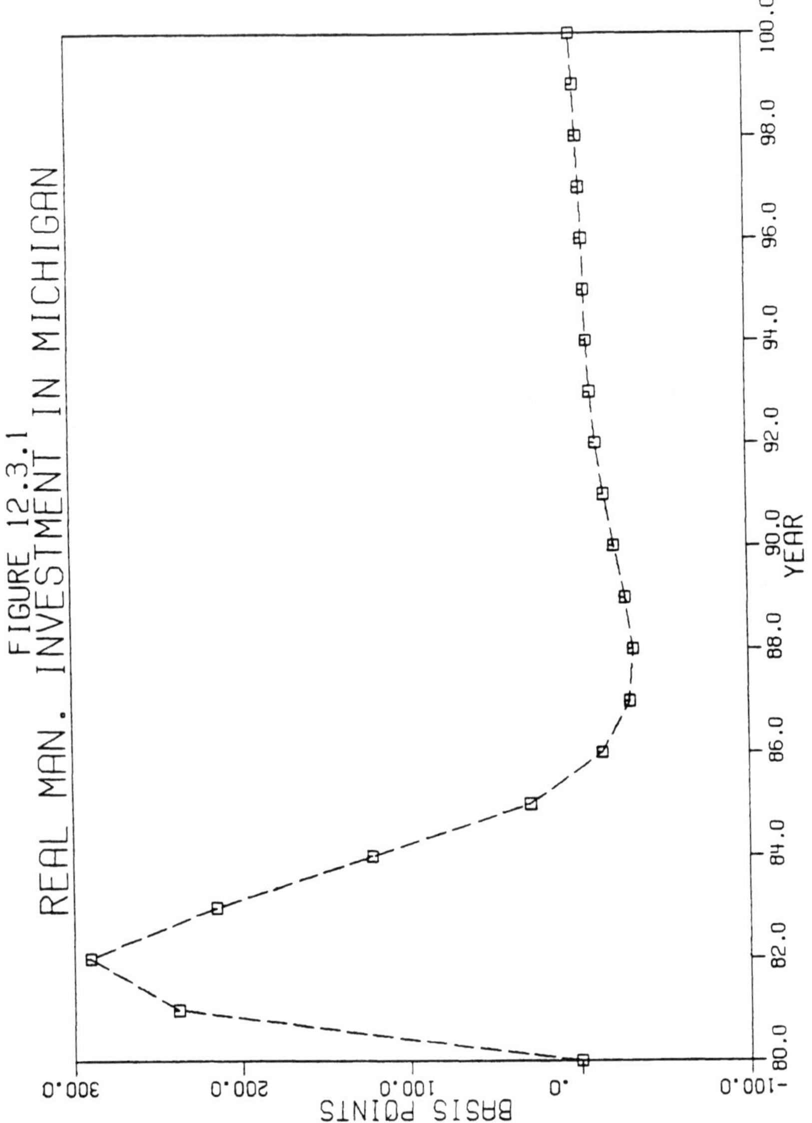
FIGURE 12.3.1
REAL MAN. INVESTMENT IN MICHIGAN
BASIS POINTS
300.0
200.0
100.0
.0
-100.0
80.0
82.0
84.0
86.0
88.0
90.0
92.0
94.0
96.0
98.0
100.0
YEAR

manufacturing output as an example, Figure 12.3.2 shows the adjustment paths for Michigan, a target state; Minnesota, a nontarget state adjacent to the target region; and the U.S. as a whole. This pattern is quite general across all states. The nontarget states' cycle lags that of the target states by about three years. At the outset of the stimulus policy the target states do very well. This prosperity spreads to other states through the trade and wage dispersion mechanisms built into ECESIS. As the policy is phased out growth in the target regions slows and begins to move back to CONTROL levels. Because of the capital stock built up during the investment program, the target states are better equipped to handle the downturn than are the nontarget states. In general the trough for target states is not as low as that for nontarget states. For the U.S. as a whole, the cycle is fairly symmetric. It should be remembered that the magnitude of the numbers involved here is quite small. Even at the extreme points in the cycle the total deviation of real manufacturing output from CONTROL for the entire U.S. is less than one billion dollars.

The initial years of the simulation behave as expected. In the target states investment increases lead to increases in manufacturing capital stocks and manufacturing output. In turn, employment and income increase and the unemployment rate falls. Also, net inmigration into the target area

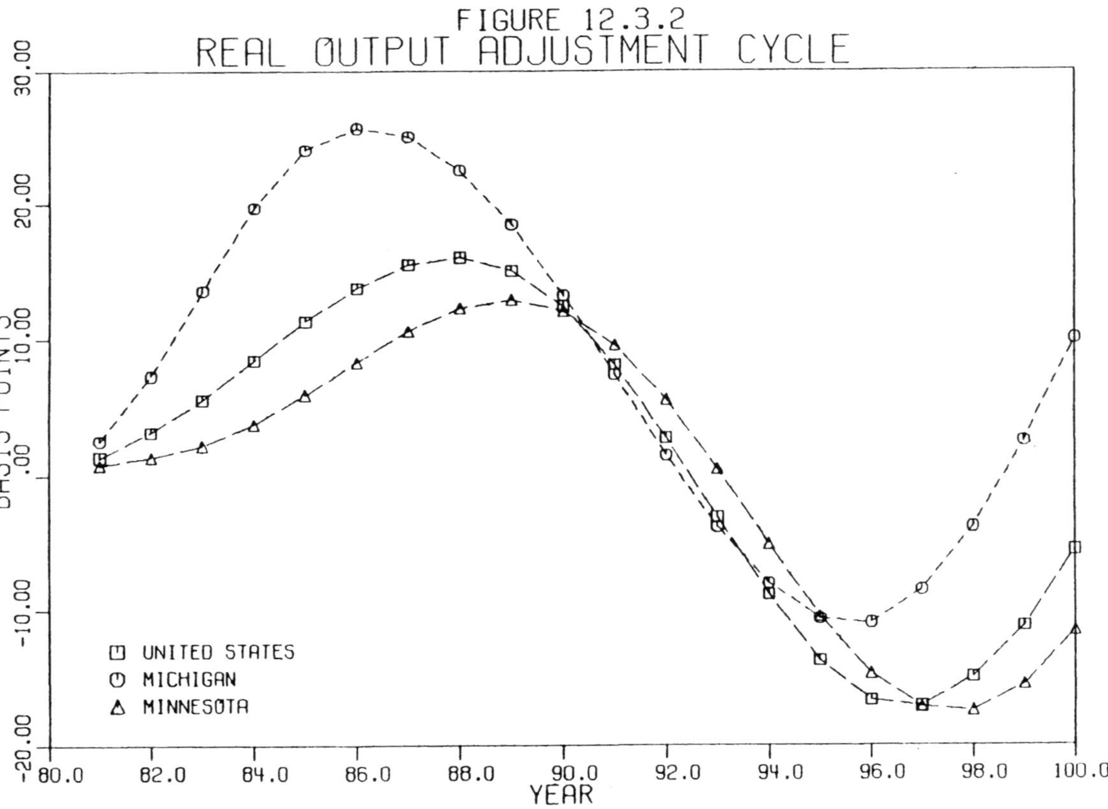
FIGURE 12.3.2
REAL OUTPUT ADJUSTMENT CYCLE
BASIS POINTS
30.00
20.00
10.00
.00
-10.00
-20.00
80.0
82.0
84.0
86.0
88.0
90.0
92.0
94.0
96.0
98.0
100.0
YEAR
UNITED STATES
MICHIGAN
MINNESOTA

increases as people move into (or fewer people move out of) the faster growing areas.

During the first part of the cycle, states contiguous to the target states naturally tend to benefit more than states in distant regions. The multilevel linkage structure of ECESIS will ensure this result. Distance is not the only factor, however. States are linked more closely by trade and migration patterns than by distance. Thus, California is economically "closer" to the target region than is, say, Nebraska. By the end of the simulation period the impact is sufficiently dispersed throughout the country that proximity not longer plays a significant role.

Only about twenty percent of total employment is in the manufacturing sector. The stimulus policy, however, directly affects the manufacturing sector so that forty percent of the new jobs created by the policy are in that industry. The bulk of those jobs are in the target states. On the other hand, during the downside of the cycle, the majority of jobs lost are also in the manufacturing sector. Other sectors of the economy are also affected by the stimulus policy. Figure 12.3.3 shows the relationship between employment in the manufacturing and nonmanufacturing sectors in Indiana (a target state) during the simulation period. The cycle in the nonmanufacturing sector has much less amplitude than the cycle for manufacturing. Since the

FIGURE 12.3.3
INDIANA EMPLOYMENT CYCLES

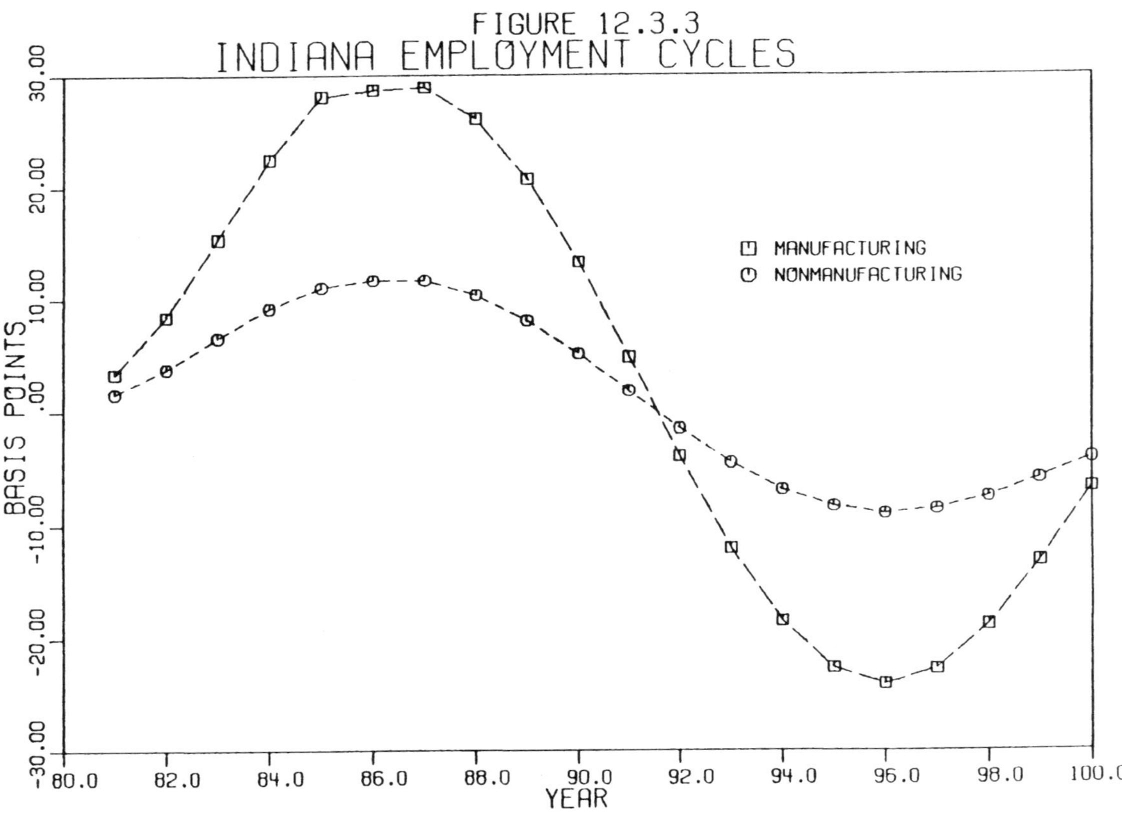

nonmanufacturing sector is about three times the size of the manufacturing sector in Indiana, about the same absolute number of jobs are involved at the cycle peak in 1987. For the entire U.S. in 1988, 52,100 new jobs are created in nonmanufacturing industries while 35,000 new jobs are created in manufacturing industries.

Because of the stimulus, the target states become more attractive destinations for migrants. By 1985, all target states except New Jersey have population levels above the CONTROL values. On the other hand, all nontarget states except New Hampshire and Massachusetts have reduced populations. The latter two states are close to the target area and benefit indirectly from the investment program. New Jersey has the misfortune of being too close to Pennsylvania and New York, both of which become very attractive destinations for migrants--including migrants from New Jersey. By 1992 the target states have attracted over twenty thousand more people than in the baseline. Most of these gains are lost during the downside of the cycle when the manufacturing sectors in the target states decline. By the year 2000 the target area has only managed to attract 2250 additional residents. In other words, people move to the target area during the boom but move out again when the slide starts. This movement accentuates the economic cycles. If the demographic model is left exogenous during the simulation so that population remains at the CONTROL levels, the adjustment paths tend to be slightly less cyclical. This is illustrated in Figure 12.3.4 using total employment in the target state Indiana. In general, other states and the U.S. as a whole follow similar patterns.

Pennsylvania is an exception to this pattern, continuing to attract migrants throughout the cycle. Consequently, by the time the manufacturing sector begins to decline in Pennsylvania the population increase creates sufficient stimulus in the nonmanufacturing sector to keep the total employment level above the CONTROL level throughout the cycle. As shown in Figure 12.3.5, Pennsylvania employment declines below the CONTROL values in the second half of the cycle when population is treated as exogenous. In this respect, Pennsylvania is the only target state in which the goal of long-term growth from the short-term investment policy has worked out. Even then, it is primarily population movements stimulating the nonmanufacturing sector rather than long-term manufacturing sector growth that achieves the desired result. The long-term effects on the total U.S. economy are minimal.

Most economists would argue that this is precisely what one would expect from such a policy. Subsidizing manufacturing capital stock development in one part of the country transfers resources from labor to capital in the

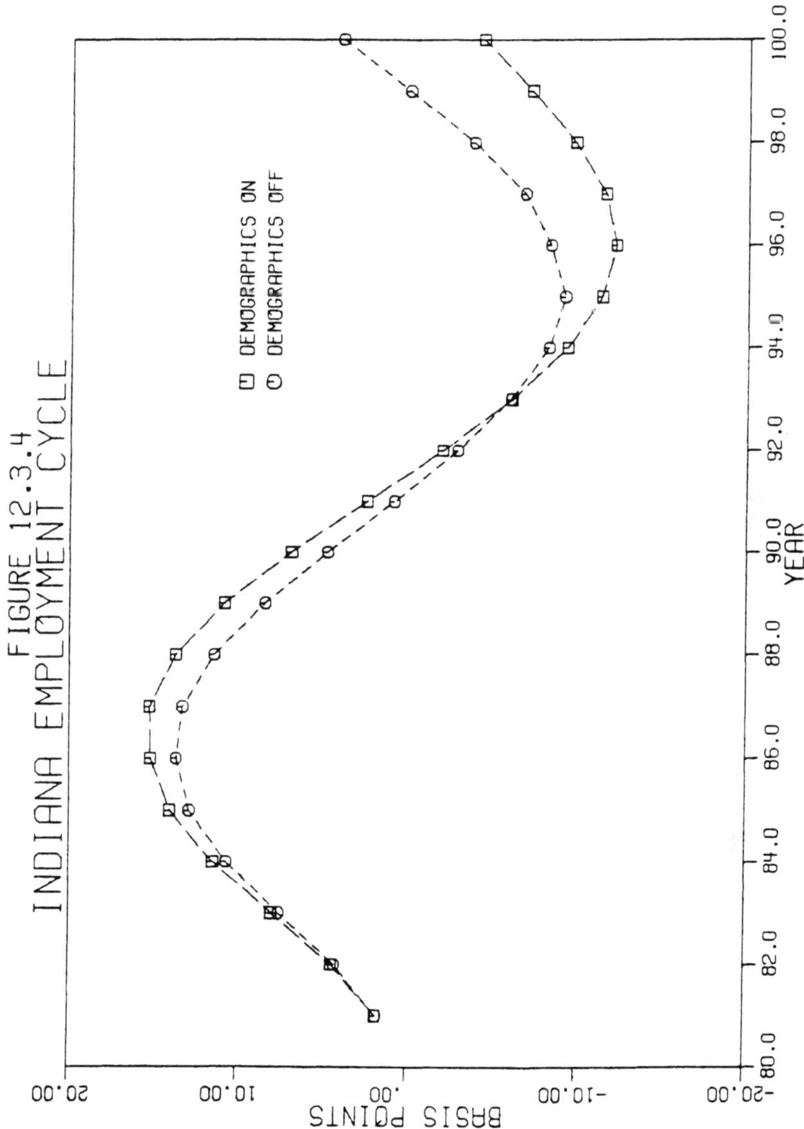
FIGURE 12.3.4
INDIANA EMPLOYMENT CYCLE
DEMOGRAPHICS ON
DEMOGRAPHICS OFF
BASIS POINTS
20.00
10.00
.00
-10.00
-20.00
YEAR
80.0
82.0
84.0
86.0
88.0
90.0
92.0
94.0
96.0
98.0
100.0

FIGURE 12.3.5
PENNSYLVANIA EMPLOYMENT CYCLE

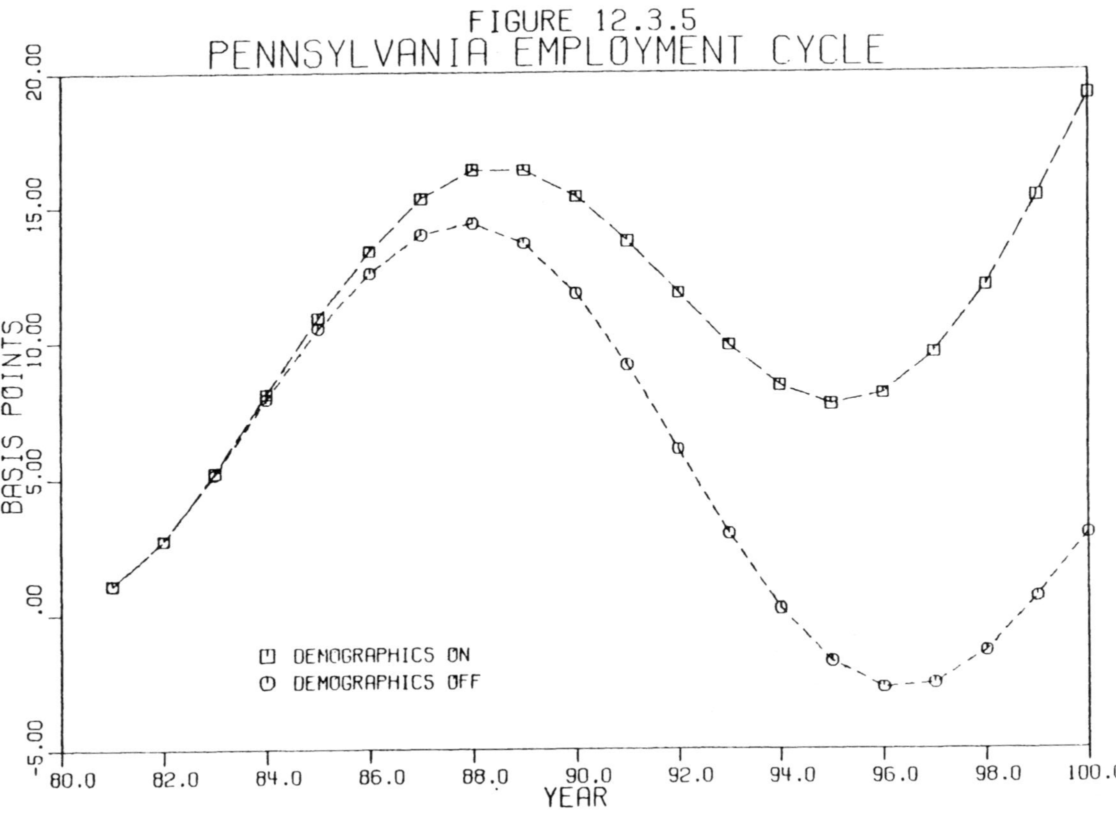

production process and lowers the production price in that region. This does give a competitive advantage to the targeted region while the subsidy is in effect. Once the subsidy is removed, however, the targeted regions find their production processes are in disequilibrium with respect to unsubsidized factor prices. The ensuing adjustment process is time consuming and costly so that the target regions quickly lose any competitive advantages they had garnered from the subsidy policy. ECESIS confirms this pattern. It is likely that ECESIS over reacts to the counter-adjustment when the subsidy is lifted but that is a characteristic of this model that has been discussed a number of times.

Both of the simulation experiments in this chapter illustrate uses for which ECESIS is particularly well suited. One can easily argue about how well ECESIS performs in these situations. Nonetheless, these experiments do demonstrate the importance of an integrated model approach. Economic-demographic interactions play an important role in such simulations--that, despite many possible criticisms, is undeniable.

CHAPTER THIRTEEN: CONCLUSION, CRITIQUE AND FUTURE RESEARCH

13.1 CONCLUSIONS

The primary goal of the ECESIS model was to link together a regional economic model and a regional demographic model and to test how that union performed under various kinds of prodding. Presumably this union should result in a model that performs at least as well as the sum of its parts and has the advantage of adding considerable detail.

The individual parts of ECESIS are themselves quite reasonable models. The fifty-one economic models of the states consist of three sectors; the largest (manufacturing) being modelled in considerable detail. For example, the production function and factor demand equations are modelled explicitly and consistently and interact with the interregional output demand equation to give the models responsiveness to both supply and demand factors. The labor market in each state is also modelled from both the supply and demand sides explicitly. In particular, the supply of labor is disaggregated by age and sex to allow for the differing trends in labor force participation rates among population cohorts in recent years. The multiplier tests discussed in Chapter Ten indicate that the economic models are quite stable and their impact, dynamic and long-run multipliers are reasonable.

The demographic model is both up-to-date and elaborate--surpassing in detail even the model used by the Bureau of the Census. Over 500 population cohorts are tracked through space and time. ECESIS is likely the first application to use the full Rees-Wilson accounting framework. The migration model is an extension and combination of the Markov and gravity models used by demographers in recent years. Over 26,000 place-to-place flows are determined. Each move considers all alternative opportunities by comparing the economic attractiveness of each possible destination.

Equally as important as the economic and demographic components are the linkages that connect the two. ECESIS has addressed most of the possible linkages suggested in the theoretical literature. Population plays an important part in the economic models; most directly in determining labor supply but also in determining output demand, wage rates, employment and some income items. State-to-state migration is directly affected by employment opportunities and competition in each state. In addition, the state economies are linked by an interregional trade model. The system is completely simultaneous; a change in any variable in any state affects the entire ECESIS model.

The tests and experiments on ECESIS discussed in Chapters Ten through Twelve indicate that economic and demographic interactions are indeed important. The qualitative properties of the model are not much changed when the demographic variables are modelled endogenously. The big factor is whether or not the state models are linked by trade flows; population flows playing a more minor role. Quantitatively, however, the demographic model turns out to be very important. Whether or not population movements are allowed in response to economic changes may make the difference between net economic growth or decline. It also matters a great deal what type of demographic model is used to determine population flows. Chapter Eleven indicates that the procedures used by the Bureau of the Census and the Bureau of Economic Analysis lead to very different results. Thus, it is not enough to simply endogenize population. One must do so in a way that takes into account the constraints of both the economic and demographic systems. Historical migration patterns are as important as current economic incentives.

There is also evidence that models such as ECESIS serve a useful purpose. The ASIA simulation experiment of Chapter Twelve could not be conducted using a model without all of the components of ECESIS. Further, issues involving both legal and illegal immigration are becoming increasingly important. Indeed, the direction of population flows has itself become an issue in recent years. There is an us versus them confrontation growing between the "frostbelt" and "sunbelt" states. If economists are to address these issues empirically then models like ECESIS will have to be used.

Perhaps most important is that, ECESIS, by looking at all components of an economic-demographic system, indicates where the greatest problems lie. Much of the theoretical literature developed so far is of little use to the modeller. Greater emphasis needs to be placed on regional versions of fertility and household formation models. Economic models that make use of populations with age-sex detail also need some attention. Though it seems obvious in retrospect, economists and demographers need a unified way of viewing their respective data. Economists tend to take a more qualitative stance when viewing their data; concerning themselves more with trends and consistency than with precision. Demographers tend to the opposite view; always revising procedures to account for the nth person even at the sake of consistency. Perhaps the greatest challenge of ECESIS was in creating a database that considered the needs and compensated for the deficiencies in the data for each of these disciplines.

Finally, it may be concluded that ECESIS performs well and, more importantly, could be made to perform better. However, refining specific equations, further disaggregation, and adding more linkages would not vastly improve ECESIS. A new type of modelling approach is required for the next generation of economic-demographic models.

13.2 A CRITIQUE OF ECESIS

The problem that is most apparent in a modelling effort such as this is the quality of the data. In many cases the appropriate economic or demographic time-series are not available and proxy variables must be used. The most notable data failures in this model are the absence of an annual time-series on in and out migration and exports and imports of goods for states. This project was begun anticipating that both of these data sets would be at least partially available. The Current Work History Sample data was reported to provide a time-series of in- and outmigration from 1969 to 1979. This source was found to be unreliable, however, and was eventually abandoned because of its poor quality.[1] Similarly, the 1977 Commodity Transportation Survey was supposed to provide a reliable

---

[1] See Isserman, Plane and McMillen (1982) for an evaluation of the CWHS data.

interstate input-output table. Funding cuts eliminated this data source.

A related problem is the poor quality of available data. In the course of the estimations many outliers were found in the data--too many to be comfortably believed. Some series exhibit a higher variance across time than is realistic. Using such data builds a certain amount of instability into the system.

Data related problems exist in all empirical exercises, including interregional economic-demographic models. Little can be done, however, to improve the data in the short-run. What is available is used and suggestions can only be made for better data collection in the future. In retrospect, more attention could be paid to proxies for missing data. For example, interstate trucking data might provide rough estimates of state exports and imports. Data issues have been addressed throughout this report. This critique will focus on other issues.

The state economic models do a good job of capturing interregional economic linkages and both supply and demand effects, but are not best suited for studying economic-demographic linkages. Too little use is made of the rich demographic data available in ECESIS. The interregional trade model is complex and creates some instabilities in the system. Emphasis should be shifted from the trade model to the economic-demographic linkages model. Industry disaggregation does not appear to aid the linkage process. Also, the particular disaggregation chosen for ECESIS is not optimal. The manufacturing sector is important for trade linkages but for the economic-demographic linkages the government sector is the most important. Also, the lack of a government sector makes policy issues difficult to analyze in ECESIS. The economic models are designed to capture short-run cycles but are also required to perform well in long-run projections. Higher priorities should be placed on the long-term growth properties of the state economies.

Fertility and mortality rates are not modelled adequately in the ECESIS demographic model. Partly this is a failure of theory. Most demographic theories are developed at the national level and do not translate easily to the regional level. ECESIS does not take full advantage of available fertility data. To do so may require a complex household decision model.

The Rees-Wilson demographic accounts model is an unnecessarily complicated version of an interregional cohort-component model. The model is very sensitive to the calculation of minor flows which are of third-order importance in any case. A simpler accounts model that ignores minor flows but puts more emphasis on age and perhaps race disaggregation would be better.

The migration model is the weakest link in ECESIS. The modified Markov approach makes clever use of available data but does not have a firm foundation in micro behavior theory. Certainly, the availability of data was a major factor here. Nonetheless, a greater effort should be made to implement a migration model that is well based in micro decision theory.

Both marriage and divorce are missing from this model, and that is in part because there is no household component in this model. However, it is also the case that state level data on marriage and divorce, as well as the exogenous variables needed to determine them, vary considerably in quality. Only thirty-two states are included in the marriage and divorce registration system, and estimates for the remaining states are not particularly good. Nonetheless, it is the case that this model is less complete for the omission of these demographic or social activities.

ECESIS suffers from the problems of scale. This model attempts to model 142 economic equations for 51 geographic units, or over 7000 endogenous equations with over 10,000 endogenous and exogenous variables. In addition, 26,000 migration flows are modelled and over 500 age-sex groups are kept track of. In order to initialize this model over 300 separate computer runs must be made. To solve ECESIS for a twenty year simulation requires about five billion bytes of memory and ninety minutes of processing time on an IBM 370 computer. This is a large amount of resources and is one of the major weaknesses of ECESIS. ECESIS is difficult to use and expensive to run and is so complex that it partially defeats its own purpose of being a useful policy tool.

13.3 SUGGESTIONS FOR FUTURE RESEARCH

The criticisms discussed in the previous section suggest the type of modelling strategy changes that ECESIS' successor should follow. Some of the criticisms might have been anticipated, but others could not. ECESIS had to be built in order to learn from its weaknesses. The model is too large and addresses too many complicated issues at once. ECESIS attempted both to examine several theoretical modelling issues and to be a reliable long-term projections model.

The key elements in an economic-demographic model are the linkages between the economic and demographic variables. These linkages include migration, marriage, fertility, labor force participation and divorce. All of these are decisions involving household formation and dissolution. Household decisions are micro level decisions and are best modelled at that level. One intriguing possibility is to develop a micro-simulation model of the household which could later be linked to aggregate economic and demographic models.

The decision to migrate involves two choices. The dichotomous choice of to move or to stay and the multivariate choice of where to move to. These choices may be modelled separately or simultaneously. The latter is preferable but more data intensive, probably requiring the use of migration data from the Decennial Censuses. In this case, it is probably better to be restricted to cross-sectional analysis than to endure the problems created by use of aggregated time-series data. A good starting point would be to estimate a micro level version of the alternative opportunities model proposed by Feder (1979 and 1980).

All of the household decisions must be determined simultaneously (Ahlburg 1979). Ignoring the migration decision for now, a micro-simulation household model could first be developed at the national level, concentrating on the best specifications. Then the issue of how to develop a regional household model could be addressed. For example, the fertility decision involves the decision of ultimate family size and the decision of the timing of the births. Family size may not be too sensitive to economic factors but the timing decisions are likely to be influenced by economic cycles. An optimal control model may prove useful in modelling the timing of births. This could be tested at the national level before being applied to regions.

Once a regional household model is developed, the issue of linking it to a regional economic model and an interregional demographic accounts model may be addressed. The economic model should be as small as possible and stress long-run growth relationships. The forte of an economic-demographic model is in analyzing long-run swings, not short-run cycles.

ECESIS is a reasonably good start at an economic-demographic model. It follows the suggestions made in the theoretical literature fairly closely. Experience from the ECESIS model has pinpointed specific problem areas that would not have been easily anticipated. The major contribution of ECESIS is that it suggests its own successor.

BIBLIOGRAPHY

Adams, F. G., Brooking, C. G., and Glickman, N. J. 1975. On the specification and simulation of a regional econometric model: a model of Mississippi. Review of Economics and Statistics 57,3: 286-298.

Ahlburg, D. A. 1979. Alternative approaches to forecasting U.S. fertility. Ph.D dissertation in economics, University of Pennsylvania.

Ahlburg, D. A. 1981. An economic-demographic model of U.S. births, marriage, divorce and female labor force participation. University of Minnesota. Mimeographed.

Ahlburg, D. A. 1982. Forecasting regional births from national birth forecasts. Paper presented at the American Statistical Association/Bureau of the Census International Conference on Forecasting Regional Population Change and its Economic Determinants and Consequences, Airlie, Virginia.

Akin, J., Guilkey, D., and Sickles, R. 1979. A randon coefficient probit model with an application to a study of migration. Journal of Econometrics 11: 233-246.

Alperovich, G., Bergman, J., and Ehemann, C. 1975. An econometric model of employment growth in U.S. metropolitan areas. Environment and Planning A 7: 833-862.

Alonso, W. 1980. Population as a system in regional development. American Economic Review 70,2: 405-509.

Anker, R. 1978. An analysis of fertility differentials in developing countries. Review of Economics and Statistics 60,1: 58-69.

Ball, R. J., ed. 1973. International Linkage of National Economic Models. Amsterdam: North-Holland.

Ballard, K. P., Gustely, R. D., and Wendling, R. M. 1980. NRIES: Structure, performance, and application of a bottom-up interregional econometric model. Washington, D.C.: U.S. Bureau of Economic Analysis, Regional Economic Analysis Division.

Bass, R., and Alexander, R. 1972. Climate, economy, and the differential migration of white and nonwhite workers. Journal of Applied Psychology 56: 518-521.

Beals, R., Levy, M., and Moses, M. 1967. Rationality and migration in Ghana. Review of Economics and Statistics 49: 480-486.

Becker, G., and Lewis, H. 1973. On the interaction between the quantity and quality of children. Journal of Political Economy 81,2/2: S278-S288.

Behman, S. 1964. Labor mobility, increasing labor demand, and money wage-rate increases in United States manufacturing. Review of Economic Studies 31: 253-266.

Beyers, W. B. 1980. Migration and the development of multiregional economic systems. Economic Geography 56,4: 320-334.

Bilsborrow, R. E., and Akin J. S. 1982. Data availability vs. data needs for analyzing the determinants and consequences of internal migration: an evaluation of U.S. survey data. Paper presented at the American Statistical Association/Bureau of the Census Internation Conference on Forecasting Regional Population Change and its Economic Determinants and Consequences, Airlie, Virginia.

Blanco, C. 1963. The determinants of interstate population movements. Journal of Regional Science 5: 77-84.

Borts, G., and Stein, J. 1964. Economic Growth in a Free Market. New York: Columbia University Press.

Brechling, F. 1973. Wage inflation and the structure of regional unemployment. Journal of Money, Credit, and Banking 5,1: 355-379.

Brown, R. S., Caves, D. W., and Christensen, L. R. 1979. Modelling the structure of cost and production for multiproduct firms. Southern Economic Journal 46,1: 256-273.

Butz, W., and Ward, M. 1979. The emergence of counter-cyclical U.S. fertility. American Economic Review 69,3: 318-328.

Cain, G., and Dooley, M. 1976. Estimation of a model of labor supply, fertility, and wages of married women. Journal of Political Economy 84,4/2: S179-S199.

Cain, G., and Weininger, A. 1973. Economic determinants of fertility: results from cross-sectional aggregate data. Demography 10,2: 205-223.

Capozza, D. R., and Van Order, R. 1977a. Pricing under spatial competition and spatial monopoly. Econometrica 45,6: 1329-1338.

Capozza, D. R., and Van Order, R. 1977b. A simple model of spatial pricing under free entry. Southern Economic Journal 44: 361-367.

Capozza, D. R., and Van Order, R. 1978. A generalized model of spatial competition. American Economic Review 68: 896-908.

Capozza, D. R., and Van Order, R. 1979. Competitive reactions in spatial monopolistic competition. Paper delivered at the Regional Science Association Meetings, Los Angeles.

Capozza, D. R., and Van Order, R. 1980. Unique equilibria, pure profits and efficiency in location models, mimeographed.

Cebula, R. J., and Vedder, R. 1973. A note on migration, economic opportunity, and the quality of life. Journal of Regional Science 13: 205-211.

Center for Human Resource Research. 1981. Handbook. Columbus, Ohio: Ohio State University, CHRR.

Chang, H. S. 1976. Tennessee Econometric Model: Phase I. Knoxvill, Tennessee: Center for Business and Economic Research, College of Business Administration, University of Tennessee.

Chau, L. 1970. An Econometric Model for Forecasting Income and Employment in Hawaii: 1951-1968. Honolulu: Economic Research Center, University of Hawaii.

Christensen, L. R., Jorgenson, D. W., and Lau, L. J. 1973. Transcendental logarithmic production frontiers. The Review of Economics and Statistics 55,1: 28-45.

Clark, G., and Ballard, K. 1980. Modeling out-migration from depressed regions: the significance of origin and destination characteristics. Environment and Planning A 12: 799-812.

Coen, R. M., and Hickman, B. G. 1970. Constrained joint estimation of factor demand and production functions. The Review of Economics and Statistics 52,3: 287-300.

Cramer, J. C. 1980. Fertility and female employment: problems of causal direction. American Sociological Review 45: 167-190.

Crow, R. T. 1979. Output determination and investment specification in macroeconometric models of open regions. Regional Science and Urban Economics, 9: 141-58.

Dahlberg, A., and Holmlund, B. 1978. The interaction of migration, income, and employment in Sweden. Demography 15,3: 259-266.

DaVanzo, J. 1976. Why Families Move: A Model of the Geographic Mobility of Married Couples. Santa Monica, CA: The Rand Corporation. R-1972-DOL.

DaVanzo, J. 1981. Repeat migration, information costs, and location-specific capital. Population and Envirnment 4,1: 45-73.

Davidson, P., and Smolensky, E. 1964. Aggregate Demand and Supply Analysis. New York: Harper and Row.

DeFronzo, J. 1976. Testing the economic theory of fertility with cross-sectional and change data. Social Biology 23,3: 226-234.

De Leeuw, F. 1979. Why capacity utilization estimates differ. Survey of Current Business 59,5: 45-55.

DeTray, D. 1973. Child quality and the demand for children. Journal of Political Economy 81,2/2: S70-S95.

Duffy, M., and Greenwood, M. 1980. Explorations in migration forecasting: time series and cross-sectional evidence. Paper presented at the Western Regional Science Association meetings, Monterey, CA.

Duncan, G., and Newman, S. 1975. People as planners: the fulfillment of residential mobility expectations. In _Five Thousand American Families: Patterns of Economic Progress_. Vol. III: Analysis of the First Six Years of the Panel Study of Income Dynamics, eds. G. Duncan, and J. N. Morgan. Ann Arbor: Institute for Social Research, The University of Michigan.

Easterlin, R. A. 1968. _Population, Labor Force, and Long Swings in Economic Growth_. New York: NBER.

Easterlin, R. A. 1973. Relative economic status and the American fertility swing. In _Family Economic Behavior: Problems and Prospects_, ed. Eleanor B. Sheldon, pp. 170-223. Philidelphia: Lippincott.

Easterlin, R. A. 1976. The conflict between aspirations and resources. _Population and Development Review_ 2,3/4: 417-425.

Easterlin, R. A., Wachter, M. L., and Wachter, S. M. 1978. Demographic influences on economic stability: the United States experience. _Population and Development Review_ 4,1: 1-22.

Eckstein, O., and Wilson, T. A. 1962. The determination of money wages in American industry. _Quarterly Journal of Economics_ 76: 379-414.

Engle, R. F. 1974. A disequilibrium model of regional investment. _Journal of Regional Science_ 14,3: 367-76.

Evans, M. K. 1969. _Macroeconomic Activity: Theory, Forecasting and Control_. New York: Harper and Row.

Feder, G. 1979. Alternative opportunities and migration: an exposition. _Annals of Regional Science_ 13,3: 57-67.

Feder, G. 1980. Alternative opportunities and migration: evidence from Korea. _Annal of Regional Science_ 14,1: 1-11.

Feeney, G. 1973. Two models for multiregional population dynamics. _Environment and Planning A_ 5: 31-43.

Feldstein, M., and Poterba, J. 1980. State and local taxes and the rate of return on nonfinancial corporate capital. National Bureau of Economic Research Working Paper #508.

Fields, G. 1976. Labor force migration, unemployment and job turnover. Review of Economics and Statistics 58,4: 407-415.

Fields, G. 1979. Place-to-place migration: some new evidence. Review of Economics and Statistics 61,1: 21-32.

Foster, E. 1978. The variability of inflation. Review of Economics and Statistics 60,3: 346-350.

Friedenberg, H., Bretzfelder, R., Johnson, K., and Trott, E. 1980. Regional and state projections of income, employment, and population to the year 2000. Survey of Current Business Nov.: 44-72.

Gerking, S. D., and Isserman, A. M. 1980. Bifurcation and the time pattern of impacts in the economic base model, mimeographed.

Gerking, S. D., and Weirick, W. N. 1983. Compensating differences in interregional wage differentials. Review of Economics and Statistics ? ?.

Ghali, M., Akiyama, M., and Fujiwara, J. 1978. Factor mobility and regional growth. Review of Economics and Statistics 60,1: 78-84.

Ghali, M., and Renaud, B. 1975. The Structure and Dynamic Properties of a Regional Economy: An Econometric Model for Hawaii. Lexington, MA: Lexington Books.

Ginzberg, E. 1982. The social security system. Scientific American 246,1: 51-57.

Gleave, D., and Cordey-Hayes, M. 1977. Migration dynamics and labour market turnover. Progress in Planning 8,1.

Glickman, N. J. 1972. An Area-Stratified Regional Econometric Model. Philidelphia: Regional Science Research Institute, Discussion Paper #58.

Glickman, N. J. 1977. Econometric Analysis of Regional Systems: Explorations in Model Building and Policy Analysis. New York: Academic Press.

Glickman, N. J. 1978. Son of the specification of regional econometric models. Papers of the Regional Science Association 32: 155-177.

Gordon, P., and Ledent, J. 1981. Towards an interregional demoeconomic model. Journal of Regional Science 21,1: 79-87.

Grant, E. K., and Vanderkamp, J. 1980. The effects of migration on income: a micro study with Canadian data 1965-71. The Canadian Journal of Economics 13,3: 381-406.

Graves, P. 1980. Migration and climate. Journal of Regional Science 20,2: 227-237.

Graves, P., and Linneman, P. 1979. Household migration: theoretical and empirical results. Journal of Urban Economics 3: 383-404.

Greenhut, M. L., and Ohta, H. 1975. Theory of Spatial Pricing and Market Areas. Durham, N.C.: Duke University Press.

Greenhut, M. L., Hwang, M., and Ohta, H. 1975. Observations on the shape and relevance of the spatial demand function. Econometrica 43: 669-682.

Greenwood, M. 1975. Research on internal migration in the United States: a survey. Journal of Economic Literature 13: 397-433.

Greenwood, M. J. 1979. The economic consequences of immigration for the United States: a survey of the findings in Interagency Task Force on Immigration Policy, Staff Report Companion Papers. Washington, D.C.: Departments of Justice, Labor, and State.

Greenwood, M., and Gormely, P. 1971. A comparison of the determinants of white and nonwhite interstate migration. Demography 9,4: 665-681.

Greenwood, M., and Sweetland, D. 1972. The determinants of migration between standard metropolitan statistical areas. Demography 9,4: 665-681.

Gregory, P., Campbell, J., and Cheng, B. 1972. A simultaneous equation model of birth rates in the United States. Review of Economics and Statistics 49,4: 374-380.

Griffith, J. 1980. Standardizing population projections required in federal fund allocations. Statistical Reporter January: 57-63.

Grossman, M., and Jacobowitz, S. 1981. Variations in infant mortality rates among counties of the United States: the roles of public policies and programs. Demography 18,4: 695-713.

Guccione, A., and Gillen, W. J. 1972. A simple disaggregation of a neoclassical investment function. Journal of Regional Science 12,2: 279-294.

Guccione, A., and Gillen, W. J. 1974. A Metzler type model for Canada. Journal of Regional Science 14: 173-190.

Hall, O. P., and Licari, J. A. 1974. Building small region econometric models: extension of Glickman's structure to Los Angeles. Journal of Regional Science 14,3: 337-353.

Haltiwanger, J. C. 1980. Implicit contract theory: A suggested reformulation. The Johns Hopkins University: Working Papers in Economics #72.

Hart, R. A., and MacKay, D. I. 1977. Wage inflation, regional policy and the regional earnings structure. Economica 44: 267-281.

Haurin, D. 1980. The regional distribution of population, migration, and climate. Quarterly Journal of Economics 95,2: 293-308.

Hendershott, P. H., and Hu, S. C. 1980a. Government-induced biases in the allocation of the stock of fixed capital in the United States. In Capital, Efficiency and Growth, ed. G. M. Von Furstenberg. Cambridge, Mass.: Ballinger Publishing Co.

Hendershott, P. H., and Hu, S. C. 1980b. A model of optimal feasible replacement investment: application to orders for producers equipment. Purdue University: Institute for Research in the Behavioral, Economics, and Management Sciences, Working Paper #723.

Hotelling, H. 1929. Stability in competition. Economic Journal 39: 41-57.

Interagency Task Force on Immigration Policy. Staff Report. Washington, D.C.: Departments of Justice, Labor, and State.

Irwin, R. 1977. Guide for Local Area Population Projections. Washington, D.C.: Bureau of the Census, Technical Paper #39.

Isserman, A. M. 1982. Multiregional demoeconomic modeling with endogeneously determined birth and migration rates: theory and prospects. Paper presented at the meetings of the Association of American Geographers, San Antonio, Texas.

Isserman, A. M., Plane, D. A., and McMillen, D. B. 1982. Internal migration in the United States: an evalutation of federal data. Review of Public Data Use 10.

Isserman, A. M., Plane, D. A., Rogerson, P., and Beaumont, P. M. 1981. Forecasting interstate migration with limited data: a demographic-economic approach. Paper presented at the Twenty-Eigth Annual North American Regional Science Association Meeting, Montreal, Canada.

Izraeli, O., and Kellman, M. 1979. Changes in money wage rates and unemployment in local labor markets: the latest evidence. Journal of Regional Science 19,3: 375-387.

Jefferson, C. W. 1978. A regional econometric model of the Northern Ireland economy. Scottish Journal of Political Economy 25,3: 253-272.

Jorgenson, D. W. 1965. Anticipation and investment. In Brookings Quarterly Econometric Model of the United States, eds. J. Duesenberry, G. Fromm, L.R. Klein, and E. Kuh, pp. 35-92. Chicago: Rand McNally.

Klein, L. R. 1969. The specification of regional econometric models. Papers and Proceedings of the Regional Science Association : 105-115.

Klein, L. R. 1974. A Textbook of Econometrics, 2nd edition. Englewood Cliffs, N.J.:Prentice-Hall, Inc.

Klein, L. R., and Glickman, N. J. 1973. An econometric model of Pennsylvania. Philadelphia: Department of Economics, University of Pennsylvania, Discussion Paper #295.

Klein, L. R., and Glickman, N. J. 1977. Econometric model building at the regional level. Philadelphia: University of Pennsylvania, mimeographed.

Klein, L. R., and Long, V. 1973. Capacity utilization: concept, measurement, and recent estimates. Brookings Papers on Economic Activity 3: 743-756.

Klein, L. R., and Preston, R. S. 1967. Some new results in the measurement of capacity utilization. American Economic Review 57,1: 34-58.

Klein, L. R., and Su, V. 1979. Direct estimates of unemployment rate and capacity utilization in macroeconometric models. International Economic Review 20,3: 725-40.

Kuznets, S. 1960. Population change and aggregate output. In Demographic and Economic Change in Developed Countries, pp. 324-340. Princeton: Princeton University Press.

Land, K. C., and McMillen, M. M. 1981. Demographic accounts and the study of social change, with applications to the post-World War II United States. In Social Accounting Systems, pp. 241-306. New York: Academic Press.

Land, K. C., and Pampel, F. C. 1980. Aggregate male and female labor force participation functions: an analysis of structural differences, 1947-1977. Social Science Research 9: 37-54.

Ledent, J. 1981. Statistical analysis of regional growth: consistent modeling of employment, population, labor force participation, and unemployment. Paper presented at the Twenty-Eigth North American Congress of the Regional Science Association, Montreal, Quebec.

Ledent, J. 1982. The migration component in multiregional economic-demographic forecasting models: using Alonso's theory of movement. Paper presented at the American Statistical Association/Bureau of the Census International Conference on Regional Population Change and its Economic Determinants and Consequences, Airlie, Virginia.

Leibenstein, H. 1954. A Theory of Economic-Demographic Development. Princeton: Princeton University Press.

Leibenstein, H. 1975. The theory of fertility decline. Quarterly Journal of Economics 89,1: 1-31.

Leibenstein, H. 1976. The problem of characterizing aspirations. Population and Development Review 2,3/4: 427-431.

Levy, M., and Wadycki, W. 1974. What is the opportunity cost of moving? Reconsideration of the effects of distance on migration. Economic Development and Cultural Change 22: 198-214.

Lewis, W. 1977. The role of age in the decision to migrate. Annals of Regional Science 11,3: 51-60.

Lichter, D. 1980. Household migration and the labor market position of married women. Social Science Research 9: 83-97.

Long, J. F. 1981. Population Deconcentration in the United States. Washington, D.C.: U.S. Bureau of the Census.

Long, J. F. 1981. Survey of federally-produced national-level demographic projections. Review of Public Data Use 9,4: 309-319.

Long, J. F. 1983. The effects of college and military populations on model of interstate migration. Socio-Economic Planning Sciences ?: ?.

Long, L. 1974. Women's labor force participation and the residential mobility of families. Social Forces 52,3: 342-348.

Long, L., and Hansen, K. A. 1979. Reasons for Interstate Migration. Current Population Reports, Series P-23, No. 81. Washington, D.C.: U.S. Government Printing Office.

Losch, A. 1967. The Economics of Location. New York: Wiley.

Lowry, I. S. 1966. Migration and Metropolitan Growth: Two Analytical Models. San Francisco, CA: Chandler Pub. Co.

Lucas, R. E. Jr., and Rapping, L. A. 1969. Real wages, employment and inflation. Journal of Political Economy 77,5: 721-754.

Lui, B-C. 1979. Differential net migration rates and the quality of life. Review of Economics and Statistics 57,3: 329-337.

MacMahon, B., Kovar, M. G., and Feldman, J. J. 1972. Infant Mortality Rates: Socioeconomic Factors. Washington, D.C.: Department of Health, Education and Welfare, Publication No. 72-1045.

Marcis, R. G., and Reed, J. D. 1974. Joint estimation of the determinants of wages in subregional labor markets in the United States: 1961-1972. Journal of Regional Science 14,2: 259-267.

Markusen, A. R., and Fastrup, J. 1978. The regional war for federal aid. The Public Interest 53, Fall.

Mason, E. S. 1939. Price and production policies of large-scale enterprises. American Economic Review 29,1: 61-74.

Mathur, V. K. 1976. The relation between rate of change of money wage rates and unemployment in local labor markets: some new evidence. Journal of Regional Science 16: 389-398.

Mehra, Y. P. 1976. Spillovers in wage determination in U.S. manufacturing industries. The Review of Economics and Statistics 58,3: 300-312.

Miller, E. 1973. Is outmigration affected by economic conditions? Southern Economic Journal 39: 396-405.

Milne, W. J. 1980. A multiregional econometric model of the United States: an application to the Northeast. Ph.D dissertation, University of Pennsylvania.

Milne, W. J. 1981. Migration in an interregional macroeconomic model of the United States: will net outmigration from the Northeast continue? International Regional Science Review 6,1: 71-83.

Milne, W. J., Glickman, N. J., and Adams, F. G. 1980. A framework for analyzing regional growth and decline: a multiregion model of the United States. Journal of Regional Science 20,2: 173-189.

Miron, J. R. 1979. Migration and urban economic growth. Regional Science and Urban Economics 9,2/3: 159-183.

Moody, H. L., and Puffer, F. W. 1969. A cross regional product approach to regional model building. Western Economic Journal 7: 291-402.

McMillen, D. B. 1983. The myths of elderly migration. Paper presented at the 1983 meetings of the American Statistical Association.

McMillen, D. B., and Long, J. F. 1981. A comparison of CWHS and CPS migration data. Paper presented at the 1981 meetings of the American Statistical Association, Social Statistics Section.

McMillen, M. M. 1980. The demographic approach to social accounting. Ph.D dissertation, University of Illinois.

McMillen, M. M., and Land, K. C. 1980. Methodological considerations in the demographic approach to social accounting. 1979 Proceedings of the Social Statistics Section, American Statistical Association.

Norton, R. D., and Rees, J. 1979. The product cycle and the spatial decentralization of American manufacturing. Regional Studies 13: 141-151.

O'Connel, M. 1983. Countercyclical fertility: a view from the trough. Washington, D.C.: Bureau of the Census, mimeographed.

Oxenfeldt, A. R. 1967. The underlying rationality of business pricing decisions. In Prices: Issues in Theory, Practice, and Public Policy, ed. A. Philips, pp. 214-227. Philadelphia: University of Pennsylvania Press.

Perry, G. L. 1973. Capacity in manufacturing. Brookings Papers on Economic Activity 3: 701-742.

Phillips, A. 1963. Industrial capacity: an appraisal of measures of capacity. American Economic Review, Papers and Proceedings 53,2: 275-292.

Plane, D. A. 1982. An information theoretic approach to the estimation of migration flows. Journal of Regional Science ?: ?.

Plane, D. A., and Isserman, A. M. 1983. U.S. interstate labor force migration: an analysis of trends, net exchanges, and migration subsystems. Socio-Economic Planning Sciences 17: ?.

Plane, D. A., and Rogerson, P. A. 1982. Spatial economic-demographic modeling of interregional migration with limited data. Paper presented at the American Statistical Association/Bureau of the Census International Conference on Forecasting Regional Population Change and its Economic Determinants and Consequences, Airlie, Virginia.

Plaut, T. 1981. An econometric model for forecasting regional population growth. International Regional Science Review 6,1: 53-70.

Puffer, F. W., and Williams, R. M. 1967. An econometric model for Southern California and forecasts for 1967. California Management Review 7: 89-92.

Raymond, R. 1972. Determinants of nonwhite migration during the 1950's: their regional significance and long-run implications. American Journal of Economic Sociology 31: 9-20.

Redwood, A. L. 1982. Forecasting subnational birth rates. Paper presented at the American Statistical Association/Bureau of the Census International Conference on Forecasting Regional Population Change and its Economic Determinants and Consequences, Airlie, Virginia.

Reed, J. D., and Hutchinson, P. M. 1976. An empirical test of a regional Phillips curve and wage rate transmission mechanism in an urban hierarchy. Annals of Regional Science 10: 19-30.

Rees, A., and Hamilton, M. T. 1967. The wage-price-productivity perplex. The Journal of Political Economy 75,1: 63-70.

Rees, P. H., and Wilson, A. G. 1977. Spatial Population Analysis. London: Edward Arnold.

Renshaw, V. 1978. Possible biases associated with errors in migration data compiled from the CWHS. Paper presented at the annual meeting of the U.S. Department of Agriculture's Regional Research Project W118-R, Snowbird, Utah.

Reza, A. M. 1978. Geographical differences in earnings and unemployment rates. The Review of Economics and Statistics ?: 201-208.

Rifkin, J., and Barber, R. 1978. The North Will Rise Again: Pensions, Politics, and Power in the 1980's. Boston: Beacon Press.

Rindfuss, R., and Bumpass, L. 1976. How old is too old? Age and the sociology of fertility. Family Planning Perspectives 8: ?.

Rodgers, G. B. 1979. Income and inequality as determinants of mortality: an international cross-section analysis. Population Studies 33,2: 343-351..

Rogers, A. 1967. A regression analysis of interregional migration in California. Review of Economics and Statistics 49,2: 262-267.

Rogers, A. 1968. Matrix Analysis of Interregional Population Growth and Distribution. Berkeley: University of California Press.

Rogers, A. 1975. An Introduction to Multiregional Mathematical Demography. New York: Wiley.

Rogerson, P. 1981. Job turnover and interregional migration. Paper presented to the American Association of Geographers, Los Angeles.

Rones, P. L. 1980. Moving to the sun: regional job growth. Monthly Labor Review March: 12-19.

Rubin, B. M. 1979. Further evidence on the metropolitan region labor market unemployment-inflation adjustment mechanism. Paper presented at the Regional Science Association Meetings, Los Angeles.

Rubin, B. M., and Erickson, R. A. 1980. Specification and performance improvements in regional econometric forecasting models: a model for the Milwaukee metropolitan area. Journal of Regional Science 20,1: 11-36.

Rutman, G. L. 1970. Migration and economic opportunities in West Virginia: a statistical analysis. Rural Sociology 35: 206-217.

Ryscavage, P. M. 1979. BLS labor force projections: a review of methods and results. Monthly Labor Review 102,4: 15-22.

Samuelson, R. D., and Roberts, P. O. 1975. A Commodity Attribute Data File for use in Freight Transportation Studies. Cambridge, MA: Massachusetts Institute of Technology, Center for Transportation Studies, CTS Report 75-20.

Sandell, S. 1977. Women and the economics of family migration. Review of Economics and Statistics 59,4: 406-414.

Sanderson, W. C. 1978. Economic-Demographic Simulation Models: A Review of Their Usefulness for Policy Analysis. Rome: Food and Agriculture Organization of the United Nations.

Santomero, A. M., and Seater, J. J. 1978. The inflation-unemployment trade-off: a critique of the literature. Journal of Economic Literature 16: 499-544.

Schultze, C. L. 1963. Uses of capacity measures for short-run economic analysis. American Economic Review, Papers and Proceedings 53,2: 292-308.

Schramm, R., and Sherman, R. 1977. A rationale for administered pricing. Southern Economic Journal 44,1: 125-135.

Simler, N. J., and Tella, A. 1980. Inflation and labor force participation. In Stagflation: the Causes, Effects, and Solutions, Special study on Economic Change, Joint Economic Committee, pg. 155-167. Washington, D.C.: U.S. Government Printing Office.

Simon, J. L. 1977. The Economics of Population Growth. Princeton: Princeton University Press.

Sjaastad, L. A. 1962. The costs and returns of human migration. Journal of Political Economy 70: S80-S93.

Smith, D. 1974. Regional growth: interstate and intersectoral factor reallocations. Review of Economics and Statistics 56,3: 353-359.

Smith, D. 1975. Neoclassical growth models and regional growth in the U.S. Journal of Regional Science 15,2: 165-181.

Smith, S. K., and Fishkind, H. H. 1981. Economic determinants of elderly migration. a time series approach, mimeographed.

Smith, T., and Slater, P. 1981. A family of spatial interaction models incorporating information flows and choice set constraints. International Regional Science Review 6,1: 15-31.

Smithies, A. 1941. Optimum location in spatial competition. The Journal of Political Economy 49: 423-439.

Sommers, P. M., and Suits, D. B. 1973. Analysis of net interstate migration. Southern Economic Journal 40: 193-201.

Stolzenberg, R. M., and Waite, L. J. 1977. Age, fertility expectations, and plans for employment. American Sociological Review 42: 769-782.

Stone, R. 1971. Demographic Accounting and Model-Building. Paris: Organisation for Economic Cooperation and Development.

Tarver, D., and Gurley, W. R. 1965. The relationship of selected variables with county net migration rates in the United States 1950 to 1960. Rural Sociology 30: 3-22.

Taylor, C. A. 1982. Demographic disaggregation in the construction of regional econometric models: a statistical evaluation. International Regional Science Review 7,1: 25-51.

Tella, A. 1964. The relation of labor force to employment. Industrial and Labor Relations Review 17: 454-469.

Tella, A. 1965. Labor force sensitivity by age, sex. Industrial Relations 4: 69-83.

The First National Bank of Boston. 1980. General Revenue Sharing Technical Papers, mimeographed.

Todaro, M. 1969. A model of labor migration and urban unemployment in less developed countries. American Economic Review 59: 138-148.

Todaro, M. 1976. Rural-urban migration, unemployment, and job probabilities: recent theoretical and empirical research. In Economic Factors in Population Growth, ed. A. Coale. New York: Macmillan.

U.S. Bureau of the Census. 1978. Current Population Reports, Series P-20, No. 331, Geographical mobility: March 1975 to March 1978. Washington, D.C.: U.S. Government Printing Office.

U.S. Bureau of the Census. 1965 (and various years). Annual Survey of Manufactures, Special Geographic Supplement to 1962-64 Data On-Book Value of Fixed Assets and Rental Payments for Buildings and Equipment. Washington, D.C.: U.S. Government Printing Office.

U.S. Bureau of the Census. 1965 (and various years). Annual Survey of Manufactures. Washington, D.C.: U.S. Government Printing Office.

U.S. Bureau of the Census. (various years). Current Population Reports, Series P-25, Annual estimates of the population of States. Washington, D.C.: U.S. Government Printing Office.

U.S. Bureau of the Census. 1980. Internal Revenue Service based Migration Files, unpublished data.

U.S. Bureau of the Census. (various years). Current Population Reports, Series P-25, Estimates of the population of States by age. Washington, D.C.: U.S. Government Printing Office.

U.S. Bureau of the Census. (various years). Current Population Reports, Series P-25, Estimates of the population of the United States and components of change. Washington, D.C.: U.S. Government Printing Office.

U.S. Bureau of the Census. 1960 Census of Population, Vol. 1, Table 16, "Age by Color and Sex". Washington, D.C.: U.S. Government Printing Office.

U.S. Bureau of the Census. 1970 Census of Population, Vol. 1, Table 20, "Age by Race and Sex 1970". Washington, D.C.: U.S. Government Printing Office.

U.S. Bureau of the Census. 1977. Current Population Reports, Series P-25, No. 704, Projections of the population of the United States: 1977 to 2050. Washington, D.C.: U.S. Government Printing Office.

U.S. Bureau of the Census. 1979. Current Population Reports, Series P-25, No. 796, Illustrative projections of State populations by age, race and sex: 1975 to 2000. Washington, D.C.: U.S. Government Printing Office.

U.S. Bureau of the Census. 1980. 1977 Census of Transportation, Commodity Transportation Survey. Transportation Division. Washington, D.C.: U.S. Government Printing Office.

U.S. Bureau of Economic Analysis. (various issues). Business Conditions Digest. Washington, D.C.: U.S. Government Printing Office.

U.S. Bureau of Economic Analysis. 1976. Regional Work Force Characteristics and Migration Data: A Handbook on the Social Security Continuous Work History Sample and Its Application. Washington, D.C.: U.S. Government Printing Office.

U.S. Bureau of Economic Analysis. (various issues and working tapes). Survey of Current Business. Washington, D.C.: U.S. Government Printing Office.

U.S. Bureau of Economic Analysis. 1976. A summary description of the sources and methods used in estimating county personal income: 1969-74. Washington, D.C.: U.S. Government Printing Office.

U.S. Department of Health, Education, and Welfare. (various issues). Monthly Vital Statistics. Washington, D.C.: U.S. Government Printing Office.

U.S. Department of Justice. 1963. Laws Applicable to Immigration and Nationality. Washington, D.C.: U.S. Government Printing Office.

U.S. Department of Justice. 1978. Statistical Yearbook of the Immigration and Naturalization Service. Washington, D.C.: U.S. Government Printing Office.

U.S. Department of Justice. 1980a. United States Immigration Laws: General Information. Washington, D.C.: U.S. Government Printing Office.

U.S. Department of Justice. 1980b. Our Immigration: A Brief Account of Immigration to the United States. Washington, D.C.: U.S. Government Printing Office.

U.S. Department of Justice. 1982. An analysis of the efficiency legislation. INS Reporter 30: 11-15.

U.S. Department of Labor. Employment and Training Administration. (various years). Area Trends in Employment and Unemployment. Washington, D.C.: U.S. Government Printing Office.

U.S. Department of Labor. Employment and Training Administration. (various years). Employment and Training Report of the President. Washington, D.C.: U.S. Government Printing Office.

U.S. Department of Labor. 1979. Employment and Earnings, States and Areas, 1939-78. Bureau of Labor Statistics, Bulletin 1370-13. Washington, D.C.: U.S. Government Printing Office.

U.S. Department of Labor. 1979. Handbook of Labor Statistics 1978. Bureau of Labor Statistics, Bulletin 2000. Washington, D.C.: U.S. Government Printing Office.

Voss, P. R., Palit, C. D., Kale, B. D., and Krebs, H. C. 1981. Forecasting State Populations Using ARIMA Time Series Techniques. Madison, WI: Wisconsin Department of Administration and the University of Wisconsin-Madison.

Wachter, M. L. 1972. A labor supply model for secondary workers. Review of Economics and Statistics 54,2: 141-151.

Wachter, M. L. 1974. A new approach to the equilibrium labour force. Economica 161,41: 35-51.

Wachter, M. L. 1975. A time-series fertility equation: the potential for a baby boom in the 1980's. International Economic Review 16,3: 609-624. Wadycki, W. 1979. Alternative opportunities and United States interstate migration: an improved econometric specification. Annals of Regional Science 13,3: 35-41.

Warnes, A. M. 1982. Longer distance migrations in older ages: some implications for local population projections. Paper presented at the American Statistical Association/Bureau of the Census International Conference on Forecasting Regional Population Change and its Economic Determinants and Consequences, Airlie, Virginia.

Weintraub, S. 1958. Approach to the Theory of Income Distribution. Philadelphia: Chilton.

Weintraub, S. 1959. A General Theory of the Price Level, Output, Income Distribution, and Economic Growth. Philadelphia: Chilton.

Weintraub, S. 1978. Capitalism's Inflation and Unemployment Crisis: Beyond Monetarism and Keynesianism. Reading, MA: Addison-Wesley.

Weiss, L. W. 1966. Business pricing policies and inflation reconsidered. Journal of Political Economy 74,2: 177-187.

Weiss, L. W. 1971. Quantitative studies of industrial organization. In Frontiers of Quantitative Economics, ed. M. D. Intriligator, pp. 362-403. Amsterdam: North-Holland Publishing Co.

Wetrogan, S., and Engels, R. 1982. Evaluation of Census and administrative data sources for migration data. Paper presented at the American Statistical Association/ Bureau of the Census International Conference on Forecasting Regional Population Change and its Economic Determinants and Consequences, Airlie, Virginia.

White, J. C. 1976. A statistical history of immigration. INS Reporter 25: 1-9.

Wrage, P. 1981. The effects of internal migration on regional wage and unemployment disparities in Canada. Journal of Regional Science 21,1: 51-63.

Wu, S. Y. 1979. An essay on monoploy power and stable price policy. American Economic Review 69,1: 60-72.

Yorden, W. J. 1961. Industrial concentration and price flexibility in inflation: price response rates in fourteen industries, 1947-1958. Review of Economics and Statistics 43,3: 287-294.

Zelomek, A. W. 1967. Business pricing: the irrational use of irrational rules of thumb. In *Prices: Issues in Theory, Practice, and Public Policy*, ed. A. Phillips, pg. 203-213. Philadelphia: University of Pennsylvania Press.

INDEX